COMBINED TREATMENTS
FOR MENTAL DISORDERS

COMBINED TREATMENTS FOR MENTAL DISORDERS

A GUIDE TO PSYCHOLOGICAL AND PHARMACOLOGICAL INTERVENTIONS

EDITED BY

MORGAN T. SAMMONS

AND NORMAN B. SCHMIDT

American Psychological Association
Washington, DC

Published by
American Psychological Association
750 First Street, NE
Washington, DC 20002
www.apa.org

To order   Tel: (800) 374-2721, Direct: (202) 336-5510
APA Order Department   Fax: (202) 336-5502, TDD/TTY: (202) 336-6123
P.O. Box 92984   Online: www.apa.org/books/
Washington, DC 20090-2984   Email: order@apa.org

In the U.K., Europe, Africa, and the Middle East, copies may be ordered from
American Psychological Association
3 Henrietta Street
Covent Garden, London
WC2E 8LU England

Typeset in Century Schoolbook by EPS Group Inc., Easton, MD

Printer: Sheridan Books, Ann Arbor, MI
Cover Designer: NiDesign, Baltimore, MD
Technical/Production Editor: Emily I. Welsh

The opinions and statements published are the responsibility of the authors, and such opinions and statements do not necessarily represent the policies of the APA.

Library of Congress Cataloging-in-Publication Data
Combined treatments for mental disorders : a guide to psychological and pharmacological interventions / edited by Morgan T. Sammons and Norman B. Schmidt.—1st ed.
       p. ; cm.
    Includes bibliographical references and index.
    ISBN 1-55798-780-7 (cb : acid-free paper)
       1. Mental illness—Chemotherapy. 2. Psychotherapy. 3. Combined modality therapy. I. Sammons, Morgan T. II. Schmidt, Norman B.
III. American Psychological Association.
    [DNLM: 1. Mental Disorders—therapy. 2. Behavior Therapy—methods.
3. Combined Modality Therapy. 4. Psychotropic Drugs—therapeutic use.
WM 400 C7305 2001]
RC483 .C59 2001
616.89′1—dc21

                                                                    2001022123

British Library Cataloguing-in-Publication Data
A CIP record is available from the British Library.

Printed in the United States of America
First Edition

Contents

Contributors

Martin M. Antony, PhD, Anxiety Treatment and Research Centre, St. Joseph's Hospital, and Department of Psychiatry and Behavioral Neurosciences, McMaster University, Hamilton, Ontario, Canada

Kathleen M. Carroll, PhD, Yale University School of Medicine, New Haven, CT

Robert D. Coursey, PhD, Psychology Department, University of Maryland, College Park, MD

Patrick H. DeLeon, PhD, JD, Office of Senator Daniel Inouye, U.S. Senate, Washington, DC

John F. Drozd, PhD, Capt, USAF, BSC, 10th Medical Group, Life Skills Center, Peterson Air Force Base, CO

Carlos M. Grilo, PhD, Yale University School of Medicine, New Haven, CT

Dorothy K. Hatsukami, PhD, Division of Neuroscience Research in Psychiatry, University of Minnesota, Minneapolis, MN

Dale L. Johnson, PhD, Department of Psychology, University of Houston, Houston, TX

Thomas E. Joiner, Jr., PhD, Department of Psychology, Florida State University, Tallahassee, FL

Margaret Koselka, PhD, Department of Medical and Clinical Psychology, Uniformed Services University of the Health Sciences, Bethesda, MD

Sharon E. Robinson Kurpius, PhD, Counseling Psychology Program, Arizona State University, Tempe, AZ

Michael J. Lambert, PhD, Brigham Young University, Salt Lake City, UT

James M. Meredith, Lt. Col., PhD, Prescribing Psychologist, US Air Force, and PACAF Psychology Consultant, Hickam Air Force Base, HI

Marc E. Mooney, MA, Clinical Science and Psychopathology Research Program, University of Minnesota, Minneapolis, MN

Charles M. Morin, PhD, School of Psychology, Laval University, Quebec, Canada

Jeremy W. Pettit, MS, Department of Psychology, Florida State University, Tallahassee, FL

Morgan T. Sammons, PhD, Mental Health Department, Naval Medical Clinic, Annapolis, MD

Norman B. Schmidt, PhD, Department of Psychology, The Ohio State University, Columbus, OH

John L. Sexton, PhD, Prescribing Psychologist, Naval Medical Center, San Diego, CA

William D. Spaulding, PhD, Department of Psychology, University of Nebraska at Lincoln, NE

Richard P. Swinson, MD, Department of Psychiatry and Behavioral Neurosciences, Faculty of Health Sciences, McMaster University, Hamilton, Ontario, Canada

Zachary R. Voelz, BA, Department of Psychology, Florida State University, Tallahassee, FL

Kelly Woolaway-Bickel, MA, Department of Psychology, The Ohio State University, Columbus, OH

COMBINED TREATMENTS FOR MENTAL DISORDERS

Introduction: Toward a Psychological Model of Pharmacological Service Provision

Morgan T. Sammons and Norman B. Schmidt

This book is aimed at psychologists and other mental health practitioners who desire to understand how psychotropic drugs can be combined with psychotherapy and other behavioral treatments to produce optimum patient outcome. Readers will discover that the science underlying combined treatments remains underdeveloped. This is in part a reflection of the inattention paid to investigating combined treatments, in part a reflection of guild-based biases that champion one form of treatment over another, and in part because of the complexity and increased costs associated with combined-treatment research designs.

As a number of chapters in this book attest, combined treatments may not represent the best option for many patients. In particular, the literature suggests that many anxiety disorders may be better treated with behavioral rather than pharmacological interventions. Behavioral treatments for phobic and other anxiety disorders are often more durable than are drug treatments, and they do not carry the risks of dependence that accompany the use of some pharmacological interventions for these disorders (the benzodiazepines). Nevertheless, not all patients are amenable to nondrug treatments because of choice, chronicity, or severity of condition. All of these factors might mitigate toward the addition of pharmacotherapy as an adjunct to behavioral treatment. It is therefore incumbent on the clinician to keep an open mind and not reject a treatment modality categorically. Clinicians who rely exclusively on psychotherapy commit as great an error as those who rely exclusively on pharmacology, for neither approach is likely to completely address the needs of all those who seek help. Flexibility in thinking and attention to the needs of the patient are far better guideposts to successful intervention than is reliance on drug company literature or the opinions of therapists who dogmatically reject all but psychotherapy.

This book will assist clinicians in understanding the research literature on combined treatments. To the extent that the literature allows, algorithms or specific treatment suggestions have been incorporated into each chapter. The book will not, in general, instruct the reader in making choices among drugs or in devising pharmacological drug regimens. To do so well requires a sound grasp of fundamental principles of pharmacology and psychopharmacology that cannot be imparted by this or any other single volume. Of course, clinical experience is the most basic prerequisite to effective prescribing, and this can be acquired only by means of appropriately supervised direct experience. In the past, acquisition of such clinical experience was limited to psychiatrists and other medical practitioners. Now, however, a number of training programs have been initiated to train psychologists, advanced-practice nurses, and other nonmedical professionals in these skills—evidence that nonmedical professions are increasingly aware of the importance and value of education in psychopharmacology.

The book is organized by diagnosis. Psychologists will recognize that there are certain perils in this approach because of the limitations of syndromic categorizations of mental distress. Depressive disorders, for example, often have significant anxiety components, and psychologists have long been sensitive to the fact that patients and their difficulties cannot be reduced to *Diagnostic and Statistical Manual of Mental Disorders*-type (4th ed., *DSM–IV*; American Psychiatric Association, 1994) checklists with rote treatment plans that are uniform for all. More than in any other health care field, the wisdom of the adage that to treat the patient, not the diagnosis, is apropos to mental health interventions.

Although this book is not a primer on psychopharmacology, each chapter provides a broad overview of current pharmacological interventions and often a preview of pending innovations in pharmacological treatment. For readers seeking an in-depth discussion of basic psychopharmacology or principles of psychotropic drug management, the following resources exist. Of the general clinical references designed to help the reader devise appropriate drug intervention strategies, those by Gelenberg and Bassuk (1997); Schatzberg and Nemeroff (1998); or Janicak, Davis, Preskorn, and Ayd (1997) are among the most complete. Readers interested in basic principles of psychopharmacology cannot do better than to add textbooks by Cooper, Bloom, and Roth (1996); Feldman, Meyer, and Quenzer (1997); or Bloom and Kupfer (1995) to their bookshelves. Stahl's (1996) book is a solid, uncomplicated general reference. Pagliaro and Pagliaro (1997, 1999) also have added to the literature by providing textbooks of basic clinical psychopharmacology that are written from a psychological perspective.

Who Should Read This Book?

The primary audience for this book are practicing clinicians who seek to incorporate scientifically informed opinion into treatment planning and case management. Psychologists, counselors, and other nonmedical practitioners engaged in behavioral treatment who seek to understand more about the pharmacology and the combined treatment of specific disorders will find this book helpful. The book will be equally helpful to medical practitioners who seek to understand more about both combined treatments and behavioral or psychotherapeutic modalities, as well as those who wish to update their knowledge regarding current pharmacological treatments. Academic psychologists and their students may also find this book of interest, for many of the chapters are written by renowned experts in their fields and represent not only state-of-the-art reviews but also a keen vision of future research and treatment.

An emerging audience for this book is the small but growing cohort of psychologists who have completed specialized training in psychopharmacology. Such psychologists are currently rare, but numerous programs around the United States are now training psychologists to prescribe. The chapters in this volume will be of use to instructors and students in such programs in that they provide a truly psychological perspective on the prescription of psychotropics. By doing so, it is hoped that this book will assist in the development of an academic model that, while providing psychopharmacological training of the highest caliber, is firmly grounded in the discipline of psychology.

Plan of the Book

Chapter 1, by Morgan T. Sammons, outlines some hypotheses as to why combined treatments have historically been neglected and offers some general clinical considerations for combining treatments. These general clinical guidelines are then expanded on in subsequent chapters that deal with specific disorders.

Ethical and professional issues involved in psychologists' acquisition of prescriptive authority are addressed in the chapter 2, by Patrick H. DeLeon, Sharon E. Robinson Kurpius, and John L. Sexton. This contribution speaks directly to the experience of psychologists in their pursuit of prescriptive authority. Although members of other professions may not at first find the material contained in this chapter to be of direct applicability, closer inspection is warranted. The ethical principles outlined in this chapter are rooted in ethical principles for psychologists, yet they are universal in their application and are just as fundamental to good psychiatric or nursing practice. Members of nonmedical professions who seek to expand their authority to use medication also will profit from examining this chapter. DeLeon et al. discuss at length the findings of the recent Pew reports on the changing scope of practice of nonmedical professions. This provides a glimpse of the future landscape of health care and the nature of expanded service provision by psychologists, nurses, and other professionals whose practices have been constrained by tradition, but not by logic, from the provision of pharmacological services.

Chapter 3, by Martin M. Antony and Richard P. Swinson, and chapter 4, by Norman B. Schmidt, Margaret Koselka, and Kelly Woolaway-Bickel, are devoted to an exploration of anxiety disorders. As noted above, some controversy exists regarding the utility of pharmacological interventions in treating anxiety disorders because of the observed durability of behavioral techniques. Certain medications, however—notably, benzodiazepines, tricyclic antidepressants, and the selective serotonin reuptake inhibitors—have also proven to be powerful tools in treating numerous anxiety-based conditions. In the last several years a number of selective serotonin reuptake inhibitors and other newer antidepressants have received a U.S. Food and Drug Administration indication for obsessive–compulsive disorder (OCD), social anxiety and social phobia, and panic disorder, making them an increasingly viable treatment option for individuals who are not responsive to behavioral intervention. Antony and Swinson, in their contribution on OCD, demonstrate that both pharmacological and behavioral approaches are of significant value in a disorder that may be mediated by perturbations in serotonergic neurotransmission. They provide valuable outlines of both pharmacological and behavioral treatments that will be of interest to clinicians working with patients with OCD. They suggest caution in applying combined treatments, largely because the few studies that have been carried out to date do not demonstrate a clear-cut advantage for such treatments. Combined treatments may be of benefit as augmentation strategies, however, or when comorbid depression or other conditions complicate the clinical picture.

In chapter 4, Schmidt et al. cautiously explore the use of combined treatments in phobic anxiety disorders. Although they note that the majority of patients with such disorders have received both medication and behavior therapy, systematic study of these treatments together has been limited. In those studies that exist, a wide range of outcome is often reported. While pharmacological interventions have demonstrated efficacy, relapse is common on discontinuation. The authors note that the timing of interventions may be an important variable in treatment, as cognitive–behaviorally based strategies may be of assistance when using fading procedures for drug treatment. They raise the notion of treatment specificity, that is, that subsets of symptoms of phobic anxiety disorders may be differentially responsive to either drug or nondrug treatment. This hypothesis requires further validation, but it seems likely that in syndromes such as bipolar disorder or schizophrenia differentially responsive symptoms exist. There is no reason to assume that symptom clusters or variable susceptibilities to a particular form of treatment do not exist for panic disorder and other phobic anxiety disorders.

Charles M. Morin, in his discussion in chapter 5 of insomnia and other sleep disorders, echoes a refrain that should be familiar at this point: that few evidence-based guidelines exist to aid the clinician in devising combined treatment strategies for this spectrum of disorders. No single approach is effective for all subtypes of sleep disorder. Pharmacological approaches are highly effective in the short-term treatment of insomnia, but tolerance to their effects, risks of dependence, and rebound on discontinuation mitigate against their prolonged use. Behavioral treatments, for individuals who respond to them, appear to be more robust. Morin suggests that combined treatments may be more effective if used concurrently —that is, an initial course of medication, coupled with behavioral management principles—but again cautions that the literature as yet provides scant support.

Depression is the most commonly treated problem in mental health offices and among the most common presenting complaints in primary care clinics. Despite its commonality and the intensity with which it has been studied, treatment is unstandardized, and the ideological divisions among various forms of intervention are wide. This is no doubt partially caused by cultural conceptions of depression (see Healy, 1997) as well as by difficulties in capturing the experience of depression under the prevailing *DSM–IV*-based nosological system. This clearly has limited the investigation of combined treatments, of which there are astonishingly few for such a common disorder, as the review in chapter 6, by Jeremy W. Pettit, Zachary R. Voelz, and Thomas E. Joiner, Jr., attests. These authors nevertheless report that combined treatment studies carried out to date suggest a modest effect for this approach. Pettit et al. also note that most studies in this area have been carried out using medications that are no longer the initial treatment of choice (e.g., the tricyclic antidepressants). They note that depression is a multifaceted problem. Some patients may do well with unimodal approaches; however, evidence suggests that many may do best with combined treatments.

Current treatments for schizophrenia and other psychotic disorders reflect two dramatic changes in the 1990s. The first was the escalating deemphasis on inpatient treatment in favor of shorter hospital stays and greater reliance on outpatient rehabilitation brought about by the advent of managed care. The second is the introduction of the atypical antipsychotic agents. As William D. Spaulding, Dale L. Johnson, and Robert D. Coursey note in chapter 7, on combined treatments in schizophrenia, these new drugs have enhanced the role of psychosocial rehabilitative efforts, because they hold the promise for long-term recovery rather than the symptom palliation afforded by earlier generations of antipsychotics. Whether the atypicals will fulfill this promise is as yet unknown, but it is clear that the contribution of psychosocial treatment in schizophrenia must be re-evaluated as necessary components in any treatment plan. As Spaulding et al. point out, the traditional psychiatric focus on symptom suppression in increasingly obsolete. A range of specific psychological and psychosocial interventions are available to assist people with schizophrenia in sustaining higher levels of recovered function, and it is more and more apparent that these interventions form a vital component of any comprehensive treatment plan. Spaulding et al. make a valuable contribution in terms of a treatment algorithm that may assist decision making in applying these interventions.

Perhaps the most strikingly successful example of combined treatments this book can offer is represented by chapter 8, Marc E. Mooney and Dorothy K. Hatsukami's contribution on treatments for tobacco cessation. Nicotine dependence is a problem with strong biological and psychological correlates. Mooney and Hatsukami successfully demonstrate that interventions addressing both behavioral and physiological components are more likely to succeed than approaches that address only one facet of the disorder. Because the long-term consequences of nicotine dependence are severe, and because combined treatments are of demonstrable robustness, psychologists should see this chapter as a true invitation to become more involved in the treatment of nicotine dependence.

Kathleen M. Carroll's chapter 9 on treatment of substance abuse (other than nicotine dependence) demonstrates a more adjunctive, yet still important role for pharmacological intervention in the treatment of addictive behavior disorders. Although the implicit thesis in Carroll's work is that behavioral principles are fundamental to successful management of substance dependence, the chapter also acknowledges the reality that no "magic bullet" exists. Clearly, the direction of the field is in seeking those appropriate combinations of treatment that best suit the individual suffering from substance abuse disorders (Boucher, Kiresuk, & Trachtenberg, 1998), and Carroll's chapter is a useful guideline for clinicians attempting to put this philosophy into practice as well as a masterful review of the substance abuse treatment literature.

Obesity is another disorder with strong physiological and psychological substrates. Both pharmacological and behavioral treatments are still evolving for this pernicious problem, which is often accompanied by significant medical comorbidity. Recent well-publicized negative outcomes associated with the "phen-fen" regimen have given pause to advocates of pharmacological interventions and, although Carlos M. Grilo notes in chapter 10 that more recent innovations, such as the lipase inhibitors, are free of these negative side effects, other problems mandate that these medications be carefully deployed. Because of the risks associated with pharmacological intervention, and because the debate as to whether purely behavioral treatments provide equivalent outcomes to drug regimens is not yet settled, a conservative approach to pharmacological management of obesity seems prudent. Nevertheless, a strong case for combined treatments can be made in cases in which high body mass indexes or medical comorbidity exist. Because of the high rate of relapse that generally follows discontinuation of pharmacological treatment, it may be reasonable to argue that the choice rests not between medication or behavioral treatment but between combined treatments versus behavioral treatment alone.

James M. Meredith, Michael J. Lambert, and John F. Drozd present in chapter 11 an outcomes assessment package that they have developed for use in a clinical setting with a focus on the Outcomes Questionnaire (OQ45.2; Lambert et al., 1996). Clinicians seeking accessible and clinically useful tools that have sound psychometric properties will find this chapter of particular interest. These authors have taken care in assembling a package of outcomes measures that largely conforms with the recommendations of the National Institute of Mental Health panel on clinical outcomes (Newman & Ciarlo, 1994). Readers will note that the measures are designed to be independent of treatment provided. This helps in meeting the requirement of clinical utility but makes it difficult to ascertain the contributions of drug and nondrug components of treatment. Are treatment-specific outcome measures necessary in clinical practice? This is a debatable question. On the one hand, it can be argued that if one uses a combination of previously validated treatments that share as mutual goals the reduction of the same set of symptoms, then treatment-specific outcomes add little to good clinical assessment. On the other hand, this answer is not likely to satisfy those who seek to isolate those factors, or combinations of factors, that contribute most to good clinical outcome. This is an area that cries out sharply for further careful research.

Ideological divisions, poorly fitting research strategies, and a gap between science-based and ordinary clinical practice have impeded a more complete understanding of the mechanisms and effectiveness of combined treatments. At the most fundamental level, the question of whether they are more efficacious than unimodal treatments has yet to be definitively answered. Yet evidence in favor is slowly accreting, at least for certain disorders and, as the chapters in this book attest, progress in other areas, however slowly, is being made. Thorny practical and ethical problems remain: From a practical perspective, is it reasonable to hope that uniform clinical decision-making strategies for selecting combined treatments can be developed? Ethically, can such strategies be developed so that they do not repeat the mistakes of the past—primarily, an excessive reliance on psychotropic agents?

Newer research models specifically designed to address combined treatments will help answer these questions. In order to have an influence on practice, however, educators and trainers in psychology must adopt and disseminate new statistical and heuristic models for understanding combined treatments. If we do not train future psychologists, both academics and clinicians, to appreciate the value of a more catholic approach toward the treatment of mental disorders, we will needlessly constrain the ability of the field to advance and to offer the widest possible range of treatment options to those whom we seek to serve.

References

American Psychiatric Association. (1994). *Diagnostic and statistical manual of mental disorders* (4th ed.). Washington, DC: Author.

Bloom, F. E., & Kupfer, D. J. (Eds.). (1995). *Psychopharmacology: The fourth generation of progress.* New York: Raven.

Boucher, T. A., Kiresuk, T. I., & Trachtenberg, A. I. (1998). Alternative therapies. In A. W. Graham, T. K. Schulz, & B. B. Wilford (Eds.), *Principles of addiction medicine* (2nd ed., pp. 371–394). Chevy Chase, MD: American Society of Addiction Medicine.

Cooper, J. R., Bloom, F. E., & Roth, R. H. (1996). *The biochemical basis of neuropharmacology* (7th ed.). New York: Oxford University Press.

Feldman, T. S., Meyer, J. S., & Quenzer, L. F. (1997). *Principles of neuropsychopharmacology.* Sunderland, MA: Sinauer Associates.

Gelenberg, A. J., & Bassuk, E. L. (Eds.). (1997). *The practitioner's guide to psychoactive drugs* (4th ed.). New York: Plenum.

Healy, D. (1997). *The antidepressant era.* Cambridge, MA: Harvard University Press.

Janicak, P. G., Davis, J. M., Preskorn, S. H., & Ayd, F. J. (1997). *Principles and practice of psychopharmacotherapy* (2nd ed.). Baltimore: Williams & Wilkins.

Lambert, M. J., Hansen, N. B., Umphress, V., Lunnen, K., Okiishi, J., Burlingame, G. M., & Reisinger, C. W. (1996). *Administration and scoring manual for the OQ45.2.* Stevenson, MD: Professional Credentialing Services.

Newman, F. L., & Ciarlo, J. A. (1994). Criteria for selecting psychological instruments for treatment outcome assessments. In M. E. Maruish (Ed.), *The use of psychological testing for treatment planning and outcome assessment* (pp. 98–110). Hillsdale, NJ: Erlbaum.

Pagliaro, L. A., & Pagliaro, A. M. (Eds.). (1997). *The pharmacologic basis of psychotherapeutics: An introduction for psychologists*. New York: Brunner/Mazel.

Pagliaro, L. A., & Pagliaro, A. M. (1999). *The psychologists' neuropsychotropic drug reference*. New York: Brunner-Routledge.

Schatzberg, A. F., & Nemeroff, C. B. (Eds.). (1998). *Textbook of psychopharmacology* (2nd ed.). Washington, DC: American Psychiatric Press.

Stahl, S. (1996). *Essential pharmacology*. New York: Cambridge University Press.

1

Combined Treatments for Mental Disorders: Clinical Dilemmas

Morgan T. Sammons

Believe those who are seeking the truth. Doubt those who find it.
—André Gide

The absence of a compelling body of evidence on combined pharmacological and nonpharmacological treatments for mental disorders is perhaps the most striking feature of the mental health clinical research literature. This lack of data—particularly in an age of evidence-based practice—about what is arguably the most common form of treatment for mental distress suggests much about the degree to which guild and financial interests shape the pursuit of scientific knowledge. My first task in this chapter is to document the prevalence of combined treatments. I then examine the academic and political phenomena that have contributed to the paucity of data on combined interventions. Obstacles, surmountable or otherwise, to our understanding of these treatments are discussed (along with some occasional successes). I then turn to more practical matters, notably, how one might proceed in developing appropriate standardized protocols that clinicians can use when formulating and applying combined interventions. Because the literature is largely silent, it is difficult to formulate clear, systematic guidelines directing clinicians toward optimum combined treatment strategies. Some tentative guidelines are be offered, but it is acknowledged that the current state of understanding renders these guidelines aspirational and, it is hoped, ephemeral, in that directives that are more solidly grounded in science will be forthcoming.

A Failure of Investigative Models: Some Flaws, Fallacies, and Conundrums

Combined drug and nondrug treatments for mental distress are poorly represented in the research and clinical literature. Nevertheless, they are

The opinions expressed by this author represent his views as a private citizen and should not be construed as representing the official opinions or positions of the U.S. Navy or Department of Defense.

widespread in clinical practice, to the extent that they may be said to constitute the norm. A significant percentage, possibly even the majority, of all patients receiving services from a psychologist or other nonprescribing mental health practitioner are also simultaneously receiving psychotropic medications, as demonstrated by a number of surveys of mental health service providers ("Mental health," 1995; Sammons, Gorny, Zinner, & Allen, 2000; Chiles, Carlin, Benjamin, & Beitman, 1991). A further telling indicator of the common nature of combined treatments is the frequency with which primary care practitioners, who are most likely to initially encounter and diagnose mental disorders, use both drugs and referral to mental health specialties. A recent survey demonstrated that 72.5% of depressed patients were given antidepressants, and 38% of these were also referred to a mental health specialist (usually a psychologist or social worker; Williams et al., 1999).

On the other hand, pharmacological treatment has become the mainstay of psychiatric service provision. Reporting on the National Ambulatory Medical Care Survey data from 1985 and 1993–1994, Olfson et al. (1998) reported that at least one antidepressant was prescribed in 48.6% of all visits to psychiatrists in 1993–1994. Using the same data set, Pincus et al. (1998) discovered that, in 1993–1994, a visit to a psychiatrist specifically for depression resulted in the prescription of a psychotropic agent in 70.9% of cases. Because not all visits to psychiatrists are for depression, the total proportion of visits in which drugs were prescribed was undoubtedly much higher. This assumption was confirmed by a survey of the practice of 148 psychiatrists in routine outpatient practice (West, Zarin, & Pincus, 1997). In this survey, 90% of all patients of psychiatrists were prescribed at least one psychotropic medication (the mean number of medications per patient was 1.8). In a further analysis of this data set, Pincus et al. (1999) reconfirmed that, in 1997, approximately 90% of patients of psychiatrists surveyed were taking medications. As the authors noted, this was a sizable increase since 1989, when 54.5% of psychiatric patients were prescribed medication. Pincus et al. (1999) also found that 55.4% of outpatients reported on in this survey received both medication and psychotherapy, with psychotherapy being provided either by the psychiatrist or another professional. It is apparent, then, that pharmacotherapy is the mainstay of current psychiatric practice but, even so, the majority of patients also receive psychotherapeutic services. Zito and colleagues (2000) also documented an extraordinary rise in the rate of prescriptions of psychotropics to preschoolers during the 1990s, indicating that the overprescription phenomenon is hardly limited to adult populations.

Unfortunately, the pervasiveness of combined treatment is poorly documented in clinical research, and its mechanisms and effectiveness remain the focus of controversy. This in large part may be because of the power of the controlled clinical trial as an investigatory heuristic. Although the benefits of controlled clinical trials cannot be disputed, in certain respects this model has led to an investigative approach that does not capture well the nuances involved in combined treatment. The literature is replete with reports of single-modality, placebo-controlled outcome studies, such as the effectiveness of cognitive–behavioral models in treating depression. Also, a reasonable number of comparative-treatment outcome studies exist for most major mental disorders. These "horse race" studies often involve head-to-head comparisons of unimodal pharmacological and psychological interventions. Although they have become somewhat less common in recent years (Beitman, 1991), these studies continue to be highly represented in the literature. At the same time, trials of combined treatments are scarce. Only a handful, of variable quality, exist for most disorders.

In part, this situation has been perpetuated by professional biases. Psychologists and nonmedical researchers may have a vested interest in demonstrating the superiority of nonpharmacological techniques. On the opposite side, psychiatric researchers, particularly those with a biological orientation, may tend to champion pharmacotherapeutic strategies. These dichotomous conceptualizations of interventions lead to difficulties in research design and provide a source of investigatory bias that can considerably influence outcome. Sources of investigatory bias are difficult to isolate precisely but are reflected by practices such as comparing the treatment being studied against one that appears equivalent but in reality is unequal. One common example of this in drug studies is the strategy of comparing a new drug against an older agent that is effective but has a less favorable side-effect profile. This practice has been found to be extremely common in schizophrenia research (Thornley & Adams, 1998). Researchers' preference for, or allegiance to, one form of treatment over another may also lead to the less favored treatment being inadequately implemented during a clinical trial (Jacobson & Hollon, 1996). A further difficulty in research design is not directly related to hidden researcher bias but is endemic in much of mental health research today. This is the familiar difficulty encountered when efficacy, rather than effectiveness, studies are performed. Efficacy studies, which I discuss in more detail later, comprise the bulk of the scientific knowledge base in mental health research. These studies, usually based on comparisons of two reasonably pure treatments applied in sterile research environments to participants who resemble each other as much as possible, result in outcomes that are poorly generalizable to the everyday treatment setting. As compared to effectiveness studies (examinations of how patients respond to treatments applied in the field; Seligman, 1995), efficacy studies have limited ability to satisfactorily inform clinicians or patients as to optimum choices among treatments (Roland & Torgerson, 1998).

Controlling Bias in Research and Practice

In light of findings that neither psychotherapeutic nor pharmacotherapeutic approaches are superior in the treatment of at least the most common form of mental distress, preference emerges as a key, if not decisive, factor in determining selection of treatment. Preference may be expressed by either the clinician or the patient. Patient choice is an important variable in determining positive outcome, but patient preferences are probably influenced by clinicians to a greater extent than is realized. Strongly held opinions about what is best for patients not only prevents clinicians from uncritically examining the data and values that shape their assumptions, but they also may make clinicians insensitive to the rights of patients to disagree (Woolf & Lawrence, 1997). In the field of mental health, clinicians are peculiarly positioned to interpret differences of opinion between therapist and patients as being rooted in psychopathology (i.e., resistance), rather than as an issue of patient choice:

> Some patients want only medications and others want only psychotherapy. Those who ask for medications only may simply want immediate relief and not care what the means is. On the other hand, those who want psychotherapy only may reject medication out of fear of some external control, preferring instead a sense of personal control. Although each of these positions may be considered resistance to oppositely oriented psychiatrists, they are more specifically resistances to the bias of the psychiatrist. (Beitman, 1991, p. 26)

The obvious challenge is to create a system in which data, and not bias, drive treatment recommendations. With such evidence, the clinician will be able to offer the patient expert advice as to the form of intervention best suited for the presenting complaint. By careful, unbiased education, patient attitudes may be changed so that they can be steered toward whatever form of intervention has been demonstrated to be most effective. The right of a patient with disabling symptoms of anxiety to demand immediate relief in the form of an anxiolytic medication must be respected, not challenged. At the same time, the clinician must take pains to educate the patient that this relief is likely to be short term and evanescent once the medication is discontinued. Such patients should be given impartial information as to the availability of potentially more effective treatments leading to longer lasting relief. This information should include a discussion of whether nonpharmacological treatment can be used in combination with medication; as a substitute for it; or if the medication will interfere with the process of behavioral treatment, as may be the case when benzodiazepines are used in conjunction with exposure-based treatments for phobic anxiety.

It is obvious that we are far from reaching the ideal of providing patients with unbiased, purely objective informed consent. Practically, this state of reason is probably impossible to attain. Biases, expectations, and differences in information processing continually affect interchanges between therapists and patients (Redelmeier, Rozin, & Kahneman, 1993). The goal should not be to eliminate such biases but to minimize their influence by making them explicit to both patient and therapist, so that each may judge the effects of their beliefs on choice of treatment.

The Burden of Reductionistic Thinking

Subtle investigator bias resulting from dichotomous thinking about mental health interventions is but one complicating factor that has led to combined treatments being understudied. Another factor that has significantly influenced research patterns has been the quest to identify, with increasing specificity, "cures" for mental disorders. This search represents something of a conundrum, which can be outlined in broad strokes as follows: Psychological distress is a heterogeneous and nonspecific concept, and its experience is unique to each sufferer. One can define, albeit in rather nebulous terms, some of the features that separate one form of psychological distress from another, but it remains true that most people with schizophrenia, or most depressed patients, share in common only the most obvious features of their diagnoses. Nevertheless, the aim of much of mental health research in the past 50 years has been to search for increasingly specific remedies. We are therefore placed in the awkward position of positing molecular cures for molar concepts that are heterogeneous, nonspecific, and experienced in an absolutely unique manner by each sufferer.

The past 50 years of mental health research has led to the successful development of many specific pharmacological and psychological treatments that have improved patient outcomes (Michels, 1999). At least in the short term, specific pharmacological interventions do assist many patients in coping with the more disabling aspects of their illness, sometimes dramatically so. Yet there is also evidence that these increasingly specific results do not translate into lasting improvement. Rates of successful treatment for schizophrenia have not appreciably changed in the past 100 years (Hegarty, Baldessarini, Tohen, Waternaux, & Oepen, 1994), despite the synthesis of effective antipsychotic drugs. New-generation antidepressants, such as the serotonin reuptake inhibitors, have not resulted in improved long-term remission rates, neither have increasingly specific psychological treatments. In the well-known (if not overstudied) Treatment of Depression Collaborative Research Project (Elkin et al., 1989), recovery rates at 18-month follow-up did not differ among any treatment. Recovery ranged from 19% for clinical management plus imipramine to 30% for cognitive–behavior therapy (CBT; Jacobson & Hollon, 1996), a less-than-splendid showing for any treatment. To a large extent, then, specificity and success do not correlate well.

Paradoxically enough, increasing the specificity of treatment has constrained our ability to perform certain types of research. Because one can demonstrate the success of specific treatments in short-term (although rarely in long-term) outcome studies, we have greater difficulty justifying the application of combined treatments. Essentially, the issue is the ability to justify a more complex, possibly more expensive treatment when simpler and cheaper remedies have been shown to be of utility. Is it ethical to impose unproven, costlier combinations on patients when less complicated alternatives, already shown to be of value, exist? This question is subject to considerable debate and arises in numerous examples throughout this chapter.

The issue of specificity pertains to diagnoses as well as treatment. It is a grave error to assume that, once having made a *Diagnostic and Statistical Manual of Mental Disorders*–type (*DSM*) diagnosis, the treatment becomes uniform. Hohagen et al. (1998) demonstrated, for example, that patients with *DSM–III–R* (American Psychiatric Association, 1987) obsessive–compulsive disorder (OCD) did best with unimodal therapy (behavioral treatment) if their symptoms were primarily compulsive but did best with combined medication and behavior treatment if their symptoms were primarily obsessive. Along similar lines, Wells and Sturm (1996) found that addition of minor tranquilizers to antidepressant therapy did nothing to improve outcomes in the treatment of major depressive disorder. Yet it is clear that a subset of patients with major depression present with significant anxiety symptoms. When these symptoms are appropriately managed with a short-term course of benzodiazepines, outcome is improved (Buysse et al., 1997; Smith, Londborg, Glaudin, & Painter, 1998).

This introduction should remind the reader that in spite of the high prevalence of combined treatment in clinical practice our knowledge of combined treatments is poor. They may not work as well as single-modality treatments for some disorders; they may provide more rapid or lasting relief in others. Because combined treatments are often not supported by the current literature, clinicians should be circumspect in devising such treatments for their patients. At the same time, clinicians should be careful to balance the needs of individual patients against the results of large-scale studies or meta-analyses, for these are poor predictors of individual response in the clinical setting (cf. Klein, 1998). For most conditions, single-modality treatments should be attempted before combined treatments are implemented and, for all conditions for which it has found to be effective, psychosocial treatment should be included in the treatment plan.

Unresolved Issues in Combined Treatments

There is bountiful support that psychopharmacotherapy provides generally incomplete and temporary relief from mental distress. There is also equally convincing evidence that credible forms of active psychotherapy are generally indistinguishable in terms of efficacy. Long-term outcome data pay no compliments to either approach. Thus, advocates of neither biological nor psychosocial approaches have much in the way of substantive data to support claims that theirs is the preferred method of intervention. Conflicts between various schools of mental health practitioners are, then, generally based in ideology (Klerman, 1991) rather than science. Because ideological allegiances have limited the study of combined treatments, clinicians lack data to guide their application. Some of the more important factors that remain poorly understood are the timing of particular components of combined treatments, our understanding of the nonspecific factors associated with any component of treatment, and how decisions about drug or nondrug treatment can be better standardized. It is to these issues that I now turn.

Timing of Interventions

If combinations of drugs and verbal therapy are used, when is it reasonable to introduce each component into the treatment plan? This largely unexplored area is of importance in determining when and if a combined strategy is indicated and how combined treatments are optimally applied in clinical settings. Miller and Keitner (1996) provided a thoughtful review on the subject and suggested that at least three strategies are possible. The first involves administering all treatments simultaneously. Providing all treatments concurrently would ensure that the patient has been exposed to all elements of potential value. This approach, however, is both costly, because greater resources are expended, and inefficient, because it is impossible (at least given the current state of understanding) to identify a priori those patients who will respond to a specific component of treatment.

A second alternative is the sequential model, wherein additional treatments are proffered on the basis of response or lack of response to previous interventions. Miller and Keitner (1996) noted that this technique is already almost universally used in drug treatment—doses are increased, or different drugs are attempted, if the first medication has proven ineffective. This, as the authors noted, is a more parsimonious and potentially cost-effective approach in that additional interventions are offered only if previous ones have failed. A potential drawback to this approach is that any beneficial synergistic effects of offering treatments together might be either deferred or lost. In addition, dose–response relations evidently exist for psychotherapies (Howard, Kopta, Krause, & Orlinsky, 1986) as well as pharmacotherapies, and this effect could be lost by adding psychotherapy later in the treatment course (i.e., too little, too late), or it could be obscured by the addition of a drug treatment.

Third, Miller and Keitner (1996) proposed a "matching" strategy, wherein various single or combined treatments are offered on the basis of an assessment of the patient's identified deficits or resources. This, they noted, is also a cost-effective model, but if treatments and patients are matched incorrectly, outcomes will be suboptimal. Because, as observed previously, one cannot easily determine in advance those components of treatment to which individual patients are likely to respond well, this may be the least preferred of the strategies for combining. Using depression as an example, it is often very difficult to clinically determine when presenting symptoms represent acute onset of a major depressive episode, an adjustment disorder, or an acute stress reaction. Although history may be of some assistance in distinguishing among disorders that may require longer term pharmacological management and those that are expected to resolve with brief treatment, this is not always the case. Suicidal ideation as a presenting complaint may result from cognitive factors (hopelessness); alternatively, patients may consider suicide as an escape from intolerable neurovegetative signs, such as severe insomnia or autonomic arousal. The dilemma here is whether to initiate a course of antidepressant therapy immediately or to see if the patient's symptoms will respond to several closely spaced sessions of psychotherapy or environmental manipulation. Delaying antidepressant treatment may be deleterious, given that patients will in any case experience a 3- to 6-week time lag in onset of antidepressant effect. Initiating treatment immediately, however, may commit the patient to an unnecessary course of medication. It is perhaps best to temporize in these situations. Some experts have recommended that, in the case of milder, less chronic, nonpsychotic depression, an extended evaluation of two to three visits be undertaken to determine those patients who will remit with nonspecific treatment alone (Depression Guideline Panel, 1993). If a patient does not respond to closely spaced therapy sessions (perhaps augmented with short-term use of a benzodiazepine to address symptoms of insomnia and autonomic arousal; Smith et al., 1998), then delay in initiating a course of antidepressants is not likely to be of lasting harm.

In many combined-treatment outcome studies, both treatments have been initiated simultaneously at the beginning of treatment (Rush & Hollon, 1991). Rush and Hollon (1991) suggested that either could be added at any point in treatment without altering the modality already used. This statement may be true in the context of augmenting suboptimal responses to unimodal treatments (a reasonably well-studied maneuver). For instance, it is commonly recommended to add psychotherapy to a medication regimen if an inadequate response is present after 6–8 weeks of treatment. By using this strategy, the additive effect of combined treatments can be estimated, but no knowledge is gained about the synergistic effects of two separate modalities applied simultaneously at some point in the treatment course, or whether reversing the order of the treatments applied would be more effective. Because no clinical outcome data exist to guide clinicians on this point, it is suggested that the following questions be asked when considering the timing of combined treatments.

First, has an adequate period of observation and assessment been accomplished? Patients presenting in acute distress present diagnostic dilemmas. A moderate to severe adjustment disorder with depressed mood may be indistinguishable from an acute stress disorder or the acute onset of a major depressive episode. Patients may demonstrate a rapid response to psychotherapy or environmental manipulation for the first two conditions and may not require initiation of pharmacotherapy. The risks of delaying treatment in a medication-responsive condition must be carefully weighed against any risk involved in the administration of drugs.

Second, have unimodal treatments already been considered or implemented? In general, pharmacotherapy alone is less effective than psychotherapy alone, especially in cases of treatment-resistant or chronic depression or when Axis II pathology or other conditions complicate the clinical picture.

Third, do contraindications exist to the use of combined modalities? Examples would be the use of a benzodiazepine during exposure-based therapy for phobias (Barlow & Lehman, 1996) or the use of relatively toxic agents, such as the tricyclic antidepressants or lithium in borderline patients or others with chronic suicidal or parasuicidal behaviors (Dimeff,

McDavid, & Linehan, 1999). There also may be medical contraindications to the use of pharmacological treatments, such as histories of cardiac difficulties in patients taking antidepressants. Although few psychotropics have been definitively linked to fetal abnormalities (Koren, Pastuszak, & Ito, 1998), research in humans is perforce limited. Some experts have recommended that women who are pregnant or contemplating pregnancy stop using antidepressants and anxiolytics unless a threat to the mother, such as suicide, exists (Diket & Nolan, 1997). This opinion is not held by all experts. Kulin et al. (1998) found no increased risk of major congenital malformations associated with antidepressant use in pregnancy in a prospective, controlled trial. Treatment of psychological disorders in the postpartum period also is understudied. The most common psychological problem in the postpartum period is depression, but a recent review identified only one controlled trial of antidepressants (Cooper & Murray, 1998). In the trial in question, both fluoxetine and counseling were found to be effective in treating postpartum depression (Appleby, Warner, Whitton, & Faragher, 1997). Numerous psychotropics are excreted in breast milk, but their effects on neonatal development are unknown (Stowe, Strader, & Nemeroff, 1998).

Fourth, for some conditions, in some individuals, combined treatments may represent optimum therapy, such as in bipolar disorder (Sachs, 1996); some forms of depression (Thase et al., 1997); for smoking cessation (Hatsukami & Mooney, 1999); and, in all probability, psychotic disorders, such as schizophrenia (Rosenheck et al., 1998; Spaulding, Johnson, & Coursey, chapter 7, this volume). Does the patient manifest characteristics that have been demonstrated to be amenable to combined treatment? It is important to understand that these characteristics are fluid, will vary throughout an episode of illness, and must be reassessed on a ongoing basis. Significant depression, for example, may be complicated by numerous manifestations of anxiety early in the treatment course. Because of the delay in onset of antidepressant drugs it is important to recognize and treat these symptoms (Smith et al., 1998).

Fifth, has the patient's history of response to either psychotherapy or pharmacotherapy been elicited? Patients whose initial response to pharmacotherapy has been positive may still require the addition of psychotherapeutic components. There is some evidence that exposure-based treatments can assist patients who initially used benzodiazepines to obtain relief from panic disorder. Benzodiazepines are effective in controlling the acute symptoms of panic but tend to provide long-term relief only with continued use. Risks of dependence (although probably overstated; Shader & Greenblatt, 1993), and the propensity for anxiolytics to interfere with exposure-based training, have led to recommendations to limit their use in the treatment of panic disorder. Bruce, Spiegel, and Hegel (1999) found that when anxiolytic agents are used, patients treated with CBT were significantly more able to discontinue alprazolam and remain symptom free at 2- to 5-year follow-up than those treated with standard management. Thus, a combination of pharmacological approaches, to ameliorate acute symptoms of the disorder, and psychotherapy, to provide long-term relief, may be an appropriate strategy in panic disorder, although further study is required before this can be recommended with certainty.

Finally, what treatment modality does the patient desire? Has he or she been given adequate informed consent about the relative efficacy of either or both treatments? Integrating pharmacotherapy with psychotherapy early in the treatment course ideally will sufficiently reduce the more florid symptoms of a mental disorder to the point that the patient is able to effectively engage in a psychotherapeutic relationship (Klerman, 1991). If this course is agreed on, patients must understand not only the risks and benefits associated with both pharmacotherapy and psychotherapy but also that the ultimate goal may be to withdraw the pharmacological agent prior to termination of therapy.

The Elusive Algorithm

During the 1990s, a number of attempts have been made to formulate rational prescribing strategies for psychotropics. In response to an emphasis on evidence-based practice and a need to manage rising health care costs, clinical guidelines have become increasingly common. Clinical guidelines are ideally evidence based, but many remain based on expert consensus or opinion (Woolf, Grol, Hutchinson, Eccles, & Grimshaw, 1999) and thus may not represent truly science-informed practice. Also, the evidence that underlies clinical guideline recommendations is intentionally biased toward highly controlled, diagnostically selective, randomized clinical trials (Shekelle, Woolf, Eccles, & Grimshaw, 1999); these generally take place in tertiary-care facilities with research capabilities. Such results likely do not translate perfectly to general treatment settings (Haycox, Bagust, & Walley, 1999), and their applicability in such settings has been challenged (Rosser, 1999). For example, the American Psychiatric Association's practice guideline for major depressive disorder (Karasu et al., 1993) has been criticized for, among other deficits, undervaluing the efficacy of cognitive therapy and overstating the value of combining behavioral or brief psychodynamic therapy with medication (Persons, Thase, & Crits-Christoph, 1996).

One common method to standardize treatment is the development of formal algorithms. These are evidence-based guidelines providing treatment options for clinicians through an episode of care. In general, commonly used drugs at low doses are selected first, with suggestions for use of drugs from other classes or other interventions should the disorder prove resistant. Algorithms have been developed for the treatment of schizophrenia (Pearsall et al., 1998) and major depression in primary care (Trivedi et al., 1998). One problem encountered in the development of algorithms is that the strength of the underlying evidence is often not very great. This is especially the case when new agents for which little clinical experience has accrued (such as the novel antipsychotics) are incorporated into an algorithm. In such instances conclusions may depend heavily on short-term, industry-funded trials (Pearsall et al., 1998).

Another problem associated with algorithms is their lack of ecological validity. Although combined treatments are common in routine practice, few algorithms address combined treatments, because these are rarely the subject of randomized clinical trials in tertiary-care settings. For example, Trivedi et al. (1998), in devising their treatment algorithm for depression in primary care, avoided any mention of referral for psychotherapy. A primary-care physician using such an algorithm to treat depression would have no prompt as to when or if a patient should be referred for psychotherapy. This is a particularly distressing oversight given the amount of evidence that psychotherapy is at least of equal efficacy (and, more controversially, occasionally superior) to pharmacotherapy in the treatment of depression (Munoz, Hollon, McGrath, Rehm, & Vanden Bos, 1994; Murphy, Carney, Knesevich, Wetzel, & Whitworth, 1995; Rush & Hollon, 1991). A solution to the current lack of ecological validity in many evidence-based guidelines would be the development of practice research networks. Such networks would enhance the ability to perform clinical trials in the primary care setting (Nutting, Beasley, & Werner, 1999) and would provide a mechanism for the systematic collection of data from potentially large numbers of participants in environments closely resembling actual practice conditions, where combined treatments are more likely to be prescribed.

Expert-consensus guidelines differ from evidence-based guidelines in that, as their name implies, they rely on the opinions of recognized specialists in the treatment of a particular disorder. Recommendations are therefore more likely to represent current standards of excellence in practice rather than treatments suggested by randomized trials. Recommendations of experts, however, may be even more subjective than evidence-based guidelines, and they are less likely to be multidisciplinary, an important element influencing the acceptability of recommendations (Shekelle et al., 1999). As noted above, past recommendations by expert panels of psychiatrists have downplayed the effectiveness of psychotherapeutic intervention. An encouraging recent development is the trend to include nonpharmacological treatments as first- or second-line interventions for various disorders, such as that for OCD (March, Frances, Carpenter, & Kahn, 1998).

Evidence-based guidelines are increasingly common, and they represent a laudable attempt to match clinical practice with the best of research knowledge. As the shortcomings already discussed suggest, however, guidelines are no panacea. Like other forms of research, they may not be appreciated or implemented by clinicians. Guidelines have also been criticized because they have failed to take into consideration the costs of treatment, although there is some evidence that this is changing (Dean, 1999). In the final analysis, algorithms or guidelines for treatment of mental disorders may fail because both the manifestations of most mental disorders and the major effects of treatment are so nonspecific as to defy quantification in the form of an algorithm or guideline.

This problem is exemplified by our ambiguous understanding of the biology of depression and the wide variety of treatments for it. No theory

advanced to date can adequately explain what, if any, biochemical perturbation leads to the subjective experience of depression (Valenstein, 1998).
It should therefore be no surprise that much remains to be understood
about the pharmacology of antidepressant agents or that any single ex-
planation of their mechanism of action is satisfactory (Shader, Fogelman,
& Greenblatt, 1998). Why so many agents with differing or even opposing
mechanisms of action produce an antidepressant response remains an unanswered question (Hollister & Claghorn, 1993).[1] Also, response to all
drugs that are antidepressants is more or less the same. A depressed patient is just as likely to respond to fluoxetine as to amitriptyline or nefazodone. Manufacturers of antidepressants often attempt to distinguish
their product by their neuroreceptor selectivity—whether a drug is more
active on serotonergic or norepinephrine-containing neurons, for example.
Although these claims reflect true pharmacological differences between
antidepressant drugs, clinically all will produce the same degree of improvement, at least insofar as group data are concerned. The selective
serotonin reuptake inhibitors (SSRIs) and other new antidepressants have
superior side-effect profiles over older drugs, but remission rates have not
improved (Burke & Preskorn, 1995). This may be, as Burke and Preskorn
(1995) speculated, because some forms of depression are not responsive to
pharmacotherapy, or because the mechanisms of action of available drugs
are not appropriate for all subtypes of the disorder. Regardless, "there are
no convincing data to suggest that regulations of adrenergic or serotonergic receptors per se [are] responsible for the therapeutic effects of antidepressant drugs" (Hyman & Nestler, 1996, p. 160). In clinical terms,
this problem is illustrated in the algorithm by Trivedi et al. (1998). For a
case of uncomplicated nonpsychotic major depression, SSRIs, nefazodone,
bupropion, venlafaxine, moclobemide, mirtazapine, and the tricyclics are
all listed as potential first interventions—a range of options that is hardly
likely to satisfy a practitioner looking for algorithmic guidance on optimum drug strategies.

The smorgasbord of pharmacological alternatives that exists for treatment of most mental disorders may be said to represent for psychopharmacotherapy what the "dodo-bird effect" represents to psychotherapy; that
is, all credible therapies tend to result in significantly greater improvement than do sham or placebo therapies, and there is little to distinguish
one credible therapy from another. The dodo-bird hypothesis has recently
been reconfirmed for psychotherapy (Wampold et al., 1997) and, because
all credible antidepressants tend to (a) result in greater improvement than
do other medications used for the same purpose and (b) result in approx-

---

[1] In spite of this it is incontestable that certain medications have a specific antidepressant effect that can be behaviorally measured and can persist over time. Chronic administration of an antidepressant compound to a severely depressed individual will have salutary
effects that are distinct from those of a placebo (although the placebo may also have beneficial effects of its own). Chronic administration of a benzodiazepine, however, to a similarly
depressed individual is not likely to result in a significant degree of improvement (Wells &
Sturm, 1996). Thus it is clear that antidepressants differ not only from placebo in their
effects, but they also differ from other classes of drugs.

imately the same rates of improvement, a dodo-bird effect can also be posited for drug treatment. If one accepts the argument that the dodo-bird principle applies to pharmacotherapy, which is buttressed by Kirsch and Sapirstein's (1998) finding that the vast majority of the effects of antidepressant drugs are nonspecific effects, then it makes little sense to develop algorithms intended to standardize their use. Nonspecific effects are difficult to incorporate into formulaic treatment strategies. This is not, however, to suggest that nonspecific effects are bereft of therapeutic benefit; far from it. One does not use specificity as a measure of how effective an intervention is. We cannot isolate the specific active components of CBT or other psychotherapies (Ablon & Jones, 1999; Jacobson et al., 1996), but CBT is an effective psychotherapy nonetheless, and to abandon it would disserve many patients. Neither should we abandon pharmacotherapy because we cannot identify active components of antidepressant treatment. As previously argued, specific treatments in fact may not be very good for many mental disorders, because they are multidimensional and, for each sufferer, uniquely experienced.

In the end, the search for an effective, universally applicable algorithm for the treatment of common mental disorders may be doomed to failure, inasmuch as it seems unlikely that the specific effects of any kind of treatment (pharmacological or not) will soon, if ever, be elucidated. Given this situation, nomothetic algorithms make little sense. As Woolf and Lawrence (1997) observed,

> universal recommendations only make sense when there is little doubt across preference groups and risk profiles about the trade-off between benefits and harms . . . when what is best for one individual also is clearly best for another. If, however, the relationship of benefits to harms is uncertain and the "best choice" is a matter of personal values, family history, and other risk factors, a single policy for everyone is improper. (p. 2106)

These cautions, although written in reference to breast cancer, are highly applicable to any attempt to create algorithms for mental distress, because personal values and family history are integral not only to the understanding of these disorders but also often to their genesis.

Proceeding in the Face of Uncertainty

It is evident that, outside of clinical trials, we have much to understand about the standards of delivery and effectiveness of both pharmacological and psychotherapeutic treatments. Nevertheless, there is some guidance, if only aspirational in nature, that can assist the clinician in selecting the appropriate form of unimodal or combined treatment. Thus, an attempt can be made to assimilate the data covered previously in this chapter into some tentative recommendations to guide the selection and timing of treatments. The reader looking for specific intervention strategies is likely to be disappointed; the preceding discussion should have educated any such seekers that we are still far from being able to delineate specific treatment recommendations.

The first task, regardless of whether unimodal or combined interventions are used, is the establishment of an accurate, objective, and comprehensive diagnosis. A firm diagnostic base is necessary before proceeding with any specific intervention. It is necessary to be alert to the presence of comorbid symptoms and evidence of dysfunction in spheres not addressed by *DSM*-based diagnoses when making the initial assessment. Here the clinician must use patient-based measures as well as clinical measures to achieve a multifactorial baseline. Consider ecological, interpersonal, intrapsychic, developmental, and biological variables. A small number of medications—for instance, some antihypertensives, steroids, or antineoplastic agents (Charney, Berman, & Miller, 1998)—have been at least tenuously linked to depression, and a careful documentation of a patient's past and current pharmacological regimen is mandatory. This should include an accurate tally of any over-the-counter, alternative, or herbal medications, or nonprescribed psychotropics (e.g., marijuana, LSD, stimulants, opiates) taken by the patient. Although somatic causes for depression are reasonably uncommon, the patient should be assessed for the presence of disease states, such as hypothyroidism, that have been associated with depression. Biological and physical workups may be especially productive in the cases of individuals with known risk factors or in cases of new-onset symptoms in older individuals with no prior history and no adequate psychosocial explanations for their current presentation. No blanket physical or laboratory workup can be recommended; these will depend on the patient's clinical presentation.

The patient's full involvement in the treatment plan must be solicited. Ethically, this is a necessity and, practically, there is evidence suggesting that patient involvement in treatment planning improves outcome (Richards, 1998). No treatment, psychological or pharmacological, should be offered without the provision of all elements of informed consent. For psychological therapies informed consent should include a description of the type of therapy, evidence supporting its effectiveness (including its effectiveness compared to no treatment at all), the demands it will impose on the patient, expected outcomes, and the frequency and cost of therapy sessions. Where evidence for the effectiveness of drug treatment exists, this alternative should also be explained to the patient. For pharmacological therapies, informed consent will include a discussion of the risks and benefits of the medication, as well as psychological treatments that may be equally effective, either singly or in combination with the drug treatment. In cases for which limited or no empirical support exists for pharmacological treatment, such as in the case of antidepressants in the treatment of depressed children and adolescents, this information should be clearly explained and available alternatives offered. The general finding that pharmacotherapies are less effective when offered without psychological interventions should be explained to the patient, and appropriate psychological, behavioral, or psychosocial modalities (not necessarily including formal psychotherapy) should be added to the treatment plan. In instances in which there is no clear evidence that one form of treatment is superior to another, the clinician must be observant of his or her inherent biases and serve as a candid, neutral source of expert advice. Strength of the evidence supporting both treatments, and the difficulties involved in translating research findings to the clinical setting, should be explained to the patient, who should then be allowed to select his or her treatment of choice. In many instances, patient choice will determine what treatment is to be applied, and clinicians must scrupulously adhere to their responsibility to provide the most expert and impartial knowledge in assisting such choices.

Observation of the nonspecific effects of intervention may assist in treatment decision making, especially decisions regarding pharmacological treatment. If the disorder improves during the assessment phase, as may be the case in the presence of a supporting and empathic therapist, a headlong rush for the prescription pad is unwise. As has been noted, some guidelines suggest that in milder, nonpsychotic or nonrecurrent depressions an extended (two- to three-session) evaluation may identify patients who will respond to nonpharmacological interventions (Depression Guideline Panel, 1993). When antidepressants are used, an excessively rapid or complete response that is not in keeping with the well-established delays in onset of effectiveness suggests that nonspecific or placebo effects are operating. These data can guide the clinician's subsequent pharmacological maneuvers and may indicate that pharmacotherapy might be safely discontinued at a relatively early point in treatment.

The effects on the therapeutic relationship of prescribing should also be considered, although admittedly there are essentially no solid data to guide clinicians here. In analyzing the limited literature on this topic, Klerman (1991) noted that most such effects were presumed to be negative. For example, the act of prescribing was thought to either diminish the effectiveness of psychotherapy by making the patient dependent on an authoritarian prescribing figure or to lead patients to forgo potentially more lasting change in favor of symptom reduction. These concerns, although worthy of some consideration, should not be dwelt on excessively. There are certain instances in which the addition of drugs may reduce the effectiveness of psychotherapy (the earlier-cited example of the use of anziolytics with exposure-based therapies). Otherwise, most opinions on the negative influence of drugs on psychotherapy are speculative.

This said, it is important not to dismiss the use of pharmacological agents when they are necessary. If levels of distress are high, particularly if they effectively preclude the establishment of a sound therapeutic liaison, consider the immediate use of combined treatment with the appropriate pharmacological agent. In catatonic or psychotic depression, other psychotic states, mania, and cases of extreme anxiety or agitation, pharmacotherapy is likely to be the first-line intervention. Even in such cases, a strong therapeutic alliance should be maintained throughout the hospitalization, and these interventions should never be offered without ongoing psychosocial intervention. Pharmacological treatments should never be offered as sole interventions. Schooler and Keith (1993) reviewed the literature on treatments for schizophrenia and found considerable evidence that currently available antipsychotic medications are effective in controlling both acute symptoms as well as in delaying or preventing relapse. Psychosocial treatments, including individual psychotherapy, individual social skills training, and family therapy, had additive or interactive roles with medication in treating both acute and long-term phases of the disorder. Family therapy was found to be a particularly effective intervention in long-term treatment. Janicak, Davis, Preskorn, and Ayd (1997) performed a meta-analysis of seven studies that examined combined psychosocial and pharmacological treatment in people with schizophrenia. Patients who received both psychoeducation and family therapy did significantly better than patients who received drugs alone.

In general, the literature suggests that unimodal treatments should be offered prior to combined treatments because of current limited evidence that combined treatments offer significant added benefit. In implementing this standard the reader should heed the caution, extensively discussed throughout this chapter, that combined treatments are more common than not and that current investigative models in all probability have underestimated the true effect of combined treatments. Where there is clear evidence that unimodal treatments may provide superior outcome, however, these should be implemented first. Such examples include many of the anxiety spectrum disorders. Behavioral treatment or CBT is the initial treatment of choice for OCD, panic disorder, and specific phobias. If adequately provided psychological therapy yields an incomplete response, it should not be discontinued, but pharmacotherapy should then be added into the treatment plan. Benzodiazepines should be largely avoided, especially in exposure-based therapies, because of their inhibition of learning responses and the risks of pharmacologic dependence.

Both pharmacological and behavioral strategies must be continually monitored and titrated throughout the treatment course. It is equally important to detect the emergence of new symptoms (and not only those associated with the initial diagnosis) at any point throughout the treatment course and modify interventions accordingly. At any stage of treatment, but particularly in the acute phase, there may be a dose–response relation between psychotherapy and clinical improvement, and the patient may require more frequent sessions. Short-term augmentation of an antidepressant regimen with a benzodiazepine may assist a depressed and anxious patient, but such treatment should be discontinued as soon as practicable. Initiation side effects must be continually monitored and managed as needed, as these can significantly affect adherence to medication regimens. If pharmacotherapy is used during maintenance and continuation phases, dosing strategies should be based on up-to-date research so as to minimize chances of recurrence. Because there is evidence that psychological therapies can also prolong time to recurrence, at least in depression, such strategies should also be maintained throughout the maintenance and continuation phases.

In any case, clinicians must keep in mind that long-term outcomes are not especially encouraging. Regardless of the modality used, most patients relapse within a few years of treatment. In one of the longer follow-up studies available, Fava and colleagues (Fava, Grandi, Zielzezny, Rafanelli, & Canestrari, 1996; Fava, Rafanelli, Grandi, Canestrari, & Morphy, 1998) examined outcomes for patients treated with either standard clinical management or CBT. All patients had initially been successfully treated with antidepressant medications. At 4-year follow-up the CBT group had significantly fewer relapses than the clinical management group, but at 6 years there was no significant difference between the two groups, although there were fewer relapses in the CBT group, and that group also experienced fewer multiple relapses.

Maintenance therapy is better than nothing, and more structured maintenance therapies, such as CBT, appear to have some advantage over standard clinical management, as the evidence reported by Fava and colleagues, 1996, 1998) indicates. Just as psychotherapies have relatively poor long-term outcome data, the results for maintenance pharmacotherapy indicate similarly poor long-term outcomes. Nevertheless, evidence suggests that patients who receive adequate pharmacological management experience fewer relapses than those who receive suboptimal management (generally in the form of insufficient dose; it is now well accepted that maintenance doses should be essentially the same as acute-phase doses) or no placebo. For instance, Keller et al. (1998) followed for 19 months patients with either major depressive disorder (MDD) or MDD and dysthymia who had responded to an acute-phase regimen of sertraline. In this study, 50% of patients treated with placebo experienced new onset of clinically significant depressive symptoms, whereas only 26% of the sertraline-treated group developed such symptoms. Although the data in favor are not overwhelming, Rush and Hollon (1991), after reviewing a number of studies, expressed limited support for the finding that cognitive therapy, whether provided singly or in combination with medication, provided better protection against relapse than pharmacotherapy.

Whatever the choice of intervention, the lowest effective dose should be used. Evidence for this is clearer when pharmacotherapies are used, but a dose–response effect in psychotherapy has been described as well (Barkham, Rees, Stiles, & Shapiro, 1996; Howard, Kopta, Krause, & Orlinsky, 1986). The patient should be continually monitored for the recurrence of symptoms to ensure that the dose is effective, particularly during maintenance and continuation phases. Clinicians must be aware of the pharmacokinetic parameters of drugs used to avoid irrational strategies, such as raising antidepressant doses before an initial response has been determined. These maneuvers do not improve outcome but put the patient at risk of developing adverse side effects and may contribute unnecessarily to the cost of treatment. The lowest effective dose strategy is particularly germane in the case of the SSRIs, because of the absence of evidence for a dose–response curve with these agents (Gelenberg, 1997). Clinicians should follow the best available evidence in regard to increasing doses or augmenting pharmacological regimens, being aware that such evidence is being continually updated. Patients should be monitored for the emergence of side effects throughout all phases of treatment, including when pharmacotherapy is discontinued.

When devising a treatment plan, consider the cost of combined or single-modality treatment options. Devising more rational strategies for deploying drugs or psychotherapy has important economic ramifications. Antidepressant drugs are among the top prescribed agents in this country. Fluoxetine was the second-ranking drug in terms of dollar sales in the first 9 months of 1998, with sertraline and paroxetine ranking fifth and seventh. Sixteen percent of all sertraline sales are to elders, and expenditure for this and other drugs may represent disproportionate demands on the income of those having fixed incomes or inadequate insurance coverage (Lagnado, 1998). The introduction of psychotherapy or behavioral management into nursing homes has been shown to reduce the frequency of prescription of psychotropics (Ray et al., 1993; Rovner, Steele, German, Clark, & Folstein, 1992), thereby presumably reducing costs, as well as risks, associated with pharmacological management.

Conclusion

This chapter has taken the reader on a sometimes arduous journey. We have traveled largely in darkness, with precious little in the way of science-based knowledge to illuminate our way. Although there is hope for a more rational future (as demonstrated by the subsequent chapters in this volume), forces other than reason direct much of the clinical practice of pyschopharmacology, and indeed much of all mental health service provision. Healy's (1997) remark that "There is a real sense at present . . . that knowledge in psychopharmacology doesn't become knowledge unless it has a certain commercial value. The survival of concepts depends on the interests with which they coincide" (p. 176) can be equally applied to both pharmacological and psychotherapeutic research. The economic and scientific forces that shape psychotherapy research and the provision of psychotherapy are more subtle than those affecting the field of psychopharmacology, but they are by no means absent. In the past, in-depth study of combined treatments for mental disorders has fallen victim to guild-associated biases that have resulted in dichotomous thinking and short-sighted investigative heuristics. This has separated clinical research from much of the reality of everyday clinical practice. Perhaps because the debate has been defined in more global, professional, and academic terms, proponents of either pharmacotherapy or psychotherapy tend to wax moralistic about their choices. It is important to resist this temptation. Psychotropics have been used extensively throughout the continuum of human history as both intoxicants and therapeutic agents. It is no more or less moral to seek relief from a pill than it is from a psychotherapist, and moral arguments, although not without inherent seduction, serve little purpose in advancing understanding of the effects of various forms of treatment. We must redefine our interests in terms of our patients. If we are successful in this redefinition, attempts to establish primacy of one form of treatment over another will fail, and we can direct our energies toward a better understanding of when truly integrated treatments serve our patients best.

References

Ablon, J. S., & Jones, E. E. (1999). Psychotherapy process in the National Institute of Mental Health Treatment of Depression Collaborative Research Program. *Journal of Consulting and Clinical Psychology, 67*, 64–75.

American Psychiatric Association. (1987). *Diagnostic and statistical manual of mental disorders* (3rd ed., rev.). Washington, DC: Author.

Appleby, L., Warner, R., Whitton, A., & Faragher, B. (1997). A controlled study of fluoxetine and cognitive–behavioural counselling in the treatment of post-natal depression. *British Medical Journal, 314*, 932–936.

Barkham, M., Rees, A., Stiles, W. B., Shapiro, D. A., Hardy, G. E., & Reynolds, S. (1996). Dose-effect relations in time-limited psychotherapy for depression. *Journal of Consulting and Clinical Psychology, 64*, 927–935.

Barlow, D. H., & Lehman, C. L. (1996). Advances in the psychosocial treatment of anxiety disorders. *Archives of General Psychiatry, 53*, 727–735.

Beitman, B. D. (1991). Medications during psychotherapy: Case studies of the reciprocal relationship between psychotherapy process and medication use. In B. D. Beitman & G. L. Klerman (Eds.), *Integrating pharmacotherapy and psychotherapy* (pp. 21–44). Washington, DC: American Psychiatric Press.

Bruce, T. J., Spiegel, D. A., & Hegel, M. T. (1999). Cognitive–behavioral therapy helps prevent relapse and recurrence of panic disorder following alprazolam discontinuation: A long term followup of the Peoria and Dartmouth studies. *Journal of Consulting and Clinical Psychology, 67*, 151–156.

Burke, M. J., & Preskorn, S. H. (1995). Short-term treatment of mood disorders with standard antidepressants. In F. E. Bloom & D. J. Kupfer (Eds.), *Psychopharmacology: The fourth generation of progress* (pp. 1053–1065). New York: Raven.

Buysse, D. J., Reynolds, C. F., Houck, P. R., Perel, J. M., Frank, E., Begley, A. E., Mazumdar, S., & Kupfer, D. J. (1997). Does lorazepam impair the antidepressant response to nortriptyline and psychotherapy? *Journal of Clinical Psychiatry, 58*, 426–432.

Charney, D. S., Berman, R. M., & Miller, H. L. (1998). Treatment of depression. In A. F. Schatzberg & C. B. Nemeroff (Eds.), *Textbook of psychopharmacology* (2nd ed., pp. 705–731). Washington, DC: American Psychiatric Press.

Chiles, J. A., Carlin, A. S., Benjamin, G. A. H., & Beitman, B. D. (1991). A physician, a nonmedical psychotherapist, and a patient: The pharmacotherapy–psychotherapy triangle. In B. D. Beitman & G. L. Klerman (Eds.), *Integrating pharmacotherapy and psychotherapy* (pp. 105–118). Washington, DC: American Psychiatric Press.

Cooper, P. J., & Murray, L. (1998). Postnatal depression. *British Medical Journal, 316*, 1884–1886.

Dean, M. (1999). A quiet clinical guideline revolution begins. *The Lancet, 353*, 651.

Depression Guideline Panel. (1993). *Depression in primary care: Volume 1. Diagnosis and detection* (Clinical Practice Guideline No. 5, AHCPR Publication No. 93-0550). Rockville, MD: U.S. Department of Health and Human Services, Public Health Services, Agency for Health Care Policy and Research.

Diket, A. L., & Nolan, T. E. (1997). Anxiety and depression: Diagnosis and treatment during pregnancy. *Obstetrics and Gynecology Clinics, 24*, 535–558.

Dimeff, L. A., McDavid, J., & Linehan, M. M. (1999). Pharmacotherapy for borderline personality disorder: A review of the literature and recommendations for treatment. *Journal of Clinical Psychology in Medical Settings, 6*, 113–138.

Elkin, I., Shea, M. T., Watkins, J. T., Imber, S. D., Stosky, S. M., Collins, J. F., Glass, D. R., Pilkonis, P. A., Leber, W. R., Doherty, J. P., Fiester, S. J., & Parloff, M. B. (1989). NIMH Treatment of Depression Collaborative Research Program I: General effectiveness of treatments. *Archives of General Psychiatry, 46*, 971–982.

Fava, G. A., Grandi, S., Zielzezny, M., Rafanelli, C., & Canestrari, R. (1996). Four year outcome for cognitive behavioral treatment of residual symptoms in major depression. *American Journal of Psychiatry, 153*(7), 945–947.

Fava, G. A., Rafanelli, C., Grandi, S., Canestrari, R., & Morphy, M. (1998). Six year outcome for cognitive behavioral treatment of residual symptoms of major depression. *American Journal of Psychiatry, 155*, 1443–1445.

Gelenberg, A. J. (1997). Introduction: The practice of pharmacotherapy. In A. J. Gelenberg & E. L. Bassuk (Eds.), *The practitioner's guide to psychoactive drugs* (4th ed., pp. 3–19). New York: Plenum.

Hatsukami, D. K., & Mooney, M. E. (1999). Pharmacological and behavioral strategies for smoking cessation. *Journal of Clinical Psychology in Medical Settings, 6*, 11–38.

Haycox, A., Bagust, A., & Walley, T. (1999). Clinical guidelines—The hidden costs. *British Medical Journal, 318*, 391–393.

Healy, D. (1997). *The antidepressant era*. Cambridge, MA: Harvard University Press.

Hegarty, J. D., Baldessarini, R. J., Tohen, M., Waternaux, C., & Oepen, G. (1994). One hundred years of schizophrenia: A meta-analysis of the outcome literature. *American Journal of Psychiatry, 151*, 1409–1415.

Hohagen, F., Winkelmann, G., Rasche-Rauchle, H., Hand, I., Honig, A., Munchau, N., Hiss, H., Geiger-Kabisch, C., Kappler, C., Schramm, P., Rey, E., Aldenhoff, J., & Berger, M. (1998). Combination of behaviour therapy with fluvoxamine in comparison with behaviour therapy and placebo: Results of a multicentre study. *British Journal of Psychiatry, 173*(Suppl. 35S), 71–78.

Hollister, L. E., & Claghorn, J. L. (1993). New antidepressants. *Annual Review of Pharmacology & Taxicology, 33*, 165–177.

Howard, K. I., Kopta, S. M., Krause, M. S., & Orlinsky, D. E. (1986). The dose effect relationship in psychotherapy. *American Psychologist, 41*, 159–164.

Hyman, S. E., & Nestler, E. J. (1996). Initiation and adaptation: A paradigm for understanding psychotropic drug action. *American Journal of Psychiatry, 153*, 151–162.

Jacobson, N. S., Dobson, K. S., Truax, P. A., Addis, M. E., Koerner, K., Gollan, J. K., Gortner, E., & Prince, S. E. (1996). A component analysis of cognitive–behavioral treatment for depression. *Journal of Consulting and Clinical Psychology, 64*, 295–304.

Jacobson, N. S., & Hollon, S. D. (1996). Cognitive behavior therapy versus pharmacotherapy: Now that the jury's returned its verdict, it is time to present the rest of the evidence. *Journal of Consulting and Clinical Psychology, 64*, 295–304.

Janicak, P. G., Davis, J. M., Preskorn, S. H., & Ayd, F. J. (1997). *Principles and practice of psychopharmacotherapy* (2nd ed.). Baltimore: Williams & Wilkins.

Karasu, T. B., Docherty, J. P., Gelenberg, A., Kupfer, D. J., Merriam, A. E., & Shadoan, R. (1993). Practice guideline for major depressive disorder in adults. *American Journal of Psychiatry, 150*(4; Suppl.), 1–26.

Keller, M. B., Kocsis, J. H., Thase, M. E., Gelenberg, A. J., Rush, J., Koran, L., Schatzberg, A., Russel, J., Hirschfeld, R., Klein, D., McCullough, J. P., Fawcett, J. A., Kornstein, S., LaVange, L., & Harrison, W. (1998). Maintenance phase efficacy of sertraline for chronic depression. *Journal of the American Medical Association, 280*, 1665–1672.

Kirsch, I., & Sapirstein, G. (1998). Listening to Prozac but hearing placebo: A meta-analysis of antidepressant medication. *Prevention and Treatment* [On-line]. Available: http://www.apa.org

Klein, D. F. (1998). Listening to meta-analysis but hearing bias. *Prevention and Treatment* [On-line]. Available: http:// www.apa.org

Klerman, G. L. (1991). Ideological conflicts in integrating pharmacotherapy and psychotherapy. In B. D. Beitman & G. L. Klerman (Eds.), *Integrating pharmacotherapy and psychotherapy* (pp. 3–19). Washington, DC: American Psychiatric Press.

Koren, G., Pastuszak, A., & Ito, S. (1998). Drugs in pregnancy. *New England Journal of Medicine, 338*, 1128–1137.

Kulin, N. A., Pastuszak, A., Sage, S. R., Schick-Boschetto, B., Spivey, G., Feldkamp, M., Ormond, K., Matsui, D., Stein-Schechman, A. K., Cook, L., Brochu, J., Reider, M., & Koren, G. (1998). Pregnancy outcome following maternal use of the new selective serotonin reuptake inhibitors. *Journal of the American Medical Association, 279*, 609–610.

Lagnado, L. (1998, November 17). Drug costs can leave elderly a grim choice: Pills or other needs. *Wall Street Journal*, pp. 1, 15.

March, J. S., Frances, A., Carpenter, D., & Kahn, D. A. (1998). The Expert Consensus Guideline Series: Treatment of obsessive compulsive disorder [On-line]. Available: http://www.psychguides.com

Mental health: Does therapy help? (1995, November). *Consumer Reports*, 743–739.

Michels, R. (1999). Are research ethics bad for our mental health? *New England Journal of Medicine, 340*, 1427–1430.

Miller, I. W., & Keitner, G. I. (1996). Combined medication and psychotherapy in the treatment of chronic mood disorders. *Psychiatric Clinics of North America, 19*(1), 151–171.

Munoz, R. F., Hollon, S. D., McGrath, E., Rehm, L. P., & Vanden Bos, G. R. (1994). On the AHCPR depression in primary care guidelines: Further considerations for practitioners. *American Psychologist, 49*, 42–61.

Murphy, G. E., Carney, R. M., Knesevich, M. A., Wetzel, R. D., & Whitworth, P. (1995). Cognitive behavior therapy, relaxation training, and tricyclic antidepressant medication in the treatment of depression. *Psychological Reports, 77*, 403–420.

Nutting, P. A., Beasley, J. W., & Werner, J. J. (1999). Practice-based research networks answer primary care questions. *Journal of the American Medical Association, 281*, 686–688.

Olfson, M., Marcus, S. C., Pincus, H. A., Zito, J. M., Thompson, J. W., & Zarin, D. A. (1998). Antidepressant prescribing practices of outpatient psychiatrists. *Archives of General Psychiatry, 55*, 310–316.

Pearsall, R., Glick, I. D., Pickar, D., Suppes, T., Tauscher, J., & Jobson, K. O. (1998). A new algorithm for treating schizophrenia. *Psychopharmacology Bulletin, 34*, 349–353.

Persons, J. B., Thase, M. E., & Crits-Christoph, P. (1996). The role of psychotherapy in the treatment of depression: Review of two practice guidelines. *Archives of General Psychiatry, 53*, 283–290.

Pincus, H. A., Tanielian, T. L., Marcus, S. C., Olfson, M., Zarin, D. A., Thompson, J., & Zito, J. M. (1998). Prescribing trends in psychotropic medications: Primary care, psychiatry, and other medical specialties. *Journal of the American Medical Association, 279*, 526–531.

Pincus, H. A., Zarin, D. A., Tanielian, T. L., Johnson, J. L., West, J. C., Pettit, A. R., Marcus, S. C., Kessler, R. C., & McIntyre, J. S. (1999). Psychiatric patients and treatments in 1997: Findings from the American Psychiatric Practice Research Network. *Archives of General Psychiatry, 56*, 441–449.

Ray, W. A., Taylor, J. A., Meador, K. G., Lichtenstein, M. J., Griffin, M. R., Fought, R., Adams, M. L., & Blazer, D. G. (1993). Reducing antipsychotic use in nursing homes: A controlled trial of provider education. *Archives of Internal Medicine, 153*, 713–721.

Redelmeier, D. A., Rozin, P., & Kahneman, D. (1993). Understanding patients' decisions: Cognitive and emotional perspectives. *Journal of the American Medical Association, 270*, 72–76.

Richards, T. (1998). Partnership with patients: Patients want more than simply information, they need involvement, too. *British Medical Journal, 316*(7125), 85–86.

Roland, M., & Torgerson, D. J. (1998). Understanding controlled trials: What are pragmatic trials? *British Medical Journal, 316*, 285.

Rosenheck, R., Tekell, J., Peters, J., Cramer, J., Fontanan, A., Xu, W., Thomas, J., Henderson, W., & Charney, D. (1998). Does participation in psychosocial treatment augment the benefit of clozapine? *Archives of General Psychiatry, 55*, 618–625.

Rosser, W. W. (1999). Application of evidence from randomised controlled trials to general practice. *The Lancet, 353*, 661–664.

Rovner, B. W., Steele, C. D., German, P., Clark, R., & Folstein, M. F. (1992). Psychiatric diagnosis and uncooperative behavior in nursing homes. *Journal of Geriatric Psychiatry and Neurology, 5*, 102–105.

Rush, A. J., & Hollon, S. D. (1991). Depression. In B. D. Beitman & G. L. Klerman (Eds.), *Integrating pharmacotherapy and psychotherapy* (pp. 121–142). Washington, DC: American Psychiatric Press.

Sachs, G. S. (1996). Bipolar mood disorder: Practical treatment strategies for acute and maintenance phase treatment. *Journal of Clinical Psychopharmacology, 16*(Suppl.), 32S–40S.

Sammons, M. T., Gorny, S., Zinner, E., & Allen, R. (2000). Prescriptive authority for psychologists: A consensus of support. *Professional Psychology: Research and Practice, 31,* 604–609.

Schooler, N. J., & Keith, S. J. (1993). The clinical research base for the treatment of schizophrenia. *Psychopharmacology Bulletin, 29,* 431–446.

Seligman, M. E. P. (1995). The effectiveness of psychotherapy: The *Consumer Reports* study. *American Psychologist, 50,* 965–974.

Shader, R. I., Fogelman, S. M., & Greenblatt, D. J. (1998). Epiphenomenal, causal, or correlational—More on the mechanism(s) of action of antidepressants. *Journal of Clinical Psychopharmacology, 18,* 265–267.

Shader, R. I., & Greenblatt, D. J. (1993). Use of benzodiazepines in anxiety disorders. *New England Journal of Medicine, 328,* 1398–1405.

Shekelle, P. G., Woolf, S. H., Eccles, M., & Grimshaw, J. (1999). Developing guidelines. *British Medical Journal, 318,* 593–596.

Smith, W. T., Londborg, P. D., Glaudin, V., & Painter, J. R. (1998). Short term augmentation of fluoxetine with clonazepam in the treatment of depression: A double blind study. *American Journal of Psychiatry, 155,* 1339–1345.

Stowe, Z. N., Strader, J. R., & Nemeroff, C. B. (1998). Psychopharmacology during pregnancy and lactation. In A. F. Schatzberg & C. B. Nemeroff (Eds.), *Textbook of psychopharmacology* (2nd ed., pp. 979–996). Washington, DC: American Psychiatric Press.

Thase, M. E., Greenhouse, J. B., Frank, E., Reynolds, C. F., Pilkonis, P. A., Hurley, K., Grochocinski, V., & Kupfer, D. J. (1997). Treatment of major depression with psychotherapy or psychotherapy–pharmacotherapy combinations. *Archives of General Psychiatry, 54,* 1009–1015.

Thornley, B., & Adams, C. (1998). Content and quality of 2000 controlled trials in schizophrenia over 50 years. *British Medical Journal, 317,* 1181–1184.

Trivedi, M. H., DeBattista, D., Fawcett, J., Nelson, C., Osser, D. N., Stein, D., & Jobson, K. (1998). Developing treatment algorithms for unipolar depression in cyberspace: International Psychopharmacology Algorithm Project. *Psychopharmacology Bulletin, 34,* 355–359.

Valenstein, E. S. (1998). *Blaming the brain*. New York: Free Press.

Wampold, B. E, Mondin, G. W., Moody, M., Stich, F., Benson, K., & Ahn, H. (1997). A meta-analysis of outcome studies comparing bona fide psychotherapies: Empirically, "all must have prizes." *Psychological Bulletin, 122,* 203–215.

Wells, K. B., & Sturm, R. (1996). Informing the policy process: From efficacy to effectiveness data on pharmacotherapy. *Journal of Consulting and Clinical Psychology, 64,* 638–645.

West, J. C., Zarin, D. A., & Pincus, H. A. (1997). Clinical and psychopharmacologic practice patterns of psychiatrists in routine practice. *Psychopharmacology Bulletin, 33,* 79–85.

Williams, J. W., Rost, K., Dietrich, A. J., Ciotti, M. C., Zyzanski, S. J., & Cornell, J. (1999). Primary care physicians' approach to depressive disorders: Effects of physician specialty and practice structure. *Archives of Family Medicine, 8,* 58–67.

Woolf, S. H., Grol, R., Hutchinson, A., Eccles, M., & Grimshaw, J. (1999). Potential benefits, limitations, and harms of clinical guidelines. *British Medical Journal, 318,* 527–530.

Woolf, S. H., & Lawrence, R. S. (1997). Preserving scientific debate and patient choice: Lessons from the Consensus Panel of Mammography Screening. *Journal of the American Medical Association, 278,* 2105–2108.

Zito, J. M., Safer, D. J., dosReis, S., Gardner, J. F., Boles, M., & Lynch, F. (2000). Trends in the prescribing of psychotropic medications to preschoolers. *Journal of the American Medical Association, 283,* 1025–1030.

2

Prescriptive Authority for Psychologists: Law, Ethics, and Public Policy

Patrick H. DeLeon, Sharon E. Robinson Kurpius, and John L. Sexton

In this chapter we briefly review the legal status of prescriptive authority for psychologists. We then discuss ethical issues that are likely to be encountered when the practice of psychology includes the administration of psychotropic agents. It is recognized that precepts of ethical conduct in prescribing have developed for physicians and other prescribers, but such a tradition has yet to develop for psychology. The standards of other professions and the American Psychological Association's (APA's) Ethical Principles of Psychologists and Code of Conduct (APA, 1992a) serve as a solid foundation, but the integration of this new skill into the practice of psychology requires development of ethical principles unique to the profession. Last, we examine from a public-policy perspective the issue of prescriptive authority for psychologists and for other nonphysician health care providers. The integration of prescriptive authority with the technological and regulatory changes that are transforming American health care is seen as fundamental to the future of psychology and other health care professions.

Legal Status

At the time of this chapter's writing, the legal ability for psychologists to prescribe medications exists in only three venues: Indiana, Guam, and certain military organizations. In a few other instances, psychologists have informally prescribed in organizations such as the Indian Health Service, the Veterans Administration, or aboard remote military facilities and ships. This prescribing occurred not as the result of the psychologist completing a formal prescription privilege training program but often informally through the personal relationship between a psychologist and a phy-

---

The opinions of John L. Sexton are his as a private citizen and do not represent the official position of the U.S. Navy or the Department of Defense.

sician. In some places, psychologists might be authorized to initiate a clinical pathway (established and monitored by physicians) that could result in a specified medication being administered. Some people may argue that this meets the definition of prescription privileges, whereas others would say it does not meet the definition of formally sanctioned or legal prescription privileges.

In Indiana, Guam, and certain military organizations, legal and credentialing criteria have been established that define the privilege to prescribe. The criteria in each venue differ. Under Indiana's 1993 modification of its psychology licensing act (Indiana Acts 140, 1993), only participants in federally funded demonstration projects could be granted limited prescription privileges, and this permission is given only after clearing a number of hurdles. A broader privilege for psychologists to prescribe is contained in Guam's Public Law B.695 (Allied Health Practices Act, 1998, Title 10). This law requires that psychologists obtain a collaborative practice agreement and approval from three boards (Pharmacy, Medical Examiners, and Allied Health Examiners).

Perhaps the broadest of all authorities for prescription privileges resides with military medical organization commanders. The federal government gives broad discretion to military medical commanders to grant clinical privileges. Military necessity dictates extreme action at times; therefore, an individual with only limited training might be authorized to perform certain procedures, such as an emergency appendectomy aboard an underway submarine. Military medical commanders have gone beyond political pressures to grant limited prescription privileges to adequately trained individuals such as corpsman, advanced-practice nurses, optometrists, podiatrists, chiropractors, and psychologists. At the time of the writing of this chapter, seven of the nine U.S. Department of Defense Psychopharmacology Demonstration Project graduates still in the military have *independent* prescription privileges, meaning they do a medical workup and prescribing, with the only oversight being the standard peer review that any other practitioner in their organization would receive. For a detailed history of prescription privileges for military psychologists, see Sexton (1998), and for the most thorough and current analysis of the performance of the Department of Defense psychologist prescribers, see the U.S. General Accounting Office (1999).

Ethical Aspects of Prescriptive Authority

Having provided a brief overview of the current legal status of prescriptive authority for psychologists, we now examine the ethical issues intertwined with this privilege. Before discussing the specific ethics, however, it is useful to briefly review Kitchener's (1984) five ethical precepts governing clinical practice:

1. *Beneficence*, "the principle of benefiting others, of accepting a responsibility to do good, underlies the profession" (Welfel & Kitchener, 1992, p. 180).

2. *Nonmaleficence*, "doing no harm, requires psychologists not to per-
   petuate physical or emotional harm or to engage in behavior that
   could result in harm to another" (Robinson-Kurpius & Fielder,
   1998, p. 55).
3. *Autonomy*, the belief that clients have the right of self-
   determination.
4. *Justice*, the requirement that psychologists act fairly and balance
   the rights of clients with those of others.
5. *Fidelity*, or the notion that psychologists remain loyal to clients,
   keep promises, and provide services in a trustworthy manner.

Of these five, perhaps those most relevant to prescriptive authority
are beneficence, nonmaleficence, and autonomy. Beneficence and nonmaleficence directly relate to psychologist responsibilities (competence),
whereas autonomy is reflected in patient rights.

Psychologist Responsibilities

Regarding competence, the first principle of the Ethical Principles of Psychologists and Code of Conduct (APA, 1992a) states that

> Psychologists strive to maintain high standards of competence in their
> work. They recognize the boundaries of their particular competencies
> and the limitations of their expertise. They provide only those services
> and use only those techniques for which they are qualified by education,
> training, or experience. Psychologists are cognizant of the fact that the
> competencies required in serving, teaching, and/or studying groups of
> people vary with the distinctive characteristics of those groups. In those
> areas in which recognized professional standards do not yet exist, psy-
> chologists exercise careful judgment and take appropriate precautions
> to protect the welfare of those with whom they work. They maintain
> knowledge of relevant scientific and professional information related to
> the services they render, and they recognize the need for ongoing ed-
> ucation. Psychologists make appropriate use of scientific, professional,
> technical, and administrative resources. (p. 1599)

Multiple issues related to prescriptive authority are subsumed under this
principle. Perhaps the most relevant aspects are education and training;
boundaries and limitations of expertise; variation in required services according to the characteristics of the individuals being served; and appropriate use of techniques, technology, and available resources.

Education and training. One of the leading arguments against psychologists attaining prescriptive authority is that they lack the necessary
education and training for this aspect of practice. In his argument against
prescription privileges, DeNelsky (1996) noted that "trying to become and
remain 'expert' in both biological and psychological interventions is not an
easy task" (p. 208) and that "psychologists who prescribe will be spending

more time studying medicine and less time learning psychology" (p. 209). As a result, they would forfeit their "position as the preeminent students of psychological interventions" (p. 208). In addition, professional education will need to focus more on basic physiology, pharmacology, and physical disease processes (Fox, Schwelitz, & Barclay, 1992) and, as a result, prescription providers may well be held to higher standard of care that will be reflected in "substantially increased malpractice insurance rates for psychologists who prescribe" (DeNelsky, 1996, p. 209). We agree that DeNelsky is very accurate about the increased breadth and depth of training needed to be a prescription provider, but we disagree that worry about the cost of insurance premiums should dictate the scope of care provided to patients.

Sammons, Sexton, and Meredith (1996) specifically addressed the basic science training needed and stressed that it is well beyond that currently offered at the predoctoral level.

> In addition to sound training in applied psychopharmacology, prescribing psychologists must have a fundamental understanding of the principles of basic and clinical pharmacology, which in turn requires a grasp of basic biochemical and physiologic processes. Prescribing psychologists will have to have a general knowledge of common medical illnesses, and will need to demonstrate competence in the physical and laboratory assessment of patients for whom they provide medication, in order to monitor for systemic or organ-system-specific effects of the agents they utilize. (p. 230)

This is a tall order that might well intimidate many, but to be an ethical prescribing provider one must have the skills and knowledge necessary for acceptable standards of care, while doing good (beneficence) and not doing harm (nonmaleficence).

The Report of the Ad Hoc Task Force on Psychopharmacology (APA, 1992b) proposed three levels of training. According to Lorion (1996), these levels parallel that "degree of involvement with and responsibility for aspects of intervention" (p. 222) desired by psychologists.

- *Level 1: Basic Psychopharmacology Education.* Competence at Level 1 implies a knowledge of the biological basis of neuropsychopharmacology, including the neurobiology of brain function and the subcellular and cellular mechanisms by which these drugs affect neurotransmitter systems. A second focus of training at this level involves mastery of the psychopharmacology of classes of medications commonly used to treat mental disorders, including both their use in treatment and their abuse (APA, 1992b, p. 7).
- *Level 2: Collaborative Practice.* Level 2 training builds on Level 1 and reflects the knowledge base necessary to participate actively in managing medications prescribed for mental disorders and integrating these medications with psychosocial treatment. Level 2 training includes more in-depth knowledge of the pharmacology of psychoactive medication and drugs of abuse, but it also includes

knowledge of psychodiagnosis, physical assessment, physical function tests, drug interactions, and drug side effects (APA, 1992b, p. 58).

- *Level 3: Prescription Privileges.* Level 3 training for psychologists would be similar to training for other professions that have independent prescription privileges limited only by scope of practice and training, for example, dentists, optometrists, podiatrists, and nurse practitioners. Under these conditions one can prescribe from a formula that is congruent with the currently accepted scope of practice. The task force acknowledged that, in some settings, optimal patient care may require psychologists to have limited prescription privileges. This would allow them to work independently of physicians but would also require a substantial commitment to training as well as a commitment to developing licensure provisions for this class of practitioner on a state-by-state basis (APA, 1992b, p. 59).

It is interesting that the vast majority of psychologists who are practitioners probably already possess the basic knowledge and skills described for Level 1 and possibly even Level 2 knowledge. More in-depth training and clinical practice under supervision is most appropriate at the postdoctoral level, because it is highly specialized training. The issue of pre- or postdoctoral specialty training is, however, another debate that we choose not to address in this chapter.

Boundaries and limitations of expertise. Taking into consideration levels of education and training, psychologists must recognize the boundaries and limits of their expertise (APA, 1992a, Ethical Standard 1.04a, Boundaries of Competence). For example, just because a psychologist has extensive experience with depressed clients and is very knowledgeable about psychotropic as well as psychosocial interventions for this mental disorder, he or she does not necessarily have the knowledge and skills to interact at the same level of expertise with physically ill, depressed clients who require psychotropic medication. Recognition of physical disease processes is of paramount importance for prescribers, but some level of expertise is also incumbent on nonprescribing psychologists who work with such clients.

> Psychologists involved in health care delivery, regardless of their ability to prescribe, should have some understanding of neurological, endocrine, metabolic, and other physical disorders that have a psychological presentation. Clinicians should be able to recognize basic manifestations of physical illness, to a sufficient extent that they can coordinate appropriate referrals. They should be well versed in the various side effects of or toxic responses to any number of non-psychotropic drugs that may be mistakenly ascribed to psychological causes. (Sammons et al., 1996, p. 234)

Again, the issue is not only knowing the effects and side effects of the medications related to the mental health concern but also knowing the potential interactions of psychotropic medications with medications being given for the physical health concern. Once a psychologist becomes a prescription writer it will not necessarily mean that he or she is competent to prescribe (or will choose to prescribe) psychotropic drugs for all clients seen in therapy. It will be incumbent on psychologists with prescription privileges to be acutely aware of the limits to their knowledge and skills and to take whatever steps are necessary to ensure ethical behavior within the boundaries of professional competence.

Characteristics of individuals being served. The above discussion leads quite naturally to the next aspect of competence: being aware of the special needs of the individual patient. Perhaps the most critical of these needs is the ability to comprehend a patient's health status, notably in those instances when psychological disturbances masquerade as an underlying physical problem. On occasion, the organic disturbance may be life threatening. Taylor (1990), in *Distinguishing Psychological From Organic Disorders*, described seven studies with nearly 4,000 participants who had an organic disturbance but who had sought treatment at an outpatient mental health facility for what they believed to be an emotional or behavioral disturbance. The percentage of those patients who had an organic malfunction as the basis for their emotional or behavioral problem ranged between 9% and 18%. To address this critical issue, all psychologists must consider the possibility of physical problems causing their patients' psychological problems and the necessity of referral of such patients for a medical workup. Substance abuse is a common precursor to psychological dysfunction, and psychologists who consider a patient's psychological disturbance to have a substance-based etiology may be required to perform (where credentialed to do so), or refer the patient for, indicated laboratory examinations. Psychologists who prescribe are required to undertake other laboratory analyses, electrographic procedures, and physical examination procedures to varying degrees.

Although psychologists with prescription privileges will primarily be focused on treating mental health patients, they will also be providing psychotherapy to patients with known medical illnesses. The interaction of the physical illness with the mental condition and the interaction of psychotropic medications with medications for the physical illness need to be clearly understood. In addition, these interactions must be understood within the context of the individual's developmental process across the life span.

There are now sophisticated computer programs that will greatly increase understanding of drugs and drug interactions, but the need to work with the patient's physician in such instances cannot be overstressed. For such patients a team approach would perhaps be most effective in providing a holistic, integrated approach to care.

Collaboration by prescribing psychologists may also have the beneficial result of reducing excessive psychotropic regimens. There are patients, such as institutionalized elderly people, who are managed only with pharmacotherapy and receive no psychosocial interventions. The responsibility of the psychologist who has prescription privileges in such instances would be to "unprescribe" as needed and to provide appropriate psychosocial interventions, such as behavioral therapy or group interventions that focus on the patients' environment and peers. The same might be true for children who have been diagnosed with attention deficit hyperactivity disorder (ADHD) and have been treated only with methylphenidate. The role of the psychologist might be to facilitate a reduced reliance on methylphenidate, to increase behavioral interventions, and to provide the family information on how to better behaviorally manage the manifestations of ADHD. From these examples it should be evident that the competent psychologist has knowledge of special patient characteristics in order to balance psychosocial interventions with psychopharmacology.

Appropriate use of technology and resources. The last area of psychologist competence focuses on the appropriate use of technology. The great danger of having sophisticated computer programs providing information about drugs and their various side effects is a potential overreliance on computer databases and decision-making aids. Although these programs can and do provide a wealth of essential information, they cannot take into consideration other aspects of patients' lives that may well influence reactions to both psychotherapy and psychopharmacology. Psychotropics cannot be reasonably provided without a careful history, accurate diagnosis, and behavioral analysis of the presenting complaint. These elements of psychological evaluation cannot be replaced by an exclusive focus on the provision of drugs. Psychologists who attain prescription privileges are well warned to not fall prey to the blandishments of algorithmic formulae for prescribing, or to otherwise desert their foundation in psychological theory and behavioral interventions.

Patient rights. Another major aspect of ethical behavior centers on patient rights. When psychologists enter into therapeutic relationships they are offering clients the highest standard of care possible, and they assume a fiduciary responsibility to their clients. This responsibility is directly stipulated in Principle D, "Respect for People's Rights and Dignity," and Principle E, "Concern for Others' Welfare," and is interwoven through all other principles and standards of the APA code. Principle D specifically states that

> psychologists accord appropriate respect to the fundamental rights, dignity, and worth of all people. They respect the rights of individuals to privacy, confidentiality, self-determination, and autonomy, mindful that legal and other obligations may lead to inconsistency and conflict with the exercise of these rights. Psychologists are aware of cultural, individual, and role differences, including those due to age, gender, race, ethnicity, national origin, religion, sexual orientation, disability, language, and socioeconomic status. (APA, 1992a, p. 1599)

Protecting these patient rights can often be challenging, particularly in the areas of informed consent and duty to protect.

Informed consent. Mandated by the APA Ethical Standards (4.02a), informed consent consists of four components: (a) knowledge of significant information regarding treatment; (b) capacity to consent; (c) voluntary expression of consent; and (d) appropriate documentation of the consent, preferably in written form. Psychologists need to provide patients with a reasonable amount of information about accepted treatments, both pharmacological and psychosocial, so that they can evaluate the benefits and risks of all of the interventions. Patients need to understand the short- and long-term benefits and risks of psychotherapy and medications commonly used for the diagnosis in question. Psychologists may not be prone to think about risks related to psychotherapy, but risks do exist, especially when a severe disturbance could result in dangerous behavior. Psychologists must keep abreast of the literature on accepted and effective interventions. Often the research does not clearly indicate the "the treatment of choice." It is the psychologist's responsibility to accurately present the accepted treatments and let the patient make the informed choice. Perhaps the most common example of this is in the treatment of moderate depression. Because the literature does not convincingly weigh in on the advantage of either pharmacotherapy or psychotherapy, the patient's choice, based on a thorough and impartial review of options by the provider, is a vital element of informed consent.

Medications always have some adverse effects. The patient should be advised about both common and less common, but potentially more serious, adverse effects. It is important to describe short- as well as long-term adverse effects to ensure a well-informed choice by the patient. For example, patients (or their legal guardians) must weigh the benefits of pharmacological treatment of psychosis with the risks for tardive dyskinesia. Because this serious adverse effect may occur in as many as 40% of patients given long-term (8 or more years) treatment with traditional antipsychotics (Kane, 1995), periodically updated informed consent, preferably in writing, is important.

Implicit in psychologists seeking prescriptive authority is the recognition that in most instances psychotropic drugs are most valuable as adjuncts to psychotherapy. To facilitate autonomy and truly informed patient decision making, psychologists need to provide information that is as complete as possible, in language patients can understand, without imposing their values on the patient through subtle, and possibly unconscious, coercion. This is especially true when guardians or other legally appointed representatives are involved in the decision-making process.

Duty to protect. Regarding the duty to protect or warn, *Tarasoff v. Board of Regents of the University of California* (1974, 1976) and other subsequent tort decisions have heightened awareness of this vital element of practice. When examined in the light of prescription privileges, the duty to warn can also be construed in terms of advising patients of potentially deleterious effects of medication regimens. This is particularly relevant in terms of iatrogenic drug dependence. One of the rights and responsibilities that accompany prescriptive authority is the responsibility to determine when pharmacological interventions are being overused or abused and to correct the situation to provide optimum care.

Doing Right for Patients: Public Policy Issues

One of the most underappreciated and yet extraordinarily powerful public policy arguments in support of professional psychology obtaining prescriptive authority is the enhancement in the quality of health care that is likely to result. Before we address this aspect of the ongoing debate surrounding psychologists obtaining prescriptive authority, however, it is important to acknowledge that within the U.S. health care system there are traditionally two distinct "tensions" involved in any proposed expansion of a profession's scope of clinical activities. The first, and somewhat surprising tension, is the initial disagreement expressed within the membership of the profession itself. The second is the to-be-expected concerns that are often raised by other potentially competing disciplines; for example, for psychology, psychiatry and, to some extent, professional nursing.

For years there has been a noticeable tension within professional psychology's practice community surrounding the issue of how (or, more candidly, even whether) to objectively determine when psychological services should be deemed "safe, effective, and appropriate"; that is, how to establish appropriate standards of care, as the federal government historically has done for new drugs and medical devices. The essence of this professional dilemma is closely related to strongly held but often admittedly conflicting views surrounding the extent to which providing psychotherapy is fundamentally an art, a science, or a combination of both. In many ways, this tension is also reflected in related policy debates surrounding where psychology's graduate students should be trained (i.e., in traditional academic departments or in professional schools) and when specialty training should occur (i.e., at the pre- or postdoctoral level).

In the future, underlying tensions regarding where training should occur may become significantly more intense, as psychology's professional schools begin to establish and operate their own comprehensive treatment facilities (i.e., possess "homes of their own" for clinical training purposes). Such developments pose substantial challenges to traditional notions of the clinical role of psychologists. The governing ethos under which psychologist-run training facilities will operate is likely to be considerably different than the treatment philosophies of traditional medically and psychiatrically oriented programs. The didactic training requirements of psychologists will likely change, as in such facilities they will assume a more central role in the management of the totality of the patient's needs, both physical and emotional. Some strife is likely as graduate programs struggle to incorporate teaching in these new areas with the academic curriculum that has historically defined the field.

Another area of considerable tension is associated with how training programs are funded (Dunivin, 1994). In recent years there has been an awakening attention of the importance of aggressively seeking training support under the various federal health care initiatives, such as Title VII of the U.S. Public Health Service Act of 1998 (the Health Professions program; Health Professions Education Parterships Act of 1998) and the Graduate Medical Education account of Medicare.

Without question, there is almost universal agreement, within psychology and the society at large that providing psychotropic medication is a health care clinical function, but such a universal agreement does not extend to other aspects of the field. Medicine and the various nonphysician disciplines that currently prescribe (e.g., nursing, dentistry, optometry, podiatry, clinical pharmacy, and physical therapy) have long adopted health care identities—both in the eyes of society and, equally important, by their own membership. Within psychology, however, it is still a very real question for many of our colleagues as to whether we are, in fact, one of the nation's "health professions" or whether we should more appropriately remain tied to our historical academic background in philosophy (Broskowski, 1995).

To fully appreciate these tensions it is important to understand that the movement toward obtaining prescriptive authority has at heart been an educational policy agenda (i.e., devising and implementing appropriate didactic and clinical training programs). At the same time, however, it has also been an initiative that, since its inception, has been driven by the practice community. In essence, the individuals seeking this expanded clinical authority have been demanding of our training institutions that they deliver programs that most are unequipped to provide. Furthermore, they have been asking traditionally oriented training institutions to focus on the needs of an entirely different student and clinical population: those already in practice, returning for specialty training, and that subset of patients who may require psychotropic medications (e.g., those afflicted with serious mental illness).

This requires a fundamentally different orientation to training, including an institutional willingness to be responsive to the obstacles inherent in interdisciplinary training. Alternative learning programs for established clinicians, such as distance learning or executive track modules (such as are already in place for physicians and other specialties), must also be considered. A further challenge lies in the fact, as noted above, that most academic training programs are bereft of treatment facilities where students have direct responsibility for the care of patients requiring psychotropic medications. Within psychology, the hands-on (vs. didactic) aspect of training is traditionally obtained away from the degree-granting institution, during the predoctoral internship. Developing viable training programs for psychologists already in practice and assuming responsibility for patients potentially requiring psychotropic medication represent new frontiers for psychology—clinically, educationally, and for our colleagues in the areas of research and public interest as well.

How, then, can we defuse the tensions that the complex prescription agenda has brought to the field? In our judgment, the key policy question for psychology has now become whether the profession has matured sufficiently to recognize itself as one of the nation's health care professions. If so, can we effectively respond to the monumental changes in patient care, scientific knowledge, and training capabilities that are evolving? Our profession's steady movement toward obtaining prescriptive authority must be viewed and understood within the public policy context and the almost unprecedented change that our nation's health care system, including its health professional training institutions, is at present experiencing.

Scope of Practice and Quality Health Care

The policy contributions of the Institute of Medicine (IOM) toward the development of a national health strategy are significant and have had significant effects on the profession of psychology. The IOM was established in 1970 by the National Academy of Sciences, an entity possessing a congressional charter to serve as a formal advisor to the federal government. On its own initiative, the IOM is authorized to identify issues of medical care, research, and education affecting the nation. Over the years, the IOM has frequently served as a health policy analysis body for the Congress, developing state-of-the-art policy documents on a wide range of issues. Recently, it convened a panel of experts (the National Roundtable on Health Care Quality) to expressly address the underlying issue of whether U.S. health policy experts can effectively evaluate the quality of care being provided within the nation's overall health care system (Chassin, Galvin, & the National Roundtable on Health Care Quality, 1998).

It has always been evident at the public policy level that practitioners are fundamentally providers of health care services, regardless of their particular clinical disciplines. Thus, many of the concerns particular to the professional practice of psychology that have been addressed within the APA may also have been addressed in the broader context of clinical service provision by the IOM roundtable. For example, the extent to which managed care's emphasis on cost effectiveness has resulted in the inappropriate overriding of practitioner clinical judgments is an issue of primary concern to clinicians in all health care endeavors, including psychology. The necessity for establishing objective standards of quality care was viewed by the commission as an urgent task. Meeting six times in formal plenary sessions between February 1996 and January 1998, the IOM roundtable convened two conferences, invited presentations from experts, and commissioned related papers. Its far-reaching and futuristic conclusion was that

> the quality of health care can be precisely defined and measured with a degree of scientific accuracy comparable with that of most measures used in clinical medicine. Serious and widespread problems exist throughout American medicine. These problems, which may be classi-

fied as underuse, overuse, or misuse, occur in small and large com-
munities alike, in all parts of the country, and with approximately
equal frequency in managed care and fee-for-service systems of care.
Very large numbers of Americans are harmed as a direct result. Quality
of care is the problem, not managed care. Current efforts to improve
will not succeed unless we undertake a major, systematic effort to over-
haul how we deliver health care services, educate and train clinicians,
and assess and improve quality. (Chassin, Galvin, & the National
Roundtable on Health Care Quality, 1998, p. 11)

Several other key policy concepts expressed in the IOM consensus statement adopted included the notions that (a) the quality of health care can
be precisely defined, as demonstrated by a wide array of scientifically valid
studies; (b) at its best, health care in the United States is superb—unfortunately, it is often not at its best; (c) a few health plans, hospitals, and
integrated delivery systems have made impressive efforts to improve their
quality of care; however, many more institutions have made little, if any,
effective effort to improve, and major obstacles lie in the way of rapid,
system-wide progress; (d) these circumstances require a major effort to
rethink and re-engineer how health care services are delivered and how
the quality of care may be accurately measured and improved.

Throughout the IOM deliberations there was a distinct focus on ensuring the promotion of what would be best for individual patients. The
roundtable participants were very careful not to merely accept or endorse
the status quo or what might be considered common practices that, although professionally accepted, had no meritorious science-based foundation. The members of the IOM roundtable stipulated that all health
care professionals must strive to stay abreast of the dynamic and ever-
expanding knowledge base evolving within their own professions and that
they must use that knowledge appropriately. They emphasized that no
matter how good one's understanding or measures of quality of care are,
professionals must always be prepared to revise them as new knowledge
is generated about what does and does not work. The underlying goal is
to produce positive outcomes for patients. Although the knowledge and
practices of individual clinicians are important for high-quality care, it was
felt that health professionals could no longer deliver high-quality care
alone. Health care professionals increasingly practice within groups and
systems of care. The functioning of those systems in preventing and minimizing errors, and the harm such errors may cause; coordinating care
among settings and various practitioners; and ensuring that relevant and
accurate health care information is available when needed were viewed
as critical in ensuring high-quality care. It is thus apparent that these
IOM conceptualizations embrace some form of coordinated or managed
care and have direct implications for psychological practice as we know it
today.

Discussing the explosion of knowledge occurring today within the
health care field, the IOM roundtable reported that whereas the randomized controlled trial has become the "gold standard" for evaluating the
efficacy of health care interventions of all sorts, it is a relatively recent

phenomenon. The results of the first controlled trial were published in 1952, and in the 30 years from 1966 through 1995 more than 76,000 journal articles were published from randomized controlled trials. The first 5 years of that period contributed less than 1% of the total; the last 5 years contributed more than the previous 25 years combined. In the face of this avalanche of rigorous data on efficacy, the current methods of training physicians and other clinicians, and the systems in place for supporting them in the delivery of health care services, have simply not kept pace. Even the rigors of today's clinical training programs have not equipped practitioners to make maximal use of a variety of methods to assess and improve their own practices. As one might predict, the members of the IOM roundtable also noted the efficacy and clinical importance of systematically using computer-assisted practice guidelines.

The direct relevance of the IOM's deliberations to public policy issues surrounding psychology's (as well as any other discipline's) obtaining prescriptive authority should be evident. First, the fact that psychiatry has traditionally been viewed as central to psychotropic clinical decisions does not preclude new roles for other professions. Second, it is becoming increasingly practical (i.e., cost effective) for comprehensive treatment systems to ensure that the basis for clinical decisions made by practitioners (including whether to use psychotropic medications) is verifiable and objectively accountable (i.e., that predetermined clinical treatment pathways are followed). Third, advances in computer and communications technology will facilitate the development of replicable clinical pathways as well as the expansion of clinical responsibilities for all disciplines. Use of such technology will enhance systematic provision of empirically validated interventions. It also will provide a mechanism by which the validity of medicine's frequent and emotionally charged allegations regarding the "public health hazard" of nonphysician prescribers can be objectively evaluated. Using data collection systems already in place in integrated health care settings, treatment decisions made by nonphysicians during actual patient care (e.g., rate of prescription of psychotropics per patient) can be tracked with relative ease, and comparative outcomes between physician and nonphysician prescribers can be assessed. Given findings from other professions that consistently indicate that nonphysician practitioners have outcomes that are just as good as their physician counterparts (e.g., Mundinger et al., 2000), it can be confidently expected that large-scale data collection will support the safety and efficacy of psychologist prescribers.

Virtual training capacities, as well as 24-hour instant on-line clinical consultations (e.g., from schools of pharmacy) will soon be readily obtainable. We suggest that these advances may lead to a fundamental reorientation of graduate education in terms of functional capacities; that is, much graduate education may be geared toward identifying the specific functional capacities required to complement the practitioner's initial training knowledge base and how such capacities can most effectively be imparted. Psychologists should soon expect the development of psychology-based prescription training modules adaptable to their own professional diagnostic capabilities and personal clinical interests (e.g., children, the elderly, women, people of color, etc.). A major challenge for professional psychology will be how to most effectively use these computer, educational, and scientific resources in developing effective treatment protocols and how to integrate these resources into doctoral and postdoctoral training.

Another major public policy player in the health and social welfare arena that has frequently been underappreciated by organized psychology has been the nation's approximately 42,000 grant-making institutions (i.e., private foundations). In 1997, U.S. independent and community foundations awarded $13.37 billion in grants to nonprofit institutions (Shmavonian, 1998). With more than $4.5 billion in assets, the Pew Charitable Trusts alone is responsible for providing approximately $190 million annually, much in the area of health care. For psychology, one of its most important initiatives is the Pew Health Professions Commission, chaired by former Senate Majority Leader George Mitchell (D-ME). In October 1998 the commission's Taskforce on Health Care Workforce Regulation released a far-reaching and futuristic report, *Strengthening Consumer Protection: Priorities for Health Care Workforce Regulation* (Finocchio, Dower, Blick, Gragnola, & the Taskforce on Health Care Workforce Regulation, 1998). The task force identified health workforce regulation as an issue of critical importance for professional organizations and the public.

> Health care workforce regulation plays a critical role in consumer protection. For most of this century, the state regulation of health care occupations and professions has established a minimum standard for safe practice and removed the egregiously incompetent. As market and regulatory forces shape the future of health care, particularly the location and content of practice, the structures and functions of state professional regulation must continue to provide consumers with important protections leading to safe and effective practice.
>
> This ostensible goal of professional regulation—to establish standards that protect consumers from incompetent practitioners—is eclipsed by a tacit goal of protecting the profession's economic prerogatives. This dichotomy of goals has created serious shortcomings that include limited public accountability, support for practice monopolies that limit access to care and lack of national uniformity. These shortcomings are further exacerbated by the current changes in health care.
>
> To become a viable element of consumer protection in health care, professional regulation must demonstrate that it unequivocally serves the public good. This will require that it evolve at the same rate as the economic, political, intellectual and technological environments in which its licensees work. In this context of consumer protection, regulators, legislators, policy makers and health care professionals face three priority areas that present the most challenges to, and promise for, improving professional regulation: health professions boards and governance structures, scopes of practice authority, and continuing competence. (Finocchio et al., 1998, p. 1)

As did the public policy experts representing the IOM, the members of this prestigious task force described a future health care environment in which traditional notions of authority and vertical decision making (i.e., where physicians per se serve as "captains of the ship" merely because of their discipline) will simply no longer be acceptable. Again, the key focus was on "what would be best for the patient" and how that could be objectively determined. The Pew task force members were acutely aware of the unprecedented advances that were occurring within the fields of technology and communications, and they correctly discerned that the primary issue was the effective use of these advances to further health care.

In addressing the various complex issues surrounding the determination of a profession's scope of practice—which is absolutely central to psychology possessing prescriptive authority—the Pew task force noted that legislative calendars across the country are flooded with bills that would regulate emerging health professions or change the practice authority of currently regulated professions. In 1995 alone, more than 800 such bills were considered, and approximately 300 laws were enacted. In 1997, 1,600 bills were introduced, and approximately 300 were enacted into public law. The task force described the legislative activity surrounding scope-of-practice decisions as one component of "turf battles," noting that often lost in these struggles among professions was consumer protection, which is regulation's ostensible primary purpose.

The Pew task force members noted that, for individual legislators, balancing the tensions between free choice by consumers and protection from harm (i.e., the "public health hazard" allegations) formed the core of their policy dilemma. Because very few elected officials have first-hand expertise in the nuances of health care, practice act decisions benefit from the strengths of state legislative activity and are subject to the vagaries of partisan politics, campaign contributions, and professional lobbying. Even health care professionals possess conflicting interests. Each profession has a valid interest in minimal restrictions for its own members, but each also benefits considerably from the anticompetitive aspect of regulation. Also, as the task force noted, it always seems to be the professions —never the public or consumer advocates—that request regulatory changes to practice acts.

The practical reality is that medicine is the only profession possessing state practice acts that cover all of health care services. With this exclusivity, little or nothing exists that can be added to the medical act, and medicine has no incentive to delete anything. Accordingly, medical professionals can (and frequently do) see every request for regulatory change from any other profession as a challenge requiring confrontation. Organized medicine has no institutional incentive to compromise because, with all-inclusive practice authority, physicians possesses the credentials, expertise, and political influence to comment on potential impacts of any proposed scope-of-practice modification laws on patients.

The Pew Commission task force further noted that a number of professions currently have scopes of practice that overlap considerably. Those that provide some or many of the same services as physicians have in recent years spent considerable time and money bolstering requests to change their practice acts to permit them to provide care that they feel is consistent with their education and training. Not surprisingly, virtually every such request has been opposed by organized medicine, often by state medical licensing boards, and sometimes by other professions as well. For example, a recent 4-year battle between California's optometrists and ophthalmologists regarding prescriptive authority cost the involved professions more than $1.8 million in campaign contributions to state legislators.

The task force also observed that individual state legislators in separate state legislatures across the nation were at a distinct disadvantage in a world increasingly driven by regional, national, and global economies and information services. Although many of the professions have adopted national standards for examination, certification, and accreditation, practice acts are still decided at the state level with little or no coordination. The differences among practice acts for single professions vary in magnitude. "The benefits and necessity of many aspects of state policy-making and policy-enforcement are numerous. However, differences from state to state in practice acts for the health professions no longer make sense" (Finocchio et al., 1998, p. 25). We re-emphasize the policy magnitude of this particular conclusionary policy statement and at the same time remind those concerned that, especially during the 1990s, this has been the policy position endorsed by the federal government in administering its own health care facilities, that is, those run by the Department of Defense, Veterans Administration, and U.S. Public Health Service. Today, all federal health care practitioners are generally required to possess a state-issued license; however, their scope-of-practice responsibilities are determined by the federal facility where they are employed, not by individual state licensing body statutes, regulations, or deliberations.

One of the Pew Commission recommendations that is particularly important to psychology is that the Congress establish a national policy advisory body to research, develop, and publish national scope-of-practice and continuing-competency standards for state legislatures to implement. The Pew Commission recommended that this body develop model legislative language for uniform practice authority acts for each of the health professions. These standards and models would be based on a wide range of evidence regarding the competence of the professions to provide safe and effective health care. The traditional state authority to regulate those health professions functioning within its geographical boundaries would essentially cease to exist. The various complex issues surrounding such recent technological advances as telehealth (or telepractice) would seem to add considerable credence to the long-term benefit of such a nationwide policy determination.

To possess the credibility required for the implementation of changes of such magnitude, the Pew Commission stressed that the proposed national policy advisory body not be captured by the interest of state regulatory agencies or by state health professions associations. The underlying objective of the national body would be to develop evidence-based models and standards in a nonpolitical forum. The intended outcomes would be evidence-based practice authority acts that would be uniform across the states. Outdated but historical precedents and individual administrative and or legislative "biases" would give way to objective policy guidance.

It was expected that by setting up guidelines in advance, particularly those that would be based on the consensus of nationally renowned experts, some of today's problems might be avoided. All individuals involved seem to agree that it is very difficult for individual state legislators to know the validity of emotional public health hazard allegations, particularly when the criticizing profession may have an interest in the outcome. The Pew task force members expected that the proposed national advisory body would assume that professions would share practice authority when appropriate and justified by the evidence at hand. To accomplish this vision, states would have to use concrete mechanisms for the collection of data on health care practice.

The Pew Commission's far-reaching and revolutionary vision of objective national standards evolving from advances in information technology, an educated consumer and patient population, and growing national concerns about health care economics can be viewed as effectively laying the policy foundation for psychology being granted the authority to practice to the fullest extent of its training (i.e., obtaining prescriptive authority). One could clearly make the public policy argument that psychology (as do each of the health care professions) has a professional responsibility to ensure that its practitioners are entitled to fully use their clinical expertise, especially if one believes that quality of care for patients will be significantly enhanced.

It is particularly interesting that the prescriptive-authority struggle in Hawaii, between psychologists and psychiatrists, was specifically referenced by the Pew task force report—but in a fashion that we would suggest the psychologists in Hawaii who were personally involved in the process would not recognize. Hawaii represented the first time in history that psychologists and psychiatrists openly engaged in a legislative battle surrounding the prescription issue. Relevant bills were introduced in both legislative bodies of the Hawaii legislature, and formal testimony was received from the administration, the public, and both professions. The Hawaii House of Representatives eventually enacted a resolution calling on the Hawaii State Judiciary Center for Alternative Dispute Resolution (ADR) to convene various roundtable meetings and report back to the legislature their ultimate recommendations. On the basis of interactions with key administrators from the ADR project, the Pew task force noted that

> during a six-month period, The Center for ADR convened three roundtable sessions that were open to anyone who wished to testify. Between 25 and 30 people attended each roundtable, and although there were many representatives of professional associations, consumers and individual professionals also participated. Center facilitators successfully carried out their charge and returned a single text document to the legislature. The legislature determined that the psychologists had not adequately proved their competence to prescribe and the proposed bill did not pass. (Finocchio et al., 1998, p. 31)

From the very beginning, however, Hawaii psychologists were definitely of the opinion that they were not charged with the responsibility of "proving their competence to prescribe." Instead, they understood that they were participating in good faith, in a collaborative effort to see if it were possible to develop a consensus position that could be endorsed by organized psychology, psychiatry and, ultimately, the consumer public. That process, in effect, provided all parties from the beginning, including psychiatry, with an absolute veto on any consensus statement. In the psychologists' view, it soon became absolutely clear that psychiatrists never intended to agree in any manner that any nonphysicians could ever safely and competently prescribe. The Pew task force is correct in stating that legislation has not yet been enacted by the Hawaii legislature that would provide psychologists with prescriptive authority; however, the difference in perceptions regarding what actually transpired in Hawaii is considerable. This last point is a cautionary one, as it has been the case in other legislative arenas that initiatives that espouse a broader role for nonphysician health care providers have been hamstrung by opposition from organized medicine. Expanding the scope of practice for nonphysician providers is in our view essential in creating a viable health care model that serves the needs of all citizens, including the now 40 million Americans who lack health care insurance.

Given the relative lack of success in pursuing this agenda in the face of stiff opposition from organized medicine, we suggest that organized psychology be quite guarded in its enthusiasm toward enacting national scope-of-practice parameters. Psychology may have "right" and objective data on its side; however, unless our colleagues are truly committed to spending the time and energy required to ensure that our position is really attended to, we are concerned that in such a highly controversial area as prescriptive authority there will be tremendous pressure on any national policy body to maintain the status quo, notwithstanding whatever lofty policy objectives might be verbally expressed and even the best of intentions. Psychology's continued presence in public policy forums will be especially critical as we are today in only the early stages of enacting permissive state legislative authority.

Conclusion

Prescription privileges for psychologists will be a topic of lively debate for some time. Currently, a few psychologists in a few jurisdictions have the privilege to prescribe, and in a few other jurisdictions the privilege exists but is not being used. Psychologists have demonstrated that ethical, high-quality care can be provided when a psychologist receives a reasonable amount of medical and pharmacological training. This demonstration of competence will serve as a springboard for states to grant certification to the hundreds of psychologists currently trained in clinical psychopharmacology, and the many who will follow them. The establishment of truly objective national standards for training and service provision may require substantial redesign of the graduate and postdoctoral curricula, but it will be in the best interests of the public and the future viability of the profession.

References

Allied Health Practices Act, 10 Guam Code Ann., §§ 12802–12827 (1998).

American Psychological Association. (1992a). Ethical principles of psychologists and code of conduct. *American Psychologist, 47,* 1597–1611.

American Psychological Association. (1992b). *Report of the Ad Hoc Task Force on Psychopharmacology.* Washington, DC: Author.

Broskowski, A. T. (1995). The evolution of health care: Implications for the training and careers of psychologists. *Professional Psychology: Research and Practice, 26,* 156–162.

Chassin, M. R., Galvin, R. W., & the National Roundtable on Health Care Quality. (1998). The urgent need to improve health care quality. Institute of Medicine National Roundtable on Health Care Quality. *Journal of the American Medical Association, 280,* 1000–1005.

DeNelsky, G. Y. (1996). The case against prescription privileges for psychologists. *American Psychologist, 51,* 207–212.

Dunivin, D. L. (1994). Health professions education: The shaping of a discipline through federal funding. *American Psychologist, 49,* 868–878.

Finocchio, L. J., Dower, C. M., Blick, N. T., Gragnola, C. M., & the Taskforce on Health Care Workforce Regulation. (1998). *Strengthening consumer protection: Priorities for health care workforce regulation.* San Francisco: Pew Health Professions Commission.

Fox, R. E., Schwelitz, F. D., & Barclay, A. G. (1992). A proposed curriculum for psychopharmacology training for professional psychologists. *Professional Psychology: Research and Practice, 23,* 216–219.

Health Professions Education Partnerships Act of 1998, Public Law 105–392.

Indiana Acts 140, Indiana Public Law 140, Indiana Code § 25–33–1–2 (1993).

Kane, J. M. (1995). Tardive dyskinesia: Epidemiological and clinical presentation. In F. E. Bloom & D. J. Kupfer (Eds.), *Psychopharmacology: The fourth generation of progress* (pp. 1485–1496). New York: Raven.

Kitchener, K. S. (1984). Intuition, critical evaluation and ethical principles: The foundation for ethical decisions in counseling psychology. *The Counseling Psychologist, 12,* 43–56.

Lorion, R. P. (1996). Applying our medicine to the psychopharmacology debate. *American Psychologist, 51,* 219–224.

Mundinger, M. O., Kane, R. L., Lenz, E. R., Totten, A. M., Tsai, W., Cleary, P. D., Friedewald, W. T., Siu, A. L., & Shelanski, M. L. (2000). Primary care outcomes in patients treated by nurse practitioners or physicians: A randomized trial. *Journal of the American Medical Association, 283,* 59–68.

Robinson-Kurpius, S. E., & Fielder, K. V. (1998). Ethical issues and the health care setting. In S. L. Roth-Roemer, S. E. Robinson-Kurpius, & C. Carmin (Eds.), *The emerging role of counseling psychology in health care* (pp. 55–73). Chicago: W. W. Norton.

Sammons, M. T., Sexton, J. L., & Meredith, J. M. (1996). Basic science training in psychopharmacology: How much is enough? *American Psychologist, 51,* 230–234.

Sexton, J. L. (1998). Military psychologists, Pioneers in prescribing. In C. Cronin (Ed.), *Military psychology: An introduction* (pp. 241–255). Needham Heights, MA: Simon & Schuster.

Shmavonian, N. K. (1998, December 13). A look at the new philanthropy. *Washington Post,* p. C3.

Tarasoff v. Board of Regents of the University of California, 118 Cal., Rptr. 129.529 P.2d 533 (1974).

Tarasoff v. Board of Regents of the University of California, 113 Cal., Rptr. 14.55 P.2d 223 (1976).

Taylor, R. L. (1990). *Distinguishing psychological from organic disorders*. New York: Springer.

U.S. General Accounting Office. (1999). *GAO/HEHS-99-98, DOD prescribing psychologists* (Report to the Chairman and Ranking Minority Member, Committee on Armed Services, U.S. Senate). Washington, DC: Author.

Welfel, E. R., & Kitchener, K. S. (1992). Introduction to the special section: Ethics education —An agenda for the '90s. *Professional Psychology: Research and Practice, 23*, 179–181.

3

Comparative and Combined Treatments for Obsessive–Compulsive Disorder

Martin M. Antony and Richard P. Swinson

This chapter is organized in five main sections. The first section reviews the nature of obsessive–compulsive disorder (OCD), including such topics as diagnostic issues, prevalence and epidemiology, and comorbidity. The second section, on assessment, includes information on interview-based assessments, self-report measures, behavioral assessment, and the use of monitoring diaries. The third section covers biological treatments for OCD and includes information on the biological underpinnings of OCD, a review of empirically supported biological treatments, and practical suggestions for providers of pharmacological treatments. The fourth section, on psychological treatments, includes an overview of psychological models and a review of the psychological treatment literature. The fifth and final section of the chapter provides information and suggestions regarding combining pharmacological and psychological treatments for OCD. Table 3.1 summarizes recommendations for assessing and treating patients with OCD.

Diagnostic Issues and Phenomenology

OCD is an anxiety disorder characterized by obsessions or compulsions causing significant distress or impairment. In the text revision of the fourth edition of the *Diagnostic and Statistical Manual of Mental Disorders (DSM–IV–TR*; American Psychiatric Association, 2000), *obsessions* are defined as recurrent thoughts, impulses, or images that are perceived by the individual as intrusive, inappropriate, and distressing. Obsessions are not simply excessive worries about real-life problems, and the individual must recognize that the obsessions are a product of his or her own mind (e.g., not caused by thought insertion). In addition, the person must attempt to ignore or suppress the obsessions or to neutralize them with another thought or action (e.g., a compulsion). *Compulsions* are repetitive behaviors or mental acts that a person performs in response to an obsession or according to specific, rigidly applied rules.

A number of investigators have conducted factor analytic studies to

Table 3.1. Recommended Steps for Assessing and Treating Patients With Obsessive–Compulsive Disorder

Phase	Steps
1: Screening for OCD (at initial sessions)	• Unstructured clinical interview with screening questions regarding obsessions and compulsions, or • Structured diagnostic interview (e.g., SCID–IV, ADIS–IV)
2: Assessment of OCD severity	• Clinician-administered assessments (e.g., Y–BOCS)—repeat periodically (e.g., every 5th session) • Self-report measures (e.g., Padua Inventory—Revised)—repeat periodically (e.g., every 5th session) • Behavioral approach test—repeat periodically (e.g., every 5th session) • Monitoring diaries (continue throughout treatment)
3: Begin initial treatment	• CBT alone, or • SSRI alone (e.g., sertraline, fluoxetine, fluvoxamine, paroxetine, citalopram), or • SSRI combined with CBT
4: Augment or switch treatments if initial treatment is ineffective or only partially effective	• If initial treatment is CBT, consider increasing frequency of CBT sessions, switching to different CBT strategies, adding an SSRI, or switching to an SSRI • If initial treatment is an SSRI, consider switching to a different SSRI or adding CBT • If initial treatment was CBT plus an SSRI, consider switching to a different SSRI, increasing the frequency of CBT sessions, or switching to different CBT strategies
5: Treatment-resistant patients	• Consider switching to clomipramine if patient has failed to respond to two or more SSRIs, or • Consider augmenting SSRI treatment with a neuroleptic (especially if patient has OCD with poor insight or comorbid tics)
6: Maintenance treatment	• Once patient has responded to acute treatment with CBT, decrease session frequency to monthly. Continue monthly sessions for up to 1 year • If patient has responded to pharmacotherapy (or combined treatment), continue medication for 1–2 years and then taper gradually, ideally while continuing CBT visits on a monthly basis

Note. OCD = obsessive–compulsive disorder; CBT = cognitive–behavioral therapy; SCID–IV = Structured Clinical Interview for *DSM–IV*; ADIS–IV = Anxiety Disorders Interview Schedule for *DSM–IV*; Y–BOCS = Yale–Brown Obsessive Compulsive Scale; SSRI = selective serotonin reuptake inhibitor.

examine the core types of OCD symptoms. Findings have been somewhat inconsistent, although washing and checking appear to consistently be categorized on different dimensions (see Antony, Downie, & Swinson, 1998, for a review) in factor analytic studies. The largest factor analytic study published to date (Leckman et al., 1997) found four factors, replicated in two independent samples. These included (a) *Obsessions and Checking* (including aggressive obsessions, sexual obsessions, religious obsessions, somatic obsessions, and checking compulsions), (b) *Symmetry and Ordering* (including symmetry obsessions), (c) *Cleanliness and Washing* (including contamination obsessions and cleaning compulsions), and (d) *Hoarding* (including hoarding obsessions).

A recent study (Summerfeldt, Richter, Antony, & Swinson, 1999) used confirmatory factor analysis to compare four models of symptom structure in 203 patients with OCD. These included a single-factor model, two-factor model (obsessions vs. compulsions), three-factor model, and four-factor model (similar to Leckman et al.'s, 1997, model). Data were analyzed at the level of discrete symptoms as well as according to a priori, higher level groupings of symptoms (from the Yale–Brown Obsessive Compulsive Scale [Y–BOCS] checklist). An adequate fit was found only for the four-factor model, confirming the findings of Leckman et al. (1997). However, the adequate model fit was only for the higher level a priori symptom groupings and did not account for the relations among discrete symptoms.

It appears that OCD is a heterogeneous condition. However, despite the presence of distinct types of OCD symptoms, many patients have symptoms from more than one domain (Rasmussen & Tsuang, 1986), and a recent study (Summerfeldt et al., 1999) has suggested that there is overlap among dimensions, especially among those representing checking and contamination-related symptoms.

Prevalence and Epidemiology

The vast majority of people in nonclinical samples experience unpleasant intrusive thoughts or engage in compulsive rituals from time to time. Although the content of these obsessions and compulsions is similar in clinical and nonclinical groups, these symptoms tend to be less frequent, less intense, and less distressing among nonclinical samples than among individuals with OCD (Muris, Merckelbach, & Clavan, 1997; Rachman & de Silva, 1978; Salkovskis & Harrison, 1984).

The prevalence of OCD has been a source of controversy in the literature. Until the 1980s, OCD was thought to be extremely rare, affecting as few as 1 in 2,000 individuals (Rudin, 1953). Over the last 10–15 years, findings from several large epidemiological studies have begun to challenge this assumption. To date, the largest study to examine the prevalence of OCD in the United States was the Epidemiologic Catchment Area (ECA) Survey (Regier et al., 1988; Robins et al., 1984). On the basis of data from structured clinical interviews conducted by trained lay interviewers, the lifetime prevalence of OCD was found to be 2.5%. This relatively high prevalence for OCD was replicated in several additional studies using similar methods (e.g., Bland, Orn, & Newman, 1988; Henderson & Pollard, 1988; Kolada, Bland, & Newman, 1994; Wittchen, 1988).

Unfortunately, the majority of these epidemiological studies have several methodological limitations (Antony, Downie, & Swinson, 1998), and recent studies have begun to challenge their findings. Nelson and Rice (1997) examined the 1-year stability of OCD lifetime diagnoses in the ECA study and found that the stability was unacceptably low (ranging from .16 to .25), suggesting that the Diagnostic Interview Schedule is neither a reliable nor valid method of diagnosing OCD. M. B. Stein, Forde, Anderson, and Walker (1997) assessed the prevalence of OCD in a community sample using (a) structured interviews conducted by lay interviewers and (b) semistructured interviews conducted by trained professionals. Whereas fully structured interviews led to a 1-month prevalence estimate of 3.1%, the 1-month prevalence of OCD using semistructured interviews was only 0.6%. The most common reasons for the overdiagnosis of OCD by the lay interviewers was the tendency to mislabel *worries* as *obsessions* and to overestimate the amount of distress and impairment associated with the OCD symptoms. In summary, the true prevalence of OCD remains unknown. Although OCD is probably more common than believed before the 1980s, it may not be as prevalent as has been suggested in recent years.

Findings regarding demographic variables and OCD are reviewed in detail elsewhere (Antony, Downie, & Swinson, 1998). To summarize, OCD begins on average in the early to mid-20s, although childhood onsets are not unusual. Whereas OCD tends to begin earlier in males than in females, the prevalence of OCD tends to be similar among adult men and women, with some evidence that OCD is slightly more common among women than men. OCD occurs across religious and ethnic groups, although it may be more common among White people than among those with an African American or Hispanic background. Findings regarding the relation between OCD and other demographic variables (e.g., income, employment, marital status, education) have been inconsistent (Antony, Downie, & Swinson, 1998).

Patterns of Comorbidity

OCD is often associated with other psychological disorders. In a sample of 87 individuals from our clinic with a principal *DSM-IV* diagnosis (American Psychiatric Association, 1994) of OCD (Antony, Downie, & Swinson, 1998), 28.7% of individuals had one additional current *DSM-IV* diagnosis, 17.2% had two additional diagnoses, and 18.4% had three or more diagnoses. The percentages of patients meeting diagnostic criteria for various additional disorders are listed in Table 3.2.

As reviewed by Antony, Downie, and Swinson (1998), these findings are fairly consistent with data from previous studies based on earlier diagnostic criteria (e.g., Crino & Andrews, 1996; Sanderson, Di Nardo, Rapee, & Barlow, 1990; Yaryura-Tobias et al., 1996), although a number of

Table 3.2. Percentages of Individuals With
Obsessive–Compulsive Disorder ($N = 87$) Who
Currently Suffer From Additional *DSM–IV*
Axis I Disorders

Comorbid diagnosis	Percentage of individuals
Social phobia	41.4
Major depressive disorder	24.1
Specific phobia	20.7
Dysthymic disorder	13.8
Panic disorder	11.5
Generalized anxiety disorder	11.5
Tic disorder	8.0
Trichotillomania	4.6

Note. Data from Antony, Downie, and Swinson (1998). All
diagnoses were determined using the Structured Clinical
Interview for *DSM–IV* (First et al., 1996). *DSM–IV = Diagnostic and Statistical Manual of Mental Disorders.*

other investigators have found that depression is the most common comorbid diagnosis among individuals with OCD. For the majority of patients
with comorbid OCD and depression the OCD symptoms typically begin
before the depression (Bellodi, Sciuto, Diaferia, Ronchi, & Smeraldi, 1992;
Demal, Lenz, Mayrhofer, Zapotoczky, & Zitterl, 1993). This is consistent
with the hypothesis that for many patients the depression is in part a
response to having OCD. In addition, there is evidence that the presence
of comorbid depression is often related to severe obsessions but not to the
severity of compulsive behaviors (Ricciardi & McNally, 1995). OCD and
related symptoms are also sometimes associated with eating disorders
(Schwalberg, Barlow, Alger, & Barlow, 1992; Thiel, Broocks, Ohlmeier, Jacoby, & Schüssler, 1995), alcohol and substance abuse (Eisen & Rasmussen, 1989; Fals-Stewart & Angarano, 1994; Riemann, McNally, & Cox,
1992), and hypochondriacal concerns (Savron et al., 1996).

Assessment of OCD

Assessment informs the clinician about the patient and the nature of his
or her OCD symptoms, which in turn helps with planning treatment.
In addition, assessment throughout the course of treatment and during
follow-up allows the clinician to evaluate the impact of the intervention.
Consistent with these two functions of assessment, we recommend that
the clinician conduct a thorough evaluation before treatment begins and
that the assessment process continue throughout the course of treatment
and periodically after treatment has been terminated. In this section we
cover the basic strategies used in the assessment of patients with OCD.
More thorough reviews on the nature and psychometric properties of var-

ious OCD assessment strategies are available elsewhere (e.g., Taylor, 1995, 1998).

Interview-Based Assessments

Semistructured diagnostic interviews. An important component of the initial evaluation for an individual presenting with OCD is a thorough diagnostic assessment. Although many clinicians use unstructured interviews to assess the symptoms of relevant *DSM–IV–TR* disorders, there are several advantages to using established semistructured interviews, such as the Anxiety Disorders Interview Schedule for *DSM–IV* (ADIS–IV; Di Nardo, Brown, & Barlow, 1994) and the Structured Clinical Interview for *DSM–IV* (SCID–IV; First, Spitzer, Gibbon, & Williams, 1996). First, earlier versions of these instruments (particularly the ADIS–IV) have been shown to be reliable for identifying individuals with OCD and associated conditions (Di Nardo, Moras, Barlow, Rapee, & Brown, 1993; Williams et al., 1992). Second, these instruments facilitate the process of distinguishing among a number of differential diagnoses. Finally, semistructured interviews ensure that the clinician does not overlook important questions. Research versions of these semistructured interviews typically take from 1 to 3 hours to complete and can take even longer for patients with numerous problems. Both the SCID–IV and ADIS–IV have briefer clinician versions that do not provide as detailed an assessment. Typically, the ADIS–IV takes longer to administer than does the SCID–IV, although it also provides a more thorough review for symptoms of OCD and the other anxiety disorders.

Y–BOCS (Goodman et al., 1989a, 1989b). The Y–BOCS has become a standard measure of OCD severity and treatment outcome. This clinician-administered measure consists of four parts: (a) definitions and examples of obsessions and compulsions, (b) a symptom checklist (consisting of a long list of obsessions and compulsions that are rated as present or absent), (c) assessment of obsessions, and (d) assessment of compulsions. It is the sections on obsessions and compulsions that form the core items of the Y–BOCS, yielding scores for severity of obsessions, severity of compulsions, and a total severity score. The core Y–BOCS items measure various aspects of OCD symptomatology (on a 5-point scale), including frequency and duration, interference in functioning, associated distress, degree of resistance, and perceived control over symptoms. As reviewed by Taylor (1998), the Y–BOCS has good psychometric properties overall, but poor discriminant validity, as it tends to correlate highly with more general measures of anxiety and depression. A revision of the Y–BOCS is in the final stages of development (Goodman, Rasmussen, & Price, 1999).

Self-Report Measures

Table 3.3 includes descriptions of some of the most commonly used self-report measures for OCD symptoms. Although most of these measures are

Table 3.3.   Selected Self-Report Measures for Obsessive–Compulsive Disorder

Measure	No. items	Description
MOCI	30	• 4 subscales: Washing, Checking, Obsessional Slowness and Repetition, Excessive Doubting and Conscientiousness • Adequate psychometric properties[a] • Assesses a limited range of symptoms[a] • Currently being revised and updated[a]
CAC	Varies	• Measures OCD-related interference for various daily activities • Does not assess OCD symptoms directly (just interference) • Several versions and revisions exist (18–62 items) • Self-report and observer-rated versions • Adequate psychometric properties (but not discriminant validity)[a]
PI	60	• 5 subscales: Checking, Contamination Fears, Mental Dyscontrol, Fear or Behavioral Dyscontrol • Developed to adequately measure obsessions as well as compulsions • Tends to correlate with general measures of worry[b]
PI–R	39	• Revised PI (by deleting items that measure general worry) • 5 subscales: Obsessional Thoughts About Harm to Oneself or Others, Obsessional Impulses to Harm Oneself or Others, Contamination Obsessions and Washing Compulsions, Checking Compulsions, Dressing and Grooming Compulsions • Good psychometric properties[a]
NIMHOCS	1	• A global rating of OCD severity (using a 15-point scale) • Commonly used in pharmaceutical trials • Psychometric properties have yet to be established • Sensitive to change following treatment[a]

Note.   OCD = obsessive–compulsive disorder; MOCI = Maudsley Obsessive Compulsive Inventory (Hodgson & Rachman, 1977); CAC = Compulsive Activity Checklist (Cottraux, Bouvard, Defayolle, & Messy, 1988; Freund, Steketee, & Foa, 1987; Marks, Hallam, Connolly, & Philpott, 1977; Philpott, 1975; Steketee & Freund, 1993); PI = Padua Inventory (Sanavio, 1988); PI–R = Padua Inventory—Revised (Burns, Keortge, Formea, & Sternberger, 1996); NIMHOCS = National Institute of Mental Health Global Obsessive Compulsive Scale (Insel et al., 1983).
[a]Taylor (1998).   [b]Freeston et al. (1994).

adequate, the revised Padua Inventory (PI–R; Sanavio, 1988) may have the most consistently strong psychometric properties (Taylor, 1998) and is relatively brief. However, this measure is also quite new, and more research is needed to establish its utility in OCD patients. In addition to the measures listed in Table 3.3 there are self-report (Baer, Brown-Beasley, Sorce, & Henriques, 1993) and computerized (Rosenfeld, Dar, Anderson, Kobak, & Greist, 1992) versions of the Y–BOCS that correlate highly with the interview version and appear to have good psychometric properties (Steketee, Frost, & Bogart, 1996). For a comprehensive review of self-report measures for OCD, see Taylor (1995, 1998).

Behavioral Approach Tests

Originally developed for assessing fear and avoidance in people with specific fears and phobias, the behavioral approach test (BAT; also called the *behavioral avoidance test*) is now a commonly used method of assessing these dimensions in people suffering from OCD (Taylor, 1998). During the BAT, patients are asked to approach one (i.e., single-task BAT) or more (i.e., multitask BAT) situations that are likely to be associated with fear. Sometimes, particularly feared situations are broken down into progressively more difficult steps and patients are asked to approach these situations in order of difficulty (i.e., multistep–multitask BAT). Overall, the BAT appears to be a psychometrically sound strategy for assessing fear and avoidance in OCD patients and is a sensitive method of measuring changes following treatment (Steketee, Chambless, Tran, Worden, & Gillis, 1996; Taylor, 1998).

The item or items chosen for the BAT should represent situations that are difficult for the patient to confront. For example, a patient who fears becoming contaminated might be asked to become increasingly close to a contaminated object and to eventually touch it. Alternatively, he or she might be asked to touch a series of increasingly contaminated objects. During the BAT, a variety of variables can be measured, including (a) the number of steps taken by the patient, (b) the patient's level of fear (using a numerical scale, e.g., from 0 to 100), (c) any obsessional thoughts that occur, (d) the intensity of urges to engage in compulsive rituals (using a numerical scale, e.g., from 0 to 100), and (e) any actual rituals engaged in by the patient. The BAT has advantages over simply asking the patient to describe his or her reaction to being exposed to the feared situation. Specifically, the BAT is less subject to biases that are inherent in retrospective self-reports. In addition, it provides the clinician with the opportunity to directly observe the behaviors associated with the patient's OCD.

Monitoring Diaries

Monitoring diaries are typically used during cognitive and behaviorally oriented therapies, although they are useful for individuals receiving pharmacological treatments as well. The purpose of diaries is to help patients and clinicians to continuously track the patient's OCD symptoms before, during, and after treatment. Patients are asked to record episodes during which they (a) experience obsessions, (b) have urges to perform compulsions, or (c) actually engage in compulsive rituals. Diaries provide an indication of the frequency and intensity of symptoms between treatment sessions. Two general approaches to monitoring may be used: event sampling and time sampling. In sampling events, the patient is asked to record each time a particular obsession or compulsion occurs (as well as the time, situation, trigger, etc.). This method is useful when the obsessions and compulsions occur infrequently (e.g., no more than a few times per day). For example, a patient who has obsessions about running over a pedestrian when driving on city streets might list each time this thought is experienced throughout the week as well as any checking rituals that occur.

For some patients, obsessions and compulsions occur too many times (or even continuously) throughout the day, so that it is not practical to record each episode. For such a patient, time sampling is a more appropriate approach. In a time sampling diary, patients are asked to record the intensity and/or frequency of obsessions and compulsions during specified time periods. For example, a patient who washes many times per day might be asked to record the percentage of time spent washing as well as the intensity of contamination obsessions (e.g., using a scale from 0 to 100) during each 1-hour period from waking until going to sleep.

Summary and Recommendations

We recommend that patients receive a semistructured diagnostic interview (e.g., SCID–IV or ADIS–IV) at the start of treatment. In addition, we suggest that they be administered the Y–BOCS, BATs, and a brief self-report questionnaire (e.g., Padua Inventory–Washington State University Revision) before treatment begins and periodically (e.g., every fifth session) throughout the course of treatment. Finally, patients should be encouraged to record their progress throughout treatment using monitoring diaries.

Biological Approaches to Treatment

Biological Views of OCD

Most of the research that has been conducted in recent years regarding the etiology of OCD has been focused on hypotheses involving brain serotonin (5-hydroxytryptamine [5-HT]) systems. 5-HT has been shown to be implicated in many behavioral systems, including mood, appetite, sexual activity, and aggression, as well as anxiety states (Murphy et al., 1996). The initial interest in the role of 5-HT in the etiology of OCD arose from the finding that clomipramine, a tricyclic antidepressant (TCA), is much more effective than are other TCAs at reducing the severity of symptoms in OCD sufferers. The addition of a chlorine atom to the basic TCA structure resulted in significant anti-obsessional activity, presumably because this enhances selectivity of the molecule for the 5-HT transporter. The hypothesized mechanism of action for clomipramine involves greater inhibition of 5-HT reuptake, relative to reuptake of other neurotransmitters (e.g., norepinephrine) that have been implicated in mood and anxiety states (Shank et al., 1988).

Zohar and Kindler (1992) demonstrated that the anti-obsessional activity of antidepressants is directly related to 5-HT reuptake inhibition. During normal neuronal activity synaptic transmission is initiated by the release of chemical neurotransmitter substances into the intracellular synaptic cleft. The impulse from the proximal cell causes the release of stored transmitter chemicals, such as 5-HT, into the synapse, where it travels to receptors on the postsynaptic cell and triggers messenger systems that propagate the impulse in that cell. Not all of the released 5-HT is used in the transmission, and a portion is taken back into the proximal cell body. In reuptake inhibition the amount taken back up is reduced, thereby making more transmitter substance available for the propagation of the next series of impulses. The specific reuptake inhibition of 5-HT is the main activity of the class of drugs named *selective serotonin reuptake inhibitors* (SSRIs).

Serotonin function can be measured peripherally, although there is no direct correlation between peripheral 5-HT activity and central 5-HT effects. Flament, Rapoport, Murphy, Berg, and Lake (1987) showed that treatment response to the SSRIs is reflected in reduction in blood platelet cell 5-HT activity. In contrast to the benefits shown by many patients with OCD to the use of SSRIs, it has been demonstrated that OC symptoms can be worsened by 5-HT agonists that compete for 5-HT receptor sites. Metachlorophenylpiperazine (mCPP) and sumatriptan (an antimigraine medication) transiently increase the severity of OC symptoms in patients with OCD while not inducing anxiety or OC symptoms in normal individuals (Zohar & Kindler, 1992). Metachlorophenylpiperazine reduces the synthesis and turnover of 5-HT and reduces the availability of 5-HT in the neural pathways; mCPP is a metabolite or byproduct of nefazodone, an antidepressant agent, and although this medication might theoretically be expected to have adverse effects in the treatment of OCD, there is no clinical evidence to support this concern.

Although there is agreement about the probable role of 5-HT in the pathophysiology of OCD, there is evidence that other brain mechanisms may be involved. Structural imaging studies have demonstrated lesions in the basal ganglia of individuals with compulsive behavior disorders. Cottraux and Gerard (1998) recently reviewed the evidence related to findings of basal ganglia changes and frontal-lobe hypometabolism. There is some evidence that children with streptococcal infections who develop antibodies to the bacterial infection may have these antibodies attack the caudate and putamen nuclei, causing a condition similar to Sydenham's chorea (Garvey, Giedd, & Swedo, 1998; Swedo et al., 1989), an uncommon disorder affecting children after streptococcal infection. It is characterized by the development of rapid, purposeless athetoid movements. Facial grimacing is also common.

Genetic studies of twins with OCD have shown evidence of transmission in a way that is consistent with a single-gene effect (Billett, Richter, & Kennedy, 1998). As yet, there is insufficient evidence to point to any particular gene, or gene complex, as being involved in the causation of OCD, but there is accumulating information that OCD complicated by tics may be associated with increased prevalence of dopamine D4 receptor genes (Cruz et al., 1997).

Review of Pharmacotherapy Studies

Numerous studies have shown that the 5-HT/serotonin reuptake inhibitors (SRIs), which include the more selective SSRIs as well as clomipramine, are effective in reducing OCD symptoms (for reviews, see Antony & Swinson, 1996; Pato, Pato, & Gunn, 1998; Pigott & Seay, 1998, 1999). One of the earliest and most frequently studied medications to be investigated in patients with OCD is clomipramine. The largest studies of clomipramine published to date are a series of two double-blind, placebo-controlled trials conducted by the Clomipramine Collaborative Study Group (1991). These studies included 520 patients (with no more than mild depression) treated for 10 weeks with clomipramine or placebo across 21 different sites. In Study 1, patients taking clomipramine (mean dosage = 234.5 mg/day) experienced a 38% decrease in Y–BOCS scores, compared to 3% for those taking placebo. These findings were essentially replicated in the second study. In both studies clomipramine was well tolerated, with common side effects including dry mouth, dizziness, tremor, fatigue, digestive problems, and urogenital symptoms. The efficacy of clomipramine for OCD has been confirmed repeatedly in a number of additional controlled trials.

More recently, investigators have begun to study the use of medications that are even more selective than clomipramine in their blocking of 5-HT reuptake: the SSRIs. These include sertraline (e.g., Chouinard et al., 1990; Greist, Chouinard, et al., 1995; Greist, Jefferson, Kobak, Chouinard, et al., 1995; Kronig et al., 1999); fluoxetine (e.g., Tollefson et al., 1994); fluvoxamine (e.g., Jenike et al., 1990; Perse, Greist, Jefferson, Rosenfeld, & Dar, 1987); paroxetine (e.g., Mundo, Bianchi, & Bellodi, 1997; Zohar, Judge, & the OCD Paroxetine Study Investigators, 1996); and, most recently, citalopram (Koponen et al., 1997; Montgomery, 1998; Mundo et al., 1997). Each of these medications has been shown to be more effective than placebo for the treatment of OCD. In general, antidepressants other than clomipramine and the SSRIs are thought to be relatively ineffective for individuals suffering from OCD (Barr, Goodman, Anand, McDougle, & Price, 1997; Jenike, Baer, Minichiello, Rauch, & Buttolph, 1997; Leonard et al., 1989; Volavka, Neziroglu, & Yaryura-Tobias, 1985).

Meta-analytic reviews of pharmacological trials have confirmed the usefulness of clomipramine and the SSRIs for treating OCD, although they have tended to show a higher effect size for clomipramine than for the SSRIs (e.g., Greist, Jefferson, Kobak, Katzelnick, & Serlin, 1995; Piccinelli, Pini, Bellantuono, & Wilkinson, 1995; D. J. Stein, Spadaccini, & Hollander, 1995). It has been argued that this difference is probably an artifact of the period during which the original clomipramine studies were conducted—a time when there were no other medications available for OCD. Specifically, trials of SSRI medications have tended to be conducted more recently than the original clomipramine trials and therefore probably included individuals who had previously failed to respond to other usually efficacious medications, such as clomipramine. In contrast, when most clomipramine trials were conducted there were no other medications approved for OCD in North America (Pigott & Seay, 1998). In fact, studies that have directly compared clomipramine with SSRIs have failed to show significant differences in efficacy (see Antony & Swinson, 1996; Pigott & Seay, 1998).

Augmentation studies. Recently, investigators have examined the usefulness of augmenting pharmacotherapy for OCD with a second medication. McDougle et al. (1994) found that adding haloperidol for patients with OCD who were refractory to treatment with fluvoxamine was more effective than augmentation with placebo. In addition, risperidone (an antipsychotic medication that blocks dopamine and 5-HT receptors) may be a useful medication for augmenting the effects of SRIs (Ravizza, Barzega, Bellino, Bogetto, & Maina, 1996; Saxena, Wang, Bystritsky, & Baxter, 1996). The method of action of the antipsychotic agents in augmenting the effects of SRIs is not clear. There is no evidence that the antipsychotics are directly anti-obsessional in activity. They may have a nonspecific effect through a calming action, or it is possible that the addition of dopamine blockade may assist in reducing compulsive behaviors. In contrast to neuroleptics, neither buspirone (an anti-anxiety medication; McDougle et al., 1993) nor lithium (a mood stabilizer; McDougle, Price, Goodman, Charney, & Heninger, 1991) appear to be useful for augmenting the effects of SSRI medications. Given the strong effects of buspirone on the 5-HT system, it is curious that this medication is not particularly useful in the treatment of OCD.

Practical Aspects of Providing Pharmacotherapy

Physical parameters to assess before prescribing. The antidepressant medications that are the first choice of treatment in OCD are generally safe and well tolerated. The efficacy of the SSRIs and clomipramine were initially established in healthy adults, but it has become clear that they can be used in children and in people with a variety of physical illnesses. One of the main limitations of the TCAs (e.g., clomipramine), particularly in higher dose ranges, is their tendency to interfere with cardiac conduction, and it is necessary to monitor heart function by means of electrocardiogram before starting treatment or when the dose is increased. The SSRIs do not have clinically significant cardiac effects in healthy young people, but caution should be taken in routinely monitoring older people or those with pre-existing cardiac conduction defects.

In most people, SSRIs are taken without problem provided that the initial dosage is fairly low. There are no absolute contraindications to the use of SSRIs except for the recent or concurrent use of a monoamine oxidase inhibitor (MAOI) such as phenelzine or tranylcypromine. Clomipramine in high doses is associated with an increased risk of seizures, and before the dose is increased beyond 200 mg per day an electroencephalogram is indicated. Liver function tests may be done before the onset of treatment if there is suspicion of possible liver impairment, particularly if there is a history of comorbid substance use or if the patient is taking other medications that are metabolized by liver pathways. Because many of the SSRIs inhibit certain hepatic enzymes (most commonly of the cytochrome P-450 family) responsible for the metabolism of a wide range of commonly taken drugs, the SSRIs (particularly fluoxetine and paroxetine) may affect the rates of metabolism of other concurrently used medications. These include the TCAs, benzodiazepines, and some antibiotics. When an SSRI is added to the medication mix of someone already taking a TCA, the resulting blood level of the tricyclic increases. Care has to be taken when a patient is switched from a TCA to an SSRI to allow sufficient time for the level of the TCA to decrease before the SSRI is added or its dose increased. Blood level monitoring of the TCA level is important when the two classes of drug are used together.

Although the accumulated evidence is that the outcome of pregnancy is not influenced by the use of any of the antidepressants, a pregnancy test may be indicated if there is a chance of an unknown early pregnancy. Appropriate informed consent is a necessity in the medication treating OCD in women who are pregnant or who may wish to become pregnant while on the medication.

Side effects. The majority of people taking SSRIs and TCAs will report some adverse effect that may be attributable to the medication. The SSRIs as a class produce similar side effects. These are described in Table 3.4, by organ system. In general, the side effects of the SSRIs are very tolerable provided the patient is informed of the range of possible symptoms and the starting dose is low.

Table 3.4. Side Effects in Patients Taking Selective Serotonin Reuptake Inhibitors

System	Side effects
Gastrointestinal	Nausea
	Intestinal cramping
	Diarrhea
	Vomiting
	Dry mouth
Central nervous system	Nervousness
	Tremulousness
	Insomnia
	Hypersomnia
	Sedation
	Anxiety
	Headache
Sexual symptoms	Delayed orgasm in men and women
Skin	Allergic reactions, rashes

Duration of pharmacotherapy. Drug treatments for OCD usually require long-term use for the onset and maintenance of therapeutic benefit. The effects of SRIs are cumulative over a period of weeks, and it is not until after about 8 weeks of use that the effectiveness of a medication can be assessed. The large trials of clomipramine and the SSRIs have all demonstrated that it takes at least 6 weeks, and perhaps as long as 12 weeks, to obtain the maximal benefit from an adequate dose of the drug used. One of the main reasons for apparent drug treatment failure is the use of too low a dose for too short a time. A major limitation of medication treatment is that the majority of responders relapse within 7 or 8 weeks after the discontinuation of the drug (Pato et al., 1998). The severity of the relapse and the proportion of patients relapsing is lessened by slow rather than rapid decrease in drug dosage. Some people maintain their improvement when the dose is reduced slowly to approximately 50% of the original effective dose.

Choosing among medications. The choice of an initial medication is between one of the available SSRIs (fluoxetine, fluvoxamine, sertraline, paroxetine, citalopram) or the use of the TCA clomipramine. The efficacy of all these agents is very similar, and the choice is usually determined by drug tolerability, safety, side effects, cost, and the patient's previous drug experience.

SSRIs are more easily tolerated than TCAs, and the initial drug of choice for most patients will be an SSRI. The specific SSRIs vary in their pharmacokinetic and pharmacodynamic properties. Fluoxetine, and its primary metabolite, have very long half-lives (i.e., the time needed for half of the medication to be metabolized by the body) compared to the other SSRIs. The advantages of a long half-life are that the drug can be taken once a day and that missed doses do not markedly affect the long-term course. The disadvantage is that if there is reason to discontinue fluoxetine because of lack of efficacy, side effects, or an uncommon allergy, it remains in circulation for a period of weeks.

Many patients require multiple medications for psychiatric and physical reasons. Sertraline and fluvoxamine have less effect on hepatic enzyme function than do fluoxetine and paroxetine and may be preferable when polydrug therapy is indicated.

Clomipramine should be given when a patient has failed adequate treatment with two of the SSRIs. It has the side-effect profile of the TCAs, including dry mouth, weight gain, sedation, cardiac conduction impairment, the potential for seizure induction, and anorgasmia. In clinical practice the large majority of patients find that clomipramine is tolerable and effective. In overdose clomipramine, as a tricyclic agent, is more hazardous than the SSRIs. At higher doses it is advisable to monitor cardiac conduction by means of a routine electrocardiogram, particularly in older people, those with pre-existing cardiac problems, those taking other medications, and when the dose is increased.

Older drugs, such as the MAOIs, have been shown to be effective, and a recent study by Jenike et al. (1997) confirmed that some patients obtain significant benefit. The MAOIs have to be used with caution because of their dietary and drug interactions that can affect blood pressure regulation in potentially dangerous ways. MAOIs must not be added to the treatment of someone who is taking or has recently discontinued SSRIs. In general, MAOIs are rarely used to treat OCD, although they may be an option for some patients who do not respond to adequate trials with SSRIs and clomipramine.

Augmentation strategies. If the chosen SSRI does not produce the desired effect at adequate dose levels given for 12 weeks or more, then it is reasonable to switch to another SSRI and then to clomipramine. If none of these strategies is sufficiently effective, then the addition of other medications to the SRI/SSRI regimen can be helpful. The evidence about the use of augmenting agents is limited. The clearest indication for the augmentation of SSRIs is in the case of OCD with a comorbid tic disorder where it has been shown that the addition of a neuroleptic, such as low-dose haloperidol, can increase efficacy significantly (McDougle et al., 1994).

Other augmenting agents have included benzodiazepines when anxiety levels are very high. Lithium is sometimes used (as in treatment-resistant depression), although evidence supporting the use of lithium as an augmenting drug in OCD is still lacking (e.g., McDougle et al., 1991). Although a range of agents has been proposed as additive to the standard approaches, most studies are anecdotal or are based on very small series. Recently, Blier and Bergeron (1996) provided data that treatment aimed at certain 5-HT receptors' reuptake inhibition can convert some nonresponsive individuals to responders. They combined an SSRI with pindolol (a beta-adrenergic blocking drug) and tryptophan (the dietary precursor to 5-HT). Tryptophan is not available in the United States but is in fairly common use in Canada as an augmenter for the treatment of depression, OCD, and insomnia.

Dosing strategies throughout treatment. SSRIs cause side effects that are often dose related, at least initially. Over time, side effects tend to become less troublesome, except for weight gain and sexual dysfunction, but the long-term acceptability of any particular drug is often determined by the initial experience. Provided the patient is well educated about potential side effects, most will tolerate a low starting dose, the equivalent of 10 mg of fluoxetine once a day. Unfortunately some patients become very tremulous and agitated on the smallest available dose of any of the SSRIs and find it extremely difficult to reach an average effective dose level.

Although there is a tendency to push the dose of SSRIs to high levels in OCD there is little evidence that this is a necessary strategy in most patients. The outcome is determined more by the length of the drug use than the maximal dose (Preskorn, 1993). The initial drug should be chosen with the patient aware of the potential side-effect profile, the drug's interactions with other medications, and the half-life of the drug used. A starting dose of 25 mg or 50 mg of sertraline, 10 mg of paroxetine, 10 mg of fluoxetine, 50 mg of fluvoxamine, or 10 mg of citalopram is tolerated in most cases. Taking medication after food is important in reducing stomach upset. Some patients will find that the drug used causes some agitation and insomnia, and they should take the medication in the morning; others find the same drug to be sedating, and nighttime dosing is appropriate for them. Once-a-day administration may increase compliance and is suitable for most cases.

The effect of the initial dose is observed for a week or two and then is usually increased according to response and tolerability. Dose-finding studies of fluoxetine (Tollefson et al., 1994) and sertraline (Greist, Chouinard, et al., 1995; Greist, Jefferson, Kobak, Chouinard, et al., 1995) have shown that only a minority of patients require high doses provided that all patients are given the necessary time to respond to the initial dose. It is currently unclear just how long the initial starting dose level should be continued. There is some evidence of a dose–response relation for fluoxetine (Tollefson et al., 1994), and it is the practice of most clinicians to increase the dose of SSRIs to 20- or 40-mg fluoxetine equivalents. OCD responds more slowly than major depression, and the time needed to judge the ultimate effect of a particular drug dose is about 8–12 weeks. In a study of long-term use of sertraline in fixed doses of 50–200 mg daily, patients improved in terms of their Y–BOCS scores until the 16th week and then maintained that improvement (Greist, Jefferson, Kobak, Chouinard, et al., 1995). Increasing the daily dose beyond sertraline 150 mg, fluoxetine 60 mg, paroxetine 40 mg, fluvoxamine 150 mg, or citalopram 40 mg should be considered only after at least 8–12 weeks at the lower doses.

The optimal length of drug treatment in OCD is not determined. There is a marked tendency for individuals to relapse after the discontinuation of medication treatment. Pato, Zohar-Kadouch, Zohar, and Murphy (1988) discontinued clomipramine treatment in 18 OCD clomipramine responders. By Week 4 postdiscontinuation there was a marked increase in symptom severity that continued to increase to the end of the study, at Week 7. From clinical experience it appears that for most responders long-term treatment (at least 1 year) is necessary to prevent relapse.

Psychosurgery

For patients who have previously failed to respond to treatment (including adequate trials of each of the SRIs, SRIs with augmentation, and cognitive–behavioral treatment), psychosurgery (e.g., cingulotomy, anterior capsulotomy) may be an option. Several long-term follow-up studies suggest that more than a quarter of patients with treatment-refractory OCD report significant benefit following psychosurgery, with relatively few side effects (e.g., Baer et al., 1995; Cumming, Hay, Lee, & Sachdev, 1995; Hay et al., 1993). Because of the intrusive nature of psychosurgery and a lack of controlled studies, these procedures are currently reserved for severe refractory cases.

Psychological Approaches to Treatment

Psychological Views of OCD

Although early psychological models came from a psychodynamic perspective (see Nemiah, 1975), there has been little empirical support for psychodynamic theories of OCD, and this perspective has had little influence on the development of effective treatments for the disorder. In contrast, cognitive and behavioral views of OCD have gained popularity in recent years and have led to the development of strategies for successfully treating OCD.

Earlier behavioral models of OCD (e.g., Rachman & Hodgson, 1980) grew out of Mowrer's (1947, 1960) two-factor model for the acquisition and maintenance of fear. Specifically, the behavioral model proposed that OCD is the result of normal thoughts, urges, and impulses being associated with anxiety through classical conditioning processes. According to this view, OCD symptoms are maintained by escape, avoidance, and undoing behaviors (e.g., compulsive rituals) that prevent the extinction of anxiety. This view led to the development of an effective behavioral treatment for OCD consisting of exposure to feared stimuli and prevention of compulsive rituals.

Some authors (e.g., Salkovskis, 1998) have argued that the traditional behavioral view is of limited usefulness. For example, many patients with OCD do not recall specific conditioning experiences that account for their OCD symptoms. Also, some individuals do not respond to exposure and response prevention alone, and those who do often achieve only a partial response to treatment. In response to these and other limitations of the behavioral model Paul Salkovskis (Salkovskis, 1985, 1989a, 1989b, 1998) developed a cognitive–behavioral model of OCD. Salkovskis has proposed that although intrusive thoughts are common in the general population it is the ways in which OCD patients interpret their cognitive intrusions that contribute to and maintain the disorder. In particular, Salkovskis has emphasized the role of perceived responsibility; that is, relative to most people, individuals with OCD believe that their actions are likely to cause or prevent the occurrence of harm to themselves or to others. Compulsions are designed as a neutralizing action to dispel the person's sense of responsibility.

The Obsessive Compulsive Cognitions Working Group (1997), which consists of a number of international experts on cognition and OCD, have proposed additional cognitive domains that may be involved in OCD, including tendencies to be perfectionistic, to believe that one's thoughts are overly important, to be overly concerned about controlling one's thoughts, to be overly intolerant of uncertainty, and to overestimate the probability of threat. As reviewed in the next section, the recent emphasis on cognitive factors in OCD has led some investigators to integrate cognitive strategies into the behavioral treatment of OCD.

Review of Psychological Treatment Studies

Over the last few decades, exposure and response prevention (ERP) has emerged as the psychological treatment of choice for OCD (Foa, Franklin, & Kozak, 1998). *Exposure* involves approaching fear-evoking situations until they no longer cause discomfort or fear. For example, individuals with contamination-related concerns might be asked to touch objects that they perceive as contaminated. Similarly, people who have intrusive religious obsessions might be asked to repeatedly expose themselves to their frightening religious thoughts and to the objects and situations that trigger these thoughts. *Response prevention*, also known as *ritual prevention* (Foa et al., 1998), involves preventing the occurrence of compulsive rituals, such as washing, checking, and counting. Although exposure and ritual prevention are each somewhat helpful on their own, they tend to target different aspects of the disorder and work best when they are implemented concurrently (Foa, Steketee, Grayson, Turner, & Latimer, 1984).

A long history of research, beginning with the work of Victor Meyer (1966), has supported the use of ERP for treating OCD. Controlled-outcome studies (e.g., Fals-Stewart, Marks, & Schafer, 1993; Foa & Goldstein, 1978; Lindsay, Crino, & Andrews, 1997) have repeatedly demonstrated a significant reduction in OCD symptoms following treatment with ERP. Furthermore, compared to pharmacological treatments with medications such as clomipramine (Marks et al., 1988; Marks, Stern, Mawson, Cobb, & McDonald, 1980; Rachman et al., 1979) and fluvoxamine (Cottraux, Mollard, Bouvard, & Marks, 1993; Cottraux et al., 1990), ERP has been shown to be at least as effective, particularly during later phases of treatment and during follow-up. The finding that ERP and pharmacotherapy with SRIs are both effective for treating OCD has been confirmed in several meta-analytic studies (e.g., Abramowitz, 1997; Cox, Swinson, Morrison, & Lee, 1993; van Balkom, van Oppen, Vermeulen, & van Dyck, 1994).

As mentioned earlier, investigators have begun to examine whether adding cognitive therapy to ERP leads to greater improvement than ERP alone. Several small-*n* studies that have used rational–emotive therapy (e.g., Emmelkamp & Beens, 1991; Emmelkamp, Visser, & Hoekstra, 1988) and self-instructional training (Emmelkamp, van der Helm, van Zanten, & Plochg, 1980) have failed to show a benefit of adding cognitive therapy to ERP. However, a more recent study based on Beck's (1976) cognitive therapy found in a larger sample of OCD patients that cognitive therapy was more effective than ERP on a limited number of measures (van Oppen et al., 1995). Studies are still needed to investigate the potential benefits of adding this form of cognitive therapy to ERP.

A number of variables appear to influence the effectiveness of ERP. Ideally, exposure should continue for 1–2 hours or until anxiety has decreased significantly (Kozak, Foa, & Steketee, 1988; Rabavilas, Boulougouris, & Stefanis, 1977). In addition, there is evidence in other anxiety disorders that more frequent exposure practices (e.g., daily) lead to more improvement than practices that are more widely spaced (e.g., weekly;

Foa, Jameson, Turner, & Payne, 1980). Therefore, it is recommended that treatment be conducted intensively, if possible. When it is not practical to see patients more frequently than once per week, it is important that patients practice ERP exercises on their own, between sessions. There is evidence that patients can benefit from self-exposure practices without a therapist present (e.g., Emmelkamp & van Kraanen, 1977). In addition, family members may be recruited to help with between-session practices.

Although abrupt exposure to increasingly difficult situations appears to be equally effective as more gradually administered exposure (Hodgson, Rachman, & Marks, 1972), gradual exposure may be more acceptable to patients. In addition, ERP appears to be equally effective when conducted individually or in groups (Fals-Stewart et al., 1993).

A number of recent treatment manuals for patients and clinicians provide detailed descriptions of how to implement ERP (e.g., Kozak & Foa, 1996; Riggs & Foa, 1993; Steketee, 1993, 1999a, 1999b). Essentially, the first step is for the patient and therapist to develop an exposure hierarchy, consisting of a list of feared situations (in order of difficulty). The patient is then instructed to stop all compulsions and rituals, which is in turn followed by gradual exposure to feared objects and situations, beginning with easier items on the hierarchy and gradually moving on to more difficult items as the fear decreases.

Because ritual prevention is often very difficult initially, it may be important for the patient and therapist to have frequent meetings (in person or by telephone) early in treatment. Some patients may refuse to stop all rituals. In such cases, the patient may initially agree to stop all rituals for an extended period (e.g., in the evenings) or in a particular location (e.g., at home) and to gradually extend the ritual prevention to other locations or other times of the day. If a patient does engage in a compulsion (e.g., washing his or her hands), he or she should be encouraged to immediately undo the effects of the ritual with further exposure (e.g., touching something that is contaminated).

Combining Medications and ERP

Review of the Literature

Several studies have been published on the efficacy of treating OCD with the combination of ERP and medication (for a thorough review, see van Balkom & van Dyck, 1998). In an early placebo-controlled study (Marks et al., 1980; Rachman et al., 1979), there were no significant differences after 7 weeks of treatment with either clomipramine, ERP, or their combination, although the combined treatment was slightly (nonsignificantly) more effective on several measures, particularly for patients who were relatively depressed. The lack of a significant advantage for the combined-treatment condition was maintained at 6-year follow-up (O'Sullivan, Noshirvani, Marks, Monteiro, & Lelliott, 1991).

In a second study by the same group (Marks et al., 1988), the combination of clomipramine and ERP was more effective than ERP plus placebo, but only during the first 8 weeks of treatment. By Week 17 this difference had disappeared. Cottraux et al. (1990) examined the combination of ERP and fluvoxamine and found a slight, nonsignificant advantage for the combined treatment over the individual component treatments. These findings were limited by the fact that many patients in the nonexposure groups engaged in self-exposure, despite instructions not to do so. In a related study, van Balkom et al. (1997) found no advantage to adding fluvoxamine to either ERP or cognitive therapy, compared to administering these psychological treatments without the medication.

Taken together, studies on combined treatments for OCD do not support the use of combination treatments over pharmacotherapy or ERP alone as a general rule, although there is limited evidence that combined treatments may be useful early in treatment (Marks et al., 1988) or for patients who are more depressed (Marks et al., 1980). However, these findings should be interpreted cautiously. Although the percentages of patients who respond to ERP, medication, or their combination tend not to differ across treatments, one should not conclude that the same patients are equally likely to respond to each treatment. In fact, clinically, we often see patients who seem to respond differentially to one treatment and not another, and combined treatment may be the treatment of choice for some individuals. Future research should try to identify methods of predicting which patients are likely to respond to particular interventions.

Practical Aspects of Combining Pharmacological and Psychological Treatments

In the short term, combined treatments are more expensive and time consuming than providing pharmacotherapy or behavior therapy alone. Furthermore, in most outcome studies the additional time and cost associated with combined treatment do not necessarily lead to greater change. Therefore, it probably makes sense to start with either SSRIs *or* behavior therapy for the typical patient with OCD. The decision of which approach to use first depends on a number of factors, including the patient's preference for one approach over the other, the availability and cost of one approach over the other, the patient's likelihood of complying with one approach versus the other, and the patient's response to previous treatments.

In 1997, March, Frances, Carpenter, and Kahn published expert consensus treatment guidelines for the treatment of OCD. For milder OCD they suggested beginning treatment either with cognitive–behavioral therapy (CBT) alone or the combination of CBT and an SRI. For more severe forms of OCD the combination of CBT and an SRI was recommended, based on the likely efficacy, speed, and durability of the treatment. CBT typically involves 13–20 weekly sessions, with continuing monthly visits during the months following the end of the acute treatment. March et al. (1997) recommended that individuals receiving pharmacotherapy also receive monthly visits for several months after they have responded to the medication. Clomipramine was recommended only for patients who have had failed trials on at least two SSRIs.

When initial treatment with either a medication or a psychological treatment alone is only partially effective, it may be warranted to augment treatment using the other strategy. For example, an individual who obtains a 50% reduction in symptoms while taking SSRIs may receive additional benefit by the addition of exposure and ritual prevention. In cases where one treatment is used to augment the other treatment, the order of interventions will depend on which approach happened to be tried first.

When patients have additional problems (such as severe depression) that are likely to influence treatment with either SSRIs or ERP alone, a combination treatment may be particularly useful. For example, if a patient is too depressed to carry out homework practices assigned by a cognitive–behavioral therapist, beginning treatment with pharmacotherapy (perhaps an SSRI) might decrease the depressive symptoms to a level at which compliance with behavioral assignments is less likely to be a problem. Similarly, beginning with medications may be helpful for patients who are too fearful to start treatment with behavior therapy. As mentioned earlier, pharmacotherapy should continue for at least a year, to minimize the chances of relapse after discontinuation. It may also be helpful to provide patients with additional sessions of CBT if and when the medication is discontinued.

When different clinicians are providing the two types of treatment, it is important that their efforts are coordinated. The effects of both treatments can be undermined if the pharmacotherapist and behavior therapist are providing contradictory messages regarding the etiology of OCD, the rationale for treatment, and the likelihood of each treatment working.

Summary and Conclusion

OCD is a relatively common anxiety disorder that tends to cause significant impairment across many domains of functioning (Antony, Roth, Swinson, Huta, & Devins, 1998). Fortunately, effective treatments have been developed from both biological and psychological perspectives. Among pharmacologically oriented treatments, medications that block the reuptake of 5-HT (e.g., clomipramine, sertraline, paroxetine, fluoxetine, fluvoxamine, and citalopram) appear to be the most effective. Cognitive–behavioral treatments, such as exposure and ritual prevention, tend to work as well as medications. Although the combination of pharmacotherapy and CBT may be the treatment of choice for some patients, studies that have examined the efficacy of combined treatments have failed to show a consistent advantage of combining treatments, compared to providing pharmacotherapy or CBT alone. Future research should attempt to identify variables that predict which patients are most likely to respond to a particular intervention.

References

Abramowitz, J. S. (1997). Effectiveness of psychological and pharmacological treatments for obsessive-compulsive disorder: A quantitative review. *Journal of Consulting and Clinical Psychology, 65*, 44–52.

American Psychiatric Association. (1994). *Diagnostic and statistical manual of mental disorders* (4th ed.). Washington, DC: Author.

American Psychiatric Association. (2000). *Diagnostic and statistical manual of mental disorders* (4th ed., text rev.). Washington, DC: Author.

Antony, M. M., Downie, F., & Swinson, R. P. (1998). Diagnostic issues and epidemiology in obsessive compulsive disorder. In R. P. Swinson, M. M. Antony, S. Rachman, & M. A. Richter (Eds.), *Obsessive compulsive disorder: Theory, research and treatment* (pp. 3–32). New York: Guilford Press.

Antony, M. M., Roth, D., Swinson, R. P., Huta, V., & Devins, G. M. (1998). Illness intrusiveness in individuals with panic disorder, obsessive compulsive disorder, or social phobia. *Journal of Nervous and Mental Disease, 186*, 311–315.

Antony, M. M., & Swinson, R. P. (1996). *Anxiety disorders and their treatment: A critical review of the evidence-based literature*. Ottawa, Ontario, Canada: Health Canada.

Baer, L., Brown-Beasley, M. W., Sorce, J., & Henriques, A. (1993). Computer-assisted telephone administration of a structured interview for obsessive–compulsive disorder. *American Journal of Psychiatry, 150*, 1737–1738.

Baer, L., Rauch, S. L., Ballantine, H. T., Jr., Martuza, R., Cosgrove, R., Cassem, E., Giriunas, I., Manzo, P. A., Dimino, C., & Jenike, M. A. (1995). Cingulotomy for intractible obsessive–compulsive disorder: Prospective long-term follow-up of 18 patients. *Archives of General Psychiatry, 52*, 384–392.

Barr, L. C., Goodman, W. K., Anand, A., McDougle, C. J., & Price, L. H. (1997). Addition of desipramine to serotonin reuptake inhibitors in treatment-resistant obsessive–compulsive disorder. *American Journal of Psychiatry, 154*, 1293–1295.

Beck, A. T. (1976). *Cognitive therapy and the emotional disorders*. New York: International Universities Press.

Bellodi, L., Sciuto, G., Diaferia, G., Ronchi, P., & Smeraldi, E. (1992). Psychiatric disorders in the families of patients with obsessive–compulsive disorder. *Psychiatry Research, 42*, 111–120.

Billett, E. A., Richter, M. A., & Kennedy, J. L. (1998). Genetics of obsessive–compulsive disorder. In R. P. Swinson, M. M. Antony, S. Rachman, & M. A. Richter (Eds.), *Obsessive compulsive disorder: Theory, research and treatment* (pp. 181–206). New York: Guilford Press.

Bland, R. C., Orn, H., & Newman, S. C. (1988). Lifetime prevalence of psychiatric disorders in Edmonton. *Acta Psychiatrica Scandinavica, 77*(Suppl. 338), 24–32.

Blier, P., & Bergeron, R. (1996). Sequential administration of augmentation strategies in treatment-resistant obsessive–compulsive disorder: Preliminary findings. *International Journal of Clinical Psychopharmacology, 11*, 37–44.

Burns, G. L., Keortge, S. G., Formea, G. M., & Sternberger, L. G. (1996). Revision of the Padua Inventory for obsessive compulsive disorder symptoms: Distinctions between worry, obsessions, and compulsions. *Behaviour Research and Therapy, 34*, 163–173.

Chouinard, G., Goodman, W., Greist, J., Jenike, M., Rasmussen, S., White, K., Hackett, E., Gaffney, M., & Bick, P. A. (1990). Results of a double-blind, placebo controlled trial of a new serotonin uptake inhibitor, sertraline, in the treatment of obsessive–compulsive disorder. *Psychopharmacology Bulletin, 26*, 279–284.

Clomipramine Collaborative Study Group. (1991). Efficacy of clomipramine in OCD: Results of a multicenter double-blind trial. *Archives of General Psychiatry, 48*, 730–738.

Cottraux, J., Bouvard, M., Defayolle, M., & Messy, P. (1988). Validity and factorial structure of the compulsive activity checklist. *Behavior Therapy, 19*, 45–53.

Cottraux, J., & Gerard, D. (1998). Neuroimaging and neuroanatomical issues in obsessive–compulsive disorder. In R. P. Swinson, M. M. Antony, S. Rachman, & M. A. Richter (Eds.), *Obsessive compulsive disorder: Theory, research and treatment* (pp. 154–180). New York: Guilford Press.

Cottraux, J., Mollard, E., Bouvard, M., & Marks, I. (1993). Exposure therapy, fluvoxamine, or combination treatment in obsessive–compulsive disorder: One-year follow-up. *Psychiatry Research*, *49*, 63–75.

Cottraux, J., Mollard, E., Bouvard, M., Marks, I., Sluys, M., Nury, A., Douge, R., & Cialdella, P. (1990). A controlled study of fluvoxamine and exposure in obsessive–compulsive disorder. *International Clinical Psychopharmacology*, *5*, 17–30.

Cox, B. J., Swinson, R. P., Morrison, B., & Lee, P. S. (1993). Clomipramine, fluoxetine, and behavior therapy in the treatment of obsessive–compulsive disorder: A meta-analysis. *Journal of Behavioral Therapy and Experimental Psychiatry*, *24*, 149–153.

Crino, R. D., & Andrews, G. (1996). Obsessive–compulsive disorder and Axis I comorbidity. *Journal of Anxiety Disorders*, *10*, 37–46.

Cruz, C., Camarena, B., King, N., Paez, F., Sidenberg, D., Ramon de la Fuente, J., & Nicolini, H. (1997). Increased prevalence of the seven-repeat variant of the dopamine D4 receptor gene in patients with obsessive–compulsive disorder with tics. *Neuroscience Letters*, *231*, 1–4.

Cumming, S., Hay, P., Lee, T., & Sachdev, P. (1995). Neuropsychological outcome from psychosurgery for obsessive–compulsive disorder. *Australia and New Zealand Journal of Psychiatry*, *29*, 293–298.

Demal, U., Lenz, G., Mayrhofer, A., Zapotoczky, H.-G., & Zitterl, W. (1993). Obsessive–compulsive disorder and depression: A retrospective study on course and interaction. *Psychopathology*, *26*, 145–150.

Di Nardo, P., Brown, T. A., & Barlow, D. H. (1994). *Anxiety Disorders Interview Schedule for DSM–IV*. San Antonio, TX: Psychological Corporation.

Di Nardo, P., Moras, K., Barlow, D. H., Rapee, R. M., & Brown, T. A. (1993). Reliability of *DSM–III–R* anxiety disorder categories: Using the Anxiety Disorders Interview Schedule–Revised (ADIS–R). *Archives of General Psychiatry*, *50*, 251–256.

Eisen, J. L., & Rasmussen, S. A. (1989). Coexisting obsessive compulsive disorder and alcoholism. *Journal of Clinical Psychiatry*, *50*, 96–98.

Emmelkamp, P. M. G., & Beens, H. (1991). Cognitive therapy with obsessive–compulsive disorder: A comparative evaluation. *Behaviour Research and Therapy*, *29*, 293–300.

Emmelkamp, P. M. G., van der Helm, M., van Zanten, B. L., & Plochg, I. (1980). Treatment of obsessive–compulsive patients: The contribution of self-instructional training to the effectiveness of exposure. *Behaviour Research and Therapy*, *18*, 61–66.

Emmelkamp, P. M. G., & van Kraanen, J. (1977). Therapist-controlled exposure *in vivo*: A comparison with obsessive–compulsive patients. *Behaviour Research and Therapy*, *15*, 491–495.

Emmelkamp, P. M. G., Visser, S., & Hoekstra, R. J. (1988). Cognitive therapy vs. exposure in vivo in the treatment of obsessive–compulsives. *Cognitive Therapy and Research*, *12*, 103–114.

Fals-Stewart, W., & Angarano, K. (1994). Obsessive–compulsive disorder among patients entering substance abuse treatment: Prevalence and accuracy of diagnosis. *Journal of Nervous and Mental Disease*, *182*, 715–719.

Fals-Stewart, W., Marks, A. P., & Schafer, J. (1993). A comparison of behavioral group therapy and individual behavior therapy in treating obsessive–compulsive disorder. *Journal of Nervous and Mental Disease*, *181*, 189–193.

First, M. B., Spitzer, R. L., Gibbon, M., & Williams, J. B. W. (1996). *Structured Clinical Interview for DSM–IV Axis I Disorders—Patient Edition* (SCID–I/P, Version 2.0). New York: Biometrics Research Department, New York State Psychiatric Institute.

Flament, M. F., Rapoport, J. L., Murphy, D. L., Berg, C. J., & Lake, C. R. (1987). Biochemical changes during clompiramine treatment of childhood obsessive–compulsive disorder. *Archives of General Psychiatry*, *44*, 219–225.

Foa, E. B., Franklin, M. E., & Kozak, M. J. (1998). Psychosocial treatments: Literature review. In R. P. Swinson, M. M. Antony, S. Rachman, & M. A. Richter (Eds.), *Obsessive compulsive disorder: Theory, research and treatment* (pp. 258–276). New York: Guilford Press.

Foa, E., & Goldstein, A. (1978). Continuous exposure and complete response prevention in the treatment of obsessive–compulsive neurosis. *Behavior Therapy*, *9*, 821–829.

Foa, E. B., Jameson, J. S., Turner, R. M., & Payne, L. L. (1980). Massed vs. spaced exposure sessions in the treatment of agoraphobia. *Behaviour Research and Therapy, 18,* 333–338.

Foa, E. B., Steketee, G., Grayson, J. B., Turner, R. M., & Latimer, P. (1984). Deliberate exposure and blocking of obsessive–compulsive rituals: Immediate and long-term effects. *Behavior Therapy, 15,* 450–472.

Freeston, M. H., Ladouceur, R., Rheaume, J., Letarte, H., Gagnon, F., & Thibodeau, N. (1994). Self-report of obsessions and worry. *Behaviour Research and Therapy, 32,* 29–36.

Freund, B., Steketee, G. S., & Foa, E. B. (1987). Compulsive Activity Checklist (CAC): Psychometric analysis with obsessive–compulsive disorder. *Behavioral Assessment, 9,* 67–79.

Garvey, M. A., Giedd, J., & Swedo, S. E. (1998). PANDAS: The search for environmental triggers of pediatric neuropsychiatric disorders. Lessons from rheumatic fever. *Journal of Child Neurology, 13,* 413–423.

Goodman, W. K., Price, L. H., Rasmussen, S. A., Mazure, D., Delgado, P., Heninger, G. R., & Charney, D. S. (1989a). The Yale–Brown Obsessive–Compulsive Scale: Part II. Validity. *Archives of General Psychiatry, 46,* 1012–1016.

Goodman, W. K., Price, L. H., Rasmussen, S. A., Mazure, D., Fleischmann, R. L., Hill, C. L., Heninger, G. R., & Charney, D. S. (1989b). The Yale–Brown Obsessive–Compulsive Scale: Part I. Development, use and reliability. *Archives of General Psychiatry, 46,* 1006–1011.

Goodman, W. K., Rasmussen, S. A., & Price, L. H. (1999). *Yale–Brown Obsessive Compulsive Scale, second edition.* Gainesville, FL: Department of Psychiatry, University of Florida College of Medicine.

Greist, J. H., Chouinard, G., Duboff, E., Halaris, A., Kim, S. K., Koran, L., Liebowitz, M., Lydiard, R. B., Rasmussen, S., White, K., & Sikes, C. (1995). Double-blind parallel comparison of three dosages of sertraline and placebo in outpatients with obsessive–compulsive disorder. *Archives of General Psychiatry, 52,* 289–295.

Greist, J. H., Jefferson, J. W., Kobak, K. A., Chouinard, G., DuBoff, E., Halaris, A., Kim, S. W., Koran, L., Liebowitz, M. R., & Lydiard, R. B. (1995). A 1 year double-blind placebo-controlled fixed-dose study of sertraline in the treatment of obsessive–compulsive disorder. *International Clinical Psychopharmacology, 10,* 57–65.

Greist, J. H., Jefferson, J. W., Kobak, K. A., Katzelnick, D. J., & Serlin, R. C. (1995). Efficacy and tolerability of serotonin transport inhibitors in obsessive–compulsive disorder: A meta-analysis. *Archives of General Psychiatry, 52,* 53–60.

Hay, P., Sachdev, P., Cumming, S., Smith, J. S., Lee, T., Kitchener, P., & Matheson, J. (1993). Treatment of obsessive–compulsive disorder by psychosurgery. *Acta Psychiatrica Scandinavica, 87,* 197–207.

Henderson, J. G., & Pollard, C. A (1988). Three types of obsessive compulsive disorder in a community sample. *Journal of Clinical Psychology, 44,* 747–752.

Hodgson, R. J., & Rachman, S. (1977). Obsessional–compulsive complaints. *Behaviour Research and Therapy, 15,* 389–395.

Hodgson, R. J., Rachman, S., & Marks, I. M. (1972). The treatment of chronic obsessive–compulsive neurosis: Follow-up and further findings. *Behaviour Research and Therapy, 10,* 181–189.

Insel, T. R., Murphy, D. L., Cohen, R. M., Alterman, I., Kilton, C., & Linnoila, M. (1983). Obsessive–compulsive disorder: A double blind trial of clomipramine and clorgyline. *Archives of General Psychiatry, 40,* 605–612.

Jenike, M. A., Baer, L., Minichiello, W. E., Rauch, S. L., & Buttolph, M. L. (1997). Placebo-controlled trial of fluoxetine and phenelzine for obsessive–compulsive disorder. *American Journal of Psychiatry, 154,* 1261–1264.

Jenike, M. A., Hyman, S. E., Baer, L., Holland, A., Minichiello, W. E., Buttolph, M. L., Summergrad, P., Seymour, R., & Ricciardi, J. (1990). A controlled trial of fluvoxamine for obsessive–compulsive disorder: Implications for a serotonergic theory. *American Journal of Psychiatry, 147,* 1209–1215.

Kolada, J. L., Bland, R. C., & Newman, S. C. (1994). Obsessive–compulsive disorder. *Acta Psychiatrica Scandinavica, 376,* 24–35.

Koponen, H., Lepola, U., Leinonen, E., Jokinen, R., Penttinen, J., & Turtonen, J. (1997). Citalopram in the treatment of obsessive–compulsive disorder: An open pilot study. *Acta Psychiatrica Scandinavica*, *96*, 343–346.

Kozak, M. J., & Foa, E. B. (1996). Obsessive–compulsive disorder. In V. B. Van Hasselt & M. Hersen (Eds.), *Sourcebook of psychological treatment manuals for adult disorders* (pp. 65–122). New York: Plenum.

Kozak, M. J., Foa, E. B., & Steketee, G. (1988). Process and outcome of exposure treatment with obsessive–compulsives: Psychophysiological indicators of emotional processing. *Behavior Therapy*, *19*, 157–169.

Kronig, M. H., Apter, J., Asnis, G., Bystritsky, A., Curtis, G., Ferguson, J., Landbloom, R., Munjack, D., Riesenberg, R., Robinson, D., Roy-Byrne, P., Phillips, K., & DuPont, I. J. (1999). Placebo-controlled, multicenter study of sertraline treatment for obsessive–compulsive disorder. *Journal of Clinical Psychopharmacology*, *19*, 172–176.

Leckman, J. F., Grice, D. E., Boardman, J., Zhang, H., Vitale, A., Bondi, C., Alsobrook, J., Peterson, B. S., Cohen, D. J., Rasmussen, S. A., Goodman, W. K., McDougle, C. J., & Pauls, D. L. (1997). Symptoms of obsessive compulsive disorder. *American Journal of Psychiatry*, *154*, 911–917.

Leonard, H. L., Swedo, S. E., Rapoport, J. L., Koby, E. V., Lenane, M. C., Cheslow, D. L., & Hamburger, S. D. (1989). Treatment of obsessive–compulsive disorder with clomipramine and desipramine in children and adolescents: A double-blind crossover comparison. *Archives of General Psychiatry*, *46*, 1088–1092.

Lindsay, M., Crino, R., & Andrews, G. (1997). Controlled trial of exposure and response prevention in obsessive–compulsive disorder. *British Journal of Psychiatry*, *171*, 135–139.

March, J. S., Frances, A., Carpenter, D., & Kahn, D. A. (Eds.). (1997). The expert consensus guideline series: Treatment of obsessive compulsive disorder. *Journal of Clinical Psychiatry*, *58*(Suppl. 4), 1–72.

Marks, I. M., Hallam, R. S., Connolly, J., & Philpott, R. (1977). *Nursing in behavioral psychotherapy*. London: Royal College of Nursing.

Marks, I. M., Lelliott, P., Basoglu, M., Noshirvani, H., Monteiro, W., Cohen, D., & Kasvikis, Y. (1988). Clomipramine, self-exposure and therapist-aided exposure for obsessive–compulsive rituals. *British Journal of Psychiatry*, *152*, 522–534.

Marks, I. M., Stern, R. S., Mawson, D., Cobb, J., & McDonald, R. (1980). Clomipramine and exposure for obsessive compulsive rituals. *British Journal of Psychiatry*, *136*, 1–25.

McDougle, C. J., Goodman, W. K., Leckman, J. F., Holzer, J. C., Barr, L. C., McCance-Katz, E., Heninger, G. R., & Price, L. H. (1993). Limited therapeutic effect of addition of buspirone in fluvoxamine refractory obsessive compulsive disorder. *American Journal of Psychiatry*, *150*, 647–649.

McDougle, C. J., Goodman, W. K., Leckman, J. F., Lee, N. C., Heninger, G. R., & Price, L. H. (1994). Haloperidol addition in fluvoxamine-refractory obsessive–compulsive disorder. *Archives of General Psychiatry*, *51*, 302–308.

McDougle, C. J., Price, L. H., Goodman, W. K., Charney, D. S., & Heninger, G. R. (1991). A controlled trial of lithium augmentation in fluvoxamine refractory obsessive compulsive disorder: Lack of efficacy. *Journal of Clinical Psychopharmacology*, *11*, 175–184.

Meyer, V. (1966). Modification of expectations in cases with obsessional rituals. *Behaviour Research and Therapy*, *4*, 273–280.

Montgomery, S. (1998, December). *Citalopram treatment of obsessive compulsive disorder: Results from a double-blind, placebo-controlled trial*. Paper presented at the meeting of the American College of Neuropsychopharmacology, Las Croabas, Puerto Rico.

Mowrer, O. H. (1947). On the dual nature of learning—A re-interpretation of "conditioning" and "problem-solving." *Harvard Educational Review*, *17*, 102–148.

Mowrer, O. H. (1960). *Learning theory and behavior*. New York: Wiley.

Mundo, E., Bianchi, L., & Bellodi, L. (1997). Efficacy of fluvoxamine, paroxetine, and citalopram in the treatment of obsessive compulsive disorder: A single blind study. *Journal of Clinical Psychopharmacology*, *17*, 267–271.

Muris, P., Merckelbach, H., & Clavan, M. (1997). Abnormal and normal compulsions. *Behaviour Research and Therapy*, *35*, 249–252.

Murphy, D. L., Greenberg, B., Altemus, M., Benjamin, J., Grady, T., & Pigott, T. (1996). The neuropharmacology and neurobiology of obsessive compulsive disorder: An update on the serotonin hypothesis. In H. G. M. Westenberg, J. A. den Boer, & D. L. Murphy (Eds.), *Advances in the neurobiology of anxiety disorders* (pp. 279–297). New York: Wiley.

Nelson, E., & Rice, J. (1997). Stability of diagnosis of obsessive–compulsive disorder in the Epidemiologic Catchment Area Study. *American Journal of Psychiatry, 154,* 826–831.

Nemiah, J. C. (1975). Obsessive compulsive neurosis. In A. M. Freedman, H. I. Kaplan, & B. J. Sadock (Eds.), *Comprehensive textbook of psychiatry* (2nd ed., Vol. 1, pp. 1241–1255). Baltimore: Williams & Wilkins.

Obsessive Compulsive Cognitions Working Group. (1997). Cognitive assessment of obsessive–compulsive disorder. *Behaviour Research and Therapy, 35,* 667–681.

O'Sullivan, G., Noshirvani, H., Marks, I., Monteiro, W., & Lelliott, P. (1991). Six-year follow-up after exposure and clomipramine therapy for obsessive compulsive disorder. *Journal of Clinical Psychiatry, 52,* 150–155.

Pato, M. T., Pato, C. N., & Gunn, S. A. (1998). Biological treatments: Clinical applications. In R. P. Swinson, M. M. Antony, S. Rachman, & M. A. Richter (Eds.), *Obsessive compulsive disorder: Theory, research and treatment* (pp. 327–348). New York: Guilford Press.

Pato, M. T., Zohar-Kadouch, R., Zohar, J., & Murphy, D. L. (1988). Return of symptoms after discontinuation of clomipramine in patients with obsessive–compulsive disorder. *American Journal of Psychiatry, 145,* 1521–1525.

Perse, T. L., Greist, J. H., Jefferson, J. W., Rosenfeld, R., & Dar, R. (1987). Fluvoxamine treatment of obsessive–compulsive disorder. *American Journal of Psychiatry, 144,* 1543–1548.

Philpott, R. (1975). Recent advances in the behavioral assessment of obsessional illness: Difficulties common to these and other measures. *Scottish Medical Journal, 20*(Suppl. 1), 33–40.

Piccinelli, M., Pini, S., Bellantuono, C., & Wilkinson, G. (1995). Efficacy of drug treatment in obsessive–compulsive disorders: A meta-analytic review. *British Journal of Psychiatry, 166,* 424–443.

Pigott, T. A., & Seay, S. (1998). Biological treatments: Literature review. In R. P. Swinson, M. M. Antony, S. Rachman, & M. A. Richter (Eds.), *Obsessive compulsive disorder: Theory, research and treatment* (pp. 298–326). New York: Guilford Press.

Pigott, T. A., & Seay, S. (1999). A review of the efficacy of selective serotonin reuptake inhibitors in obsessive–compulsive disorder. *Journal of Clinical Psychiatry, 60,* 101–106.

Preskorn, S. (1993). Pharmacokinetics of anti-depressants: Why and how they are relevant to treatment. *Journal of Clinical Psychiatry, 54*(Suppl. 9), 14–34.

Rabavilas, A. D., Boulougouris, J. C., & Stefanis, C. (1977). Compulsive checking diminished when over-checking instructions were disobeyed. *Journal of Behavior Therapy and Experimental Psychiatry, 8,* 111–112.

Rachman, S., Cobb, J., Grey, S., McDonald, B., Mawson, D., Sartory, G., & Stern, R. (1979). The behavioural treatment of obsessional–compulsive disorders, with and without clomipramine. *Behavior Research and Therapy, 17,* 467–478.

Rachman, S., & de Silva, P. (1978). Abnormal and normal obsessions. *Behaviour Research and Therapy, 16,* 233–248.

Rachman, S. J., & Hodgson, R. J. (1980). *Obsessions and compulsions.* Englewood Cliffs, NJ: Prentice-Hall.

Rasmussen, S. A., & Tsuang, M. T. (1986). Clinical characteristics and family history in *DSM–III* obsessive–compulsive disorder. *American Journal of Psychiatry, 143,* 317–322.

Ravizza, L., Barzega, G., Bellino, S., Bogetto, F., & Maina, G. (1996). Therapeutic effect and safety of adjunctive risperidone in refractory obsessive–compulsive disorder (OCD). *Psychopharmacology Bulletin, 32,* 677–682.

Regier, D. A., Boyd, J. H., Burke, J. D., Jr., Rae, D. S., Myers, J. K., Kramer, M., Robins, L. N., George, L. K., Karno, M., & Locke, B. Z. (1988). One-month prevalence of mental disorders in the United States: Based on five Epidemiologic Catchment Area sites. *Archives of General Psychiatry, 45,* 977–986.

Ricciardi, J. N., & McNally, R. J. (1995). Depressed mood is related to obsessions, but not to compulsions, in obsessive compulsive disorder. *Journal of Anxiety Disorders*, *9*, 249–256.

Riemann, B. C., McNally, R. J., & Cox, W. M. (1992). The comorbidity of obsessive compulsive disorder and alcoholism. *Journal of Anxiety Disorders*, *6*, 105–110.

Riggs, D. S., & Foa, E. B. (1993). Obsessive compulsive disorder. In D. H. Barlow (Ed.), *Clinical handbook of psychological disorders* (2nd ed., pp. 189–239). New York: Guilford Press.

Robins, L. N., Helzer, J. E., Weissman, M. M., Orvaschel, H., Gruenberg, E., Burke, J. D., & Regier, D. A. (1984). Lifetime prevalence of specific psychiatric disorders in three sites. *Archives of General Psychiatry*, *41*, 949–958.

Rosenfeld, R., Dar, R., Anderson, D., Kobak, K. A., & Greist, J. H. (1992). A computer-administered version of the Yale–Brown Obsessive–Compulsive Scale. *Psychological Assessment*, *4*, 329–332.

Rudin, E. (1953). Ein beitrag zur frage der zwangskrankheit insebesondere ihrere hereditaren beziehungen. [A contribution to the question concerning obsessive–compulsive disorder, specifically with respect to its hereditary relationship.] *Archiv der Psychiatrischen Nervenkrankheit*, *191*, 14–54.

Salkovskis, P. M. (1985). Obsessional–compulsive problems: A cognitive–behavioural analysis. *Behaviour Research and Therapy*, *23*, 571–583.

Salkovskis, P. M. (1989a). Cognitive–behavioural factors and the persistence of intrusive thoughts in obsessional problems. *Behaviour Research and Therapy*, *27*, 677–682.

Salkovskis, P. M. (1989b). Obsessive and intrusive thoughts: Clinical and non-clinical aspects. In P. M. G. Emmelkamp, W. T. A. M. Everaerd, & M. J. M. van Son (Eds.), *Fresh perspectives on anxiety disorders* (pp. 197–212). Amsterdam: Swets & Zeitlinger.

Salkovskis, P. M. (1998). Psychological approaches to the understanding of obsessional problems. In R. P. Swinson, M. M. Antony, S. Rachman, & M. A. Richter (Eds.), *Obsessive compulsive disorder: Theory, research and treatment* (pp. 33–50). New York: Guilford Press.

Salkovskis, P. M., & Harrison, J. (1984). Abnormal and normal obsessions: A replication. *Behaviour Research and Therapy*, *22*, 549–552.

Sanavio, E. (1988). Obsessions and compulsions: The Padua Inventory. *Behaviour Research and Therapy*, *26*, 169–177.

Sanderson, W. C., Di Nardo, P. A., Rapee, R. M., & Barlow, D. H. (1990). Syndrome comorbidity in patients diagnosed with a *DSM–III–R* anxiety disorder. *Journal of Abnormal Psychology*, *99*, 308–312.

Savron, G., Fava, G. A., Grandi, S., Rafanelli, C., Raffi, A. R., & Belluardo, P. (1996). Hypochondriacal fears and beliefs in obsessive–compulsive disorder. *Acta Psychiatrica Scandinavica*, *93*, 345–348.

Saxena, S., Wang, D., Bystritsky, A., & Baxter, L. R. (1996). Risperidone augmentation of SRI treatment for refractory obsessive–compulsive disorder. *Journal of Clinical Psychiatry*, *57*, 303–306.

Schwalberg, M. D., Barlow, D. H., Alger, S. A., & Howard, L. J. (1992). Comparison of bulimics, obese binge eaters, social phobics, and individuals with panic disorder on comorbidity across *DSM–III–R* anxiety disorders. *Journal of Abnormal Psychology*, *101*, 675–681.

Shank, R. P., Vaught, J. L., Pelley, K. A., Setler, P. E., McComsey, D. F., & Maryanoff, B. E. (1988). McN-5652: A highly potent inhibitor of serotonin uptake. *Journal of Pharmacology and Experimental Therapies*, *247*, 1032–1038.

Stein, D. J., Spadaccini, E., & Hollander, E. (1995). Meta-analysis of pharmacotherapy trials for obsessive-compulsive disorder. *International Clinical Psychopharmacology*, *10*, 11–18.

Stein, M. B., Forde, D. R., Anderson, G., & Walker, J. R. (1997). Obsessive–compulsive disorder in the community: An epidemiologic survey with clinical reappraisal. *American Journal of Psychiatry*, *154*, 1120–1126.

Steketee, G. S. (1993). *Treatment of obsessive compulsive disorder*. New York: Guilford Press.

Steketee, G. S. (1999a). *Overcoming obsessive compulsive disorder* (client manual). Oakland, CA: New Harbinger.

Steketee, G. S. (1999b). *Overcoming obsessive compulsive disorder* (therapist protocol). Oakland, CA: New Harbinger.

Steketee, G. S., Chambless, D. L., Tran, G. Q., Worden, H., & Gillis, M. M. (1996). Behavioral avoidance test for obsessive compulsive disorder. *Behaviour Research and Therapy, 34*, 73–83.

Steketee, G. S., & Freund, B. (1993). Compulsive Activity Checklist (CAC): Further psychometric analyses and revision. *Behavioural Psychotherapy, 21*, 13–25.

Steketee, G., Frost, R., & Bogart, K. (1996). The Yale–Brown Obsessive Compulsive Scale: Interview versus self-report. *Behaviour Research and Therapy, 34*, 675–684.

Summerfeldt, L. J., Richter, M. A., Antony, M. M., & Swinson, R. P. (1999). Symptom structure in obsessive compulsive disorder: A confirmatory factor-analytic study. *Behaviour Research and Therapy, 37*, 297–311.

Swedo, S. E., Rapoport, J. L., Cheslow, D. L., Leonard, H. L., Ayoub, E. M., Hosier, D. M., & Wald, E. R. (1989). High prevalence of obsessive–compulsive symptoms in patients with Sydenham's chorea. *American Journal of Psychiatry, 146*, 246–249.

Taylor, S. (1995). Assessment of obsessions and compulsions: Reliability, validity, and sensitivity to treatment effects. *Clinical Psychology Review, 15*, 261–296.

Taylor, S. (1998). Assessment of obsessive compulsive disorder. In R. P. Swinson, M. M. Antony, S. Rachman, & M. A. Richter (Eds.), *Obsessive compulsive disorder: Theory, research and treatment* (pp. 229–257). New York: Guilford Press.

Thiel, A., Broocks, A., Ohlmeier, M., Jacoby, G. E., & Schüssler, G. (1995). Obsessive–compulsive disorder among patients with anorexia nervosa and bulimia nervosa. *American Journal of Psychiatry, 152*, 72–75.

Tollefson, G. D., Rampey, A. H., Potvin, J. H., Jenike, M. A., Rush, A. J., Dominguez, R. A., Koran, L. M., Shear, M. K., Goodman, W., & Genduso, L. A. (1994). A multicenter investigation of fixed-dose fluoxetine in the treatment of obsessive–compulsive disorder. *Archives of General Psychiatry, 51*, 559–567.

van Balkom, A. J. L. M., de Haan, E., van Oppen, P., Spinhoven, P., Hoogduin, K. A. L., & van Dyck, R. (1997, May). *Cognitive behavioral therapy versus the combination with fluvoxamine in the treatment of obsessive compulsive disorder*. Paper presented at the meeting of the American Psychiatric Association, San Diego, CA.

van Balkom, A. J. L. M., & van Dyck, R. (1998). Combination treatments for OCD. In R. P. Swinson, M. M. Antony, S. Rachman, & M. A. Richter (Eds.), *Obsessive compulsive disorder: Theory, research and treatment* (pp. 349–366). New York: Guilford Press.

van Balkom, A. J., van Oppen, P., Vermeulen, A. W., & van Dyck, R. (1994). A meta-analysis on the treatment of obsessive compulsive disorder: A comparison of antidepressants, behavior, and cognitive therapy. *Clinical Psychology Review, 14*, 359–381.

van Oppen, P., de Haan, E., van Balkom, A. J., Spinoven, P., Hoogduin, K., & van Dyck, R. (1995). Cognitive therapy and exposure *in vivo* in the treatment of obsessive compulsive disorder. *Behaviour Research and Therapy, 33*, 379–390.

Volavka, J., Neziroglu, F., & Yaryura-Tobias, J. A. (1985). Clomipramine and imipramine in obsessive–compulsive disorder. *Psychiatry Research, 14*, 83–91.

Williams, J. B. W., Gibbon, M., First, M. B., Spitzer, R. L., Davis, M., Borus, J., Howes, M. J., Kane, J., Pope, H. G., Rounsaville, B., & Wittchen, H.-U. (1992). The Structured Clinical Interview for *DSM–III–R* (SCID): II. Multisite test–retest reliability. *Archives of General Psychiatry, 49*, 630–636.

Wittchen, H.-U. (1988). Natural course and spontaneous remissions of untreated anxiety disorders: Results of the Munich Follow-up Study (MFS). In I. Hand & H.-U. Wittchen (Eds.), *Panic and phobias 2: Treatment and variables affecting course and outcome* (pp. 3–17). New York: Springer-Verlag.

Yaryura-Tobias, J., Todaro, J., Grunes, M. S., Mckay, D., Stockman, R., & Neziroglu, F. A. (1996, November). *Comorbidity versus continuum of Axis I disorders in OCD*. Paper presented at the meeting of the Association for Advancement of Behavior Therapy, New York.

Zohar, J., Judge, R., & the OCD Paroxetine Study Investigators. (1996). Paroxetine versus clomipramine in the treatment of OCD. *British Journal of Psychiatry, 169*, 468–474.

Zohar, J., & Kindler, S. (1992). Serotonergic probes in obsessive compulsive disorder. *International Clinical Psychopharmacology, 7*, 39S–40S.

4

Combined Treatments for Phobic Anxiety Disorders

Norman B. Schmidt, Margaret Koselka, and Kelly Woolaway-Bickel

The 1990s have seen significant advances in both psychosocial treatment, notably cognitive–behavioral therapy (CBT) and pharmacological treatments for phobic anxiety disorders (i.e., panic disorder, social and specific phobia). Given the widely acknowledged efficacy of both forms of treatment, it seems reasonable to consider that the combination of approaches should yield an extremely potent treatment strategy. Moreover, findings suggest that a majority of patients with phobic anxiety conditions have received medication and psychotherapy (Taylor et al., 1989). Data from our research laboratory, which specializes in treatment of anxiety conditions, suggests that 75% of patients with panic disorder have received at least one medication trial and that 65% of these patients are currently receiving pharmacotherapy at the time of their assessment (Schmidt, 1997). These findings indicate that combined treatments appear to be commonplace in day-to-day clinical practice. Because combined treatments are a reality in psychological practices, a question of great importance is whether the combination of medications and psychotherapy conveys additive benefits relative to singular treatments.

In this chapter we summarize scientific evidence for the singular and combined treatment approaches to these conditions. In some cases, it appears that combined treatments yield immediate and short-term benefits above those provided by either pharmacological treatment or CBT alone. In the long term, however, the benefit of combined treatment disappears. Other data indicate that the sequencing of pharmacotherapy and CBT may be important, particularly when benzodiazepines are used in treatment or when one goal of treatment is the elimination of benzodiazepines. Although conclusions should be considered preliminary because of the lack of combined treatment outcome studies, combined treatments do not ap-

This report was supported by Uniformed Services University of the Health Sciences (USUHS) Grant RO72CF. The opinions or assertions contained herein are the private ones of the authors and are not to be construed as official or reflecting the views of the Department of Defense or the USUHS.

pear to be the treatment of choice for patients with phobic anxiety conditions.[1]

This chapter is organized by condition: Panic disorder, social phobia, and the specific phobias are considered separately. For each condition, only methodologically sound and appropriately controlled outcome studies were evaluated for determining the singular and combined effectiveness of psychosocial and pharmacological treatments. Each section is designed to answer several questions relating to the combined pharmacological and psychotherapeutic treatment: (a) what is the efficacy of the singular treatments? (b) what is the evidence for the efficacy of combined treatments? and (c) what implications do these research findings have for clinical practice?

Panic Disorder

Epidemiological data suggest that panic disorder afflicts millions and has a markedly negative impact on quality of life (Markowitz, Weissman, Ouellette, Lish, & Klerman, 1989; Telch, Schmidt, Jaimez, Jacquin, & Harrington, 1995; Weissman, 1991). Panic disorder has received far more attention, in terms of controlled treatment outcome studies, compared to the other phobic anxiety conditions. This literature clearly indicates high efficacy for several classes of medication as well as CBT. The picture with combined treatments is less clear, as there are no compelling data to indicate that CBT and pharmacotherapy synergistically interact in a positive fashion in these patients.

Singular Treatments

Efficacy of pharmacotherapy. Since Klein's early work on the pharmacological dissection of panic and anxiety (Klein, 1964; Klein & Fink, 1962), a tremendous amount of research has been generated on the etiology and treatment of panic from a biological perspective. Within this perspective, treatment has focused on the elimination of panic attacks through pharmacotherapy (Sheehan, 1982). Many advances in the pharmacological treatment of panic have emerged during the 1990s. Several classes of medication—including tricyclic antidepressants (TCAs) and monoamine oxidase inhibitors (MAOIs), as well as the benzodiazepines— have demonstrated panic-blocking efficacy in a number of double-blind placebo controlled trials (Sheehan, 1985; Telch, Tearnan, & Taylor, 1983;

---

[1]The *DSM* anxiety disorders include a number of additional diagnoses such as generalized anxiety disorder, posttraumatic stress disorder, and obsessive–compulsive disorder. Although these conditions are considered similar in terms of nosology, important phenomenological, etiological, and treatment differences exist among these conditions. As such, a single chapter describing all of these conditions would likely prove to be cumbersome. Therefore, we focus only on the so-called phobic anxiety conditions (panic disorder, social phobia, and specific phobias) in which phobic avoidance is a predominant feature.

Zitrin, Klein, Woerner, & Ross, 1983). More recently, serotonin reuptake inhibitors (SRIs) have also been found to be effective for panic disorder (Schneier et al., 1990).

The TCAs were the first pharmacological agents with demonstrated efficacy for panic disorder (Klein, 1964). Many controlled trials with TCAs, particularly imipramine, have demonstrated their efficacy in decreasing panic attack frequency and other anxiety symptoms (Lydiard et al., 1993; Zitrin et al., 1983). More recently, data suggest that the serotonergic TCA clomipramine may be superior to other TCAs (Modigh, Westberg, & Eriksson, 1992). Despite the effectiveness of TCAs, many patients report considerable difficulty tolerating the side effects produced by TCAs, and these often result in a substantial discontinuation rates (Noyes, Garvey, & Cook, 1989).

MAOIs have also been found to have considerable efficacy in the treatment of anxiety. For example, in an open trial of phenelzine, 97% of patients completing 6 months of treatment were panic free (Buiges & Vallego, 1987). Controlled trials have reported substantially lower rates of panic-free status, however, with as many as 40% of patients reporting partial or no improvement following treatment (Sheehan, Ballenger, & Jacobsen, 1980). Despite their efficacy, MAOIs have been limited in their use because of significant side effects, dietary restrictions, and the possibility of fatal hypertensive reactions. Newer, reversible MAOIs, such as moclobemide, are safer, do not require a specific diet, and appear to be promising in terms of treatment efficacy (Tiller, Bouwer, & Behnke, 1997).

The SRIs have been widely used in the treatment of depression because of their efficacy, safety, and favorable side-effect profile. Recent controlled trials also suggest that SRIs are effective for panic disorder (Schneier et al., 1990). Fluvoxamine has been the best studied SRI to date, but other controlled trials using paroxetine (Ballenger, Wheadon, Steiner, Bushnell, & Gergel, 1998; Dunbar, 1995) and sertraline (DuBoff et al., 1995; Pohl, Wolkow, & Clary, 1998; Rapaport, Wolkow, & Clary, 1998) have demonstrated that these agents have shown better efficacy than placebo and, in some cases, other antipanic agents. Although SRIs have a generally well-tolerated side-effect profile, it is notable that 20%–30% of patients with panic disorder do not tolerate the restlessness and increased anxiety associated with the initial dosing.

Benzodiazepines are unique among antipanic pharmacological agents because of their rapid efficacy. Benzodiazepines are also much better tolerated relative to antidepressants, resulting in dropout rates that are 50% lower than for antidepressants in clinical trials (Broocks et al., 1998; Charney et al., 1986). Alprazolam has been the best studied benzodiazepine and was included in a large cross-national collaborative study (Ballenger et al., 1988). Findings from this study indicated that 55% of patients in the alprazolam group, compared to 32% of those in the placebo group, attained panic-free status. Despite a relatively favorable side-effect profile, sedation often limits dosing with benzodiazepines for many patients (Pollack, Otto, Kaspi, Hammerness, & Rosenbaum, 1994).

A summary of the efficacy of pharmacological treatments for panic disorder appears in Table 4.1. Michelson and Marchione (1991) devised a useful method for calculating the overall efficacy of treatments. Their method of summary is based on a hypothetical cohort, but the numbers are derived from available empirical studies. An overall efficacy index is calculated for each class of medications based on three factors: (a) level of attrition, (b) percentage of patients achieving high end-state functioning (i.e., clinically significant improvement across the relevant clinical facets of panic disorder), and (c) relapse rates (see Michelson & Marchione, 1991, for more details).

The overall efficacy index shows very low efficacy for beta blockers and low-potency benzodiazepines. It is notable that this level of efficacy is only somewhat improved for the high-potency benzodiazepines despite the higher percentage of patients who achieve clinically significant gains with the high-potency benzodiazepines. The high levels of relapse, or "rebound panic," following discontinuation of these medications contributes to overall low levels of efficacy using this index. The MAOIs achieve somewhat better overall efficacy, limited mainly by high attrition, with the TCAs and SRIs achieving the highest levels of efficacy among the pharmacological agents.

Many patients with panic disorder, outside of controlled clinical trials, receive several classes of medication. The most typical combination includes an antidepressant in conjunction with a high-potency benzodiazepine (often prescribed on an as-needed basis for acute anxiety episodes). Controlled clinical trials that evaluate combinations of medications are scarce, so it is unclear whether the potency of single medication classes described above is an underestimate of the typical pharmacological efficacy achieved for patients receiving multidrug treatment.

Efficacy of psychosocial treatments. In addition to pharmacological treatments, there is encouraging evidence to suggest that many patients with panic disorder can be effectively treated with nondrug, psychosocial

Table 4.1. Overall Efficacy for Pharmacological Treatment in a Hypothetical Cohort of 100 Patients

| Medication | Attrition | | Improvement | | Relapse | | Overall efficacy index |
	%	(n_{rem})	%	(n_{rem})	%	(n_{rem})	
Beta blockers	20	80	10	8	90	1	1
Benzos (low)	10	90	15	13	85	2	2
Benzos (high)	10	90	60	54	90	6	6
MAOIs	35	65	45	29	40	17	17
TCAs	25	75	60	45	35	29	29
SRIs	20	80	65	52	35	34	34

Note. Adapted from Michelson and Marchione (1991). n_{rem} = number of patients remaining; Benzos (low) = low-potency benzodiazepines; Benzos (high) = high-potency benzodiazepines; MAOIs = monoamine oxidase inhibitors; TCAs = tricyclic antidepressants; SRIs = serotonin reuptake inhibitors.

treatments. Historically, the practice of encouraging patients to repeatedly confront situations that produce intense fear and avoidance (i.e., in vivo exposure) has been the hallmark of behavioral treatments for agoraphobia and panic (Mathews, Teasdale, Munby, Johnston, & Shaw, 1981). In the mid-1980s, cognitive models of panic were proposed that offered new directions for intervention (Beck, 1988; Beck & Emery, 1985; D. M. Clark, 1986). Within the cognitive framework, panic attacks are conceptualized as the result of catastrophic misinterpretation of benign bodily sensations that are typically involved in the normal anxiety response (e.g., heart palpitations, dizziness, dyspnea).

Psychological treatments, termed *cognitive–behavioral therapy*, derived from this cognitive framework, have been initiated at several research centers (Barlow, Craske, Cerney, & Klosko, 1989; Schmidt, Staab, Trakowski, & Sammons, 1997; Telch et al., 1993). These newer treatments focus on correcting the patient's hypersensitivity to bodily sensations and the misinterpretation of these sensations as signaling immediate threat. The main treatment components typically include (a) education, (b) training in cognitive reappraisal, (c) repeated exposure to bodily sensations connected to the fear response (i.e., interoceptive exposure), and (d) repeated exposure to external situations connected to the fear response (i.e., in vivo exposure).

More cognitively oriented treatment programs derived from Beck's cognitive model (Beck & Emery, 1985) emphasize the correction of catastrophic misinterpretation through cognitive restructuring and behavioral experiments (D. M. Clark & Salkovskis, in press). Based on Beck's cognitive model of panic (Beck & Emery, 1985), which emphasizes the causal role of catastrophic appraisals of physical sensations, specific cognitive techniques have been incorporated into most of the psychological treatments that directly target panic. This treatment component involves helping the patient to identify and alter his or her dysfunctional appraisals of threat and catastrophe associated with certain bodily sensations.

Alternatively, David Barlow and his colleagues have developed a treatment protocol that places greater emphasis on interoceptive exposure as a means for reducing anxiety sensitivity or the set of beliefs associated with fear of bodily perturbations (Barlow et al., 1989). On the basis of "fear of fear" conceptualizations of panic disorder (Goldstein & Chambless, 1978) and recent cognitive models of panic that place central importance on the misinterpretation of certain bodily sensations (D. M. Clark, 1986), Barlow and others have turned to the purposeful induction of unpleasant bodily sensations as a treatment procedure for panic disorder. Treatment outcome data from these research efforts suggests that both forms of CBT are highly effective in alleviating panic as well as the other major clinical facets of panic disorder (see Chambless & Gillis, 1994, for a review).

Table 4.2 depicts the relative efficacy of these treatments on the same overall efficacy index used for the pharmacological outcome studies. As can be seen in Table 4.2, older studies that have used in vivo exposure produced fairly substantial gains but are somewhat limited by relapse. More recent CBT studies that focus on cognitive restructuring are some-

Table 4.2. Overall Efficacy for Cognitive–Behavioral Treatment in a Hypothetical Cohort of 100 Patients

Therapy	Attrition		Improvement		Relapse		Overall efficacy index
	%	(n_{rem})	%	(n_{rem})	%	(n_{rem})	
In vivo exposure	15	85	65	55	20	44	44
Cognitive tx	15	85	75	64	20	51	51
In vivo exposure + cognitive tx	15	85	75	64	20	51	51
CBT with interoceptive exposure	15	85	80	68	20	54	54

Note. Adapted from Michelson and Marchione (1991). n_{rem} = number of patients remaining; tx = treatment; CBT = cognitive–behavioral treatment.

what more effective than in vivo exposure. The combination of in vivo exposure with cognitive restructuring is comparable to cognitive therapy alone. Treatments that implement interoceptive exposure appear to be the most promising, with large clinical changes and a fairly low rate of relapse.

Combined Treatments

Rationale. Treatment is inextricably derived from theoretical considerations; that is, one's understanding of the etiology of a disorder often dictates thinking about its treatment. In the case of panic disorder, theories of etiology tend to be somewhat divergent. Psychological approaches emphasize cognition, whereas biological approaches emphasize neurotransmitter imbalances. However, rationales can be made for combining psychological and biological interventions. The most commonly used rationales for combining psychosocial and pharmacological treatments include (a) treatment specificity, (b) facilitation of psychosocial treatment vis à vis pharmacotherapy, and (c) facilitation of pharmacotherapy vis à vis psychosocial treatment (see Telch & Lucas, 1994).

Treatment specificity rests on the assumption that drug and psychological treatments affect different facets of the anxiety condition. In the case of panic disorder, Klein (1964) originally argued that different classes of medications exerted specific effects on panic attacks versus generalized anxiety (i.e., the so-called pharmacological dissection of panic disorder). On the basis of early data, Klein believed that medication combinations were needed to adequately treat the different facets of panic disorder. To the extent that the premise of treatment specificity is accurate and that different treatment modalities uniquely affect somewhat independent aspects of the disorder, the combined use of medications and psychotherapy should prove more efficacious than the singular treatments.

A second rationale for combined treatment suggests that the primary mode of treatment should be psychological but the adjunctive use of medication may be indicated in some cases. Common examples provided for this rationale include cases in which the individual with panic disorder is also substantially depressed or extremely distressed. In such cases it may be difficult to implement psychological treatments, so the short-term administration of antidepressants or benzodiazepines may be useful in assisting during the initial phases of treatment.

The final rationale describes the opposite situation. Some patients taking medications may be assisted with the addition of psychological interventions. For example, many patients with panic disorder report substantial reservations or even fears regarding prolonged medication use (Telch, 1988). For these patients, specific psychological interventions targeting medication fears may be beneficial.

Current knowledge. Knowledge regarding combined treatments for panic disorder is limited, so firm conclusions cannot be made. The present review is based on controlled studies that have compared a drug-plus-psychotherapy treatment condition with the singular condition (either drug or psychotherapy). At the time of the National Institute of Mental Health consensus conference for the treatment of panic disorder held in 1991, there were only 11 published reports that conducted such comparisons (Telch & Lucas, 1994). Since the consensus conference, there have only been about a half dozen additional reports. It is also notable that there have been very few studies that have evaluated the newer combined CBT modality. Only the in vivo exposure component of the more recent multifaceted treatment protocols has been thoroughly investigated. However, several more recent studies have evaluated the combination of TCAs with the more recent CBT treatment protocol (Barlow & Lehman, 1996). There are also preliminary data evaluating the singular and combined effects of SRIs and newer versions of CBT (Sharp & Power, 1998; Sharp et al., 1996) and one study that has evaluated buspirone and CBT (Bouvard, Mollard, Guerin, & Cottraux, 1997).

There are several other limitations worth noting. Most of the combined-treatment studies have reported only on the short-term effectiveness of treatment combinations, whereas few studies have examined long-term outcomes. It is noteworthy that despite the widespread use of benzodiazepines relatively little is known about their combined effects with CBT. The majority of studies in this literature have also systematically excluded patients with little or no phobic avoidance (i.e., patients with panic disorder without agoraphobia have been excluded from many studies). Despite the fact that patients without an agoraphobia diagnosis constitute a substantial percentage of all patients with panic disorder, this subgroup has not been satisfactorily evaluated.

Short-term efficacy. Keeping these limitations in mind, what can be determined regarding the efficacy of combined treatments? One important index of efficacy is the rapidity of change or short-term effectiveness, such as evaluation of change at posttreatment. At the time of the consensus conference, Telch and Lucas (1994) provided a summary of change at posttreatment across combined treatment studies for panic disorder, and the addition of later studies does not change the conclusions that were made more than 5 years ago.

In general, extant data can be summarized to suggest that the relative effect sizes indicate an additive effect for the combined treatment. For example, Bouvard et al. (1997) found some advantage for patients treated with buspirone plus CBT relative to CBT alone. Consistent with the treatment-specificity hypothesis, combined treatment appears to have added benefit relative to either singular treatment. Moreover, some studies indicate that this relative benefit is fairly substantial as indexed by moderate to large effect-size differences.

Long-term efficacy. Although combined treatments appear to offer clear immediate advantages over singular treatments, it is also critical to examine the long-term impact of these treatments after a follow-up period. As noted above, fewer data are available to address this issue, but these data stand in contrast to the short-term efficacy findings. Studies evaluating long-term efficacy indicate that the preliminary benefits of combined treatment are lost during follow-up and that, in some cases, combined treatment may yield poorer outcome in the long term.

In the case of combined treatments using TCAs, the superiority of the combined treatment compared to psychological treatment is lost over time, with increased relapse among patients receiving combined treatment along with continued improvement for patients who had received in vivo exposure (Marks et al., 1983). When the combination of benzodiazepines and in vivo exposure is compared with in vivo exposure alone, it appears that patients receiving combined treatment, despite initial improvements, displayed poorer outcome at follow-up relative to those receiving psychological treatment alone (Marks et al., 1993). This turnabout is largely due to the high rates of relapse for patients when taken off of benzodiazepines and is consistent with earlier reports suggesting that benzodiazepines may interfere with the effectiveness of exposure therapy (Chambless, Foa, Groves, & Goldstein, 1979). Similarly, Bouvard et al. (1997) reported that the short-term advantages of combining buspirone with CBT were lost at 1-year follow-up.

In summary, data suggest that combined treatments may promote beneficial effects in the short term. In the long term, however, combined treatments may lose their advantage and in some cases (e.g., the combination of exposure plus benzodiazepines) may have deleterious effects.

An important caveat to the combined-treatment literature is worth noting. Several recent studies have made it clear that the sequencing of cognitive–behavioral and pharmacological interventions may be important. Studies from three separate research laboratories have suggested that the addition of CBT to pharmacotherapy will assist a substantial number of patients in successfully discontinuing medications (Otto et al., 1993; Schmidt et al., 1997; Speigel, Bruce, Gregg, & Nuzzarello, 1994). Each of these studies indicates that brief psychosocial interventions designed to facilitate drug discontinuation, in the context of a very slow drug taper, appear to minimize relapse rates as well as return to medication use at follow-up.

Treatment algorithm for unmedicated patients. What do these data suggest for clinicians? Treatment algorithms can be recommended on the basis of the current state of knowledge. When an unmedicated patient presents for treatment, it is most conservative to start this patient with a trial of CBT without pharmacological intervention, because the data suggest that the singular effects of CBT will be highly effective for the majority of individuals. There will be some instances when CBT should be immediately combined with pharmacological intervention. If the patient is extremely distressed, medications may be beneficial or necessary for his or her adequate participation in a CBT protocol. For example, some highly distressed patients may benefit from a brief trial of benzodiazepines that can be faded as their symptoms become more tolerable and manageable. Another common example involves a patient with comorbid and severe mood pathology. Severely depressed patients may not be capable of undertaking a CBT trial and should be considered for a combination of CBT plus antidepressant medication.

When motivation is a problem, medications may also be initiated jointly with CBT. Many patients desire a quick and easy solution to their distress and are not willing to endure the rigors that are a necessary part of most CBT protocols. Other patients may not want CBT or may not accept nonbiological explanations for their anxiety. For some of these patients, a combined treatment approach may be the only method for them to receive any psychosocial intervention.

Finally, there will be some instances in which medications should be added at some point during a CBT trial. Medications should be considered when the patient shows little or no clinical improvement or a significant worsening of symptoms. Some patients, for any number of reasons, are noncompliant with the protocol and should also be considered candidates for medication (most likely an SRI) during CBT.

Treatment algorithm for medicated patients. A treatment algorithm is also suggested for medicated patients. Although data do not clearly indicate that the addition of CBT to medications will benefit most patients, CBT appears to be helpful for fading medications. It is not surprising that the majority of medicated patients who seek psychosocial treatment express the desire to be free from medications. In the case of high-potency benzodiazepines, it is important to wait until the patient shows clinically significant improvement prior to initiating a medication-fading procedure. In our experience, approximately 8 sessions of a CBT protocol focusing on education, cognitive restructuring, interoceptive exposure, and in vivo exposure, delivered over a 2-month period, is typically a sufficient preparatory period. At that point most patients show substantial clinical gains and are prepared to begin the fading procedure. The taper itself should be conducted at an extremely slow rate (0.25 mg alprazolam equivalent/week) to minimize the likelihood of withdrawal effects and so-called rebound panic.

In the case of antidepressants, we are aware of no published accounts of systematic medication fading. In a recent study, however, Schmidt, Woolaway-Bickle, Trakowski, Santiago, & Vasey (in press) found that patients could successfully discontinue antidepressants following a trial of CBT without adverse consequences. In some cases, it may be desirable to have the patient fade the antidepressant in the context of the CBT trial. The patient's history of mood pathology as well as current mood symptoms should be carefully considered prior to this recommendation. Given the lack of studies in this area, it seems prudent to recommend a longer duration of CBT, such as 12 sessions delivered over 3 months, prior to initiating the taper. Once again, because of the sensitivity that many of these patients have in regard to internal bodily perturbations, an unusually slow taper schedule is recommended to avoid rebound anxiety from sensations induced by pharmacological changes.

Summary of Panic Disorder Treatments

Empirical studies are clearly lacking in the area of combined treatments for panic disorder. Existing data are also not entirely clear. Some reviews of this literature indicate that the combination of medications and psychotherapy impair the effectiveness of CBT (Basoglu, 1992). Others have suggested that combinations of pharmacotherapy and CBT may be beneficial (Mavissakalian, 1991). The present review suggests that this picture is more complex when short- versus long-term outcomes are considered. In the short term, patients appear to benefit from multifaceted treatment, whereas these benefits are lost in the long term. Until additional studies are completed, combined treatments cannot currently be recommended as a first-line option for most cases of panic disorder. Data indicate, however, that treatment combination for the specific purpose of benzodiazepine discontinuation is likely to benefit many patients.

Social Phobia

Like panic disorder, social phobia is a highly prevalent and often debilitating disorder (Kessler et al., 1994; Marshall, Schneier, Fallon, Feerick, & Liebowitz, 1994). Social phobia has not received the same degree of attention as has panic disorder, but a number of treatment outcome studies have suggested that social phobia is responsive to both psychosocial and pharmacological interventions (Turner, Cooley-Quille, & Beidel, 1996). We review each of these therapies separately as well as the few studies that have assessed combined treatments. In our review of social phobia we refer at times to studies that have evaluated the generalized form of social phobia and to other studies that have examined a specific subtype of social phobia. *Generalized social phobia* refers to individuals with pervasive social evaluation fears. The social phobia subtype that is most often studied typically includes individuals with severe public-speaking or performance anxiety who do not show a more generalized fear of negative evaluation.

Singular Treatments

Efficacy of pharmacotherapy. A variety of medications appear to be efficacious in treating social phobia, with some trials suggesting that a majority of patients (60%–90%) exhibit clinical improvement (Turner et al., 1996). The most well-studied medications in the treatment of social phobia include antidepressants, benzodiazepines, beta receptor antagonists, and buspirone (see Table 4.3).

Antidepressants—SRIs. SRIs have been found to be effective in treating social phobia and may be particularly useful in patients with co-occurring psychiatric conditions, such as depression, which are also ameliorated by SRIs (Marshall & Schneier, 1996). Fluoxetine appears to have a potent effect, with 58%–70% of medicated patients showing clinical improvement up to a 6-month follow-up (Liebowitz et al., 1991; Roy-Byrne, Wingerson, Cowley, & Dager, 1993). Sertraline also has been found to be effective relative to placebo. For example, 50% of the patients receiving sertraline were rated moderately or markedly improved on the basis of clinical global impressions compared to only 9% of a control group (Katzelnick et al., 1995). Sertraline appears to be particularly beneficial for patients with co-occurring obsessive–compulsive spectrum disorders such as trichotillomania and obsessive–compulsive disorder (Schneier, Chin, Hollander, & Liebowitz, 1992). Finally, paroxetine has also been found to be effective in the treatment of generalized social phobia (Stein et al., 1998).

Antidepressants—MAOIs. MAOIs can be reversible (moclobemide, brofaromine) or irreversible (phenelzine). Reversible MAOIs selectively inhibit MAO-A, which results in a lower threat of a hypertensive reactions (due to less interference in the metabolism of tyramine in food), thereby creating fewer dietary restrictions relative to irreversible MAOIs. None of the reversible MAOIs have been approved for use in the United States but have been studied in Europe.

The irreversible MAOI phenelzine has been touted as the "gold standard" for treatment of social phobia (Agras, 1990) and has been widely studied. Overall, phenelzine outperforms beta blockers in controlled studies. Phenelzine has been shown to create improvement in approximately 70% of individuals compared to only about 30% improvement with atenolol (Liebowitz et al., 1988, 1990). These treatment gains have typically been maintained for medicated patients at follow-up (see Table 4.3).

Reversible MAOIs have been found to be highly effective. For example, brofaromine created clinical improvement in 73% of the patients with so-

Table 4.3. Effect Sizes (ESs) for Treatments of Social Phobia

Outcome measure	Pharmacological (d)	Psychosocial (d)	Combined (d)
Clinician ratings	0.75 (Sertraline)[a] 0.93–5.61 (Phenelzine)[e,f,g] 1.78 (Clonazepam)[j] 0.72–0.91 (Brofaramine)[k] 0.75–1.33 (Atenolol)[e,m]	1.03–2.00 (EXP)[b,c] 1.33 (SD)[h] 2.32 (SD)[j] 1.33 (SST)[h] 2.32 (SST)[j] 1.33 (Flooding)[h] 1.77 (Flooding)[m]	0.93 (SST + propanolol)[d] 1.44 (EXP and unspecified anxiolytic)[l]
Average ES	1.40	1.63	1.19
Patient rating	0.62–0.76 (Sertraline)[a] 1.50–6.91 (Phenelzine)[f,g] 1.11–1.44 (Clonazepam)[j] 0.46 (Buspirone)[q] 0.67 (Brofaromine)[k] 0.40 (Atenolol)[m]	0.67–2.81 (EXP)[c,n,o,p] 0.96–2.33 (CBT)[r] 0.29–0.97 (ES)[r] 0.73–3.68 (SST)[j,s] 3.68 (SD)[j] 0.94 (Flooding)[m] 1.10 (CBT + placebo)[q]	1.23–1.41 (CBT + buspirone)[q]
Average ES	1.53	1.28	1.30
Behavioral approach task	0.34 (Atenolol)[m]	1.10–2.42 (EXP)[h,n,p] 2.41 (SST)[h] 1.43–2.42 (Flooding)[h,m]	1.23–1.25 (SST + propanolol)[d]
Average ES	0.34	1.80	1.24
Overall average ES	0.76	1.57	1.26

Note. EXP = exposure; SST = social skills training; SD = systematic desensitization; CBT = cognitive–behavioral therapy; ES = education and supportive therapy.

[a]Katzelnick et al. (1995). [b]Scholing & Emmelkamp (1993). [c]Butler et al. (1984). [d]Falloon et al. (1981). [e]Liebowitz et al. (1988). [f]Liebowitz et al. (1992). [g]Versiani et al. (1992). [h]Shaw (1979). [i]Munjack et al. (1990). [j]Trower et al. (1978). [k]van Vliet et al. (1992). [l]Alstrom et al. (1984). [m]Turner et al. (1994). [n]Newman et al. (1994). [o]Mattick & Peters (1988). [p]Mattick et al. (1989). [q]Clark & Agras (1991). [r]Heimberg et al. (1993). [s]Stravynski et al. (1982).

cial phobia (van Vleit, den Boer, & Westenberg, 1992). The main side effect noted by patients taking brofaromine was middle sleep disturbance, but it is notable that no patients dropped out of the medication condition of this study, suggesting a high level of tolerance. However, some studies have reported relatively few differences between reversible MAOIs and placebo (Schneier et al., 1998).

The overall efficacy of reversible and irreversible MAOIs appears to be comparable. For example, some reports suggest high levels of improvement for both phenelzine (92% improved) and moclobemide (82% improved; Versiani et al., 1992). It is important to point out, however, that moclobemide appears to be better tolerated by most patients and produced fewer side effects compared to phenelzine (Marshall et al., 1994; Scholing & Emmelkamp, 1990). Unfortunately, treatment gains with both phenelzine or moclobemide are lost after the medications are discontinued, resulting in high levels of relapse among patients who have terminated pharmacotherapy (Turner et al., 1996).

Antidepressants—TCAs. Few controlled studies have examined the effect of TCAs on social phobia. Earlier anecdotal evidence and uncontrolled clinical trials suggested that TCAs were not effective in treating social phobia (Agras, 1990; Roy-Byrne et al., 1993). More recent case reports suggest that clomipramine and imipramine possess some efficacy (Lydiard & Falsetti, 1995). There is also some suggestion that imipramine may be particularly helpful in treating social phobics who have mitral valve prolapse (Liebowitz, 1991). In general, however, there is no compelling evidence to recommend TCAs for social phobia.

Buspirone. The non-benzodiazepine anxiolytic buspirone has accrued a mixed clinical record in terms of efficacy findings but has the advantage of producing minimal side effects. Some evidence suggests that efficacy findings may be related to dose effects. In moderate doses, the effects of buspirone have been indistinguishable from placebo (Marshall et al., 1994). A single-blind placebo study, however, found that 67% of patients who could tolerate higher doses of buspirone (45 mg/day or more) showed clinical improvement (Schneier et al., 1993). Although buspirone has been highly touted as a potent anxiolytic, data are too preliminary to unconditionally recommend its use in social phobia when other medications have demonstrated greater effectiveness.

Benzodiazepines. In the 1970s, benzodiazepines became the medication of choice for anxiety disorders because of advantages over earlier anxiolytics such as the barbiturates, including a higher therapeutic-to-toxicity ratio (Coyle, 1979). The literature is mixed regarding the efficacy of benzodiazepines in the treatment of social phobia. Gelernter et al. (1991) compared CBT, alprazolam, phenelzine, and placebo in the treatment of social phobia. All treatments showed some efficacy; however, when more stringent improvement criteria were applied, 69% of phenelzine patients were considered treatment responders compared to 38% responders in the alprazolam-treated group (Gelernter et al., 1991). On the other hand, several studies of another high-potency benzodiazepine, clonazepam, have indicated good efficacy. Clonazepam, compared to placebo, produced moderate to marked improvement in 70% of the patients compared to only 10% in the control group, although only in high doses (average dose 2.5 mg/day; Munjack, Baltazar, Bohn, Cabe, & Appleton, 1990).

On the whole, benzodiazepines appear to have some efficacy in the treatment of social phobia. There are drawbacks to the use of benzodiazepines, however, as diazepam has been shown to impair performance in social phobics (Scholing & Emmelkamp, 1990) and may actually produce disinhibited behavior in high doses (Marshall & Schneier, 1996). Also, benzodiazepines require a tapered dosage regimen when patients wish to discontinue the medication, and patients often relapse when benzodiazepines are withdrawn (Hope, Holt, & Heimberg, 1993; Sands, 1996).

Beta receptor antagonists. Beta receptor antagonists, commonly known as *beta blockers*, are frequently found in medication studies compared with MAOIs. On the whole, beta blockers do not appear to be as effective as MAOIs. A variety of studies have suggested that atenolol is indistinguishable from placebo and fares more poorly than MAOIs (Liebowitz et al., 1988, 1990, 1992). Propanolol has also been found to be no better than placebo (Marshall et al., 1994).

Beta blockers are likely to be more efficacious when they are used in the treatment of more specific subtypes of social phobia. The *Diagnostic and Statistical Manual of Mental Disorders* (4th ed., *DSM–IV*; American Psychiatric Association, 1994) categorizes social phobia patients as "generalized" when their fears include most social situations, whereas a patient will be diagnosed with the "specific" subtype when fear occurs in discrete situations, such as speaking in public or performing on stage. It appears that beta blockers are not effective for generalized social phobics (Lydiard & Falsetti, 1995). However, atenolol has been found to reduce anxiety in individuals with more circumscribed performance anxiety when given 1–1.5 hours prior to performance (Roy-Byrne et al., 1993).

Follow-up analyses. Little evidence has been provided on the long-term course of pharmacotherapy in social phobia. The few studies providing follow-up data suggest that patients who are continued on medications during the follow-up period often maintain treatment gains and may continue to make progress (Gelernter et al., 1991; Liebowitz et al., 1992; van Vliet et al., 1992; Versiani et al., 1992). On the other hand, patients whose medications are discontinued show very high rates of relapse during follow-up (Roy-Byrne et al., 1993).

MAOIs appear to be an efficacious pharmacological treatment for social phobia, whereas SRIs are also effective and have a considerably better side-effect profile (although newer reversible MAOIs produce fewer side effects and do not require dietary restrictions). Beta blockers and benzodiazepines may be useful for instances of acute anxiety, or for more circumscribed cases of social phobia (e.g., performance anxiety). Unfortunately, relapse is very common in each of these agents when the medication is withdrawn.

Efficacy of psychosocial treatments. A variety of psychosocial treatments have been found to be effective in the treatment of social phobia. Many current treatment protocols involve multiple interventions, although some studies have demonstrated the effectiveness of several specific intervention components (e.g., in vivo exposure, social skills training).

In vivo exposure. Exposure-based treatments, whether they include in vivo exposure, imaginal exposure, or exposure in the context of role play, tend to produce substantial clinical gains for patients with social phobia (Heimberg & Barlow, 1991; Hope et al., 1993; Mattick, Peters, & Clarke, 1989; see Table 4.3). There is some suggestion that applied relaxation, when used during exposure treatments, may facilitate treatment progress (Lydiard & Falsetti, 1995). Applied relaxation may be especially useful in patients with subtypes of social phobia who are physiological reactors (Heimberg & Barlow, 1991; Öst, Jerremalm, & Johannsson, 1981). Several studies have found that exposure-based treatments outperform beta blockers (Turner, Biedel, & Jacob, 1994), but their efficacy relative to more potent pharmacological agents (e.g., MAOIs) is unclear.

Social skills training. Social skills training has generally been found to be effective for social phobia (Lucock & Salkovskis, 1988) and appears to be comparable to exposure-based treatments in its effectiveness (Shaw, 1979; Trower, Yardley, Bryant, & Shaw, 1978). Not all people with social phobia possess social skills deficits, however, so it is not surprising that treatments integrating social skills training components are most efficacious when used with individuals found to be lacking social skills (Agras, 1990; Lydiard & Falsetti, 1995; Scholing & Emmelkamp, 1990; Wlazlo, Schroeder-Hartwig, Hand, Kaiser, & Munchau, 1990). Adding cognitive restructuring to social skills training was not found to be more effective than social skills alone in one trial (Stravynski, Marks, & Yule, 1982).

Other studies indicate differential responding to social skills training based on a subtyping of social phobia (Öst et al., 1981). Öst and his colleagues categorized social phobics as physiological reactors (responding to anxiety with physiological responses) and behavioral reactors (responding to anxiety primarily through behavior, such as avoidance). Öst et al. (1981) found that social skills training was more efficacious in behavioral reactors and that relaxation was more helpful to physiological reactors.

Combined cognitive–behavioral interventions. In general, the literature suggests that the newer CBT treatment protocols that include both cognitive and behavioral components are somewhat more effective than singular interventions (e.g., in vivo exposure alone) in treating social phobia. A group-administered cognitive–behavioral treatment, compared to an education and supportive treatment condition, produced significant clinical improvement in approximately 75% of patients receiving CBT compared to less than 50% of those receiving education and support (Heimberg et al., 1990). Combined CBT also appears to be more effective than exposure alone (Agras, 1990; Mattick & Peters, 1988; Turner et al., 1996). For example, Mattick et al. (1989) compared exposure therapy, cognitive restructuring, and their combination and found that the combination condition proved more efficacious than exposure alone as well as cognitive restructuring alone. Treatment gains from combined CBT interventions appear to be maintained over time. At 6-month follow-up, 81% of the patients in a CBT condition were classified as improved, compared to 47% of the education-plus-support group (Heimberg & Barlow, 1991), with comparable levels of improvement being evidenced as long as 5 years following treatment (Heimberg, Salzman, Holt, & Blendell, 1993).

Combined Treatments

Although a variety of treatment outcome studies of social phobia have contrasted the effects of pharmacotherapy and psychosocial therapy, only a handful of studies have examined the effectiveness of these combined treatments. In general, there is no evidence to clearly suggest that combined treatments offer an advantage over singular treatments, but firm conclusions cannot be made from such a limited sample of studies.

Falloon, Lloyd, and Harpin (1981) compared social skills training (conducted by nonprofessional volunteers) plus placebo with social skills training plus propanolol (160–320 mg/day). There were no significant group differences, with both treatments producing significant improvements at posttreatment. At 6-month follow-up there continued to be no group differences with a general maintenance of treatment gains. Clark and Agras (1991) compared buspirone, placebo, CBT plus placebo, and CBT plus buspirone. Findings suggest that buspirone was not significantly better than placebo and that groups who received CBT improved more than groups that did not receive CBT.

Treatment algorithm. On the whole, the treatment algorithm for social phobia, along with the appropriate cautions, is similar to that recommended for panic disorder. In the case of social phobia, however, there is some suggestion that different subtypes (i.e., specific vs. generalized) should be treated differently. For example, the specific subtype may be effectively treated with as-needed doses of beta blockers or benzodiazepines, whereas these treatments have shown no efficacy for the generalized subtype. Similarly, generalized social phobics often benefit from social skills training, but many patients with more specific performance fears do not show social skills deficits.

Unmedicated patients. It is recommended that unmedicated patients be started with a trial of CBT without pharmacological intervention, because the empirical data suggest that the singular effects of CBT will be highly effective for the majority of individuals without the problem of high rates of relapse associated with medications. The specific set of problems or skills deficits presented by each patient should be used to weight the emphasis on each type of CBT intervention (e.g., cognitive restructuring vs. social skills training). There may be instances, such as when the patient is highly distressed or unmotivated to comply with a CBT regimen, when it will be useful to combine CBT with pharmacological interventions. Medications should be considered when the patient shows little or no clinical improvement or a significant worsening of symptoms during the CBT trial. When a medication is considered, SRIs are likely to be the best choice for most generalized social phobics because of their high efficacy and relatively few side effects.

Medicated patients. It is our assumption that many medicated patients who seek out psychosocial treatment will express the desire to be free from medications. In the case of more circumscribed social phobias (e.g., public speaking), the patient will often take a beta blocker or benzodiazepine as needed when a speaking event can be anticipated. Cognitive–behavioral interventions should be geared toward assisting the patient in fading medication use in this context (e.g., substitution of alternative coping skills, such as diaphragmatic breathing or use of cognitive restructuring during anxiety). Cognitive restructuring in combination with in vivo exposure practice should provide the patient with a means for gradual tapering of the medication. In the case of a more generalized social phobia, medication tapering should be considered following significant symptomatic relief (i.e., usually occurring after 8–12 sessions).

Summary of Social Phobia Treatments

A variety of medication classes have shown good efficacy with respect to the treatment of social phobia. MAOIs appear to produce the highest levels of clinical improvement, but SRIs also appear to be effective without the problematic dietary restrictions and potential for severe side effects associated with irreversible MAOIs. Always problematic, however, is the issue of high rates of relapse following medication discontinuation. Psychosocial treatments also appear to be comparable to pharmacological interventions and may be superior to medication in effecting change of phobic avoidance behaviors (see Table 4.3). There are few combined pharmacological and psychological treatments and, although these studies suggest good efficacy, these levels of effectiveness do not appear to be superior to those produced by singular treatment strategies.

Specific Phobia

Community samples suggest that specific phobias are highly prevalent and may occur in 10%–11% of the population, although only a small percentage of these individuals will present for treatment (Agras, Sylvester,

& Oliveau, 1969). In part because of the relatively lower numbers of individuals who seek out treatment for specific phobias, knowledge of treatment efficacy has lagged behind that of the other phobic anxiety conditions, particularly in the area of pharmacological and combined psychosocial and pharmacological treatments. There are clear and abundant data, however, suggesting that cognitive–behavioral treatments are highly effective for specific phobias regardless of the specific focus of the phobia (e.g., animals, heights, enclosed spaces).

Singular Treatments

Efficacy of pharmacotherapy. Knowledge of pharmacological treatment of specific phobia is limited and quite variable. Specific phobia has been found to be only minimally or markedly responsive to drug therapy depending on the medication and the type of phobia (Noyes, Chaudry, Dewat, & Domingo, 1986; Roy-Byrne et al., 1993). There is also consistent evidence to suggest high rates of relapse once the medication is withdrawn (McGlynn, 1994; Noyes, 1991; Sartory, 1983). Only two classes of medication, beta receptor antagonists and benzodiazepines, have been more thoroughly evaluated in specific phobia. The singular effects of these agents are reviewed below.

Beta receptor antagonists. There is no evidence that would recommend beta receptor antagonists (beta blockers) for the treatment of specific phobia. Beta blockers have shown little or no efficacy for specific phobia (Liebowitz & Strauman, 1988). Despite the suggestion that the efficacy of beta blockers may depend on the cardioreactivity of the patient (Hugdahl, 1988), beta blockers have been found to decrease cardiac symptoms without affecting levels of subjective anxiety (Bernadt, Silverstone, & Singleton, 1980).

Benzodiazepines. Benzodiazepines have shown moderate effectiveness in the treatment of specific phobias (Noyes, 1991). For example, acute alprazolam administration was efficacious when administered prior to flights in the treatment of flying phobia (Liebowitz, 1991). Diazepam given prior to exposure to the feared stimuli also produced significant improvements on behavioral approach tasks compared to placebo (Bernadt et al., 1980; Whitehead, Blackwell, & Robinson, 1978). It appears that some forms of specific phobia (e.g., acrophobia) will respond well to benzodiazepines.

Efficacy of psychosocial treatments. Psychosocial interventions, particularly exposure, have been the most widely used intervention modality in the treatment of specific phobia. Other skills-based interventions, including cognitive restructuring and relaxation procedures, have also been found to be reasonably effective in the treatment of specific phobia (see Table 4.4). Each of these treatment techniques is reviewed.

Table 4.4. Effect Sizes (ESs) for Treatments of Specific Phobia

Outcome measure	Pharmacological (d)	Psychosocial (d)	Combination (d)
Clinician rating	—	2.4–3.8 (SD)[a] 2.9 (Multicomponent CBT)[c] 1.6–2.5 (BT + P)[d]	3.0 (Diazepam + flooding)[b] 1.2–2.2 (ST/BT + I)[e]
Average ES		3.0	2.6
Patient rating	5.2 (Diazepam)[e]	2.9–4.7 (PM)[f,g] 5.2–7.3 (PM + SD)[d] 2.9–7.1 (SD)[a] 1.9 (Flooding)[b] 1.1–3.8 (EXP)[e,h] 1.0 (PM + SIT)[i] 2.1 (CR)[j] 3.6 (BF)[k] 3.6 (PMRT)[k]	—
Average ES	5.2	3.6	
Behavioral approach task	9.2 (Diazepam)[e]	2.6–4.3 (PM)[h,g] 8.9–12.1 (PMw/SD)[h] 2.0–2.4 (SD)[a,l] 1.2 (Flooding)[f] 3.6–3.8 (EXP)[g,j,m] 1.5 (CR)[j] 1.3 (PM + SIT)[i]	—
Average ES	9.2	3.9	—
Overall average ES	7.2	3.5	2.6

Note. SD = systematic desensitization; CBT = cognitive–behavioral therapy; BT = behavior therapy; P = placebo; ST = supportive therapy; I = imipramine; PM = participant modeling; EXP = exposure; SIT = self-instructional training; CR = cognitive restructuring; BF = biofeedback; PMRT = progressive muscle relaxation.
[a]Rosen et al. (1976). [b]Zitrin et al. (1978). [c]Denholtz & Mann (1975). [d]Marks et al. (1972). [e]Whitehead et al. (1978). [f]Marshall (1985). [g]Williams et al. (1984). [h]Bandura et al. (1975). [i]Ladouceur (1983). [j]Biran & Wilson (1981). [k]Miller, Murphy, & Miller (1978). [l]Kimura et al. (1972). [m]Leitenberg & Callahan (1973).

Exposure. In vivo exposure to anxiety cues has been widely established as an effective treatment for specific phobia (Noyes, 1991). In reviews of phobia treatment studies that have used exposure, it was found to be more effective than control procedures 73% of the time (Taylor & Arnow, 1988). It appears that duration of exposure is a critical parameter in determining its effectiveness. Brief exposure does not appear to be effective in many cases, whereas prolonged exposure has typically produced better outcomes (Marshall, 1985).

There are several popular variations of exposure, including *flooding*, which is an exposure technique in which the patient is exposed to highly anxiety-provoking stimuli with the prevention of avoidance behaviors, and *systematic desensitization*, which is exposure in the context of a relaxation procedure. Both have been found to be effective (Marshall, 1985). Fortunately, systematic desensitization, a far less aversive procedure, produces significant clinical gains in a high percentage of patients with specific phobia, and there is no suggestion that flooding procedures yield more rapid or more complete recovery (Öst, 1996).

It appears that exposure can be enhanced with various techniques, including participant modeling in which the therapist models successful completion of exposure to the feared stimulus (Öst, 1996). For example, a person with a snake phobia would watch the therapist handle the snakes successfully in the context of exposure trials. Williams, Dooseman, and Kleifield (1984) compared participant modeling with self-exposure and a no-treatment control group. Although both treatments were effective in this study, participant modeling produced a relatively greater effect size (see Table 4.4).

Relaxation, biofeedback, and breathing retraining. Progressive muscle relaxation (PMR), biofeedback, and breathing retraining are relaxation skills that are often used in the context of other cognitive and behavioral interventions but appear to have efficacy when administered singularly. In one study that compared electromyographic (EMG) biofeedback, PMR, and a no-treatment control, PMR and EMG feedback yielded significantly greater effects compared to the control condition, with the effect sizes for the treatment conditions being essentially equivalent for anxiety reduction (Miller, Murphy, & Miller, 1978). Öst and his colleagues reported high levels of efficacy for applied relaxation skills, with this treatment producing a clinically significant effect in 86% of a claustrophobic sample (Öst, Johannsson, & Jerremalm, 1982). Applied muscle tension, used to increase blood pressure and decrease the likelihood of vasovagal syncope, produced a clinically significant effect in 85% of a blood–injury phobic sample (Öst, Fellenius, & Sterner, 1991). Breathing control procedures, or diaphragmatic breathing, also has been efficacious (Lum, 1981).

Cognitive therapy. Cognitive therapy and guided exposure have been compared and found to be equally efficacious (Biran & Wilson, 1981). In addition, there are cases in which the combination of cognitive therapy with behavior therapy may produce gains beyond the singular effects of exposure alone (Taylor & Arnow, 1988).

Follow-up studies. In a review of follow-up evaluation of specific phobia for periods ranging from 6 months to 10 years (Öst, 1996) there was a wide range of outcomes, with as many as 100% of individuals achieving high end-state functioning, but also as few as 6% maintaining treatment gains. Initial follow-up evaluations typically indicate that continued treatment gains occur during the short-term follow-up period (Bandura, Adams, & Beyer, 1977; Biran & Wilson, 1981; Marshall, 1985). Moreover, Öst (1989) found that the effects of psychological intervention were generally maintained at longer term follow-up (>6 months). On average, 11% of total improvement for patients took place during the follow-up period (Öst, 1989).

Combined Treatments

Only benzodiazepines and TCAs have been used in conjunction with psychological treatment modalities for specific phobias. Whitehead, Robinson, Blackwell, and Stutz (1978) compared flooding plus diazepam (5 mg administered three times per day) with flooding plus placebo. The results suggested that diazepam administration had no effect on the length of time required for the successful completion of treatment (see Table 4.4). The authors concluded that diazepam did little to enhance the effectiveness of flooding therapy (Whitehead et al., 1978).

Only one study has evaluated specific phobia and the combination of behavior therapy and antidepressants. In this case, patients with specific phobias received either behavioral treatment plus imipramine, supportive therapy plus imipramine, or behavioral therapy plus placebo (Zitrin, Klein, & Woerner, 1978; Zitrin et al., 1983). Zitrin et al. (1978, 1983) found that imipramine did not produce improved treatment response beyond the effects of behavior therapy plus placebo.

Treatment algorithm. Unmedicated patients who seek treatment for specific phobias should be recommended for exposure-based CBT. For patients taking stable doses of medication, it may be beneficial to discontinue medication prior to or during CBT for the various reasons delineated in previous sections. Patients taking medication as needed should also have the opportunity to participate in exposure exercises without the use of medication. Administration of benzodiazepines may be necessary in some cases to provide relief from acute, overwhelming anxiety that would otherwise prevent the patient from taking part in treatment. If benzodiazepines are used, they should be administered 3–4 hours before CBT begins because of evidence suggesting that exposure will be most effective when levels of medication are below peak levels (Sartory, 1983).

Summary of Specific Phobia Treatments

Cognitive–behavioral treatment, particularly exposure-based treatment, appears to be empirically justified as the treatment of choice for social phobia. Some pharmacological treatments have been effective in decreasing anxiety, but psychosocial treatments alone have consistently been found to demonstrate equal or better efficacy and do not possess the high relapse rates and side-effect profiles that are associated with pharmacotherapy (McGlynn, 1994). Combined-treatment data also are very limited, and there are no data to recommend concurrent psychosocial and pharmacological treatment.

Phobic anxiety conditions are highly debilitating. A patient's distress may tempt clinicians to conduct a comprehensive treatment program that uses all available interventions, including both mediations and CBT. Unfortunately, empirical investigations across each of the phobic anxiety conditions have not supported this type of "shotgun" approach. Instead, it appears that combined treatments do not outperform singular treatments, and in some instances combined treatments may even lead to poorer outcomes.

It is somewhat surprising that combined treatments are not more clearly beneficial for patients with phobic anxiety disorders. A variety of factors may contribute to the lack of clear-cut benefits that many practitioners likely believe exist. These factors, including the method (or lack thereof) of explaining the treatment approach, underreliance on cognitive–behavioral skills, and misattribution of gains, may partly account for this failure to obtain additive or synergistic benefits. In these final few sections we discuss these factors as a caution to mental health professionals in implementing combined treatment strategies.

Delivery of a Deterministic Biological or Psychological Model

Patients can be discouraged from alternative treatment modalities when their physician or therapist provides an overly narrow and compelling case for either a biological or psychological model of the disorder. When combined treatments are being delivered it is critically important to provide a compelling rationale for their integration. Too many patients in research protocols express confusion regarding discrepant etiologies that have been provided to them by different health care professionals. Only the most deterministic neurobiological models propose that a neurological imbalance is both necessary and sufficient for the development of the disorder.

Integrated biopsychological models, models that most mental health professionals feel more closely approximate reality, incorporate the possibility of neurochemical imbalances as one of many possible factors that contribute to anxiety. As such, neurological triggers are only one of several steps necessary for the generation of fear, as perceptual processes constitute additional necessary steps. According to these models, perceptual or attributional problems are central components. When anxiety is viewed as a biological dysregulation, it is treated with drugs designed to correct the neurochemical imbalance. When anxiety is viewed as a perceptual problem, interventions are designed to provide the patient with corrective information to change these attributions. An integrated conceptual model encompasses the possibility of biological dysregulation but treats it as only one of several factors for intervention. The integrated model therefore accommodates both biological and psychological treatment intervention.

Medication Overreliance

Another potential pitfall that may occur in combined treatments is the temptation for patients to overrely on medications in the context of both acute and chronic anxiety. By necessity, cognitive–behavioral interventions require that patients use skills and knowledge in the context of feared stimuli in order to learn that they can master their anxiety. Patients who routinely take medications prior to fear-provoking situations may not have the opportunity to practice cognitive–behavioral skills because of relatively low levels of anxiety. There is also the possibility that the patient may experience state-dependent learning when under the influence of medications that may interfere with the emotional processing of fear that should take place during exposure. We have found that it is very useful for patients to practice in fear-provoking situations without the use of medications or any other medication-related "safety aids." For example, some patients may not take medications, but they will continue to carry their pill bottle with them. It is important for these patients to continue to practice cognitive and behavioral interventions without the availability of any of these medication-related safety aids.

Medication Misattribution

Many patients engaging in combined treatments express the concern that even though their symptoms have improved, they believe that they are at risk for relapse once the medications are removed. Other patients who have been taking medications for many years but achieve substantial clinical gains only after completing a CBT trial appear to overattribute their positive end-state functioning to their medication use. These misattribution problems appear to be particularly prevalent for patients using benzodiazepines. It is obviously critical to restructure questionable attributions but, once again, one of the most potent strategies of avoiding misattribution problems is to have medicated patients discontinue their use of medications in the context of the CBT trial.

Final Thoughts

Examination of studies across the phobic anxiety conditions suggests that a fair amount is known about singular treatments but relatively little is known about combined treatments. This is particularly unfortunate given the wide use and acceptance of combined treatments in clinical practice. At best, it appears that combined treatments are no better than singular intervention strategies in the long term (although there may be some short-term benefits). In the absence of compelling data in this regard, we would generally recommend unimodal treatment for most phobic anxiety conditions.

These recommendations are necessarily tentative insomuch as there has been so little work on integrated treatments. Despite findings from this review, we believe that combination treatments have promise. We hope that future research will offer new insights and understanding into effective combination treatments, including methods for effectively sequencing different treatment modalities.

References

Agras, W. S. (1990). Treatment of social phobias: 143rd annual meeting of the American Psychiatric Association. *Journal of Clinical Psychiatry, 51*(Suppl.), 52–55.

Agras, W. S., Sylvester, D., & Oliveau, D. (1969). The epidemiology of common fears and phobias. *Comprehensive Psychiatry, 10,* 151–156.

Alstrom, J. E., Nordlund, C. L., Persson, G., Harding, M., & Ljungqvist, C. (1984). Effects of four treatment methods on social phobic patients not suitable for insight-oriented psychotherapy. *Acta Psychiatrica Scandinavica, 70,* 97–110.

American Psychiatric Association. (1994). *Diagnostic and statistical manual of mental disorders* (4th ed.). Washington, DC: Author.

Ballenger, J. C., Burrows, G. D., DuPont, R. L., Jr., Lesser, I. M., Noyes, R., Jr., Pecknold, J. C., Rifkin, A., & Swinson, R. P. (1988). Alprazolam in panic disorder and agoraphobia: Results from a multicenter trial. I: Efficacy in short-term treatment. *Archives of General Psychiatry, 45,* 413–422.

Ballenger, J. C., Wheadon, D. E., Steiner, M., Bushnell, W., & Gergel, I. P. (1998). Double-blind, fixed-dose, placebo-controlled study of paroxetine in the treatment of panic disorder. *American Journal of Psychiatry, 155,* 36–42.

Bandura, A., Adams, N. E., & Beyer, J. (1977). Cognitive processes mediating behavioral change. *Journal of Personality and Social Psychology, 35,* 125–139.

Bandura, A., Jeffery, R. W., & Gajdos, W. (1975). Generalizing change through participant modeling with self-directed mastery. *Behaviour Research and Therapy, 13,* 141–152.

Barlow, D. H., Craske, M. G., Cerney, J. A., & Klosko, J. S. (1989). Behavioral treatment of panic disorder. *Behavior Therapy, 20,* 261–282.

Barlow, D. H., & Lehman, C. L. (1996). Advances in the psychosocial treatment of anxiety disorders: Implications for national health care. *Archives of General Psychiatry, 53,* 727–735.

Basoglu, M. (1992). Pharmacological and behavioral treatment of panic disorder. *Psychotherapy and Psychosomatics, 58,* 57–59.

Beck, A. T. (1988). Cognitive approaches to panic disorder: Theory and therapy. In S. Rachman & J. Maser (Eds.), *Panic: Psychological perspectives* (pp. 91–109). Hillsdale, NJ: Erlbaum.

Beck, A. T., & Emery, G. (1985). *Anxiety disorders and phobias: A cognitive perspective.* New York: Basic Books.

Bernadt, M. W., Silverstone, T., & Singleton, W. (1980). Behavioural and subjective effects of beta-adrenergic blockade in phobic subjects. *British Journal of Psychiatry, 137,* 452–457.

Biran, M., & Wilson, G. T. (1981). Treatment of phobic disorders using cognitive and exposure methods: A self-efficacy analysis. *Journal of Consulting and Clinical Psychology, 49,* 886–889.

Bouvard, M., Mollard, E., Guerin, J., & Cottraux, J. (1997). Study and course of the psychological profile in 77 patients experiencing panic disorder with agoraphobia after cognitive behavioral therapy with or without buspirone. *Psychotherapy and Psychosomatics, 66,* 27–32.

Broocks, A., Badelow, B., Pekrun, G., George, A., Meyer, T., Bartmann, U., Hillmer-Vogel, U., & Ruther, E. (1998). Comparison of aerobic exercise, clomipramine, and placebo in the treatment of panic disorder. *American Journal of Psychiatry, 155,* 603–609.

Buiges, J., & Vallego, J. (1987). Therapeutic response to phenelzine in patients with panic disorder and agoraphobia with panic attacks. *Journal of Clinical Psychiatry, 48,* 55–59.

Butler, G., Cullinton, A., Munby, M., Amies, P., & Gelder, M. (1984). Exposure and anxiety management in the treatment of social phobia. *Journal of Consulting and Clinical Psychology, 52,* 642–650.

Chambless, D. L., Foa, E. B., Groves, G. A., & Goldstein, A. J. (1979). Flooding with Brevital in the treatment of agoraphobia: Countereffective? *Behaviour Research & Therapy, 17,* 243–251.

Chambless, D. L., & Gillis, M. M. (1994). A review of psychosocial treatments for panic disorder. In B. E. Wolfe & J. D. Maser (Eds.), *Treatment of panic disorder* (pp. 149–173). Washington, DC: American Psychiatric Press.

Charney, D. S., Woods, S., Goodman, W., Rifkin, B., Kinch, M., Aiken, B., Quadrino, L., & Heninger, G. (1986). Drug treatment of panic disorder: The comparative efficacy of imipramine, alprazolam, and trazodone. *Journal of Clinical Psychiatry, 47,* 580–586.

Clark, D. B., & Agras, W. S. (1991). The assessment and treatment of performance anxiety in musicians. *American Journal of Psychiatry, 148,* 598–605.

Clark, D. M. (1986). A cognitive approach to panic. *Behaviour Research and Therapy, 24,* 461–470.

Clark, D. M., & Salkovskis, P. M. (in press). *Cognitive therapy with panic and hypochondriasis.* Oxford, England: Pergamon.

Coyle, J. T. (1979). Pharmcotherapy for anxiety. *Psychiatric Annals, 9*(10), 10–15.

Denholtz, M. S., & Mann, E. T. (1975). An automated audiovisual treatment of phobias administered by non-professionals. *Journal of Behavioral Therapy and Experimental Psychiatry, 6,* 111–115.

DuBoff, E., England, D., Ferguson, J. M., Londborg, P. D., Rosenthal, M. H., Smith, W., Weise, C., & Wolkow, R. M. (1995). Double-blind comparison of three fixed doses of sertraline and placebo in patients with panic disorder. *European Neuropsychopharmacology, 5,* 287.

Dunbar, G. (1995, May). *A double-blind placebo controlled study of paroxetine and clomipramine in the treatment of panic disorder.* Paper presented at the 148th annual meeting of the American Psychiatric Association, Miami, FL.

Falloon, I. R., Lloyd, G. G., & Harpin, R. E. (1981). The treatment of social phobia, real-life rehearsal with nonprofessional therapists. *Journal of Nervous and Mental Disorders, 169,* 180–184.

Gelernter, C. S., Uhde, T. W., Cimbolic, P., Arnkoff, D. B., Vittone, B. J., Tancer, M. E., & Bartko, J. J. (1991). Cognitive–behavioral and pharmacological treatments of social phobia: A controlled study. *Archives of General Psychiatry, 48,* 938–945.

Goldstein, A. J., & Chambless, D. L. (1978). A reanalysis of agoraphobia. *Behavior Therapy, 9,* 47–59.

Heimberg, R. G., & Barlow, D. H. (1991). New developments in cognitive–behavioral therapy for social phobia. *Journal of Clinical Psychiatry, 52*(11, Suppl.), 21–30.

Heimberg, R. G., Dodge, C. S., Hope, D. A., Kennedy, C. R., Zollo, L. J., & Becker, R. E. (1990). Cognitive behavioral group treatment for social phobia: Comparison to a credible placebo control. *Cognitive Therapy and Research, 14,* 1–23.

Heimberg, R. G., Salzman, D. G., Holt, C. S., & Blendell, K. A. (1993). Cognitive–behavioral group treatment for social phobia: Effectiveness at five-year follow up. *Cognitive Therapy and Research, 17,* 325–339.

Hope, D. A., Holt, C. S., & Heimberg, R. G. (1993). Social phobia. In T. R. Giles (Ed.), *Handbook of effective psychotherapy* (pp. 227–251). New York: Plenum.

Hugdahl, K. (1988). Psychophysiological aspects of phobic fears. *Neuropsychobiology, 20,* 194–204.

Katzelnick, D., Kobak, K., Greist, J., Jefferson, J., Mantle, J., & Serlin, R. (1995). Sertraline for social phobia: A double-blind, placebo-controlled crossover study. *American Journal of Psychiatry, 152,* 1368–1370.

Kessler, R. C., McGonagle, K. A., Zhao, S., Nelson, C. B., Hughes, M., Eshleman, S., Wittchen, H. U., & Kendler, K. S. (1994). Lifetime and 12 month prevalence of *DSM-III–R* psychiatric disorder in the United States: Results from the National Comorbidity Survey. *Archives of General Psychiatry, 51,* 8–19.

Kimura, H. K., Kennedy, T. D., & Rhodes, L. E. (1972). Recurring assessment of changed in phobic behavior during the course of desensitization. *Behaviour Research and Therapy, 10,* 279–282.

Klein, D. F. (1964). Delineation of two drug-responsive anxiety syndromes. *Psychopharmacologia, 5,* 397–408.

Klein, D. F., & Fink, M. (1962). Psychiatric reaction patterns to imipramine. *American Journal of Psychiatry, 119,* 432–438.

Ladouceur, R. (1983). Participant modeling with or without cognitive treatment for phobias. *Journal of Consulting and Clinical Psychology, 51,* 942–944.

Leitenberg, H., & Callahan, E. J. (1973). Reinforced practice and reduction of different kinds of fears in adults and children. *Behaviour Research and Therapy, 11,* 19–30.

Liebowitz, M. R. (1991). Psychopharmacological management of social and simple phobias. In W. Coryell & G. Winokur (Eds.), *The clinical management of anxiety disorders* (pp. 63–78). New York: Oxford University Press.

Liebowitz, M. R., Gorman, J. M., Fyer, A. J., Campeas, R., Levin, A., Sandberg, D., Hollander, E., Papp, L., & Goetz, D. (1988). Pharmacotherapy of social phobia: An interim report of a placebo-controlled comparison of phenelzine and atenolol. *Journal of Clinical Psychiatry, 49,* 252–258.

Liebowitz, M. R., Schneier, R., Campeas, R., Gorman, J., Fyer, A., Hollander, E., Hatterer, J., & Papp, L. (1990). Phenelzine and atenolol in social phobia. *Psychopharmacology Bulletin, 26,* 123–125.

Liebowitz, M. R., Schneier, F., Campeas, R., Hollander, E., Hatterer, J., Fyer, A., Gorman, J., Papp, L., Davies S., Gully, R., & Klein, D. (1992). Phenelzine vs atenolol in social phobia: A placebo controlled comparison. *Archives of General Psychiatry, 49,* 290–301.

Liebowitz, M. R., Schneier, F., Hollander, E., Welkowitz, L., Saoud, J., Feerick, J., Campeas, R., Fallon, B., Street, L., & Gitow, A. (1991). Treatment of social phobia with drugs other than benzodiazepines. *Journal of Clinical Psychiatry, 52*(11 Suppl.), 10–15.

Liebowitz, M. R., & Strauman, T. J. (1988). Social phobia. In J. G. Howells (Ed.), *Modern perspectives in psychosocial pathology* (pp. 203–220). New York: Brunner/Mazel.

Lucock, M. P., & Salkovskis, P. M. (1988). Cognitive factors in social anxiety and its treatment. *Behaviour Research and Therapy, 26,* 297–302.

Lum, S. (1981). Hyperventilation and anxiety state. *Journal of the Royal Society of Medicine, 74,* 1–4.

Lydiard, R. B., & Falsetti, S. A. (1995). Treatment options for social phobia. *Psychiatric Annals, 25,* 570–576.

Lydiard, R., Morton, W., Emmanuel, N., Zealberg, J., Laraia, M., Stuart, G., O'Neil, P., & Ballenger, J. (1993). Preliminary report: Placebo-controlled, double-blind study of the clinical and metabolic effects of desimipramine in panic disorder. *Psychopharmacology Bulletin, 29,* 183–188.

Markowitz, J. S., Weissman, M. M., Ouellette, R., Lish, J. D., & Klerman, G. L. (1989). Quality of life in panic disorder. *Archives of General Psychiatry, 46,* 984–992.

Marks, I. M., Gray, S., Cohen, D., Hill, R., Mawson, D., Ramm, E., & Stern, R. S. (1983). Imipramine and brief therapist-aided exposure in agoraphobics having self-exposure homework. *Archives of General Psychiatry, 40,* 153–162.

Marks, I. M., Swinson, R. P., Basoglu, M., Kuch, K., Noshirvani, H., O'Sullivan, G., Lelliott, P. T., Kirby, M., McNamee, G., Sengun, S., & Wickwire, K. (1993). Alprazolam and exposure alone and combined in panic disorder with agoraphobia: A controlled study in London and Toronto. *British Journal of Psychiatry, 162,* 776–787.

Marks, I. M., Viswanathan, R., Lirsedge, M. S., & Gardner, R. (1972). Enhanced relief of phobias by flooding during waning diazepam effect. *British Journal of Psychiatry, 12,* 493–505.

Marshall, R. D., & Schneier, F. R. (1996). An algorithm for the pharmacotherapy of social phobia. *Psychiatric Annals, 26,* 210–216.

Marshall, R. D., Schneier, F. R., Fallon, B. A., Feerick, J., & Liebowitz, M. R. (1994). Medication therapy for social phobia. *Journal of Clinical Psychiatry, 55,* 33–37.

Marshall, W. L. (1985). The effects of variable exposure in flooding therapy. *Behavior Therapy, 16,* 117–135.

Mathews, A. M., Teasdale, J., Munby, M., Johnston, D., & Shaw, P. (1981). *Agoraphobia: Nature and treatment.* New York, Guilford Press.

Mattick, R. P., & Peters, L. (1988). Treatment of severe social phobia: Effects of guided exposure with and without cognitive restructuring. *Journal of Consulting and Clinical Psychology, 56,* 251–260.

Mattick, R. P., Peters, L., & Clarke, J. C. (1989). Exposure and cognitive restructuring for severe social phobia. *Behavior Therapy, 20,* 3–23.

Mavissakalian, M. (1991). Agoraphobia. In B. D. Beitman & G. L. Klerman (Eds.), *Integrating pharmacotherapy and psychotherapy* (pp. 165–181). Washington, DC: American Psychiatric Press.

McGlynn, F. D. (1994). Simple phobia. In M. Hersen & R. T. Ammerman (Eds.), *Handbook of prescriptive treatments for adults* (pp. 179–196). New York: Plenum.

Michelson, L., & Marchione, K. (1991). Behavioral, cognitive and pharmacological treatments of panic disorder with agoraphobia: Critique and synthesis. *Journal of Consulting and Clinical Psychology, 59,* 100–114.

Miller, M. P., Murphy, P. J., & Miller, T. P. (1978). Comparison of electromyographic feedback and progressive relaxation training in treating circumscribed anxiety stress reactions. *Journal of Consulting and Clinical Psychology, 46,* 1291–1298.

Modigh, K., Westberg, P., & Eriksson, E. (1992). Superiority of clomipramine over imipramine in the treatment of panic disorder: A placebo-controlled trial. *Journal of Clinical Psychopharmacology, 12,* 251–261.

Munjack, D., Baltazar, P., Bohn, P., Cabe, D., & Appleton, A. (1990). Clonazepam in the treatment of social phobia: A pilot study. *Journal of Clinical Psychiatry, 51*(5 Suppl.), 35–41.

Newman, M., Hofmann, S., Trabert, W., Roth, W., & Taylor, C. B. (1994). Does behavioral treatment of social phobia lead to cognitive changes? *Behavior Therapy, 25,* 503–517.

Noyes, R., Jr. (1991). Treatments of choice for anxiety disorders. In W. Coryell & G. Winokur (Eds.), *The clinical management of anxiety disorders* (pp. 140–153). New York: Oxford University Press.

Noyes, R., Chaudry, D. R., Dewat, R., & Domingo, D. V. (1986). Pharmacologic treatment of phobic disorders. *Journal of Clinical Psychiatry, 47,* 445–452.

Noyes, R., Garvey, M., & Cook, B. (1989). Follow-up study of patients with panic disorder treated with tricyclic antidepressants. *Journal of Affective Disorders, 16,* 249–257.

Öst, L. G. (1989). A maintenance program for behavioral treatment of anxiety disorders. *Behaviour Research and Therapy, 27,* 123–130.

Öst, L. G. (1996). Long term effects of behavioral therapy for specific phobia. In M. Mavissakalian & R. Prien (Eds.), *Long term treatments of anxiety disorders* (pp. 121–170). Washington, DC: American Psychiatric Press.

Öst, L. G., Fellenius, J., & Sterner, U. (1991). Applied tension, exposure *in vivo,* and tension only in the treatment of blood phobia. *Behaviour Research and Therapy, 29,* 561–574.

Öst, L. G., Jerremalm, A., & Johannsson, J. (1981). Individual response patterns and the effects of different behavioral methods in the treatment of social phobia. *Behaviour Research and Therapy, 19,* 1–16.

Öst, L. G., Johannsson, J., & Jerremalm, A. (1982). Individual response patterns and the effects of different behavioral methods in the treatment of claustrophobia. *Behaviour Research and Therapy, 20,* 445–460.

Otto, M. W., Pollack, M. H., Sachs, G. S., Reiter, S. R., Meltzer-Brody, S., & Rosenbaum, J. F. (1993). Discontinuation of benzodiazepine treatment. *American Journal of Psychiatry, 150,* 1485–1490.

Pohl, R. B., Wolkow, R. M., & Clary, C. M. (1998). Sertraline in the treatment of panic disorder: A double-blind multicenter trial. *American Journal of Psychiatry, 155,* 1189–1195.

Pollack, M. H., Otto, M. W., Kaspi, S., Hammerness, P., & Rosenbaum, J. (1994). Cognitive–behavior therapy for treatment-refractory panic disorder. *Journal of Clinical Psychopharmacology, 13*, 257–263.

Rapaport, M. H., Wolkow, R. M., & Clary, C. M. (1998). Methodologies and outcomes from the Sertraline Multicenter Flexible-Dose Trials. *Psychopharmacology Bulletin, 34*, 183–189.

Rosen, G. M., Glasgow, R. E., & Barrera, M., Jr. (1976). A controlled study to assess the clinical efficacy of totally self-administered systematic desensitization. *Journal of Consulting and Clinical Psychology, 44*, 208–217.

Roy-Byrne, P., Wingerson, D., Cowley, D., & Dager, S. (1993). Psychopharmacologic treatment of panic, generalized anxiety disorder, and social phobia. *Psychiatric Clinics of North America, 16*, 719–735.

Sands, B. F. (1996). Generalized anxiety disorder, social phobia, and performance anxiety: Pharmacotherapy and aspects of integration with psychotherapy. In J. Ellison (Ed.), *Integrative treatment of anxiety disorders* (pp. 1–51). Washington, DC: American Psychiatric Press.

Sartory, G. (1983). Benzodiazepines and behavioral treatment of phobic anxiety. *Behavioural Psychotherapy, 11*, 204–217.

Schmidt, N. B. (1997). [Medication use in patients with panic disorder]. Unpublished raw data.

Schmidt, N. B., Staab, J. P., Trakowski, J. H., & Sammons, M. (1997). Efficacy of a brief psychosocial treatment for panic disorder in an active duty sample: Implications for military readiness. *Military Medicine, 162*, 123–129.

Schmidt, N. B., Woolaway-Bickle, K., Trakowski, J., Santiago, H. T., & Vasey, M. (in press). Antidepressant discontinuation in the context of cognitive behavioral therapy for panic disorder. *Behaviour Research & Therapy*.

Schneier, F. R., Chin, S. J., Hollander, E., & Liebowitz, M. R. (1992). Fluoxetine in social phobia. *Journal of Clinical Psychopharmacology, 12*, 62–63.

Schneier, F. R., Goetz, D., Campeas, R., Fallon, B., Marshall, R., & Liebowitz, M. R. (1998). Placebo-controlled trial of moclobemide in social phobia. *British Journal of Psychiatry, 172*, 70–77.

Schneier, F. R., Leibowitz, M. R., Davies, S. O., Fairbanks, J., Hollander, E., Campeas, R., & Klein, D. F. (1990). Fluoxetine and panic disorder. *Journal of Clinical Psychopharmacology, 10*, 119–121.

Schneier, F. R., Saoud, J., Campeas, R., Fallon, B., Hollander, E., Coplan, J., & Liebowitz, M. R. (1993). Buspirone in social phobia. *Journal of Clinical Psychopharmacology, 13*, 251–255.

Scholing, A., & Emmelkamp, P. M. G. (1990). Social phobia: Nature and treatment. In H. Leitenberg (Ed.), *Handbook of social and evaluation anxiety* (pp. 269–324). New York: Plenum.

Scholing, A., & Emmelkamp, P. M. G. (1993). Cognitive and behavioral treatments of fear of blushing, sweating or trembling. *Behaviour Research and Therapy, 31*, 155–170.

Sharp, D. M., & Power, K. G. (1998). Psychologist, patient, and general practitioner ratings of outcome of pharmacological and psychological treatments for panic disorder and agoraphobia in primary care. *Behavioural and Cognitive Psychotherapy, 26*, 13–27.

Sharp, D. M., Power, K. G., Simpson, R. J., Swanson, V., Moodie, E., Anstee, J. A., & Ashford, J. J. (1996). Fluvoxamine, placebo, and cognitive behaviour therapy used alone and in combination in the treatment of panic disorder and agoraphobia. *Journal of Anxiety Disorders, 10*, 219–242.

Shaw, P. (1979). A comparison of three behavior therapies in the treatment of social phobia. *British Journal of Psychiatry, 134*, 620–623.

Sheehan, D. V. (1982). Panic attacks and phobias. *New England Journal of Medicine, 307*, 156–158.

Sheehan, D. V. (1985). Monoamine oxidase inhibitors and alprazolam in the treatment of panic disorder and agoraphobia. *Psychiatric Clinics of North America, 8*, 49–62.

Sheehan, D. V., Ballenger, J., & Jacobsen, G. (1980). Treatment of endogenous anxiety with phobic, hysterical, and hypochondriacal symptoms. *Archives of General Psychiatry, 37*, 51–59.

Speigel, D. A., Bruce, T. J., Gregg, S. F., & Nuzzarello, A. (1994). Does cognitive behavior therapy assist in slow-taper alprazolam discontinuation in panic disorder? *American Journal of Psychiatry, 151*, 876–881.

Stein, M. B., Liebowitz, M. R., Lydiard, B., Pitts, C. D., Bushnessl, W., & Gergel, I. (1998). Paroxetine treatment of generalized social phobia. *Journal of the American Medical Association, 280*, 708–713.

Stravynski, A., Marks, I., & Yule, W. (1982). Social skills problems in neurotic outpatients: Social skills training with and without cognitive modification. *Archives of General Psychiatry, 39*, 1379–1383.

Taylor, C. B., & Arnow, B. (1988). *The nature and treatment of anxiety disorders.* New York: Free Press.

Taylor, C. B., King, R., Margraf, J., Ehlers, A., Telch, M., Roth, W. T., & Agras, W. S. (1989). Use of medication and *in vivo* exposure in volunteers for panic disorder research. *American Journal of Psychiatry, 146*, 1423–1426.

Telch, M. J. (1988). Combined pharmacological and psychological treatments for panic sufferers. In S. Rachman & J. Maser (Eds.), *Panic: Psychological perspectives* (pp. 167–187). Hillsdale, NJ: Erlbaum.

Telch, M. J., & Lucas, R. A. (1994). Combined pharmacological and psychological treatment of panic disorder: Current status and future directions. In B. E. Wolfe & J. Maser (Eds.), *Treatment of panic disorder* (pp. 177–179). Washington, DC: American Psychiatric Press.

Telch, M. J., Lucas, J. A., Schmidt, N. B., Hanna, H. H., Jaimez, T. L., & Lucas, R. (1993). Group cognitive–behavioral treatment of panic disorder. *Behaviour Research and Therapy, 31*, 279–287.

Telch, M. J., Schmidt, N. B., Jaimez, L., Jacquin, K., & Harrington, P. (1995). The impact of cognitive–behavioral therapy on quality of life in panic disorder patients. *Journal of Consulting and Clinical Psychology, 63*, 823–830.

Telch, M. J., Tearnan, B. H., & Taylor, C. B. (1983). Antidepressant medication in the treatment of agoraphobia: A critical review. *Behaviour Research and Therapy, 21*, 505–517.

Tiller, J. W. G., Bouwer, C., & Behnke, K. (1997). Moclobemide for anxiety disorders: A focus on moclobemide for panic disorder. *International Clinical Psychopharmacology, 12*, S27–S30.

Trower, P., Yardley, K., Bryant, B., & Shaw, P. (1978). The treatment of social failure: A comparison of anxiety reduction and skills acquisition procedures on two social problems. *Behavior Modification, 2*, 41–60.

Turner, S. M., Beidel, D. C., & Jacob, R. G. (1994). Social phobia: A comparison of behavior therapy and atenolol. *Journal of Consulting and Clinical Psychology, 62*, 350–358.

Turner, S. M., Cooley-Quille, M. R., & Beidel, D. C. (1996). Behavioral and pharmacological treatment for social phobia. In M. Mavissakalian & R. F. Prien (Eds.), *Long-term treatments of anxiety disorders* (pp. 343–371). Washington, DC: American Psychiatric Press.

van Vleit, I., den Boer, J., & Westenberg, H. (1992). Psychopharmacological treatment of social phobia: Clinical and biochemical effects of brofaromine, a selective MAO-A inhibitor. *European Neuropsychopharmacology, 2*, 21–29.

Versiani, M., Nardi, A. E., Mundim, F. D., Alves, A., Liebowitz, M. R., & Amrein, R. (1992). Pharmacotherapy of social phobia: A controlled study with moclobemide and phenelzine. *British Journal of Psychiatry, 161*, 353–360.

Weissman, M. M. (1991). Panic disorder: Impact on quality of life. *Journal of Clinical Psychiatry, 52*, 6–8.

Whitehead, W. E., Blackwell, B., & Robinson, A. (1978). Effects of diazepam on phobic avoidance behavior and phobic anxiety. *Biological Psychiatry, 13*, 59–64.

Whitehead, W. E., Robinson, A., Blackwell, B., & Stutz, R. M. (1978). Flooding treatment of phobias: Does chronic diazepam increase effectiveness? *Journal of Behavior Therapy and Experimental Psychiatry, 9*, 219–225.

Williams, S. L., Dooseman, G., & Kleifield, E. (1984). Comparative effectiveness of guided mastery and exposure treatments for intractable phobias. *Journal of Consulting and Clinical Psychology, 52*, 505–518.

Wlazlo, Z., Schroeder-Hartwig, K., Hand, I., Kaiser, G., & Munchau, N. (1990). Exposure *in vivo* vs social skills training for social phobia: Long-term outcome and differential effects. *Behaviour Research and Therapy, 28,* 181–193.

Zitrin, C. M., Klein, D., & Woerner, M. G. (1978). Behavior therapy, supportive psychotherapy, imipramine, and phobias. *Archives of General Psychiatry, 35,* 303–321.

Zitrin, C. M., Klein, D. F., Woerner, M. G., & Ross, D. C. (1983). Treatment of phobias: Comparison of imipramine hydrochloride and placebo. *Archives of General Psychiatry, 40,* 125–138.

5

Combined Treatments of Insomnia

Charles M. Morin

Sleep disorders affect large segments of the population on a situational, recurrent, or chronic basis. They may involve trouble sleeping at night (insomnia), problems staying awake during the day (hypersomnia), or abnormal behaviors (night terrors, somnambulism) occurring during the sleep period. Insomnia is, by far, the most common sleep disorder and the most likely complaint to be encountered in clinical practice, either as a primary condition or in association with psychological or medical disorders. Psychological and pharmacological treatments for insomnia have been extensively evaluated, but each treatment modality has its own limitations, and no single approach is effective with all patients and for all subtypes of insomnia. Despite repeated calls from several panels of experts for greater integration of behavioral and pharmacological therapies (National Institutes of Health, 1984, 1991, 1996), there are still few evidence-based guidelines for practitioners to determine how to best integrate these treatments in the clinical management of insomnia. In this chapter I summarize the current status of psychopharmacological therapies for insomnia, with a discussion of their benefits and risks, and their respective advantages and limitations. Guidelines for selecting among psychological, pharmacological, and combined therapies are provided, and optimal models for their integration are discussed.

Epidemiology

Insomnia is among the most frequent complaints brought to the attention of health care practitioners. Epidemiological surveys indicate that between 9% and 15% of the adult population complains of chronic insomnia, with an additional 15%–20% reporting occasional trouble sleeping (Ford & Kamerow, 1989; Mellinger, Balter, & Uhlenhuth, 1985). Insomnia is more prevalent among women, older adults, and patients with medical or psychiatric disorders. Chronic insomnia is not a benign problem; it can adversely affect a person's life, causing substantial psychosocial, occupational, health, and economic repercussions (Simon & VonKorff, 1997). For

Preparation of this chapter was supported in part by Grant MH 55469 from the National Institute of Mental Health.

example, individuals with chronic sleep disturbances report more psychological distress and impairments of daytime functioning relative to good sleepers; in addition, they take more sick leave and use health care resources more often than good sleepers. Persistent insomnia is also associated with prolonged use of hypnotic medications and with increased risks of major depression (Becker, Brown, & Jamieson, 1991; Ford & Kamerow, 1989; Mellinger et al., 1985; Vollrath, Wicki, & Angst, 1989).

Despite its high prevalence and negative psychosocial and economic impact, insomnia remains for the most part untreated. In a National Institute of Mental Health survey of psychotherapeutic drug use, 7% of the respondents, and only 15% of those reporting serious insomnia, had used either a prescribed or over-the-counter sleeping aid within the previous year (Mellinger et al., 1985). Most patients who decide to initiate treatment will resort to a host of self-help remedies (e.g., alcohol, over-the-counter drugs) of limited value; when insomnia is brought to professional attention, typically to a primary care physician, treatment is usually limited to pharmacotherapy. Nearly 50% of patients consulting for insomnia in medical practice are prescribed a hypnotic medication, and the majority of those will continue using their medications almost daily for more than 1 year (Hohagen et al., 1993; Ohayon & Caulet, 1996). Although health care professionals are receptive to nondrug therapies for insomnia, specific behavioral interventions, other than general sleep hygiene advises (e.g., reduce caffeine and exercise more), are not well known and are infrequently used in clinical practice (Rothenberg, 1992).

Evaluation and Diagnostic Considerations

Insomnia is a heterogeneous complaint reflecting impaired quality, duration, or efficiency of sleep. It may involve difficulties initiating sleep; trouble staying asleep, such as frequent or prolonged awakenings; or early morning awakening with an inability to return to sleep. The primary complaint may also involve nonrestorative sleep or diminished sleep quality, resulting in daytime fatigue and low energy. In treatment outcome research, insomnia is usually operationalized as a latency to sleep onset and/ or wake-after-sleep onset greater than 30 minutes, with a corresponding sleep efficiency (ratio of time asleep to time spent in bed) lower than 85%. Insomnia may be situational, lasting a few days and often associated with stressful life events; episodic; or evolve into more chronic sleep difficulties persisting over months or even years (Morin, 1993).

Insomnia is often a symptom of an underlying medical or psychiatric condition or another sleep disorder, but it can also be a syndrome or a disorder in itself. According to the *Diagnostic and Statistical Manual of Mental Disorders* (4th ed., *DSM–IV*; American Psychiatric Association, 1994), the essential feature of primary insomnia is a complaint of difficulty initiating or maintaining sleep, or nonrestorative sleep, that lasts for at least 1 month and causes clinically significant distress or impairment in social, occupational, or other important areas of functioning. The sleep disturbance does not occur exclusively during the course of another sleep disorder or mental disorder and is not due to the direct physiological effects of a substance or a general medical condition. The diagnosis of primary insomnia is often made by exclusion (i.e., after ruling out several other conditions); in addition, it is based exclusively on the subjective complaint of an individual, which can be problematic because there may be significant discrepancies between subjective reports and objective recordings of sleep. A diagnosis of secondary insomnia is made when the sleep disturbance is judged to be related temporally and causally to another psychiatric, medical, or sleep disorder. Because sleep disturbances are common features of other mental disorders, an additional diagnosis of insomnia related to another mental disorder is made only when the sleep disturbance is a predominant complaint and is sufficiently severe to warrant independent clinical attention. Some estimates suggest that between 35% and 40% of all insomnia cases are associated with an underlying psychopathology, with affective and anxiety disorders being the two most common comorbid psychological disorders (Buysse et al., 1994; Morin & Ware, 1996). At times, it may be difficult to determine whether insomnia is primary or secondary to another condition, such as major depression or generalized anxiety disorder. Insomnia may also be due to a medical condition (e.g., hyperthyroidism) or a chronic pain syndrome, or it may be associated with prescribed medications (e.g., some beta blockers or activating antidepressants) that may secondarily interfere with sleep. Finally, it is also possible that insomnia is the presenting complaint but that the main problem is with an underlying sleep disorder, such as restless legs syndrome/periodic limb movements or sleep apnea. Whenever insomnia is secondary to another psychiatric, medical, or sleep disorder, treatment should focus initially on the underlying condition.

The differential diagnosis of insomnia requires a detailed and multifaceted evaluation, involving a clinical interview; psychological screening assessment; a physical examination; daily sleep monitoring and, when an underlying sleep disorder (e.g., restless legs/periodic limb movements, sleep apnea) is suspected, a sleep laboratory evaluation. A detailed sleep history is particularly useful to elicit the type of complaint, its duration and course, exacerbating and alleviating factors, and so on. In light of the high comorbidity between sleep disturbances and psychopathology, the history should identify relative onset and course of each condition in order to establish whether the sleep disorder is primary or secondary in nature. As part of the clinical evaluation it is also very important to obtain a medical history as well as a detailed history of alcohol and drug use and use of both prescribed and over-the-counter medications (for more information about assessment, see Morin, 1993; Morin & Edinger, 1997; Spielman & Glovinsky, 1991).

Pharmacotherapy

Several classes of medications are used in the treatment of insomnia. They include the benzodiazepines (BZD), non-BZD hypnotics, antidepressants, and over-the-counter medications. There are six BZDs that are specifically marketed as hypnotics in the United States or in Canada: flurazepam, temazepam, triazolam, estazolam, quazepam, and (in Canada only) nitrazepam. Several other BZDs (e.g., lorazepam, clonazepam, oxazepam), which are primarily marketed as anxiolytics, are frequently used for insomnia as well. In addition, there are three newer hypnotics (zolpidem, zaleplon, and zopiclone) which, although non-BZD agents, act primarily on the same BZD and GABA (Gamma Amino Butyric Acid) receptors. Unlike the true BZDs, which all have hypnotic, anxiolytic, and anticonvulsant properties, these newer drugs may have more selective/specific hypnotic effects. In Table 5.1 are presented a list of BZD-receptor agents commonly used in the management of insomnia.

Antidepressants with sedating properties (e.g., trazodone, amitriptyline, doxepin) are often used in the treatment of insomnia (Walsh & Engelhardt, 1992). These agents are used in much smaller doses for treating primary insomnia (e.g., 10–20 mg of amitriptyline) than are those prescribed for depression. Although numerous studies have documented the effects of antidepressants on the sleep of individuals with major depression, few studies have examined the efficacy and safety of those agents when used as hypnotics with nondepressed insomniacs (e.g., Hohagen et al., 1994; Nierenberg, Adler, Peselow, Zomberg, & Rosenthal, 1994; Scharf & Sachais, 1990). For this reason, antidepressants are usually not recommended as the first line of treatment for primary insomnia. Antihistamine (e.g., diphenhydramine) is the active ingredient of most over-the-counter medicines that are advertised and sold to promote sleep (e.g., Sominex, Nytol, Sleep-Eze, Unisom). Most of those agents produce drowsiness, but there is limited evidence that they are efficacious in the treatment of insomnia (Rickels et al., 1983). Melatonin is another popular agent

Table 5.1. Benzodiazepine-Receptor Agents Commonly Prescribed for Insomnia

Benzodiazepines	Equivalent dosage (mg)	Usual dosage (mg)	Half-life (hr)[a]
Bromazepam[b] (Lectopam®)	3	1.5–6	8–19
Clonazepam (Klonopin®)	0.25	0.5–2	20–60
Estazolam (ProSom®)	1	1.0–2.0	8–24
Flurazepam (Dalmane®)	15	15–30	48–100
Lorazepam (Ativan®)	1	0.5–2	10–20
Nitrazepam[b] (Mogadon®)	10	5–10	16–18
Oxazepam (Serax®)	15	10–30	5–10
Temazepam (Restoril®)	15	7.5–30	8–17
Triazolam (Halcion®)	0.25	0.125–0.25	2–4
Quazepam (Doral®)	15	7.5–30	40–120
Zaleplon (Sonata®)	5	5–10	1
Zopiclone[b] (Imovane®)	3.75	3.75–7.5	4–6
Zolpidem (Ambien®)	5	5–10	1.5–5

[a]May be longer in older adults.   [b]Not available in the United States.

that is increasingly used as a sleep aid. It is a naturally occurring hormone produced by the pineal gland at night. Although it may be promising for some forms of circadian sleep disturbances associated with shift work and jet lag, the benefits of melatonin for insomnia are equivocal, and the adverse effects with long-term usage are unknown (Mendelson, 1997). Thus, although it is widely available in over-the-counter preparations, the clinical use of melatonin for insomnia is premature at this time. There are several other natural health products (e.g., St. John's Wort, Valerian) that are promoted as sleep aids but for which there is little empirical support.

Most sleep experts agree that, when a sleep medication is indicated for insomnia, it should be a BZD-receptor agent (BRAs, i.e., BZDs, zaleplon, zopiclone, and zolpidem). The remaining discussion will focus on those agents. Hypnotic medications, such as the BZDs and the newer non-BZD agents, present a lower risk of physical dependence and lethal overdose than older drugs, such as chloral hydrate and the barbiturates (American Psychiatric Association, 1990; Roy-Byrne & Cowley, 1991). Their therapeutic, abuse-potential, and side-effect profiles are comparable, although hypnotics with rapid onset and short-to-intermediate duration of actions may present the highest ratio of benefits to residual effects (Roth & Roehrs, 1991). The main differences among the BZD-receptor agents are their pharmacokinetic properties: absorption, distribution, and elimination. The rate of absorption and rate of distribution determine the speed of onset of the drug effect; elimination half-life and rate of distribution determine the length of time during which the drug effects persist. Combined with the dosage, these properties mediate the effects of the drugs on sleep and on daytime functioning (Greenblatt, 1991).

Evidence for Efficacy

Controlled clinical trials have shown that all BRAs are more effective than placebo in the acute and short-term phases of insomnia treatment (Holbrook, Crowther, Lotter, Cheng, & King, 2000; Kupfer & Reynolds, 1997; Nowell et al., 1997; Parrino & Terzano, 1996; Roth & Roehrs, 1991). Hypnotic medications improve sleep continuity and efficiency through a reduction of sleep onset latency and time awake after sleep onset. These agents also reduce the number of awakenings and stage shifts through the night. Their effects on sleep stages vary with the specific class of medications. All hypnotic drugs increase Stage 1 and Stage 2 sleep. BZDs tend to reduce the proportion of slow-wave (Stages 3–4) sleep and, to a lesser extent, REM sleep. These last changes are less pronounced with zolpidem and zopiclone (Hoehns & Perry, 1993; Scharf, Roth, Vogel, & Walsh, 1994; Wadworth & McTavish, 1993).

In a recent meta-analysis of 22 placebo-controlled trials ($n = 1,894$), BZDs and zolpidem were found to produce reliable improvements of sleep onset latency (mean effect size = .56), number of awakenings (.65), total sleep time (.71), and sleep quality (.62; Nowell et al., 1997). Another meta-analysis (Holbrook et al., 2000) showed that BZDs reduced sleep latency by a modest 10 minutes and increased total sleep duration by about 1 hour. Thus, hypnotic medications are efficacious for the acute and short-term management of insomnia. In addition, there is high level of satisfaction with BZD treatment among patients who are willing to take such medications (Balter & Uhlenhuth, 1992). However, because the median treatment duration in controlled studies is only 1 week (range: 4–35 days), and follow-ups are virtually absent, the long-term efficacy of hypnotic medications remains unknown.

Risks and Limitations

The main limitations of hypnotic medications are their residual effects the next day and their associated risks of tolerance and dependence. The most common residual effects are daytime drowsiness; dizziness or lightheadedness; and impairments of cognitive and psychomotor functions, including memory impairments and slower reaction times (Holbrook et al., 2000; Johnson & Chernik, 1982). In general, hypnotic medications have relatively few side effects, when used at the appropriate doses. Also, short-acting agents have less residual effects the next day than long-acting ones. Long-acting BZDs (e.g., flurazepam and quazepam) are more likely to produce next-day residual effects, such as drowsiness and impairments of psychomotor and cognitive functions (Roehrs, Kribbs, Zorick, & Roth, 1986; Roth & Roehrs, 1991). These residual effects are more pronounced in elderly people because of slower drug metabolism as a consequence of aging (Hart, Morin, & Best, 1995). Long-acting BZDs result in an increased rate of falls and hip fractures (Ray, 1992) and motor vehicle accidents in the elderly population (Hemmelgarn, Suissa, Huang, Boivin, & Pinard, 1997). BZDs can cause respiratory depression, a problem that is more likely to occur in people who already have severe sleep apnea or chronic obstructive pulmonary disease. Another potential residual effect is anterograde amnesia, a problem that is more likely with shorter acting agents. When used on a prolonged basis, hypnotics may lead to tolerance, and it may be necessary to increase the dosage to maintain therapeutic effects. This tolerance effect, however, varies across agents and individuals, and some people may remain on the same dosage for prolonged periods of time. Whether this prolonged usage is a sign of continued effectiveness or of fear of discontinuing the medication is unclear. Rebound insomnia is a common problem associated with discontinuation of BZD hypnotics; it is more pronounced with short-acting drugs and can be attenuated with a gradual tapering regimen (Greenblatt, 1991). Zolpidem and zopiclone may produce less rebound insomnia on discontinuation (Hoehns & Perry, 1993; Wadworth & McTavish, 1993). Finally, all sleep-promoting medications, prescribed or over-the-counter, carry some risk of dependence (American Psychiatric Association, 1990), which is often more psychological than physical (Morin, 1993).

Clinical Indications and Contraindications

The main indication for using hypnotic medications is situational insomnia, usually arising from acute stress, medical illness or hospitalization, and changes in the sleep environment or sleep schedules (jet lag, shift work; National Institutes of Health, 1984). For chronic insomnia, a short-term trial of sleep medications may be indicated during the initial treatment phase in order to break the cycle of sleeplessness and emotional distress. For individuals who are unresponsive to psychological interventions, hypnotic medications may prove a useful alternative. Sleep medications may also be a useful adjunct for insomnia secondary to psychopathology (e.g., major depression and generalized anxiety disorders), although the main focus of treatment should be on the underlying condition. The same principle applies to the management of insomnia associated with another sleep disorder (e.g., restless legs/periodic limb movements) or with a medical condition (e.g., pain).

Hypnotic medications are contraindicated among patients who are actively abusing alcohol or drugs. BZDs should be avoided in patients with severe sleep apnea because it may worsen the breathing problem and its associated cardiovascular complications. Sleep medications are also contraindicated in pregnant women and in individuals who are on call (e.g., nurses, fireman, etc.) and might need to awake rapidly and go to work during their usual sleep period. Hypnotics would then interfere with alertness and cognitive functions. Use of sleep medications should be monitored carefully among older adults (National Institutes of Health, 1991) and patients with hepatic, renal, or pulmonary diseases and among patients with severe psychiatric conditions, such as psychoses and borderline personality disorders (Stepanski, Zorick, & Roth, 1991).

Prescribing Guidelines

Selection of a hypnotic medication is partly dependent on the nature of the insomnia complaint, the individual's age, and the presence of any associated medical or psychological condition. The best hypnotic drug will promote sleep at night and will have no or minimal residual effects the next day. As such, speed of onset of action and duration of effects are two important considerations in selecting a sleep medication. Drugs with a rapid absorption rate and a short half-life (e.g., zolpidem, zalephon, triazolam) are better suited for sleep-onset insomnia, whereas those with an intermediate half-life (temazepam, lorazepam, oxazepam) are more effective for sleep-maintenance problems. Drugs with a long duration of action (e.g., flurazepam) should be avoided in older adults because they take longer to metabolize drugs that affect the central nervous system and are more likely to experience daytime residual effects. On the other hand, this residual sedation may be therapeutic for a younger person with significant daytime anxiety. In this latter case, a long-acting agent may promote sleep at night and produce residual anxiolytic effects the next day.

A general principle that applies to all hypnotic medications is to use the lowest effective dosage for the shortest period of time. Recommended dosages for the various hypnotic drugs are provided in Table 5.1. It is always best to start with the smallest dosage and to increase it only if necessary. Higher dosages will prolong the duration of action and are more likely to produce adverse effects. A drug that is available in different dosages may be easier to taper at the end of treatment. The standard recommendation is to use sleep medications only as needed (prn schedule) and not to exceed two or three times per week (National Institutes of Health, 1984, 1991). Although this pattern of intermittent usage may prevent tolerance, it may also promote dependency through a negative conditioning process. For example, after being awake for more than an hour (an aversive stimulus), the individual who takes a sleeping pill only occasionally is likely to associate this behavior with a quick relief from sleeplessness. As such, the pill-taking behavior is negatively reinforced and is likely to recur in the near future. For this reason, some clinicians have suggested to patients to take sleep medications every night, over a limited period time, in order to avoid reinforcing this conditioning between sleeplessness and the pill-taking behavior (Stepanski et al., 1991). For the same reason, it may be preferable to use sleep medication at a predetermined time (i.e., bedtime) rather than simply waiting 1 or 2 hours of wakefulness to get back up to take the medication.

Duration of treatment is also dependent on the course of insomnia. For acute insomnia, sleep medications may be used for several consecutive nights. Treatment duration ideally should not exceed 4 weeks, to avoid tolerance and minimize the risk of dependency. If insomnia is a recurring problem and is predictable (e.g., when traveling), it may be necessary to repeat this treatment regimen periodically. For chronic insomnia, sleep medications may be used for a few nights (up to 2–3 weeks) to break the cycle of performance anxiety, but the main focus of therapy should be non-pharmacological. Because insomnia is often a recurrent problem (Mendelson, 1995; Vollrath et al., 1989), it may be necessary to develop new treatment maintenance models, such as intermittent-dosing strategies. Although this treatment maintenance model has yielded interesting results with antidepressant medications for major depression, it remains to be validated for insomnia treated with BZD hypnotics.

In summary, hypnotic medications are effective for the acute and short-term management of insomnia; they have a quick onset of action, often producing significant therapeutic benefits on the very first night of usage. These benefits last several nights and, in some cases, up to a few weeks. There is currently little evidence of sustained sleep benefits on drug discontinuation or of continued efficacy with prolonged usage. No single agent can achieve complete control of insomnia. In addition, all benzodiazepine hypnotics carry some risk of dependence, particularly with prolonged usage. As several panels of insomnia experts have already concluded, the primary indication for hypnotic medications is for situational sleep difficulties; their role in the clinical management of chronic insomnia should be as an adjunct to behavioral interventions (National Institutes of Health, 1984, 1991, 1996).

Psychological Therapies

Recognition that psychological and behavioral factors play an important mediating role in insomnia has led to the use of more than a dozen nonpharmacological interventions (mostly cognitive–behavioral in content) for treating this condition. Treatment modalities that have been adequately evaluated in controlled clinical trials include stimulus control therapy, sleep restriction, relaxation-based interventions, cognitive therapy, and sleep hygiene education. These treatments seek to modify maladaptive sleep habits, reduce autonomic and cognitive arousal, alter dysfunctional beliefs and attitudes about sleep, and educate patients about healthier sleep practices (see Table 5.2). Cognitive–behavioral interventions are structured, short term, and sleep focused. Treatment duration typically lasts 4–6 hours and is implemented over a period of 4–8 weeks. A summary of these treatments is provided next; more extensive descriptions are available from other sources (Espie, 1991; Hauri, 1991; Lichstein & Morin, 2000; Morin, 1993).

Relaxation-Based Interventions

Relaxation is the most commonly used nonpharmacological therapy for insomnia. There are several forms of relaxation-based interventions. Some methods (e.g., progressive muscle relaxation, autogenic training, biofeed-

Table 5.2. Psychological Treatments for Insomnia

Therapy	Description
Relaxation training	Methods aimed at reducing somatic tension (e.g., progressive muscle relaxation, autogenic training, biofeedback) or intrusive thoughts (e.g., imagery training, hypnosis, thought stopping) interfering with sleep.
Stimlus control	Go to bed only when sleepy, get out of bed when unable to sleep, use the bed/bedroom for sleep only (no reading, watching tv, etc.), arise at the same time every morning, no napping.
Sleep restriction	Curtail time in bed to the actual sleep time, thereby creating mild sleep deprivation, which results in more consolidated and more efficient sleep.
Cognitive therapy	Psychotherapeutic method aimed at changing dysfunctional beliefs and attitudes about sleep and insomnia (e.g., unrealistic sleep expectations, fear of the consequences of insomnia).
Sleep hygiene	Avoid stimulants (e.g., caffeine and nicotine) and alcohol around bedtime; do not eat heavy or spicy meals too close to bedtime; exercise regularly but not too late in the evening; maintain a dark, quiet, and comfortable sleep environment.

back) focus primarily on reducing somatic arousal (e.g., muscle tension), whereas attention-focusing procedures (e.g., imagery training, meditation, thought stopping) target mental arousal in the forms of worries, intrusive thoughts, or a racing mind. Biofeedback is another self-regulation method designed to train a patient to control some physiological parameters (e.g., frontalis electromyographic tension) through visual or auditory feedback.

Stimulus Control Therapy

Chronic insomniacs often become apprehensive around bedtime and associate the bed or bedroom with frustration and arousal. This conditioning process may take place over several weeks or even months outside of the patient's awareness. Stimulus control therapy consists of a set of instructions designed to reassociate temporal (bedtime) and environmental (bed and bedroom) stimuli with rapid sleep onset. This is accomplished by postponing bedtime until sleep is imminent, getting out of bed when unable to sleep, and curtailing sleep-incompatible activities (overt and covert). The second objective of stimulus control is to establish a regular circadian sleep–wake rhythm by enforcing a strict adherence to a regular arising time and avoidance of daytime naps (Bootzin, Epstein, & Wood, 1991).

Sleep Restriction

Poor sleepers often increase their time in bed in a misguided effort to provide more opportunity for sleep, a strategy that is more likely to result in sleep that is fragmented and of poor quality. Sleep restriction therapy consists of curtailing the amount of time spent in bed to the actual amount of time asleep (Spielman, Saskin, & Thorpy, 1987). Time in bed is subsequently adjusted on the basis of sleep efficiency ([SE] ratio of total sleep/time in bed × 100%) for a given period of time (usually a week). For example, if a person reports sleeping an average of 6 hours/night out of 8 hours spent in bed, the initial prescribed sleep window (i.e., from initial bedtime to final arising time) would be 6 hours. The subsequent allowable time in bed is increased by about 20 minutes for a given week when SE exceeds 85%, decreased by the same amount of time when SE is lower than 80%, and kept stable when SE falls between 80% and 85%. Adjustments are made weekly until an optimal sleep duration is achieved. Sleep restriction produces a mild state of sleep deprivation and may alleviate sleep anticipatory anxiety. To prevent excessive daytime sleepiness, time in bed should not be restricted to less than 5 hours/night in bed.

Cognitive Therapy

Cognitive therapy seeks to alter dysfunctional sleep cognitions (e.g., beliefs, attitudes, expectations, attributions). The basic premise of this approach is that appraisal of a given situation (sleeplessness) can trigger negative emotions (fear, anxiety) that are incompatible with sleep. For example, when a person is unable to sleep at night and begins thinking about the possible consequences of sleep loss on the next day's performance, this can set off a spiral reaction and feed into the vicious cycle of insomnia, emotional distress, and more sleep disturbances. Cognitive therapy is designed to identify dysfunctional cognitions and reframe them into more adaptive substitutes in order to short-circuit the self-fulfilling nature of this vicious cycle. Specific treatment targets include unrealistic expectations ("I must get my 8 hours of sleep every night"), faulty causal attributions ("my insomnia is entirely due to a biochemical imbalance"), amplification of the consequences of insomnia ("insomnia may have serious consequences on my health"), and misconceptions about healthy sleep practices (Morin, 1993). These factors play an important mediating role in insomnia, particularly in exacerbating emotional arousal, performance anxiety, and learned helplessness as related to sleeplessness.

Sleep Hygiene Education

Sleep hygiene education is concerned with health practices (e.g., diet, exercise, substance use) and environmental factors (e.g., light, noise, temperature) that may interfere with sleep (Hauri, 1991). Although these factors are rarely of sufficient severity to be the primary cause of insomnia, they may potentiate sleep difficulties caused by other factors. Sleep hygiene is typically incorporated with other interventions to minimize interference from poor sleep hygiene practices. Basic recommendations involve avoidance of stimulants (e.g., caffeine, nicotine) and alcohol; exercising regularly; and minimizing noise, light, and excessive temperature. Some may also include advice about maintaining a regular sleep schedule and avoiding napping, although these instructions are part of the standard stimulus control therapy.

There are several additional nonpharmacological interventions that have been used in the treatment of insomnia, including paradoxical intention, acupuncture, ocular relaxation, electrosleep therapy, and so on. Although these methods may be useful in clinical practice, they have not been evaluated as extensively in controlled clinical trials as the interventions just described. Psychotherapy has also been advocated to address predisposing factors to insomnia, but there has been no controlled evaluation of such a recommendation.

Evidence for Efficacy

Two meta-analyses recently summarized the findings of more than 50 clinical studies (involving more than 2,000 patients) of nonpharmacological interventions for insomnia (Morin, Culbert, & Schwartz, 1994; Murtagh & Greenwood, 1995). The data indicate that behavioral treatment (lasting an average of 4–6 weeks) produces reliable changes in several sleep parameters of individuals with chronic insomnia. For example, almost identical effect sizes have been reported in both meta-analyses for sleep onset latency (.87 and .88), the main target symptom in studies of sleep-onset insomnia. An effect size of this magnitude indicates that, on average, insomnia patients are better off (fall asleep faster) after treatment than about 80% of untreated control individuals. Reliable effect sizes, falling in the range of what is conventionally defined as moderate to large, have also been reported for other sleep parameters, including total sleep time (.42–.49), number of awakenings (.53–.63), duration of awakenings (.65), and sleep quality ratings (.94). These effect sizes are comparable to those reported with BZDs and zolpidem (Nowell et al., 1997). In terms of absolute changes, sleep onset latency is reduced from an average of 60–65 minutes at baseline to about 35 minutes at posttreatment. The duration of awakenings is similarly decreased from an average of 70 minutes at baseline to about 38 minutes following treatment. Total sleep time is increased by a modest 30 minutes, from 6 hours to 6.5 hours after treatment, but perceived sleep quality is significantly enhanced with treatment. Overall, the magnitude of these changes indicates that between 70% and 80% of treated patients benefit from treatment. These results represent conservative estimates of efficacy because they are based on average effect sizes computed across all treatment modalities.

Numerous studies have compared the relative effectiveness of various psychological treatments. In general, but not always, stimulus control therapy and sleep restriction have been shown the most effective single-treatment modalities. However, most psychological interventions are not incompatible with each other and can be effectively combined (Lichstein & Riedel, 1994). The best outcome is obtained from multifaceted interventions that incorporate behavioral, educational, and cognitive components (Jacobs, Benson, & Friedman, 1993; Morin, Kowatch, Barry, & Walton, 1993).

Durability and Generalizability of Changes

Cognitive–behavioral treatment for insomnia produces stable therapeutic changes over time. Posttreatment improvements of sleep parameters and satisfaction with those changes are well maintained up to 24 months later. In addition, although increases in total sleep time are fairly modest during the initial treatment period, these gains are typically enhanced at follow-ups, with total sleep time often exceeding 6.5 hours. Although promising, these data must be interpreted cautiously, because less than 50% of studies have reported long-term follow-ups and, among those that have, attrition rates increase substantially over time.

Another important issue that arises is whether the findings obtained in those studies would generalize to patients typically seen in clinical practice, that is, those with comorbid medical or psychiatric disorders. The large majority of behavioral (and pharmacological) treatment studies have focused on primary insomnia in otherwise healthy and medication-free patients. Findings from three uncontrolled clinical case series (Chambers

& Alexander, 1992; Jacobs, Benson, & Friedman, 1996; Morin, Stone, McDonald, & Jones, 1994) have yielded promising results suggesting that patients with medical and psychiatric conditions, or even those using hypnotic medications, can benefit from behavioral treatment for sleep disturbances. Because those studies have a more naturalistic focus and are not as rigorously controlled as randomized controlled trials, these conclusions are only tentative at this time.

The evidence indicates that behavioral treatment produces reliable and durable sleep improvements in primary insomnia. Although the majority (70%–80%) of treated patients benefit from treatment, only a minority of individuals become good sleepers, and a small proportion of patients do not respond at all to treatment. Nonetheless, cognitive–behavioral treatment often leads to a greater sense of personal control over sleep and a reduced need for hypnotic medications. Behavioral interventions require more time to improve sleep patterns relative to drug therapy, but these changes are fairly durable over time.

Integrated Psychopharmacological Approaches

Despite the extensive literature reporting on the separate effects of behavioral and pharmacological therapies, only a handful of studies have directly evaluated the combined or differential effects of those treatment modalities (Hauri, 1997; McClusky, Milby, Switzer, Williams, & Wooten, 1991; Milby et al., 1993; Morin, Colecchi, Stone, Sood, & Brink, 1999). Three of those studies compared triazolam with relaxation (McClusky et al., 1991; Milby et al., 1993) or sleep hygiene (Hauri, 1997), and the other one (Morin et al., 1999) compared cognitive–behavior therapy (CBT) with temazepam. The data from those studies collectively indicate that both treatment modalities are effective in the short term. Drug therapy produces quicker and slightly better results in the acute phase (first week) of treatment, whereas behavioral and drug therapies are equally effective in the short-term interval (4–8 weeks). Combined interventions appear to have a slight advantage over a single-treatment modality during the initial course of treatment. Furthermore, long-term effects have been fairly consistent for the single-treatment modalities but more equivocal for the combined approach. For instance, sleep improvements are well sustained after behavioral treatment, and those obtained with hypnotic drugs are quickly lost after discontinuation of the medication. Combined biobehavioral interventions may yield a slightly better outcome during initial treatment, but long-term effects are more equivocal. Studies with short-term follow-ups (<1 month) indicate that a combined intervention (i.e., triazolam plus relaxation) produces more sustained benefits than drug therapy alone (McClusky et al., 1991; Milby et al., 1993), whereas the only two investigations with follow-ups exceeding 6 months in duration reported more variable long-term outcomes among patients receiving a combined intervention relative to those treated with behavioral treatment alone (Hauri, 1997; Morin et al., 1999). It appears that some of those patients retain their initial sleep improvements, whereas others return to their baseline values. Thus, despite the intuitive appeal in combining drug and nondrug interventions, it is not entirely clear when, how, and for whom it is indicated to combine behavioral and drug treatments for insomnia.

An integrated biobehavioral intervention should theoretically optimize treatment outcome by capitalizing on the more immediate and potent effects of drug therapy and the more sustained effects of psychological interventions. In practice, however, the limited evidence available is not entirely clear as to whether a combined intervention has an additive or subtractive effect on long-term outcome (Kendall & Lipman, 1991; Morin, 1996). In light of the mediating role of psychological factors in chronic insomnia, behavioral and attitudinal changes may be essential to sustain improvements in sleep patterns. When combining behavioral and drug therapies, patients' attributions of the initial benefits may be critical in determining long-term outcomes. Attribution of therapeutic benefits to the drug alone, without integration of self-management skills, may place a patient at significantly greater risk for relapse once the drug is discontinued. Additional research is needed to evaluate the effects of single and combined drug and nondrug treatments for insomnia and to examine potential mechanisms of changes mediating short- and long-term outcomes. Likewise, clinical strategies to facilitate discontinuation of hypnotic medications are currently under evaluation (Morin et al., 1998).

Clinical Guidelines for Selecting Single Versus Combined Interventions

Despite the limited empirical evidence available on the integration of behavioral and pharmacological approaches for insomnia, some general principles can guide practitioners in selecting optimal treatment strategies. These guidelines are functions of several factors, including the nature (primary vs. secondary), duration, and course of insomnia; the presence of comorbid psychological or medical conditions; prior usage of hypnotic medications and, importantly, consumer's preference.

For acute and situational insomnia, treatment should focus on alleviating the precipitating factors (i.e., stress, medical illness) when possible. In some instances (e.g., bereavement, divorce, jet lag) a hypnotic medication may be necessary and very useful to alleviate sleep difficulties. For chronic and primary insomnia, behavioral treatment should represent the main intervention, with hypnotic medications serving as an adjunct.

The presence of comorbid medical or psychological disorders is another factor to consider in selecting the most appropriate treatment for insomnia. Several contraindications (e.g., renal and hepatic diseases) to using hypnotic medications were discussed earlier in this chapter. When insomnia is associated with another psychopathology or with another medical condition, the general principle is to treat the underlying condition first. However, this is not always possible; neither does this approach always resolve the concurrent sleep difficulties. For example, treatment of chronic pain or major depression does not always alleviate the often-associated sleep disturbances. In such instances, it may be necessary to introduce a treatment, behavioral or pharmacological, that focuses directly on sleep disturbances.

Prior usage of hypnotic drugs is another important consideration in selecting the most appropriate treatment for insomnia. Two different scenarios are likely to arise in clinical practice. The first one, most commonly encountered by psychologists, involves a patient who has already been on hypnotic medications for a prolonged period and is unable to discontinue his or her sleeping pills. In such an instance of hypnotic-dependent insomnia, the most appropriate intervention would involve a gradual tapering from hypnotic medications, accompanied by CBT (Morin et al., 1998). In the second scenario, a patient may have used hypnotic medications only infrequently or not at all in the past. In such instance, a short-term trial on hypnotic medications could be very useful during the initial period of treatment in order to provide some immediate relief and reduce performance anxiety. CBT would be initiated simultaneously and maintained on drug withdrawal.

Patient preference is another important factor for selecting psychological and pharmacological therapy. Regardless of how effective a treatment is, if a patient fails to comply with the clinician's recommendation its clinical utility will be rather limited. Thus, if a patient is unwilling to use a sleep medication, behavioral interventions may be the only alternative left. Likewise, if a patient is unwilling to invest time and efforts in the behavioral approach, medication may be a better choice of treatment. Although behavioral approaches are generally more acceptable than drug treatments to patients with insomnia (Morin, Gaulier, Barry, & Kowatch, 1992), this issue of treatment preference needs to be addressed systematically when discussing the various treatment options with a patient.

Data are still limited on how to best integrate sleep medications and behavioral interventions. The few studies available on this issue have initiated and discontinued drug and nondrug approaches at the same time. To take full advantages of the quicker results from drug therapy and the more sustained effects of behavioral intervention, a sequential approach might be preferable to a combined (concurrent) approach. Unlike with a combined method, in which both treatments are initiated and discontinued at the same time, in a sequential approach drug treatment is initiated first and gradually discontinued while the behavioral intervention is implemented concurrently. This method would ensure that patients are still in treatment after drug tapering; it would provide them with the opportunity to fully integrate newly learned self-management skills, especially at a time when rebound insomnia is likely to reinforce the belief that medication is needed indefinitely.

Criteria for Outcome Evaluation

There is currently no consensus as to how treatment effectiveness should be measured and what the optimal outcome should be when treating insomnia. Clinical studies have focused almost exclusively on symptom reductions, that is, reduction of the time required to fall asleep or the frequency and duration of nocturnal awakenings and increase in the amount of total sleep time. Although these sleep indexes are important in evaluating outcome, insomnia is more than just a complaint about poor sleep. It is often the emotional distress about sleep loss and the fear of its consequences (e.g., fatigue, impaired daytime functioning), rather than insomnia per se, that prompt individuals to seek treatment. Thus, an important marker of progress should be the perception of control over sleep. Likewise, measures of functional impairments, mood disturbances, psychological well-being, and quality of life, and even use of health-care services and hypnotic medications, would provide more clinically meaningful indexes to capture the impact of treatment.

Summary and Conclusion

Psychological and pharmacological therapies produce reliable changes in several sleep parameters, but each treatment modality has its own advantages and limitations, and neither approach is effective for all patients and all subtypes of insomnia. Some patients fail to respond to treatment, regardless of its nature, and the majority of responders do not necessarily become "good sleepers." In terms of trajectory of changes, drug therapy produces acute changes in sleep patterns, but these benefits are typically not maintained after discontinuation of the medication. Given that insomnia is often a recurrent condition, short-term drug treatment is unlikely to be sufficient for the clinical management of this condition. Behavioral interventions are more time consuming and take longer to produce therapeutic benefits. However, these gains are well sustained over time. Combined approaches have yielded short-term outcomes that are either equivalent to or slightly better than either form of therapy alone. Long-term effects have been mixed. Although integrated approaches are preferable to drug therapy alone, it is yet unclear whether the addition of sleep medications to behavioral treatment enhances outcome. Additional research is needed to design and evaluate more efficient models for integrating biobehavioral approaches, using multifaceted and sequential therapies.

References

American Psychiatric Association. (1990). *Benzodiazepine dependence, toxicity, and abuse: A task force report of the American Psychiatric Association.* Washington, DC: Author.

American Psychiatric Association. (1994). *Diagnostic and statistical manual of mental disorders* (4th ed.). Washington, DC: Author.

Balter, M. B., & Uhlenhuth, E. H. (1992). New epidemiologic findings about insomnia and its treatment. *Journal of Clinical Psychiatry, 53*(Suppl.), 34–42.

Becker, P. M., Brown, W. D., & Jamieson, A. O. (1991). Impact of insomnia: Assessment with the Sickness Impact Profile. *Sleep Research, 20,* 206.

Bootzin, R. R., Epstein, D., & Wood, J. M. (1991). Stimulus control instructions. In P. Hauri (Ed.), *Case studies in insomnia* (pp. 19–28). New York: Plenum.

Buysse, D. J., Reynolds, C. R., Kupfer, D. J., Thorpy, M. J., Bixler, E., Manfredi, R., Kales, A., Vgontzas, A., Stepanski, E., Roth, T., Hauri, P., & Mesiano, D. (1994). Clinical diagnoses in 216 insomnia patients using the International Classification of Sleep Disorders (ICSD), *DSM-IV* and *ICD-10* categories: A report from the APANIMH *DSM-IV* field trial. *Sleep, 17,* 630-637.

Chambers, M. J., & Alexander, S. D. (1992). Assessment and prediction of outcome for a brief behavioral insomnia treatment program. *Journal of Behavior Therapy and Experimental Psychiatry, 23,* 289-297.

Espie, C. A. (1991). *The psychological treatment of insomnia.* Chichester, England: Wiley.

Ford, D. E., & Kamerow, D. B. (1989). Epidemiologic study of sleep disturbances and psychiatric disorders: An opportunity for prevention? *Journal of the American Medical Association, 262,* 1479-1484.

Greenblatt, D. J. (1991). Benzodiazepine hypnotics: Sorting the pharmacokinetic facts. *Journal of Clinical Psychiatry, 52*(Suppl.), 4-10.

Hart, R. P., Morin, C. M., & Best, A. M. (1995). Neuropsychological performance in elderly insomnia patients. *Aging and Cognition, 2,* 268-278.

Hauri, P. J. (Ed.). (1991). *Case studies in insomnia.* New York: Plenum.

Hauri, P. J. (1997). Insomnia: Can we mix behavioral therapy with hypnotics when treating insomniacs? *Sleep, 20,* 1111-1118.

Hemmelgarn, B., Suissa, S., Huang, A., Boivin, J. F., & Pinard, G. (1997). Benzodiazepine use and the risk of motor vehicle crash in the elderly. *Journal of the American Medical Association, 278,* 27-31.

Hoehns, J. D., & Perry, P. J. (1993). Zolpidem: A nonbenzodiazepine hypnotic for treatment of insomnia. *Clinical Pharmacology, 12,* 814-828.

Hohagen, F., Montero, R. F., Weiss, E., Lis, S., Schonbrunn, E., Dressing, H., Riemann, D., & Berger, M. (1994). Treatment of primary insomnia with trimipramine: An alternative to benzodiazepine hypnotics? *European Archives of Psychiatry and Clinical Neuroscience, 244,* 65-72.

Hohagen, F., Rink, K., Kappler, C., Schramm, E., Riemann, D., Weyerer, S., & Berger, M. (1993). Prevalence and treatment of insomnia in general practice: A longitudinal study. *European Archives of Psychiatry and Clinical Neuroscience, 242,* 329-336.

Holbrook, A. M., Crowther, R., Lotter, A., Cheng, C., & King, D. (2000). Meta-analysis of the use of benzodiazepines for insomnia. *Canadian Medical Association Journal, 162,* 225-233.

Jacobs, G. D., Benson, H., & Friedman, R. (1993). Home-based central nervous system assessment of a multifactor behavioral intervention for chronic sleep-onset insomnia. *Behavior Therapy, 24,* 159-174.

Jacobs, G. D., Benson, H., & Friedman, R. (1996). Perceived benefits in behavioral-medicine insomnia program: A clinical report. *American Journal of Medicine, 100,* 212-216.

Johnson, L. C., & Chernik, D. A. (1982). Sedative-hypnotics and human performance. *Psychopharmacology, 76,* 101-113.

Kendall, P. C., & Lipman, A. J. (1991). Psychological and pharmacological therapy: Methods and modes for comparative outcome research. *Journal of Consulting and Clinical Psychology, 59,* 78-87.

Kupfer, D. J., & Reynolds, C. R. (1997). Management of insomnia. *New England Journal of Medicine, 336,* 341-346.

Lichstein, K. L., & Morin, C. M. (2000). *Treatment of late-life insomnia.* Newbury Park, CA: Sage.

Lichstein, K. L., & Riedel, B. W. (1994). Behavioral assessment and treatment of insomnia: A review with an emphasis on clinical application. *Behavior Therapy, 25,* 659-688.

McClusky, H. Y., Milby, J. B., Switzer, P. K., Williams, V., & Wooten, V. (1991). Efficacy of behavioral versus triazolam treatment in persistent sleep-onset insomnia. *American Journal of Psychiatry, 148,* 121-126.

Mellinger, G. D., Balter, M. B., & Uhlenhuth, E. H. (1985). Insomnia and its treatment: Prevalence and correlates. *Archives of General Psychiatry, 42,* 225-232.

Mendelson, W. B. (1995). Long-term follow-up of chronic insomnia. *Sleep, 18,* 698-701.

Mendelson, W. B. (1997). A critical evaluation of the hypnotic efficacy of melatonin. *Sleep, 20,* 916-919.

Milby, J. B., Williams, V., Hall, J. N., Khuder, S., McGill, T., & Wooten, V. (1993). Effectiveness of combined triazolam–behavioral therapy for primary insomnia. *American Journal of Psychiatry, 150*, 1259–1260.

Morin, C. M. (1993). *Insomnia: Psychological assessment and management*. New York: Guilford Press.

Morin, C. M. (1996). Introduction: Psychosocial and pharmacological treatments in behavioral medicine. *Clinical Psychology Review, 16*, 453–456.

Morin, C. M., Bastien, C., Radouco-Thomas, M., Guay, B., Leblanc, S., Blais, F., & Gagné, A. (1998). Late-life insomnia and chronic use of benzodiazepines: Medication tapering with and without behavioral interventions. *Sleep, 21*(Suppl.), 99.

Morin, C. M., Colecchi, C. A., Stone, J., Sood, R., & Brink, D. (1999). Behavioral and pharmacological therapies for late-life insomnia: A randomized clinical trial. *Journal of the American Medical Association, 281*, 991–999.

Morin, C. M., Culbert, J. P., & Schwartz, S. M. (1994). Nonpharmacological interventions for insomnia: A meta-analysis of treatment efficacy. *American Journal of Psychiatry, 151*, 1172–1180.

Morin, C. M., & Edinger, J. D. (1997). Sleep disorders: Evaluation and diagnosis. In S. M. Turner & M. Hersen (Eds.), *Adult psychopathology and diagnosis* (3rd ed., pp. 483–507). New York: Wiley.

Morin, C. M., Gaulier, B., Barry, T., & Kowatch, R. (1992). Patient's acceptance of psychological and pharmacological therapies for insomnia. *Sleep, 15*, 302–305.

Morin, C. M., Kowatch, R. A., Barry, T., & Walton, E. (1993). Cognitive behavior therapy for late-life insomnia. *Journal of Consulting and Clinical Psychology, 61*, 137–146.

Morin, C. M., Stone, J., McDonald, K., & Jones, S. (1994). Psychological management of insomnia: A clinical replication series with 100 patients. *Behavior Therapy, 25*, 291–309.

Morin, C. M., & Ware, C. (1996). Sleep and psychopathology. *Applied and Preventive Psychology, 5*, 211–224.

Murtagh, D. R. R., & Greenwood, K. M. (1995). Identifying effective psychological treatments for insomnia: A meta-analysis. *Journal of Consulting and Clinical Psychology, 63*, 79–89.

National Institutes of Health. (1984). Drugs and insomnia: The use of medication to promote sleep. *Journal of the American Medical Association, 18*, 2410–2414.

National Institutes of Health. (1991). Consensus development conference statement: The treatment of sleep disorders of older people. *Sleep, 14*, 169–177.

National Institutes of Health. (1996). NIH releases statement on behavioral and relaxation approaches for chronic pain and insomnia. *American Family Physician, 53*, 1877–1880.

Nierenberg, A. A., Adler, L. A., Peselow, E., Zomberg, G., & Rosenthal, M. (1994). Trazodone for antidepressant-associated insomnia. *American Journal of Psychiatry, 151*, 1069–1072.

Nowell, P. D., Mazumdar, S., Buysse, D. J., Dew, M. A., Reynolds, C. F., & Kupfer, D. J. (1997). Benzodiazepines and zolpidem for chronic insomnia: A meta-analysis of treatment efficacy. *Journal of the American Medical Association, 278*, 2170–2177.

Ohayon, M., & Caulet, M. (1996). Psychotropic medication and insomnia complaints in two epidemiological studies. *Canadian Journal of Psychiatry, 41*, 457–464.

Parrino, L., & Terzano, M. G. (1996). Polysomnographic effects of hypnotic drugs: A review. *Psychopharmacology, 126*, 1–16.

Ray, W. A. (1992). Psychotropic drugs and injuries among the elderly: A review. *Journal of Clinical Psychopharmacology, 12*, 386–396.

Rickels, K., Morris, R. J., Newman, H., Rosenfeld, H., Schiller, H., & Weinstock, R. (1983). Diphenhydramine in insomniac family practice patients: A double-blind study. *Journal of Clinical Pharmacology, 23*, 234–242.

Roehrs, T., Kribbs, N., Zorick, F., & Roth, T. (1986). Hypnotic residual effects of benzodiazepines with repeated administration. *Sleep, 9*, 309–316.

Roth, T., & Roehrs, T. (1991). A review of the safety profiles of benzodiazepine hypnotics. *Journal of Clinical Psychiatry, 52*, 38–41.

Rothenberg, S. A. (1992). A pilot survey in the medical community on the use of behavioral treatments for insomnia. *Sleep Research, 21*, 355.

Roy-Byrne, P. P., & Cowley, D. S. (Eds.). (1991). *Benzodiazepines in clinical practice: Risks and benefits*. Washington, DC: American Psychiatric Press.

Scharf, M. B., Roth, T., Vogel, G. W., & Walsh, J. K. (1994). A multicenter, placebo-controlled study evaluating zolpidem in the treatment of chronic insomnia. *Journal of Clinical Psychiatry, 55*, 192–199.

Scharf, M. B., & Sachais, B. A. (1990). Sleep laboratory evaluation of the effects and efficacy of trazodone in depressed insomniac patients. *Journal of Clinical Psychiatry, 51*(Suppl.), 13–17.

Simon, G., & VonKorff, M. (1997). Prevalence, burden, and treatment of insomnia in primary care. *American Journal of Psychiatry, 154*, 1417–1423.

Spielman, A. J., & Glovinsky, P. B. (1991). The varied nature of insomnia. In P. Hauri (Ed.), *Case studies in insomnia* (pp. 1–15). New York: Plenum.

Spielman, A. J., Saskin, P., & Thorpy, M. J. (1987). Treatment of chronic insomnia by restriction of time in bed. *Sleep, 10*, 45–56.

Stepanski, E., Zorick, F., & Roth, T. (1991). Pharmacotherapy of insomnia. In P. Hauri (Ed.), *Case studies in insomnia* (pp. 115–129). New York: Plenum.

Vollrath, M., Wicki, W., & Angst, J. (1989). The Zurich Study: VIII. Insomnia: Association with depression, anxiety, somatic syndromes, and course of insomnia. *European Archives of Psychiatry and Clinical Neuroscience, 239*, 113–124.

Wadworth, A. N., & McTavish, D. (1993). Zopiclone: A review of its pharmacological properties and therapeutic efficacy as an hypnotic. *Drugs and Aging, 3*, 441–459.

Walsh, J. K., & Engelhardt, C. L. (1992). Trends in the pharmacologic treatment of insomnia. *Journal of Clinical Psychiatry, 53*(Suppl.), 10–17.

6

Combined Treatments for Depression

Jeremy W. Pettit, Zachary R. Voelz,
and Thomas E. Joiner, Jr.

Depression mars the lives of millions of individuals, and its incidence appears to be steadily increasing (Cross-National Collaborative Group, 1992; Klerman & Weissman, 1989; Lewinsohn, Rohde, Seeley, & Fischer, 1993). It is estimated that at least 1 out of 10 individuals suffers from depression during a lifetime, with acuteness and chronicity of the illness varying remarkably from person to person. More specifically, estimates place the prevalence of depression from 3% to 13% in the general population, with as many as 20% of adults experiencing depressive symptoms at any given time (Amenson & Lewinsohn, 1981; Kessler et al., 1994; Oliver & Simmons, 1985, as cited in Antonuccio, Danton, & DeNelsky, 1995; Thase & Kupfer, 1996). Depending on inclusion criteria, the lifetime incidence rates have been estimated to be between 5% and 25% (Blazer, Kessler, McGonagle, & Swartz, 1994) or 20%–55%, with the rate for females double that for males (Antonuccio et al., 1995; Antonuccio, Danton, DeNelsky, Greenberg, & Gordon, 1999; Antonuccio, Thomas, & Danton, 1997). In addition, as the risk for depression among younger populations continues to grow, the age of onset for the disorder appears to be decreasing (Klerman & Weissman, 1989; M. M. Weissman, Bruce, Leaf, Florio, & Holzer, 1991). Individuals who have experienced depression once appear vulnerable to experiencing it again. Research has found that approximately 75%–80% of patients who experience a major depressive episode will have recurrent episodes of depression, even after receiving different forms of psychotherapy or drug treatments (Frank et al., 1990; Thase & Sullivan, 1995).

There is currently much debate, disagreement, and uncertainty among various groups concerning the most effective treatment available for depression. There are cogent arguments that medications that alter neurotransmitter functions in the brain are the best way to deal with the disorder (for a history of biological processes in mood disorders, see Thase & Howland, 1995). Others have argued convincingly that psychotherapies that address patterns of thinking, interpersonal relationships, and past experiences produce the best results in the treatment of depression. Decades of research on psychotherapy outcome support this view. There are also those who agree that both views have strengths and weaknesses and that both pharmacotherapy and psychotherapy are effective ways to treat depression. Our key tasks, consequently, are to determine which approaches are most efficacious under a given set of circumstances (e.g., particular subtypes of depression) and under what circumstances combinations of psychological and pharmacological treatments are better than either therapy administered singly in the treatment and prevention of depression.

Pharmacotherapy for Depression

Pharmacological treatments have gained popularity during the last 50 years as a method of treatment intervention for depression as well as for many other psychological disorders. They have been proven effective in ameliorating the symptoms for a large percentage of depressed individuals and are now the most common form of treatment for depression (Narrow, Regier, Rae, Manderscheid, & Locke, 1993). The constraints of this chapter do not allow for a detailed discussion of antidepressant medications, but we briefly present them below.

Commonly Used Medications

Antidepressant medications are classified depending on their chemical structure and how they work, and all categories of antidepressants tend to be comparably efficacious (Depression Guideline Panel, 1993). They can be categorized into four basic groups: (a) tricyclics (TCAs), (b) monoamine oxidase inhibitors (MAOIs), (c) serotonin reuptake inhibitors (SRIs), and (d) atypical drugs (see Tables 6.1–6.4). Medications in the current anti-

Table 6.1. Tricyclic Antidepressants

Chemical name	Trade name
Amitriptyline	Elavil, Endep
Amoxapine	Asendin
Clomipramine	Anafranil
Desipramine	Norpramin, Pertofrane
Dothiepin[a]	
Doxepin	Sinequan, Adapin
Imipramine	Tofranil, Tipramine, Norfranil
Lofepramine[a]	
Maprotiline	Ludiomil
Mianserin[a]	
Nortriptyline	Pamelor, Aventyl
Protriptyline	Vivactil
Trimipramine	Surmontil

[a]Not available in the United States.

Table 6.2. Monoamine Oxidase Inhibitors

Chemical name	Trade name
Brofaromine[a]	Consonar
Isocarboxazid	Marplan
Moclobemide[a]	Manerex
Phenelzine	Nardil
Tranylcypromine	Parnate

[a]Reversible monoamine-A inhibitors, not available in the United States.

depressant pharmacopoeia are in general hypothesized to work by altering the activity of biogenic amine neurotransmitters (e.g., acetylcholine, norepinephrine, serotonin, and dopamine). This view is oversimplified, as antidepressants also affect presynaptic receptors, postsynaptic second messengers, and neurophysiologic response systems (Barden, Reul, & Holsboer, 1995; Manji, 1992; Thase & Kupfer, 1996; Wachtel, 1990).

In terms of efficacy of antidepressants, the superiority of TCAs to placebo in treating unipolar major depression has been repeatedly demonstrated in randomized clinical trials (e.g., Brotman & Falk, 1987; Klein & Davis, 1980; Klerman & Cole, 1965), although TCAs have received somewhat less support for the treatment of other depressive variants, such as atypical or subsyndromal depression (Quitkin et al., 1990). MAOIs are comparably effective to TCAs and may be more effective than TCAs and SRIs in treating individuals with atypical depression or reversed vegetative symptoms (e.g., hypersomnia, hyperphagia, and behavioral activation; D. L. Murphy, Aulakh, & Garrick, 1987; Quitkin et al., 1993; Thase, Trivedi, & Rush, 1995). Their efficacy with severe levels of depression, however, is less certain, as some research indicates that they are not as effective as TCAs or SRIs (Brotman & Falk, 1987). In addition, the use of MAOIs has been constrained by an unfavorable side-effect profile as well as drug interactions and dietary restrictions prohibiting the ingestion of tyramine-containing foodstuffs (generally, aged or fermented foods and certain fruits and alcoholic beverages). The recent development of the "re-

Table 6.3. Serotonin-Specific Reuptake Inhibitors

Chemical name	Trade name
Citalopram	Celexa
Fluoxetine	Prozac
Fluvoxamine	Luvox
Paroxetine	Paxil
Sertraline	Zoloft

Table 6.4. Atypical Antidepressants

Chemical name	Trade name
Bupropion	Wellbutrin
Mirtazapine	Remeron
Nefazodone	Serzone
Reboxetine[a]	Edronax
Trazadone	Desyrel, Trazon, Trialodine
Venlaxafine	Effexor

[a]Not available in the United States.

versible" MAOIs, which promise a more favorable side-effect profile and fewer dietary and drug interactions, may increase their currency as first-line agents against depression (Janicak, Davis, Preskorn, & Ayd, 1997; Krishnan, 1998).

SRIs have fewer adverse side effects and are far less lethal in overdose than are TCAs and irreversible MAOIs (Kapur, Mieczkowski, & Mann, 1992; Preskorn & Burke, 1992). This in large part accounts for their popularity and the frequency of their use. Because of their relatively benign side-effect profiles and low toxicity, their use has become commonplace. The efficacy of and response time to SRIs are similar to those of TCAs (Rickels & Schweizer, 1990).

Certain other drugs, although they do not fit into any of the first three major categories of TCAs, MAOIs, or SRIs, are classified as "atypical" and have also been found to be effective for treating depressive symptoms. Examples of atypical antidepressants currently available are trazodone, nefazodone, bupropion, venlafaxine, and reboxetine.

Effects on Depressive Episodes and Relapse Prevention

Most antidepressant medications have a fairly high success rate of ameliorating depressive symptoms (Anderson & Tomenson, 1994; Depression Guideline Panel, 1993; M. Fava & Rosenbaum, 1991; Song et al., 1993). For instance, TCAs have been found to be effective in treating depression among approximately 50% of patients who begin treatment and among approximately 65% of those who complete treatment (Depression Guideline Panel, 1993). Several meta-analyses, studies, and reviews have demonstrated the efficacy of antidepressants over placebos in treating depression (Davis, Wang, & Janicak, 1993; R. P. Greenberg, Bornstein, Greenberg, & Fisher, 1992; Joffe, Sokolov, & Streiner, 1996; Morris & Beck, 1974; Song et al., 1993). The average treatment response difference between medication and placebo ranges from 20% to 40% (Depression Guideline Panel, 1993). A recent analysis of the Food and Drug Administration's database for Phase 3 clinical trials suggested an average placebo response rate of approximately 30% (Khan, Warner, & Brown, 2000).

Antidepressants, however, are much less successful at preventing the relapse or recurrence of depression if they are discontinued shortly after the remission of symptoms (Hollon, Shelton, & Loosen, 1991; Thase, 1990). Thase (1999) reported that up to 50% of patients relapse unless treated 4–6 months after the initial acute phase. Administration of the drugs can be continued for long periods of time, in which case they are more effective in preventing relapse or recurrence (Anton, Robinson, Roberts, & Kensler, 1994; M. Fava & Kaji, 1994; Feiger et al., 1999). Thus, it is commonly recommended that successful pharmacological treatment of depression be followed by at least 6 months of continued treatment (Depression Guideline Panel, 1993; Prien & Kupfer, 1986). In addition, individuals with chronic depression or a history of recurrent depressive episodes may be candidates for maintenance therapy lasting for years (Kupfer, 1991; Prien & Kocsis, 1995; Thase, 1993).

Relative Advantages of Pharmacological Treatment

One benefit of pharmacotherapy for depression is a decreased amount of time spent in treatment by both therapist and patient. Administering pharmacotherapy allows the patient to simply take a drug and routinely check in with the physician to monitor progress or, if indicated, drug level. No long-term "talking therapy" sessions are required, thus saving the therapist and patient both time and energy. Antidepressant medications also tend to produce relatively rapid results. Whereas a patient may spend months in psychotherapy before progress is made, antidepressant medications usually have a positive effect within the first 6–8 weeks of treatment (Depression Guideline Panel, 1993).

Relative Disadvantages of Pharmacological Treatment

Disadvantages of pharmacotherapy include adverse side effects of medication, treatment nonadherence, treatment dropout, and possible overdose. No medication is completely free of side effects, and antidepressants are no exception. A large number of antidepressant side effects have been reported (Frazer, 1997; Richelson, 1994). Common side effects for TCAs include sedation, weight gain, dry mouth, blurred vision, constipation, urinary retention, sinus tachycardia, orthostatic hypotension, and short-term memory impairment.

MAOIs produce side effects more commonly than do TCAs and SRIs and have dangerous interactions with specific foods and medicines. Common MAOI side effects involve orthostatic hypotension, weight gain, edema, sexual dysfunction, insomnia, sweating, dizziness, blurred vision, weakness, drowsiness, and constipation. Foods containing large amounts of tyramine (e.g., certain types of alcohol, cheese, nuts, chocolate, yeast, caffeine, meat extracts) may cause a life-threatening hypertensive reaction, the so-called "cheese reaction" (Blackwell, 1963; Cooper, 1989). Meperidine (Demerol) and many medications containing sympathomimetic compounds taken in conjunction with MAOIs may cause a potentially lethal central serotonin syndrome (Kaplan & Sadock, 1993).

SRIs tend to produce fewer side effects than other antidepressants (Kaplan & Sadock, 1993). Some common side effects of SRIs involve the central nervous system and the gastrointestinal system and include headaches, nervousness, insomnia, drowsiness, dizziness, tremor, anxiety, agitation, anorexia, nausea, constipation, and diarrhea (Grimsley & Jann, 1992; Rickels & Schweizer, 1990). A fairly common side effect is sexual dysfunction, including decreased libido, erectile dysfunction, decreased vaginal lubrication, and delayed orgasm or anorgasmia (Settle, 1992; Sussman, 1999). Sexual dysfunction may occur in more than half of individuals taking SRIs (Ellison, 1998).

The side effects of antidepressant medications in the atypical category depend on the chemical composition of the drug. Several of these medications produce anticholinergic effects, orthostatic hypertension, sedation, and priapism. Bupropion lowers the seizure threshold to a significantly greater degree than do other antidepressants. As a result, it is contraindicated in patients at higher risk for development of seizures (specifically, those with histories of eating disorders or seizures). Nefazodone, a recently introduced drug, has a reasonably benign side-effect profile, although it may cause sedation and has some adverse interactions with other medications.

Withdrawal from all four classes of antidepressants (TCAs, MAOIs, SRIs, and atypical antidepressants) has the potential to produce a discontinuation syndrome. Symptoms can consist of gastrointestinal distress, anxiety, sleep disturbances, changes in appetite, movement disorders, mania or hypomania, and panic attacks. Discontinuation symptoms vary in severity according to the class of drug and pharmacokinetic properties. Symptoms associated with TCAs and SRIs are typically mild, but those associated with MAOIs may be more serious (Lejoyeux & Ades, 1997). Drugs with long elimination half-lives (e.g., fluoxetine) are less likely to produce withdrawal problems; the opposite is true for drugs with shorter half-lives (e.g., venlafaxine, sertraline), and these should be gradually tapered to prevent such problems. Finally, withdrawal of antidepressants may lead to a rebound or recurrence of depression.

Although antidepressants are effective in treating 50%–70% of the depressed individuals to whom they are administered (Depression Guideline Panel, 1993; Miller, Norman, & Keitner, 1990), the remaining 30%–50% of individuals do not recover as a result of the medications. Thus, antidepressant medications are still ineffective among a large percentage of depressed individuals. Some investigators have argued that this observed lack of efficacy in both clinical trials and in practice is due to undertreatment, either because of inadequate doses or prematurely terminated trials (Keller et al., 1982; Rush & Hollon, 1991). As a result, the overall efficacy of antidepressants may be underestimated.

Psychotherapy for Depression

Commonly Used Therapies

Numerous forms of psychotherapy have been and continue to be applied in the treatment of depression (see Exhibit 6.1). Some of these therapies are backed by empirical support, whereas others remain largely unsubstantiated. Proponents of various theoretical orientations debate the effectiveness of their preferred forms of psychotherapy, but cognitive (e.g., Beck, 1967, 1976; Ellis, 1962) and cognitive–behavioral theories (e.g., Lewinsohn & Clark, 1984; Rehm, Kaslow, & Rabin, 1987) have received the most empirical support for the treatment of depression. Other therapies, such as interpersonal psychotherapy (IPT; Klerman, Weissman, Rounsaville, & Chevron, 1984) and social skills training (e.g., Bellack, Hersen, & Himmelhoch, 1981; Monti, Corriveau, & Curran, 1980), have been shown to be effective interventions as well.

Effects on Depressive Episodes and Relapse Prevention

Both psychotherapy and pharmacotherapy have approximately the same response rate of 50%–70% (Miller et al., 1990). Accordingly, meta-analyses involving psychotherapeutic and pharmacological treatments reveal similar levels of efficacy when applied to mild to moderate depressive episodes (Depression Guideline Panel, 1993; Dobson, 1989). Although it has been clinically presumed that severe depression is more responsive to pharmacotherapy, DeRubeis, Gelfand, Tang, and Simons (1999) concluded after comparing the results of four trials that cognitive behavior therapy was as effective as pharmacotherapy, even when applied to patients with severe depression. These findings present some challenge to the belief that more severe forms of the disorder are preferentially responsive to medication.

The most well-researched psychotherapies for depression are cognitive and cognitive behavioral therapies. Cognitive therapy (CT) is a brief intervention (10–20 sessions) that focuses on the patient's thinking pro-

Exhibit 6.1.   Psychotherapies Used to Treat Depression

Behavioral therapy
Cognitive therapy
Cognitive–behavioral therapy
Interpersonal psychotherapy
Marital therapy
Brief psychodynamic therapy
Rational–emotive therapy
Relaxation therapy
Social skills training

cesses, particularly errors in cognitions made by depressed individuals. According to the cognitive theory of depression, individuals can develop negative beliefs regarding themselves, their worlds, and their futures. These dysfunctional views are referred to as the *cognitive triad* and are posited to serve as a vulnerability factor to depression. A wide base of empirical data supports the efficacy of CT (e.g., Beck, Hollon, Young, Bedrosian, & Budenz, 1985; Blackburn, Bishop, Glen, Whalley, & Christie, 1981; Covi & Lipman, 1987; Elkin et al., 1989; G. E. Murphy, Simons, Wetzel, & Lustman, 1984; Rush, Beck, Kovacs, & Hollon, 1977; Teasdale, Fennel, Hibbert, & Amies, 1984).

A similar treatment, cognitive–behavioral therapy (CBT), also focuses on dysfunctional and irrational cognitions as well as on deficits in behavior and motivation. Numerous studies have supported the efficacy of different cognitive–behavioral approaches to treatment. For example, Cuijpers (1998) recently conducted a meta-analysis of Lewinsohn's "Coping With Depression" course (Lewinsohn, Antonuccio, Breckenridge, & Teri, 1984) and found it to be comparably effective to other treatment modalities for depression. Robinson, Berman, and Neimeyer (1990) conducted an earlier meta-analysis of 58 studies that compared CBT with other methods of treatment. They concluded that CBT was more effective than other psychotherapeutic interventions and showed a trend toward outperforming pharmacological interventions. In addition, group cognitive, behavioral, and cognitive–behavioral treatments for depression have been widely supported (e.g., Brown & Lewinsohn, 1984; Comas-Diaz, 1981; Peterson & Halstead, 1998; Rehm et al., 1987; Scott & Stradling, 1990; Zettle & Rains, 1989).

IPT is a brief treatment (usually 12–16 weeks) that focuses on the patient's interpersonal functioning as it relates to current depression and the onset of depression (Klerman et al., 1984). In IPT, individuals work toward developing appropriate interpersonal skills for dealing with problems such as grief, role issues, and interpersonal deficits (Otto, Pava, & Sprich-Buckminster, 1996). The superiority of IPT to placebo has been demonstrated for the treatment of acute depression (e.g., DiMascio et al., 1979; Elkin et al., 1989; M. M. Weissman et al., 1979) and the prevention of relapse (e.g., Frank, Kupfer, Wagner, McEachran, & Cornes, 1991; M. M. Weissman, Klerman, Prusoff, Sholomskas, & Padian, 1981). A recent study by Mufson, Weissman, Moreau, and Garfinkel (1999) found IPT to be significantly more effective than clinical management in the treatment of depressed adolescents.

Benefits and Drawbacks of Psychotherapy

A large amount of research suggests that psychotherapy typically yields lower relapse rates relative to the relapse rates following medication trials (Blackburn, Eunson, & Bishop, 1986; Evans et al., 1992; Frank et al., 1991; Hersen, Bellack, Himmelhoch, & Thase, 1984; Hollon & Beck, 1994; Hollon, Shelton, & Davis, 1993; Kovacs, Rush, Beck, & Hollon, 1981; Mc-

Lean & Hakistian, 1990; Shea et al., 1992; Simons, Murphy, Levine, & Wetzel, 1986). This greater relapse prevention possibly arises from lasting changes in behavioral and cognitive patterns resulting from psychotherapy. Nevertheless, as mentioned earlier in the chapter, maintenance treatment with pharmacotherapy does appear to be comparably effective in the prevention of relapse.

Disadvantages of psychotherapy include an increased amount of time spent in treatment, possibly slower results than are achieved with pharmacotherapy, and potentially increased cost (Klerman et al., 1994). Psychotherapy during the acute treatment phase can be much more expensive to administer than pharmacotherapy. This, however, may be a misleading representation of actual cost; that is, if psychotherapy is more effective at preventing relapse or recurrence, then it may be cheaper in the long run to administer psychotherapy at one time period than to repeatedly administer pharmacotherapy. For an in-depth analysis of the costs associated with pharmacotherapy and psychotherapy, we refer readers to works by Antonuccio et al. (1997); Hersh and Lazar (1999); Lave, Frank, Schulberg, and Kamlet (1998); Montgomery and Kasper (1998); and Von Korff et al. (1998). Clearly, further research needs to be conducted concerning the long-term costs associated with treatments of depression.

Combined Pharmacotherapy and Psychotherapy for Depression

Combined therapy is frequently used in the treatment of depression. In fact, combination treatments probably represent the most common form of treatment received by depressed individuals. Unfortunately, this topic has received relatively little attention from researchers compared to psychotherapy and pharmacotherapy administered singly. Much more extensive research needs to be conducted to conclusively determine the efficacy, advantages, and disadvantages of combined therapy.

Frequently Used Combinations

Virtually any combination of antidepressant medication and psychotherapy can be used, but common sense and ethical practice and research dictate that those of greatest benefit (or theorized benefit) to the patient be used. The various combinations of therapies used in the studies reviewed in this chapter are listed in Table 6.5. As can be seen, the most frequent combinations involved either CT, CBT, or IPT, along with various TCAs (i.e., amitriptyline, desipramine, or nortriptyline). Studies in which SRIs were used are as yet poorly represented in the clinical literature.

Effects on Depressive Episodes and Relapse Prevention

In the following section we review several empirical studies that were conducted in the 1990s on combined therapy for depression. The infor-

Table 6.5. Summary of Combined Therapy Studies Conducted During the 1990s: Acute, Continuation, and Maintenance Treatments

Study	Patient characteristics	Psytx	Pharmtx	Cells and ns	Outcome measures	Length of treatment	Results
Bowers (1990)	$N = 30$, Ages 18–60, mean age = 36, 80% female, 20% male, all Caucasian	Cognitive Therapy (CT; 12 sessions) or relaxation therapy (RT; 12 sessions)	Nortriptyline (D): starting dosage = 25–75 mg/day, discharge dosage = 100–200 mg/day	(1) CT&D, 10 (2) RT&D, 10 (3) D only, 10	BDI HRSD DAS ATQ HS	4 weeks (avg, inpatient), "acute treatment"	(1) > (2), significant, and (2) > (3), significant
Evans et al. (1992)	$N = 44$; these patients were successfully treated during acute tx of Hollon et al.'s (1992) study	CT administered during acute tx only and discontinued during follow-up	Imipramine hydrochloride (D): administered during acute tx in all drug conditions; used only in D&Cont condition for follow-up	(1) D&No Cont, 10 (2) D&Cont, 11 (3) CT only, 10 (4) CT&D, 13 D&Cont was only condition to receive continuation tx during follow-up	BDI HRSD RDS MMPI–D	24 months (outpatient), "Continuation treatment & follow-up"	(1) = 50% relapse (2) = 32% relapse (3) = 21% relapse (4) = 15% relapse
G. A. Fava, Rafanelli, Grandi, Conti, & Belluardo (1998)	$N = 40$; all patients had already received 3 to 5 months of antidepressant tx and were judged to be in remission	Cognitive–behavioral therapy (CBT), administered for 20 weeks following end of acute tx	Various medications tapered until discontinued . . . (Dt); medications were tapered over 20 weeks following end of acute tx and then discontinued	(1) CBT&Dt, 20 (2) ClinMan& Dt, 20	Paykel Clinical Interview	20 weeks of continuing CBT or ClinMan while tapering off medications; followed up for next 2 years	(1) = 25% relapse (2) = 80% relapse
Hollon et al. (1992)	$N = 107$; Ages 18–62, mean age = 33, 80% female, 20% male, 91% Caucasian	CT (maximum of 20 sessions)	Imipramine Hydrochloride (D): starting dosage = 75 mg/day, discharge dosage = 200–300 mg/day	(1) D only, 32 (2) CT only, 16 (3) CT&D, 16	HRSD RDS GAS BDI MMPI–D	12 weeks (outpatient), "acute treatment"	(3) > (1), nonsignificant (3) > (2) nonsignificant (1) = (2)

Study	Sample	Medication (D)	Psychotherapy (P)	Groups, N	Measures	Duration	Results
Macaskill & Macaskill (1996)	N = 20; ages 18–65, mean age = 38, 70% female, 30% male, all had high levels of cognitive dysfunction based on DAS	Lofepramine (D): starting dosage = 35 mg b.i.d. max. final dosage = 280 mg/day	Rational–Emotive Therapy (RET; maximum of 30 sessions), aspects of cognitive therapy were incorporated in certain problem areas	(1) D only, 10 (2) D&RET, 10	BDI HRSD SAS DIS GII	24 weeks (max.) (outpatient) OR until remission of depressive symptomatology for 3 continuous weeks, "acute treatment"	(2) > (1) significant
Miller et al. (1990)	N = 69; ages 18–65, mean age = 35, 81% female, 19% male, patients divided into HCD and LCD based on DAS scores	Amitriptyline (D) (minimum of 150 mg/day) or Desipramine (D) (minimum of 150 mg/day)	Cognitive–Behavioral Therapy (P) or Social Skills Training (P)	High Cognitive Dys. (1) D only, 17 (2) D&P, 14 Low Cognitive Dys. (3) D only, 24 (4) D&P, 14	BDI mod–HRSD DAS CBQ	Hospital stay plus 20 weeks outpatient tx, "acute treatment"	(2) > (1) significant (2) > (3) significant (2) > (4) significant (3) = (4)
Reynolds, Frank, et al. (1999)	N = 107, ages ≥59, mean age = 67, all recovered after acute tx and shown to be stabilized after 16 wks of continuation tx with interpersonal psychotherapy (IPT) and medicine	Nortriptyline hydrochloride (D) (80–120 ng/ml steady state level)	IPT	(1) D only, 24 (2) Pl only, 29 (3) IPT&D, 22 (4) IPT&Pl, 21 All treatments were administered monthly	Recurrence of major depressive episode (MDE)	Up to first recurrence or maximum of 3 years, "maintenance treatment"	(1) = 43% recurrence (2) = 90% recurrence (3) = 20% recurrence (4) = 64% recurrence
Reynolds, Miller, et al. (1999)	N = 80, ages ≥50, all experienced bereavement-related MDEs due to recent loss of spouse or loved one	Nortriptyline (D)	IPT	(1) D only, 25 (2) Pl only, 22 (3) IPT&D, 16 (4) IPT&Pl, 17	HRSD	16 weeks (or shorter if remission requirements were met), "acute treatment"	(1) = 56% remission (2) = 45% remission (3) = 69% remission (4) = 29% remission

Table continues

Table 6.5. (*Continued*)

Study	Patient characteristics	Psytx	Pharmtx	Cells and *n*s	Outcome measures	Length of treatment	Results
Reynolds et al. (1996)	Two separately controlled studies: *n* = 148, elderly patients, mean age = 67.9, and *n* = 214, midlife patients, mean age = 38.5	IPT	Nortriptyline (D; 80–120 ng/ml, for the elderly patients) Imipramine (D; enough to produce steady state plasma levels of 225 ng/ml, for the midlife patients)	(1) IPT&D (elderly), 148 (2) IPT&D (midlife), 214	HRSD	Until remission requirements were met during acute tx, then received 16 or 20 weeks of continuing tx, "acute and continuation treatment"	(1) = 78% remission (2) = 70% remission (1) = 16% relapse (2) = 7% relapse
Savard et al. (1998)	*N* = 6, 1 male, 5 females, mean age = 35.2, all patients were HIV positive	CT (P; sixteen 50-min sessions)	Fluoxetine treatment (D) (20 mg/day)	(1) D&P, 3 (2) D, then P&D after 2 months, 2 (3) D, then P&D after 4 months, 1	VAS BDI–SF HADS–D	Variable lengths of treatment, "acute treatment and up to 1-yr follow-up"	The addition of cognitive tx resulted in significant improvement of symptoms in 5 of 6 patients, beyond the effects of drug tx alone

Note. Psytx = psychotherapy treatment; Pharmtx = pharmacological treatment; BDI = Beck Depression Inventory; HRSD = Hamilton Rating Scale for Depression; DAS = Dysfunctional Attitudes Scale; ATQ = Automatic Thoughts Questionnaire; HS = Hopelessness Scale; Cont = continuation of treatment; RDS = Raskin Depression Scale; MMPI–D = Minnesota Multiphasic Personality Inventory—Scale 2 (Depression); ClinMan = clinical management addressing problems associated with tapering off medication; Pl = placebo; VAS = Visual Analogue Scale; BDI–SF = Beck Depression Inventory—Short Form; HADS–D = Depression scale of the Hospital Anxiety and Depression Scale.

mation and conclusions drawn from studies prior to 1990 are included in the form of previous reviews conducted by M. M. Weissman (1979); Conte, Plutchik, Wild, and Toksoz (1986); Manning and Frances (1990); Wexler and Cicchetti (1992); and Thase, Greenhouse, Frank, Reynolds, Pilkonis, Hurley, Grochocinski, and Kupfer (1997). Information regarding patient characteristics, forms and lengths of treatments, outcome measures, and results from each of the studies is presented in Table 6.6.

Previous Reviews of Combined Treatment Studies

M. M. Weissman (1979), in one of the earliest reviews of combined therapy, examined 17 clinical trials completed between 1974 and 1979 that tested the efficacy of various psychological, pharmacological, and combined treatments. On the basis of the resulting data, Weissman concluded that combined therapy was more effective than either type of treatment alone.

Conte et al. (1986) reviewed all studies on combined therapy for depression from 1974 to 1984. Most of the investigations used either amitriptyline, clomipramine, or nortriptyline. Psychotherapies included marital therapy, IPT, social skills training, CT, behavior therapy, and psychodynamically oriented group therapy. Overall, combined therapy was slightly more effective than psychotherapy or pharmacotherapy alone.

In perhaps the most comprehensive review that has been performed to date, Manning and Frances (1990) examined 17 combined-therapy studies completed between 1969 and 1989, concluding that combined treatment was at least as effective as either treatment alone. In some cases, combined therapy demonstrated small advantages over psychotherapy or pharmacotherapy alone. Overall, however, the authors found the differences among combined therapy, psychotherapy, and pharmacotherapy to be relatively inconsequential.

Wexler and Cicchetti (1992) found similar results in a review of treatment outcome studies. They attempted to determine whether pharmacotherapy, psychotherapy, or a combination of the two produced superior results than the other two methods of treatment. The studies they reviewed used three types of psychotherapy: IPT, CT, or behavioral therapy. Pharmacotherapy usually consisted of 200–300 mg/day of amitriptyline or imipramine, and treatment lasted from 12 to 16 weeks. The authors found an overall success rate of 67% for combined therapy, 62% for psychotherapy alone, and 52% for pharmacotherapy alone, based on change in Depression Inventory (Beck, Rush, Shaw, & Emery, 1979; Beck & Steer, 1987) scores. None of these differences reached statistical significance. Pharmacotherapy regimens had significantly higher failure and dropout rates than either combined therapy or psychotherapy alone; these last two did not differ significantly. Wexler and Cicchetti concluded that psychotherapy alone was the treatment of choice for depression because (a) there was no difference in the effectiveness of the three treatments; (b) combined therapy incurred higher costs and more negative side effects; and (c) pharmacotherapy involved more side effects, higher treatment failure, and higher dropout rates.

Thase et al. (1997) examined six studies of combined therapy and psychotherapy alone for depression, looking specifically at CBT, IPT, nortriptyline, and imipramine. The results of this clinical outcome review indicated that psychotherapy alone was the best treatment for individuals with moderate to low levels of depression because the addition of medication would simply increase cost, side effects, and treatment resistance without providing improvement beyond the effects of psychotherapy. For patients with more severe levels of depression, however, it appeared that the combination of psychotherapy and pharmacotherapy was superior to psychotherapy alone.

Miller et al. (1990) investigated the relative merits of pharmacotherapy versus combined therapy in groups of inpatients using Beck's (1976) classification as either low cognitive dysfunction (LCD) or high cognitive dysfunction (HCD). Patients with LCD responded best to pharmacotherapy alone during hospitalization, whereas patients with HCD responded equally well to pharmacotherapy and combined therapy. Twenty weeks after discharge, however, patients with LCD responded equally to pharmacotherapy and combined therapy, whereas patients with HCD responded better to combined therapy. These results led to the conclusion that LCD depressed individuals were best served by pharmacotherapy alone, as the addition of psychotherapy tended to slow response to treatment. For HCD depressed individuals, on the other hand, the addition of psychotherapy (CBT, in particular) to pharmacotherapy led to superior outcomes compared to pharmacotherapy alone. This finding is consistent with Beck's model of depression in that individuals holding a high number of faulty beliefs and dysfunctional attitudes (i.e., HCD) were most responsive to the addition of a therapy focused on changing these beliefs. Accordingly, individuals not possessing these faulty beliefs (i.e., LCD) did not benefit from such a therapy.

Bowers (1990) compared nortriptyline therapy, CT and nortriptyline therapy combined, and relaxation and nortriptyline therapies combined. He found the combination of CT and nortriptyline to be most effective in reducing depression, followed by the combination of relaxation therapy and nortriptyline, and finally nortriptyline alone. The results of this study indicated that pharmacotherapy for depression was enhanced by supplementation with some form of psychotherapy, with CT providing more benefit than relaxation therapy.

In a study that compared CT, imipramine hydrochloride, pharmacotherapy, and CT and imipramine therapy combined, Hollon et al. (1992) found no differences between CT and imipramine. It is notable, however, that combined therapy showed a nonsignificant trend toward higher response rates than either therapy alone. The authors concluded that combined therapy may be advantageous relative to either therapy alone but that a larger sample would be necessary to detect this difference.

Macaskill and Macaskill (1996) reported that the TCA lofepramine (which is not available in the United States) combined with rational–emotive therapy (RET) led to greater improvement on a number of depression-relevant scales than lofepramine alone. Patients completed 24 weeks of treatment, with the majority of the improvement occurring within the first 10 weeks. Furthermore, there was negligible improvement among patients who received lofepramine alone (a finding inconsistent with previous findings of the drug's effectiveness). The conclusion, therefore, was that combined RET and lofepramine therapy were superior to lofepramine alone in the treatment of major depressive episodes.

Reynolds, Miller, et al. (1999) investigated the relative efficacy of nortriptyline therapy, IPT, and a combination of these two therapies among patients older than age 50 who were experiencing bereavement-related depressive episodes. The remission rate was 69% for combined nortriptyline and IPT, 56% for nortriptyline and clinical management, 29% for IPT and placebo, and 45% for placebo and clinical management. In addition, attrition rates were lowest in the combined-treatment group. The difference between combined therapy and nortriptyline alone did not reach statistical significance, although both treatment modalities were more effective than IPT plus placebo. Nevertheless, the high rate of remission seen with combined treatment, when considered with its low rate of attrition, made it more attractive than either therapy administered singly.

Finally, results from a large multicenter study of nefazodone and psychotherapy suggest that combined therapy is a more effective treatment for chronic depression than psychotherapy or pharmacotherapy alone (Keller et al., 2000). The combination of nefazodone and a variant of CBT (the cognitive–behavioral analysis system of psychotherapy) led to a reduction or elimination of depressive symptoms among 85% of patients. Nefazodone alone and CBT alone led to a reduction or elimination of symptoms among just over half of the patients who received these treatments. Although providing somewhat differing conclusions, these studies tend to support the use of combined therapy to treat unipolar depression. Although some of the studies led to contrary conclusions, the summation of the various results suggests that combined therapy may be more effective than psychotherapy or pharmacotherapy alone, especially when treating individuals with severe or chronic levels of depression.

Effects on Preventing Relapse and Recurrence

As a continuation of the Hollon et al. (1992) study mentioned in the previous section, Evans et al. (1992) conducted a 2-year follow-up of patients treated with imipramine hydrochloride, CT, or a combination of the two. The pharmacotherapy-alone group manifested a significantly higher relapse rate and earlier relapse times than did those in the CT or combined conditions. The CT and the combined-therapy conditions did not differ significantly. In addition, receiving CT during the course of the depressive episode was found to be as effective in preventing relapse as receiving continued medication after the episode. Thus, the administration of CT during acute treatment, either alone or combined with medication, was effective in preventing relapse (Evans et al., 1992).

G. A. Fava, Rafanelli, Grandi, Canestrari, and Morphy (1998) found similar results while investigating the effects of 3–5 months of antidepressant therapy during the course of a major depressive episode, followed by 20 weeks of CBT maintenance. The CBT group showed a significantly lower level of symptoms after discontinuation of medication compared to the clinical management group. The CBT group had a relapse rate of 25%, compared to 80% for the clinical management group. Thus, the addition of CBT as pharmacotherapy is being tapered appears to be an effective means of preventing recurrent episodes of depression over relatively short periods. Nevertheless, G. A. Fava, Rafanelli, Grandi, Canestrari, and Morphy (1998) found the protective effects of CBT to be greatly reduced after 6 years, with differences in relapse rates between the CBT and clinical management groups failing to reach significance. It is notable, however, that patients in the CBT group had significantly fewer depressive episodes than did patients in the clinical management group.

Reynolds, Frank, et al. (1999) extended these findings to the prevention of relapse in geriatric settings. In elderly populations, maintenance treatment with IPT and nortriptyline was shown to be effective at preventing the recurrence of depression. In particular, this combined treatment outperformed placebo treatments, IPT alone, and showed a nonsignificant trend toward outperforming nortriptyline maintenance alone. The combination of IPT and nortriptyline led to a 3-year relapse rate of 20%, compared to 43% for nortriptyline alone, 64% for IPT alone, and 90% for placebo treatment. The results of this study suggest that, among the elderly population, maintenance treatment with nortriptyline or IPT was superior to placebo, and a combination of nortriptyline and IPT was preferable to either treatment administered singly.

Furthermore, Reynolds, Frank, Kupfer, et al. (1996) examined the efficacy of a combination of IPT and imipramine among middle-aged adults. The combination of IPT and imipramine proved to be an effective form of treatment, as 69.6% of patients improved during acute treatment, and only 6.7% relapsed. Unfortunately, the efficacy of this form of treatment was not compared with single-modality therapy or placebo, limiting the conclusions that could be drawn from this study.

These four studies on relapse prevention all provide evidence suggesting that combined therapy tends to outperform pharmacotherapy alone or psychotherapy alone with respect to preventing relapse into depressive episodes. Because all four studies found such similar results, it is less likely that these findings were due to extraneous factors or confounding variables. Possible explanations for the superiority of combined therapy in preventing relapse better than either psychotherapy or pharmacotherapy alone are discussed briefly in the Conclusion section.

Advantages of Combined Treatments

As Conte et al. (1986) speculated, the effectiveness of combined treatment for depression may result from its broader coverage of individual differences—that is, some individuals may respond better to pharmacotherapy than to psychotherapy, whereas others may respond better to psychotherapy than to pharmacotherapy. In the event of combined therapy, both groups of individuals receive a form of the therapy that is most likely to benefit them, thus leading to a higher overall rate of success. Hollon, DeRubeis, and Evans (1990) accurately described this phenomenon by noting that "combined (cognitive therapy–pharmaco) therapy provides the benefits of either single modality while compensating for the limitations of each" (p. 59). Some interesting work, primarily by Thase, Simons, Reynolds, and their colleagues, has sought to identify factors that predict treatment response to CBT, CT and, to a lesser extent, antidepressants (see also Bielski & Friedel, 1976; Klerman, Weissman, & Prusoff, 1982; Miller et al., 1990; Prusoff, Weissman, Klerman, & Rounsaville, 1980; Simons, Gordon, Monroe, & Thase, 1995; Simons, Lustman, Wetzel, & Murphy, 1985; Spangler, Simons, Monroe, & Thase, 1997; Thase, Fasiczka, Berman, Simons, & Reynolds, 1998; Thase et al., 1994; Thase, Simons, Cahalane, McGeary, & Harden, 1991; Thase, Simons, & Reynolds, 1993, 1996; Zuckerman, Prusoff, Weissman, & Padian, 1980). The majority of this research has centered on CBT or CT, although some has focused on treatment response to pharmacotherapy. One interesting hypothesis that has arisen from this body of literature is the speculation that specific forms of treatment are best suited for types of depression that are either psychological or biological in origin. For example, some research has suggested that biologically mediated depression, as measured by abnormal sleep electroencephalogram profiles, may predict poor response to CBT, although this is subject to some dispute (e.g., Thase et al., 1991). If subtypes of depression can be determined to have a predominantly psychologic or biologic foundation, treatment specificity may be enhanced.

A number of parameters, including psychological and psychosocial variables, clearly play a role in determining response to biological treatments such as pharmacotherapy. Factors related to a good response to TCAs such as imipramine and amitriptyline include upper socioeconomic class, insidious onset, anorexia, weight loss, middle and late insomnia, and psychomotor disturbance. Poor prognosis with TCAs may be indicated by neurotic, hypochondriacal, and hysterical traits; multiple prior episodes; and delusions.

It is important to note, however, as Otto et al. (1996) observed, that the attempt to match biological interventions to biological disruptions has been largely unsuccessful; that is, the fact that depression is related to certain biological abnormalities does not necessarily mean that biological treatments are the most effective way to treat the disorder, and the reverse is also true (i.e., psychological abnormalities may be best treated with biological therapies).

In sum, despite identifying certain factors at least weakly predictive of treatment response to CBT and TCAs, research that differentiates responders to pharmacotherapy and psychotherapy is lacking (see Miller et al., 1990, for a notable exception). Thus, an important direction for future research will be to distinguish individuals who respond better to one form of treatment than the other, then apply the appropriate therapy. This would theoretically result in more efficient and probably more effective treatment. The notion that matching patient variables to corresponding treatment modalities will produce better outcomes has intuitive appeal, but it remains to be seen whether it is pragmatically effective. Therefore, until a relation between patient characteristics and likely treatment response is empirically established, combined therapy appears to be the most effective form of treatment, as it has a wider range of coverage than either therapy administered singly.

Another benefit of combined therapy for depression is its coverage of different times during the course of depression. For example, medications may produce quicker responses than psychotherapy, but psychotherapy may reduce the rate of relapse. Thus, combined therapy leads to a quicker response rate than psychotherapy while also reducing the risk of later recurrence of the disorder. The course of the disorder is more completely covered by combined therapy than either of the two therapies singly. Of course, maintenance pharmacotherapy and psychotherapy would have similar time coverage but would increase the cost, time, and potential adverse effects associated with continued therapy. We are of the opinion that, if combined therapy administered over a relatively brief period can be as effective (and perhaps more effective) than either therapy administered indefinitely, combined therapy is the treatment of choice.

Disadvantages of Combined Treatments

One drawback to applying combined therapy to the treatment of depression is the addition of adverse side effects incurred by medication (when medication is added to psychotherapy). The experience of medication side effects not only causes the patient discomfort but also decreases the likelihood of treatment adherence and increases the risk of premature termination of treatment (e.g., McElroy, Keck, & Friedman, 1995). Finally, the issue of overdose is always a necessary concern when administering medications to depressed individuals in an outpatient setting.

The addition of psychotherapy to a pharmacological treatment plan, compared to pharmacological treatment alone, increases the amount of time spent by both patient and therapist. This is especially the case if the patient must go to a physician for medication checkups and to a psychologist or other nonmedical therapist for psychotherapy sessions. In today's time-driven environment each additional component of therapy may be viewed as a drawback by patients and third-party payers alike.

Issues of cost become more salient when treatment plans are expanded. This area needs little elaboration, as the addition of either pharmacotherapy or psychotherapy will lead to increased costs to both patient and third-party payers. Again, this issue is complex, because it is possible that long-range cost may be lower for combined therapy than the other two forms of treatment. Certainly, combined therapy is the most expensive option during the acute treatment phase, but it may be cheaper over the course of many years if it is more effective in preventing relapse and recurrence.

Analytical Limitations of Combined Treatment Studies

A number of potential limitations arise when aggregating data from multiple studies (as has been done in this chapter), and these must be considered when synthesizing the results of diverse studies. We discuss below a few of the most relevant limitations to our review of combined treatment research.

First, a number of the studies reviewed have lacked adequate statistical power to detect differences between the various forms of therapy used. Studies with small cell sizes of individuals receiving different treatments lack power to find true and significant effects of the treatments being investigated. A larger statistical problem occurs when attempting to measure additive effects of two relatively equipotent treatments. Because adding two equally effective treatments together is not likely to double the treatment effect size, interactive effects, although important, may be dismissed as nonsignificant. This becomes a major issue in the analysis of combined treatments for depression, because most studies have found psychotherapy and pharmacotherapy to be in general of equal potency in treating depression. Finally, combined treatment studies will require numerous cells and large sample sizes to detect significant differences, making such investigations costly and difficult to perform.

Even though the treatments used in depression studies have previously been shown to be effective (as mentioned earlier), the possibility of a placebo effect still threatens the validity of treatment outcome findings in this area. Unfortunately, only two new studies reviewed here (Reynolds, Frank, et al., 1999; Reynolds, Miller, et al., 1999) included a placebo control group in assessing the results of combined therapy. Hence, it is possible that some of the conclusions drawn from these studies would have been quite different if control groups had been included and treatment groups had not differed significantly from control groups.

In addition, variations across studies in the dosages and durations of therapies present a problem in drawing conclusions in combined-treatment research. Studies included in our review vary in length of psychotherapy sessions provided to patients from only 4 weeks (Bowers, 1990) up to 3 years (Reynolds, Miller, et al., 1999). Considerable variations also occurred in the relative dosages of antidepressants. This may be in part attributable to uncertainties regarding the most effective dosage of medications. Doses less than maximally effective are often used in order to minimize potential side effects and risks associated with the drugs. Consequently, a large percentage of patients may be "undertreated" in regard to the most effective level of medication. Certain researchers (e.g., Hollon et al., 1992), however, experimented with higher dosages in an attempt to maximize treatment effectiveness. The large variability in dose ranges encountered in such studies limits generalizability and limits the findings of systematic reviews of pharmacological interventions. A fourth potential problem area in compiling data across studies involves the grouping of diverse forms of psychotherapy under the general guise of psychotherapy. In unpublished preliminary data, Thase et al. (1997) reported on the comparability of IPT and CBT, finding similar recovery rates, but other data regarding comparisons among other forms of psychotherapy as components of combined protocols are limited. It should be noted that this problem is applicable to the use of various pharmacotherapies as well. All but two studies reviewed here (Keller et al., 2000; Savard et al., 1998) used TCAs. This may allow for some conclusions to be drawn regarding TCAs as a class, but it does not allow for comparability of drugs within the TCA class. Nevertheless, it allows for a greater degree of confidence than if SRIs or MAOIs had been commonly used. Future studies with newer agents will require comparison with findings generated from studies of TCAs.

Conclusion

The results of the empirical studies on combined treatment for depression vary somewhat but tend to converge on a single theme: Combined therapy may be more effective than psychotherapy alone or pharmacotherapy alone in the treatment of depressive episodes. This appears to be particularly the case with respect to patients with severe or chronic depressions. Throughout the literature on combined therapy versus pharmacotherapy or psychotherapy alone, a modest effect exists indicating that combined therapy is the treatment of choice. This effect is not large as measured by available investigations, but appears to be large enough to merit attention, especially considering that an effect for combined treatments is found in both acute and relapse prevention studies. It is worth noting, however, that our review suggests a less aggressive, single-treatment modality is likely to be sufficient in relatively uncomplicated, less severe cases of depression. In instances where there is less severe depression, it appears that patients would best be treated by either pharmacotherapy or psychotherapy alone, rather than increasing the cost, time, and effort of treatment by adding a relatively inconsequential second dimension to therapy. In our opinion, psychotherapy would be preferable to pharmacotherapy in such cases, because of the fewer adverse side effects and the higher treatment compliance associated with psychotherapy. In addition, psychotherapy seems to lead to lower relapse rates than pharmacotherapy after discontinuation of treatment (e.g., Evans et al., 1992).

There are still no specific findings indicating that certain antidepressant medications are superior to others in treating depression, although the general category of SRIs is often favored, largely because SRIs lead to fewer negative side effects. All but one study (Savard et al., 1998) on combined treatment reviewed in this chapter used TCAs rather than SRIs. This implies that a discrepancy might exist between currently available clinical research and clinical practice; that is, researchers have tested the effects of pharmacotherapy using TCAs, whereas clinicians are treating their patients with SRIs. This discrepancy between research and practice should disappear as clinical experience accumulates with the SRIs, an assumption borne out by the fact that recent studies have found no difference in the efficacies of TCAs and SRIs. In reference to psychotherapies,

CTs and CBTs have received the most support and have been the focus of the most empirical research conducted with depression. Other therapies, such as IPT, have also received some degree of empirical support.

Treatment Algorithm

On consideration of the research on various treatments available for unipolar depression, we have limned a treatment algorithm providing guidance for appropriate treatment strategies regarding depressed patients (see Figure 6.1). In an effort to actively engage patients in the therapeutic process, we feel that patients should be presented with the treatment options of psychotherapy, pharmacotherapy, or combined therapy, including general information regarding their effectiveness, cost, time involvement,

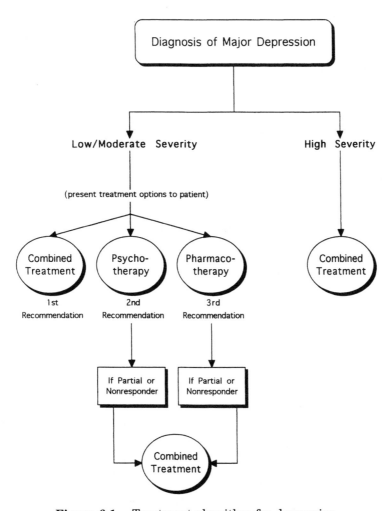

Figure 6.1.   Treatment algorithm for depression.

and potential side effects. This way, patients can weigh their options and have some say in the form of treatment they will undertake.

We recognize that not all patients will be able to make this decision (e.g., severely depressed, hospitalized patients) and that many will look for guidance from the mental health professional. In the event of severe depression, combined treatment appears to be the most beneficial form of treatment and is recommended as the initial treatment strategy. Moreover, when finances allow, research supports the implementation of combined treatment for mild and moderate levels of depression. Often, however, finances are limited, and patients with mild to moderate depression may be forced to choose between psychotherapy and pharmacotherapy. In this case, we recommend the administration of psychotherapy over pharmacotherapy, as psychotherapy appears to be as effective as pharmacotherapy during the acute treatment phase, typically prevents relapse at a higher rate, does not suffer from the adverse side effects associated with antidepressants, and may not be more expensive than pharmacotherapy over the long-term course of treatment (i.e., maintenance pharmacotherapy). In the event of partial or no response to psychotherapy, we recommend that antidepressant treatment be added to the current psychological treatment.

In addition to selecting the treatment modality to be offered, clinicians must also choose the specific form of treatment to be used within each modality. Regarding psychotherapy, empirical evidence supports the selection of CT, CBT, or IPTs. The various pharmacotherapies currently available appear to be similarly efficacious, although SRIs generally produce fewer adverse side effects than TCAs or MAOIs. Antidepressants should be selected and monitored on the basis of each patient's response to a particular drug.

References

Amenson, C. S., & Lewinsohn, P. M. (1981). An investigation into the observed sex difference in prevalence of unipolar depression. *Journal of Abnormal Psychology, 90,* 1–13.

Anderson, I. M., & Tomenson, B. M. (1994). The efficacy of selective serotonin reuptake inhibitors in depression: A meta-analysis of studies against tricyclic antidepressants. *Journal of Psychopharmacology, 8,* 238–249.

Anton, S. F., Robinson, D. S., Roberts, D. L., & Kensler, T. T. (1994). Long-term treatment of depression with nefazadone. *Psychopharmacology Bulletin, 30,* 165–169.

Antonuccio, D. O., Danton, W. G., & DeNelsky, G. Y. (1995). Psychotherapy versus medication for depression: Challenging the conventional wisdom with data. *Professional Psychology: Research and Practice, 26,* 574–585.

Antonuccio, D. O., Danton, W. G., DeNelsky, G. Y., Greenberg, R. P., & Gordon, J. S. (1999). Raising questions about antidepressants. *Psychotherapy and Psychosomatics, 68,* 3–14.

Antonuccio, D. O., Thomas, M., & Danton, W. G. (1997). A cost-effective analysis of cognitive behavior therapy and fluoxetine (Prozac) in the treatment of depression. *Behavior Therapy, 28,* 187–210.

Barden, N., Reul, J. M., & Holsboer, F. (1995). Do antidepressants stabilize mood through actions on the hypothalamic–pituitary–adrenocortical system? *Trends in Neuroscience, 18*(1), 6–11.

Beck, A. T. (1967). *Depression: Clinical, experimental and theoretical aspects.* New York: Harper & Row.

Beck, A. T. (1976). *Cognitive therapy and the emotional disorders*. New York: International Universities Press.

Beck, A. T., Hollon, S. D., Young, J. E., Bedrosian, R. C., & Budenz, D. (1985). Treatment of depression with cognitive therapy and amitriptyline. *Archives of General Psychiatry, 42*, 142–148.

Beck, A. T., Rush, A. J., Shaw, B., & Emery, G. (1979). *Cognitive therapy of depression*. New York: Guilford Press.

Beck, A. T., & Steer, R. A. (1987). *Manual for the revised Beck Depression Inventory*. San Antonio, TX: Psychological Corporation.

Bellack, A. S., Hersen, M., & Himmelhoch, J. (1981). Social skills training for depression: A treatment manual. *Catalog of Selected Documents in Psychology, 10*, 92.

Bielski, R. J., & Friedel, R. O. (1976). Prediction of tricyclic antidepressant response: A critical review. *Archives of General Psychiatry, 33*, 1479–1489.

Blackburn, I. M., Bishop, S., Glen, A. I., Whalley, L. J., & Christie, J. E. (1981). The efficacy of cognitive therapy in depression: A treatment trial using cognitive therapy and pharmacotherapy, each alone and in combination. *British Journal of Psychiatry, 139*, 181–189.

Blackburn, I. M., Eunson, K. M., & Bishop, S. (1986). A two-year naturalistic follow-up of depressed patients treated with cognitive therapy, pharmacotherapy, and a combination of both. *Journal of Affective Disorders, 10*, 67–75.

Blackwell, B. (1963). Hypertensive crisis due to monoamine oxidase inhibitors. *The Lancet, 11*, 849–851.

Blazer, D. G., Kessler, R. C., McGonagle, K. A., & Swartz, M. S. (1994). The prevalence and distribution of major depression in a national community sample: The National Comorbidity Survey. *American Journal of Psychiatry, 151*, 979–986.

Bowers, W. A. (1990). Treatment of depressed in-patients: Cognitive therapy plus medication, relaxation plus medication, and medication alone. *British Journal of Psychiatry, 156*, 73–78.

Brotman, A. W., & Falk, W. E. (1987). Pharmacologic treatment of acute depressive subtypes. In H. Y. Meltzer (Ed.), *Psychopharmacology: The third generation of progress* (pp. 1031–1040). New York: Raven Press.

Brown, R. A., & Lewinsohn, P. M. (1984). A psychoeducational approach to the treatment of depression: Comparison of control group, individual, and minimal contact procedures. *Journal of Consulting and Clinical Psychology, 52*, 774–783.

Comas-Diaz, L. (1981). Effects of cognitive and behavioral group treatment on the depressive symptomatology of Puerto Rican women. *Journal of Consulting and Clinical Psychology, 49*, 627–632.

Conte, H. R., Plutchik, R., Wild, K. V., & Toksoz, B. K. (1986). Combined psychotherapy and pharmacotherapy for depression: A systematic analysis of the evidence. *Archives of General Psychiatry, 43*, 471–479.

Cooper, A. J. (1989). Tyramine and irreversible monoamine oxidase inhibitors in clinical practice. *British Journal of Psychiatry, 155*(Suppl. 6), 38–45.

Covi, L., & Lipman, R. S. (1987). Cognitive–behavioral group psychotherapy combined with imipramine in major depression. *Psychopharmacology Bulletin, 23*, 173–176.

Cross-National Collaborative Group. (1992). The changing rate of major depression: Cross-national comparisons. *Journal of the American Medical Association, 268*, 3098–3105.

Cuijpers, P. (1998). A psychoeducational approach to the treatment of depression: A meta-analysis of Lewinsohn's "Coping With Depression" course. *Behavior Therapy, 29*, 521–533.

Davis, J. M., Wang, Z., & Janicak, P. G. (1993). A quantitative analysis of clinical drug trials for the treatment of affective disorders. *Psychopharmacology Bulletin, 29*, 175–181.

Depression Guideline Panel. (1993, April). *Depression in primary care: Vol. 1. Detection and diagnosis* (Clinical Practice Guideline No. 5, AHCPR Publication No. 93-0550). Rockville, MD: U.S. Department of Health and Human Services, Public Health Service, Agency for Health Care Policy and Research.

DeRubeis, R. J., Gelfand, L. A., Tang, T. Z., & Simons, A. D. (1999). Medications versus cognitive behavior therapy for severely depressed outpatients: Mega-analysis of four randomized comparisons. *American Journal of Psychiatry, 156*, 1007–1013.

DiMascio, A., Weissman, M. M., Prusoff, B. A., Neu, C., Zwilling, M., & Klerman, G. L. (1979). Differential symptom reduction by drugs and psychotherapy in acute depression. *Archives of General Psychiatry, 36*, 1450–1456.

Dobson, K. S. (1989). A meta-analysis of the efficacy of cognitive therapy of depression. *Journal of Consulting and Clinical Psychology, 57*, 414–419.

Elkin, I., Shea, M. T., Watkins, J. T., Imber, S. D., Sotsky, S. M., Collins, J. F., Glass, D. R., Pilkonis, P. A., Leber, W. R., Docherty, J. P., Fiester, S. J., & Parlof, M. B. (1989). National Institute of Mental Health Treatment of Depression Collaborative Program: General effectiveness of treatments. *Archives of General Psychiatry, 46*, 971–982.

Ellis, A. (1962). *Reason and emotion in psychotherapy*. Secaucus, NJ: Prentice-Hall.

Ellison, J. M. (1998). Antidepressant-induced sexual dysfunction: Review, classification, and suggestions for treatment. *Harvard Review of Psychiatry, 6*, 177–189.

Evans, M. D., Hollon, S. D., DeRubeis, R. J., Piasecki, J. M., Grove, W. M., Garvey, M. J., & Tuason, V. B. (1992). Differential relapse following cognitive therapy and pharmacotherapy for depression. *Archives of General Psychiatry, 49*, 802–808.

Fava, G. A., Rafanelli, C., Grandi, S., Canestrari, R., & Morphy, M. A. (1998). Six-year outcome for cognitive behavioral treatment of residual symptoms in major depression. *American Journal of Psychiatry, 155*, 1443–1445.

Fava, G. A., Rafanelli, C., Grandi, S., Conti, S., & Belluardo, P. (1998). Prevention of recurrent depression with cognitive behavioral therapy: Preliminary findings. *Archives of General Psychiatry, 55*, 816–820.

Fava, M., & Kaji, J. (1994). Continuation and maintenance treatments of major depressive disorder. *Psychiatric Annals, 24*, 281–290.

Fava, M., & Rosenbaum, J. F. (1991). Suicidality and fluoxetine: Is there a relationship? *Journal of Clinical Psychiatry, 52*, 108–111.

Feiger, A. D., Bielski, R. J., Bremner, J., Heiser, J. F., Trivedi, M., Wilcox, C. S., Roberts, D. L., Kensler, T. T., McQuade, R. D., Kaplita, S. B., & Archibald, D. G. (1999). Double-blind, placebo-substitution study of nefazodone in the prevention of relapse during continuation treatment of outpatients with major depression. *International Journal of Clinical Psychopharmacology, 14*, 19–28.

Frank, E., Kupfer, D. J., Perel, J. M., Cornes, C., Jarret, D. B., Mallinger, A. G., Thase, M. E., McEachran, A. B., & Grochocinski, V. J. (1990). Three-year outcomes for maintenance therapies in recurrent depression. *Archives of General Psychiatry, 47*, 1093–1099.

Frank, E., Kupfer, D. J., Wagner, E. F., McEachran, A. B., & Cornes, C. (1991). Efficacy of interpersonal psychotherapy as a maintenance treatment of recurrent depression: Contributing factors. *Archives of General Psychiatry, 48*, 1053–1059.

Frazer, A. (1997). Antidepressants. *Journal of Clinical Psychiatry, 58*(Suppl. 6), 9–25.

Greenberg, R. P., Bornstein, R. F., Greenberg, M. D., & Fisher, S. (1992). A meta-analysis of antidepressant outcome under "blinder" conditions. *Journal of Consulting and Clinical Psychology, 60*, 664–669.

Grimsley, S. R., & Jann, M. W. (1992). Paroxetine, sertraline, and fluoxetine: New selective serotonin reuptake inhibitors. *Clinical Pharmacy, 11*, 930–957.

Hersen, M., Bellack, A. S., Himmelhoch, J. M., & Thase, M. E. (1984). Effects of social skill training, amitriptyline, and psychotherapy in unipolar depressed women. *Behavior Therapy, 15*, 21–40.

Hersh, E. K., & Lazar, S. G. (1999). Cost-effectiveness of psychotherapy for depression. In D. Spiegel (Ed.), *Efficacy and cost-effectiveness of psychotherapy: Clinical practice* (Vol. 45, pp. 125–132). Washington, DC: American Psychiatric Association.

Hollon, S. D., & Beck, A. T. (1994). Cognitive and cognitive–behavioral therapies. In A. E. Bergin & S. L. Garfield (Eds.), *Handbook of psychotherapy and behavior change* (pp. 428–466). New York: Wiley.

Hollon, S. D., DeRubeis, R. J., & Evans, M. D. (1990). Combined cognitive therapy and pharmacotherapy in the treatment of depression. In D. W. Manning & A. J. Frances (Eds.), *Combined pharmacotherapy and psychotherapy for depression* (pp. 37–64). Washington, DC: American Psychiatric Press.

Hollon, S. D., DeRubeis, R. J., Evans, M. D., Wiemer, M. J., Garvey, M. J., Grove, W. M., & Tuason, V. B. (1992). Cognitive therapy and pharmacotherapy for depression: Singly and in combination. *Archives of General Psychiatry, 49*, 774–781.

Hollon, S. D., Shelton, R. C., & Davis, D. D. (1993). Cognitive therapy for depression: Conceptual issues and clinical efficacy. *Journal of Consulting and Clinical Psychology, 61*, 270–275.

Hollon, S. D., Shelton, R. C., & Loosen, P. T. (1991). Cognitive therapy and pharmacotherapy for depression. *Journal of Consulting and Clinical Psychology, 59*, 88–99.

Janicak, P. G., Davis, J. M., Preskorn, S. H., & Ayd, F. J., Jr. (1997). *Principles and practices of psychopharmacotherapy* (2nd ed.). Baltimore: Williams & Wilkins.

Joffe, R., Sokolov, S., & Streiner, D. (1996). Antidepressant treatment of depression: A meta-analysis. *Canadian Journal of Psychiatry, 41*, 613–616.

Kaplan, H. I., & Sadock, B. J. (1993). *Pocket handbook of psychiatric drug treatment*. Baltimore: Williams & Wilkins.

Kapur, S., Mieczkowski, T., & Mann, J. J. (1992). Antidepressant medication and the relative risk of suicide attempt and suicide. *Journal of the American Medical Association, 268*, 3441–3445.

Keller, M. B., Klerman, G. L., Lavori, P. W., Fawcett, J. A., Coryell, W., & Endicott, J. (1982). Treatment received by depressed patients. *Journal of the American Medical Association, 248*, 1848–1855.

Keller, M. B., McCullough, J. P., Klein, D. N., Arnow, B., Dunner, D. L., Gelenberg, A. J., Markowitz, J. C., Nemeroff, C. B., Russel, J. M., Thase, M. E., Trivedi, M. H., & Zajecka, J. (2000). A comparison of nefazodone, the cognitive behavioral analysis system of psychotherapy and their combination for the treatment of chronic depression. *New England Journal of Medicine, 342*, 1462–1470.

Kessler, R. C., McGonagle, K. A., Zhao, S., Nelson, C. B., Hughes, M., Eshleman, S., Wittchen, H., & Kendler, K. S. (1994). Lifetime and 12-month prevalence of *DSM–III–R* psychiatric disorders in the United States. *Archives of General Psychiatry, 51*, 8–19.

Khan, A., Warner, H. A., & Brown, W. D. (2000). Symptom reduction and suicide risk in patients treated with placebo in antidepressant clinical trials: An analysis of the Food and Drug Administration database. *Archives of General Psychiatry, 5*, 311–317.

Klein, D. F., & Davis, J. M. (1980). *Diagnosis and drug treatment of psychiatric disorders* (2nd ed.). Baltimore: Williams & Wilkins.

Klerman, G. L., & Cole, J. O. (1965). Clinical pharmacology of imipramine and related antidepressant compounds. *Pharmacology Review, 17*, 101–141.

Klerman, G. L., & Weissman, M. M. (1989). Increasing rates of depression. *Journal of the American Medical Association, 261*, 2229–2235.

Klerman, G. L., Weissman, M. M., Frank, E., Kocsis, J. H., Markowitz, J. C., & Montgomery, S. (1994). Evaluating drug treatments of depressive disorders. In R. F. Prien & D. S. Robinson (Eds.), *Clinical evaluation of psychotropic drugs: Principles and guidelines* (pp. 281–325). New York: Raven Press.

Klerman, G. L., Weissman, M. M., & Prusoff, B. A. (1982). RDC endogenous depression as a predictor of response to antidepressant drugs and psychotherapy. *Advances in Biochemical Psychopharmacology, 32*, 165–174.

Klerman, G. L., Weissman, M. M., Rounsaville, B. J., & Chevron, E. S. (1984). *Interpersonal psychotherapy of depression*. New York: Basic Books.

Kovacs, M., Rush, A. J., Beck, A. T., & Hollon, S. D. (1981). Depressed outpatients treated with cognitive therapy or pharmacotherapy: A one-year follow-up. *Archives of General Psychiatry, 38*, 33–39.

Krishnan, K. R. R. (1998). Monoamine oxidase inhibitors. In A. F. Schatzberg & C. B. Nemeroff (Eds.), *Textbook of psychopharmacology* (2nd ed., pp. 239–250). Washington, DC: American Psychiatric Press.

Kupfer, D. J. (1991). Long-term treatment of depression. *Journal of Clinical Psychiatry, 52*, 28–42.

Lave, J. R., Frank, R. G., Schulberg, H. C., & Kamlet, M. S. (1998). Cost-effectiveness of treatments for major depression in primary care practice. *Archives of General Psychiatry, 55*, 645–651.

Lejoyeux, M., & Ades, J. (1997). Antidepressant discontinuation: A review of the literature. *Journal of Clinical Psychiatry*, *58*(Suppl. 7), 11–16.

Lewinsohn, P. M., Antonuccio, D. O., Breckenridge, J. S., & Teri, L. (1984). *The "Coping With Depression" course*. Eugene, OR: Castalia.

Lewinsohn, P. M., & Clarke, G. N. (1984). Group treatment of depressed individuals: The "Coping With Depression" course. *Advances in Behavior Research and Therapy*, *6*, 99–114.

Lewinsohn, P. M., Rohde, P., Seeley, J. R., & Fischer, S. A. (1993). Age-cohort changes in the lifetime occurrence of depression and other mental disorders. *Journal of Abnormal Psychology*, *102*, 110–120.

Macaskill, N. D., & Macaskill, A. (1996). Rational–emotive therapy plus pharmacotherapy versus pharmacotherapy alone in the treatment of high cognitive dysfunction depression. *Cognitive Therapy and Research*, *20*, 575–592.

Manji, H. K. (1992). G proteins: Implications for psychiatry. *American Journal of Psychiatry*, *149*, 746–760.

Manning, D. W., & Frances, A. J. (1990). Combined therapy for depression: Critical review of the literature. In D. W. Manning & A. J. Frances (Eds.), *Combined pharmacotherapy and psychotherapy for depression* (pp. 3–33). Washington, DC: American Psychiatric Press.

McElroy, S. L., Keck, P. E., & Friedman, L. M. (1995). Minimizing and managing antidepressant side effects. *Journal of Clinical Psychiatry*, *56*(Suppl. 2), 49–55.

McLean, P. D., & Hakistian, A. R. (1990). Relative endurance of unipolar depression treatment effects: Longitudinal follow-up. *Journal of Consulting and Clinical Psychology*, *58*, 482–488.

Miller, I. W., Norman, W. H., & Keitner, G. I. (1990). Treatment response of high cognitive dysfunction depressed inpatients. *Comprehensive Psychiatry*, *30*, 61–72.

Montgomery, S. A., & Kasper, S. (1998). Side effects, dropouts from treatment and cost consequences. *International Clinical Psychopharmacology*, *13*(Suppl. 2), 1–5.

Monti, P. M., Corriveau, D., & Curran, J. P. (1980). Social skills training for psychiatric patients: Treatment and outcome. In J. P. Curran & P. M. Monti (Eds.), *Social skills training* (pp. 185–223). New York: Guilford Press.

Morris, J. B., & Beck, A. T. (1974). The efficacy of antidepressant drugs: A review of research (1958 to 1972). *Archives of General Psychiatry*, *30*, 667–674.

Mufson, L., Weissman, M. M., Moreau, D., & Garfinkel, R. (1999). Efficacy of interpersonal psychotherapy for depressed adolescents. *Archives of General Psychiatry*, *56*, 573–579.

Murphy, D. L., Aulakh, C. S., & Garrick, N. A. (1987). Monoamine oxidase inhibitors as antidepressants: Implications for the mechanism of action of antidepressants and the psychobiology of the affective disorders and some related disorders. In H. Y. Meltzer (Ed.), *Psychopharmacology: The third generation of progress* (pp. 545–552). New York: Raven Press.

Murphy, G. E., Simons, A. D., Wetzel, R. D., & Lustman, P. J. (1984). Cognitive therapy and pharmacotherapy: Singly and together in the treatment of depression. *Archives of General Psychiatry*, *41*, 33–41.

Narrow, W. E., Regier, D. A., Rae, D. S., Manderscheid, R. W., & Locke, B. Z. (1993). Use of services by persons with mental and addictive disorders: Findings from the National Institute of Mental Health Epidemiological Catchment Area Program. *Archives of General Psychiatry*, *50*, 95–107.

Oliver, J. M., & Simmons, M. E. (1985). Affective disorders and depression as measured by the Diagnostic Interview Schedule and the Beck Depression Inventory in an unselected adult population. *Journal of Clinical Psychology*, *41*, 469–477.

Otto, M. W., Pava, J. A., & Sprich-Buckminster, S. (1996). Treatment of major depression: Applications and efficacy of cognitive–behavioral therapy. In M. H. Pollack, M. W. Otto, & J. F. Rosenbaum (Eds.), *Challenges in clinical practice* (pp. 31–52). New York: Guilford Press.

Peterson, A. L., & Halstead, T. S. (1998). Group cognitive behavior therapy for depression in a community setting: A clinical replication series. *Behavior Therapy*, *29*, 3–18.

Preskorn, S. H., & Burke, M. (1992). Somatic therapy for major depressive disorder: Selection of an antidepressant. *Journal of Clinical Psychiatry*, *53*(Suppl. 9), 5–18.

Prien, R. F., & Kocsis, J. H. (1995). Long-term treatment of mood disorders. In F. E. Bloom & D. J. Kupfer (Eds.), *Psychopharmacology: The fourth generation of progress* (pp. 1067–1079). New York: Raven Press.

Prien, R. F., & Kupfer, D. J. (1986). Continuation drug therapy for major depressive episodes: How long should it be maintained? *American Journal of Psychiatry, 143*, 18–23.

Prusoff, B. A., Weissman, M. M., Klerman, G. L., & Rounsaville, B. J. (1980). Research diagnostic criteria subtypes of depression: Their role as predictors of differential response to psychotherapy and drug treatment. *Archives of General Psychiatry, 37*, 796–801.

Quitkin, F. M., McGrath, R. J., Stewart, J. W., Harrison, W., Tricamo, E., Wager, S. G., Ocepek-Welikson, K., Nunes, E., Rabkin, J. G., & Klein, D. F. (1990). Atypical depression, panic attacks, and response to imipramine and phenelzine. *Archives of General Psychiatry, 47*, 935–941.

Quitkin, F. M., Stewart, J. W., McGrath, P. J., Tricamo, E., Rabkin, J. G., Ocepek-Welikson, K., Nunes, E., Harrison, W., & Klein, D. F. (1993). Columbia atypical depression: A subgroup of depressives with better response to MAOI than to tricyclic antidepressants or placebo. *British Journal of Psychiatry, 163*, 30–34.

Rehm, L. P., Kaslow, N. J., & Rabin, A. S. (1987). Cognitive and behavioral targets in a self-control therapy program for depression. *Journal of Consulting and Clinical Psychology, 55*, 60–67.

Reynolds, C. F. III, Frank, E., Kupfer, D. J., Thase, M. E., Perel, J. M., Mazumdar, S., & Houck, P. R. (1996). Treatment outcome in recurrent major depression: A post hoc comparison of elderly ("young old") and midlife patients. *American Journal of Psychiatry, 153*, 1288–1292.

Reynolds, C. F. III, Frank, E., Perel, J. M., Imber, S. D., Cornes, C., Miller, M. D., Mazumdar, S., Houck, P. R., Dew, M. A., Stack, J. A., Pollock, B. G., & Kupfer, D. J. (1999). Nortriptyline and interpersonal psychotherapy as maintenance therapies for recurrent major depression: A randomized controlled trial in patients older than 59 years. *Journal of the American Medical Association, 281*, 39–45.

Reynolds, C. F. III, Miller, M. D., Pasternak, R. E., Frank, E., Perel, J. M., Cornes, C., Houck, P. R., Mazumdar, S., Dew, M. A., & Kupfer, D. J. (1999). Treatment of bereavement-related major depressive episodes in later life: A controlled study of acute and continuation treatment with nortriptyline and interpersonal psychotherapy. *American Journal of Psychiatry, 156*, 202–208.

Richelson, E. (1994). The pharmacology of antidepressants at the synapse: Focus on newer compounds. *Journal of Clinical Psychiatry, 55*(9, Suppl. A), 34–39.

Rickels, K., & Schweizer, E. (1990). Clinical overview of serotonin reuptake inhibitors. *Journal of Clinical Psychiatry, 51*(12, Suppl. B), 9–12.

Robinson, L. A., Berman, J. S., & Neimeyer, R. A. (1990). Psychotherapy for the treatment of depression: A comprehensive review of controlled outcome research. *Psychological Bulletin, 108*, 30–49.

Rush, A. J., Beck, A. T., Kovacs, M., & Hollon, S. (1977). Comparative efficacy of cognitive therapy and pharmacotherapy in the treatment of depressed outpatients. *Cognitive Therapy and Research, 1*, 17–37.

Rush, A. J., & Hollon, S. D. (1991). Depression. In B. D. Beitman & G. L. Klerman (Eds.), *Integrating pharmacotherapy and psychotherapy* (pp. 121–142). Washington, DC: American Psychiatric Press.

Savard, J., Laberge, B., Gauthier, J. G., Fournier, J., Bouchard, S., Baril, J., & Bergeron, M. G. (1998). Combination of fluoxetine and cognitive therapy for the treatment of major depression among people with HIV infection: A time-series analysis investigation. *Cognitive Therapy and Research, 22*, 21–46.

Scott, M. J., & Stradling, S. G. (1990). Group cognitive therapy for depression produces clinically significant reliable change in community based settings. *Behavioural Psychotherapy, 18*, 1–19.

Settle, E. C. (1992). Antidepressant side effects: Issues and options [Monograph]. *Journal of Clinical Psychiatry, 10*, 48–61.

Shea, M. T., Elkin, I., Imber, S. D., Sotsky, S. M., Watkins, J. T., Collins, J. F., Pilkonis, P. A., Beckham, E., Glass, D. R., Dolan, R. T., & Parloff, M. B. (1992). Course of depressive symptoms over follow-up: Findings from the National Institute of Mental Health Treatment of Depression Collaborative Research Program. *Archives of General Psychiatry, 49*, 782–787.

Simons, A. D., Gordon, J. S., Monroe, S. M., & Thase, M. E. (1995). Toward an integration of psychologic, social, and biologic factors in depression: Effects on outcome and course of cognitive therapy. *Journal of Consulting and Clinical Psychology, 63*, 369–377.

Simons, A. D., Lustman, P. J., Wetzel, R. D., & Murphy, G. E. (1985). Predicting response to cognitive therapy of depression: The role of learned resourcefulness. *Cognitive Therapy and Research, 9*, 79–89.

Simons, A. D., Murphy, G. E., Levine, J. L., & Wetzel, R. D. (1986). Cognitive therapy and pharmacotherapy for depression: Sustained improvement over one year. *Archives of General Psychiatry, 43*, 43–48.

Song, F., Freemantle, N., Sheldon, T. A., House, A., Watson, P., Long, A., & Mason, J. (1993). Selective serotonin reuptake inhibitors: Meta-analysis of efficacy and acceptability. *British Medical Journal, 306*, 683–687.

Spangler, D. L., Simons, A. D., Monroe, S. M., & Thase, M. E. (1997). Response to cognitive–behavioral therapy in depression: Effects of pretreatment cognitive dysfunction and life stress. *Journal of Consulting and Clinical Psychology, 65*, 568–575.

Sussman, N. (1999). The role of antidepressants in sexual dysfunction [Monograph]. *Journal of Clinical Psychiatry, 17*, 9–14.

Teasdale, J. D., Fennel, M. J., Hibbert, G. A., & Amies, P. L. (1984). Cognitive therapy for major depressive disorder in primary care. *British Journal of Psychiatry, 144*, 400–406.

Thase, M. E. (1990). Relapse and recurrence in unipolar major depression: Short-term and long-term approaches. *Journal of Clinical Psychiatry, 51*(6, Suppl.), 51–57.

Thase, M. E. (1993). Maintenance treatments of recurrent affective disorders. *Current Opinion in Psychiatry, 6*, 16–21.

Thase, M. E. (1999). Redefining antidepressant efficacy toward long-term recovery. *Journal of Clinical Psychiatry, 60*(Suppl. 6), 15–19.

Thase, M. E., Fasiczka, A. L., Berman, S. R., Simons, A. D., & Reynolds, C. F. III. (1998). Electroencephalographic sleep profiles before and after cognitive behavior therapy of depression. *Archives of General Psychiatry, 55*, 138–144.

Thase, M. E., Greenhouse, J. B., Frank, E., Reynolds, C. F. III, Pilkonis, P. A., Hurley, K., Grochocinski, V., & Kupfer, D. J. (1997). Treatment of major depression with psychotherapy–pharmacotherapy combinations. *Archives of General Psychiatry, 54*, 1009–1015.

Thase, M. E., & Howland, R. H. (1995). Biological processes in depression: An updated review and integration. In E. E. Beckham & W. R. Leber (Eds.), *Handbook of depression* (2nd ed., pp. 213–279). New York: Guilford Press.

Thase, M. E., & Kupfer, D. J. (1996). Recent developments in the pharmacotherapy of mood disorders. *Journal of Consulting and Clinical Psychology, 64*, 646–659.

Thase, M. E., Reynolds, C. F. III, Frank, E., Simons, A. D., McGeary, J., Fasiczka, A. L., Garamoni, G. G., Jennings, J. R., & Kupfer D. J. (1994). Do depressed men and women respond similarly to cognitive behavior therapy? *American Journal of Psychiatry, 151*, 500–505.

Thase, M. E., Simons, A. D., Cahalane, J., McGeary, J., & Harden, T. (1991). Severity of depression and response to cognitive behavior therapy. *American Journal of Psychiatry, 148*, 784–789.

Thase, M. E., Simons, A. D., & Reynolds, C. F. III. (1993). Psychobiological correlates of poor response to cognitive behavior therapy: Potential indications for antidepressant pharmacotherapy. *Psychopharmacology Bulletin, 29*, 293–301.

Thase, M. E., Simons, A. D., & Reynolds, C. F. III. (1996). Abnormal electroencephalographic sleep profiles in major depression: Association with response to cognitive behavior therapy. *Archives of General Psychiatry, 53*, 99–108.

Thase, M. E., & Sullivan, L. R. (1995). Relapse and recurrence of depression: A practical approach for prevention. *CNS Drugs, 4*, 261–277.

Thase, M. E., Trivedi, M. H., & Rush, A. J. (1995). MAOIs in the contemporary treatment of depression. *Neuropsychopharmacology, 12,* 185–219.

Von Korff, M., Katon, W., Bush, T., Lin, E. H., Simon, G. E., Saunders, K., Ludman, E., Walker, E., & Unutzer, J. (1998). Treatment costs, cost offset, and cost-effectiveness of collaborative management of depression. *Psychosomatic Medicine, 60,* 143–149.

Wachtel, H. (1990). The second messenger dysbalance hypothesis of affective disorders. *Pharmacopsychiatry, 23,* 27–32.

Weissman, M. M. (1979). The psychological treatment of depression: Evidence for the efficacy of psychotherapy alone, in comparison with, and in combination with pharmacotherapy. *Archives of General Psychiatry, 36,* 1261–1269.

Weissman, M. M., Bruce, M. L., Leaf, P. J., Florio, L. P., & Holzer, C. (1991). Affective disorders. In L. N. Robins & D. S. Regier (Eds.), *Psychiatric disorders of America: The epidemiologic catchment area of study* (pp. 53–80). New York: Free Press.

Weissman, M. M., Klerman, G. L., Prusoff, B. A., Sholomskas, D., & Padian, N. (1981). Depressed outpatients: Results one year after treatment with drugs and/or interpersonal psychotherapy. *Archives of General Psychiatry, 38,* 52–55.

Weissman, M. M., Prusoff, B. A., DiMascio, A., Neu, C., Goklaney, M., & Klerman, G. L. (1979). The efficacy of drugs and psychotherapy in the treatment of acute depressive episodes. *American Journal of Psychiatry, 136,* 555–558.

Wexler, B. E., & Cicchetti, D. V. (1992). The outpatient treatment of depression: Implications of outcome research for clinical practice. *Journal of Nervous and Mental Disease, 180,* 277–286.

Zettle, R. D., & Rains, J. C. (1989). Group cognitive and contextual therapies in the treatment of depression. *Journal of Clinical Psychology, 45,* 436–445.

Zuckerman, D. M., Prusoff, B. A., Weissman, M. M., & Padian, N. S. (1980). Personality as a predictor of psychotherapy and pharmacotherapy outcome for depressed outpatients. *Journal of Consulting and Clinical Psychology, 48,* 730–735.

7

Combined Treatments and Rehabilitation of Schizophrenia

William D. Spaulding, Dale L. Johnson, and Robert D. Coursey

This chapter is for mental health practitioners who work with clients who have schizophrenia or similar disorders, as a member of an interdisciplinary treatment and rehabilitation team. Psychopharmacology usually plays a significant role in the work of such teams. Although a physician member of the team usually has direct responsibility for prescribing the medications, all team members should share responsibility for identifying targets for treatment, monitoring medication effects, and integrating pharmacological and psychosocial approaches. Psychologists are often the team members most knowledgeable and experienced in assessment of cognition and behavior, including changes produced by psychopharmacological treatment. They are also often the most knowledgeable and experienced in conducting treatment and rehabilitation as a sequence of controlled clinical trials and in analyzing and interpreting the data generated by such trials. Treatment and rehabilitation rely heavily on these skills for optimum outcome. Consequently, the team's overall effectiveness is determined not only by psychologists' expertise in assessment and experimental design but also by their ability to apply this expertise to issues of psychopharmacology in the comprehensive treatment and rehabilitation of schizophrenia.

In recent years many psychosocial approaches have demonstrated effectiveness for improving the personal and social functioning and quality of life of people with severe and disabling psychiatric disorders. These approaches are increasingly included, along with specialized pharmacotherapeutic approaches, under the umbrella term *psychiatric rehabilitation* (Anthony, Cohen, & Farkas, 1990; Liberman, 1992).[1] The concept of

---

[1] The term *psychiatric rehabilitation* may be confused with *psychosocial rehabilitation*, and the two are sometimes used interchangeably. In practice, both are sometimes used as a contraction of *biopsychosocial rehabilitation*. However, *psychosocial rehabilitation* sometimes specifically refers to a particular type of program, associated with specific prototypes, such as Fountain House in New York and Thresholds in Chicago. For example, a recent set of practice guidelines (McEvoy, Scheifler, & Frances, 1999) explicitly distinguished between psychiatric and psychosocial rehabilitation in this way.

rehabilitation de-emphasizes traditional allopathic treatment goals, such as "cure" or even "resolution of symptoms," and instead emphasizes the importance of acquiring skills necessary to manage the disorder, minimize the impact of disabilities, and get on with life. Achievement of these goals constitutes *recovery*. This reorientation obviates old debates about whether schizophrenia should be viewed as a medical problem requiring medical treatment and creates a conceptual environment wherein both biological and psychosocial approaches can work in complementary ways toward common ends. It is in this context that the goal of recovery is now best understood not as escaping an illness but as overcoming the consequences of an illness that cannot at present be fully eliminated, using combinations of pharmacological and psychosocial techniques. Psychologists and other nonmedical mental health professionals have an essential role in setting the stage for a rehabilitation and recovery agenda and in making it possible (Johnson, 1990).

New developments in treatment and rehabilitation have appeared, and the clinical armamentarium is growing. In the area of psychosocial treatment, specific intervention modalities are available for an increasing number of the particular functional impairments associated with schizophrenia and similar disorders, including interpersonal functioning, stress management and emotional regulation, and various domains of cognition. Helpful techniques are increasingly available not only to mental health professionals but also to families, friends, employers, spouses, and the affected individuals themselves. Psychopharmacotherapy has reached a new and exciting level with the advent of the atypical antipsychotic drugs. These medications tend to produce more effective relief of major psychotic symptoms, and they may also produce better cognitive functioning as well. Because they cause fewer side effects, they are more likely to be taken as prescribed. Medication nonadherence is a major (but not the only) factor in exacerbation of symptoms or relapse. These advances in medical treatment have not made psychosocial treatments less important; on the contrary, they have made them more important. With the new medications and psychosocial interventions it is now possible to expect not only symptom relief but also some degree of recovery in most patients.

Effective Modalities in Treatment and Rehabilitation

The past 30 years have seen much systematic research on the efficacy of various treatment approaches for schizophrenia, both pharmacological and psychosocial. Interpretation of this research is difficult and complex, for several reasons. First, schizophrenia is a complex condition that changes over time. Treatment most applicable or efficacious during one phase of the disorder is not necessarily equally so during other phases. Second, the heterogeneity of people with schizophrenia complicates outcome research just as it complicates etiological research. The approach or combination of approaches optimal for one individual is not necessarily optimal for the next. Third, individual circumstances may mediate the effectiveness of any particular approach. This is especially true for psychosocial approaches that emphasize adaptation to certain environments, as opposed to adaptability to environments in general. For example, family-focused interventions are more important for patients who have regular contact with their families and less important for those who do not. Fourth, treatment trials often combine a number of specific modalities in a single experimental condition. This reflects the multimodal nature of rehabilitation, and it permits conclusions about overall efficacy, but it does not permit conclusions about the unique contributions of specific modalities.

The complexity and heterogeneity of the schizophrenic syndrome produces a multiplicity of treatment and rehabilitation goals, and this affects outcome research. Different but equally important outcomes include reduction of psychotic symptoms, reduction of other problem behaviors, normalization of affective experience and self-esteem, and improvement of skill performance in many domains of personal and social functioning. Progress on any one of these can be quite independent of progress on the others. Different modalities usually target different goals, so experimental comparison of modalities often has limited value. For example, there is little value in showing that a modality designed to improve social skills does so better than a modality designed to improve housekeeping skills. As a result, comparative-outcome studies that pit two contending interventions against each other are less often of interest in rehabilitation than in other areas. *Additive* outcome trial designs are more useful in that they evaluate the unique contribution of a particular modality to some outcome when used in conjunction with other modalities (see Spaulding, 1992). For example, social skills training would be added to a larger regimen of rehabilitation services to determine whether it uniquely enhances improvement on a measure of social competence. The rehabilitation services are a standard regimen, provided to all participants, not a separate condition in the study design. In an additive design control conditions are used to control for placebo and related artifacts, not to determine the differential efficacy of the conditions.

It is important to understand that there has been much simplistic and unhelpful debate about the efficacy of treatments for schizophrenia over the entire 20th century. Much of this is attributable to unreflective acceptance of a simplistic view of schizophrenia as a unitary, homogeneous disorder. Similarly, parochial attitudes about science have polarized the mental health community. In the 1960s, even as psychoanalysis was losing credibility as the principal paradigm of psychopathology and mental health, the insights of social critics such as Erving Goffman (1961) and the experimental work of social psychologists such as the Braginskys (Braginsky, Braginsky, & Ring, 1969) elucidated the pathogenic role of mental hospitals and other social institutions, especially for severe mental illness. Previous views of schizophrenia as a biological disorder yielded to the view that it is a psychosocial phenomenon. Within 10 years, with the advent of antipsychotic drugs, opinion swung to the other pole, and views of schizophrenia again became dominated by naive biological reductionism. Psychosocial treatment was viewed by some as a form of welfare (e.g., Klein,

1980). As the limitations of pharmacological treatment became evident in the late 1970s, there was renewed interest in psychosocial treatment.

Throughout these vacillations, research on both pharmacological and psychosocial treatment followed a progression that should be quite familiar to psychologists. As with the history of psychotherapy research, treatment benefits tend to appear first as nonspecific; that is, people in general benefit from treatment in general. As research progresses, the active components of treatment and their relations to specific recipient characteristics are gradually identified. It was evident early on that, in general, any antipsychotic medication tends to be more beneficial than none, and any psychosocial service tends to be more beneficial than the neglect and squalor to which people with severe mental illness have been subjected historically. Today science has reached an intermediate stage of progress in schizophrenia treatment research. The mechanisms and active components of nonspecific treatment effects are just now being identified. No treatment should be devalued simply because its effects are nonspecific; ultimately, the best outcome is achieved with a full understanding of specific and nonspecific treatment effects.

Professional practice guides to treatment of schizophrenia are increasingly available (see Smith & Docherty, 1998). The *Guidelines for Treatment of Schizophrenia* prepared by the American Psychiatric Association (1997) are intended to provide practical advice for the prescribing physician including in regard to dosing strategies, management of comorbid conditions, and side effects. These guidelines also list the panoply of psychosocial approaches of known effectiveness but do not describe them or give much further information. The *Expert Consensus Guideline Series Treatment of Schizophrenia 1999* (McEvoy, Scheifler, & Frances, 1999), an update of an earlier set (Francis, Docherty, & Kahn, 1996), include detailed protocols for selecting pharmacological and psychosocial treatments and related services. *Schizophrenia Treatment Outcomes Research* (Lehman, Thompson, Dixon, & Scott, 1995) is a thorough review of the efficacy and effectiveness of treatments for schizophrenia. Finally, a special issue of the *Journal of Consulting and Clinical Psychology*, edited by Kendall (1998), is devoted to empirically supported psychological therapies and includes material relevant to the treatment of schizophrenia. Mental health professionals whose practice includes people with schizophrenia should be familiar will all four of these sources.

Despite the existence of guidelines and a robust outcome literature, a cardinal rule in treatment of schizophrenia is to emphasize tailoring of treatment to the individual recipient. Functional assessment and a hypothetico–deductive approach to evaluating treatment response for the individual case are the main tools in the tailoring process. This is a maxim familiar to psychologists in assessment and treatment of all behavior problems, but the complexity and heterogeneity of schizophrenia make it particularly applicable to psychiatric rehabilitation.

An integration of the various guidelines, reviews, meta-analyses, and outcome studies in the professional and scientific literature yields the following list of specific modalities of known effectiveness that should be considered essential elements of the service repertoire for people with schizophrenia. Although not all these modalities may be needed for all people with schizophrenia, a service system that serves all people with disabling psychiatric disorders should be expected to have the capability of providing any or all when needed.

Enlightened Psychopharmacotherapy

There is some recognition in the psychiatric literature that the complexity of schizophrenia and the unpredictability of its response to treatment demand a somewhat unconventional approach to pharmacotherapy (Falloon & Liberman, 1983; Liberman, Corrigan, & Schade, 1989; Liberman, Falloon & Wallace, 1984). There are two key principles: (a) Although antipsychotic drugs are a sine qua non in treating schizophrenia, they are almost never sufficient by themselves, and so special attention must be given to coordinating pharmacological and psychosocial treatment, and (b) nothing can be taken for granted about the effectiveness of any particular drug intervention, and so each intervention must be systematically, comprehensively, and objectively evaluated in a hypothetico–deductive, trial-and-test approach to treatment.

Rehabilitation Counseling

Rehabilitation counseling, primarily associated with the work of William Anthony and his colleagues (Anthony et al., 1990), represents a fusion of key concepts and principles from traditional physical rehabilitation and traditional client-centered psychotherapy. Rehabilitation counseling typically involves a periodic meeting of the client and at least one other member of the treatment and rehabilitation team. Both directive and nondirective psychotherapy techniques are used to identify the problems that require treatment and rehabilitation, the client's desires and concerns, and resources to be applied. The initial objective is to reach consensus about the client's needs and what the team can do about them. A subsequent objective is to construct an individualized treatment and rehabilitation plan that integrates the team's goals (remember that the client is a member of the team) and objectives with specific interventions and other services. All the pharmacological and psychosocial modalities to be used in the client's treatment and rehabilitation are included on this plan, and it thus takes on a key role in consolidating each team member's understanding of the purpose and importance of each modality and service. This is seen as crucial to maximally engaging the client in rehabilitation and ensuring high-fidelity implementation of the treatment plan. As the treatment plan is implemented, the focus of counseling turns to appraisal and evaluation of progress, with the ongoing objective of reinforcing the client's experience of success and self-efficacy. Counseling continues until the treatment plan goals have been met and recovery is as complete as possible.

There have been no controlled experimental analyses of the unique contribution of rehabilitation counseling to outcome. It plays such a central role that comprehensive psychiatric rehabilitation would be difficult to provide, if not impossible, without it.

Social Skills Training

This modality is familiar to behaviorally oriented psychologists, having been widely applied to a diversity of recipient populations. They are highly developed and manualized versions designed specifically for recipients with severe and persistent schizophrenia. The most widely researched and used are disseminated by Robert Liberman and his colleagues at the University of California, Los Angeles (UCLA) Center for Research on Treatment and Rehabilitation of Psychosis, along with related therapist training materials.[2] Original research studies and a meta-analysis of 27 controlled trials (Benton & Schroeder, 1998) are consistent in showing that formal social skills training improves personal and social functioning and reduces hospital recidivism in participants with schizophrenia.

Social skills training of the type known to be effective for schizophrenia is an energetic, highly structured, highly interactive modality. It involves almost continuous use of role-playing exercises, with all group members serving as observers and assistants when not actually role playing. It is necessary for the therapist to engage the trainees and achieve their active participation throughout treatment. Unfortunately, "social skills" groups in mental health settings are often quite a bit less than this. The availability of therapist training materials and related resources make it possible for most mental health settings to be able to provide high-quality services, but only if the training is actually done and high fidelity to training precepts is assured by quality-assurance mechanisms.

Independent Living Skills Training

This modality also is familiar to behaviorally oriented psychologists. People with schizophrenia and related disorders often lose or fail to develop skills associated with routine daily living, such as keeping a daily schedule, housekeeping, cooking, management of personal funds, and using public resources. Acquisition of these skills contributes importantly to the ability to live safely and comfortably outside institutions.

Trainees receive classroom instruction and in vivo coaching to establish the knowledge base and performance ability necessary to use specific skills. The required therapist skills are often in the professional training

---

[2]Materials developed by the UCLA Center for Research on Treatment and Rehabilitation of Psychosis can be obtained by submitting a request to Psychiatric Rehabilitation Consultants, P.O. Box 2867, Camarillo, CA 93011-2867.

of psychiatric nurses, occupational therapists, and other mental health professionals besides psychologists.

Occupational Skills Training

Occupational functioning incorporates both "work" and "play." In the work domain, occupational skills are generally understood to be those that are important for any work-related activity, for example, punctuality, proper workplace grooming, staying on task, following instructions, and managing relationships with coworkers and supervisors. These should not be confused with vocational skills, which are more specific to particular kinds of work. Leisure and recreational skills, including identifying interests and planning activities, are as important to stable functioning and a decent quality of life as are work skills. Occupational skills training should not be confused with occupational therapy, a specific modality provided by certified occupational or recreational therapists.

Disorder Management Training

This modality has gradually differentiated itself from related social and living skills approaches, reflecting a growing recognition that specialized skills are needed to manage psychiatric disorders, comparable to skills needed to manage severe and persistent physical conditions, such as diabetes. Students learn about the episodic and persistent symptoms of their disorder, the relation between these symptoms and functional impairments, pharmacological and other techniques (e.g., relaxation and stress management) for controlling the symptoms, drug side effects, identification of warning signs of an impending relapse, and various other aspects of their disorder and its management. Behavioral skills indirectly relevant to disorder management are included, for example, the assertive skills necessary for dealing with the doctor and the doctor's receptionist in getting an appointment for a medication review.

Skill training packages have been developed by the UCLA dissemination center, including materials for training therapists. The UCLA medication management and symptom management modalities have proven effective in enhancing medication adherence and preventing relapse (Eckman, Liberman, Phipps, & Blair, 1990).

Recently, disorder management training for schizophrenia has begun to benefit from relapse prevention and related techniques (e.g., Birchwood, 1995; Bradshaw, 1996; Kavanagh, 1992; O'Connor, 1991). Well known for application in substance abuse, many of the techniques of relapse prevention are well suited to the episodic nature of schizophrenia and the important role of the identified patient in managing those episodes. The original application of relapse prevention is also of interest, as people with schizophrenia often have substance abuse problems as well. So far there have been no controlled trials of the unique contribution of relapse prevention techniques to disorder management in schizophrenia.

Family Psychoeducation

A broad spectrum of family processes and therapies have long been of interest in schizophrenia research. In the 1950s, many people believed that families, and parents in particular, have a causal role in the etiology of the disorder. This view was never empirically supported and today is largely discredited. Nevertheless, family members often experience guilt and distress in this regard. Furthermore, they are usually overwhelmed by the burden of living with and trying to help a person with a serious mental illness. Clinicians should always be vigilant in watching for these problems and should intervene with corrective information when indicated (Johnson, 1995).

In controlled-outcome trials, family services that include psychoeducation, coping skills and problem-solving training, behavioral management, and social support have been found to reduce relapse and recidivism rates (e.g., Falloon, McGill, Boyd, & Pederson, 1987; Hogarty et al., 1991; Leff, Kuipers, Berkowitz, & Sturgeon, 1985; Lam, 1991).

A variant of this approach to family services uses multifamily psychoeducational groups to build supportive social networks and to teach coping and problem-solving skills (McFarlane & Cunningham, 1996). In controlled comparative studies the multifamily format has been superior to a single-family format in reducing relapse (McFarlane, Link, Dushay, Marchal, & Crilly, 1995; McFarlane, Lukens, et al., 1995).

Controlled trials of briefer family education and support modalities, ranging from 1 to 8 sessions, have been found to increase family members' sense of support from the treatment team, increase their knowledge about schizophrenia and its treatment and rehabilitation, improve their self-reported coping, reduce distress and self-blame, and increase satisfaction with services (Abramowitz & Coursey, 1989; Posner, Wilson, Kral, Lander, & McIlraith, 1992). However, the briefer modalities have not been shown to reduce relapse or hospital recidivism.

Mueser and Gingrich (1995) provided a book that serves as a manual for family members undergoing psychoeducation. In addition to didactically presented information, it included "workbook" materials for learning and practicing behavioral analysis and problem solving, making it ideally suited as a resource for education and support groups. Similar, more comprehensive, materials are available for professionals (Mueser & Glynn, 2000).

Contingency Management

Contingency management is a genre of techniques that evolved from learning and social-learning theories in the 1960s. They are especially important in psychiatric inpatient settings (see Corrigan & Liberman, 1994).

Nevertheless, contingency management is one of the most underused technologies in adult mental health services. Implementation is complicated by the need for administrative mechanisms to review and approve individual treatment plans, because of the potentially restrictive nature of the approach and the fact that it is often used to address problems with people who are involuntary patients.

The earliest applications of contingency management for schizophrenia, in the form of token economies in psychiatric hospitals, provided strong empirical evidence of effectiveness in promoting adaptive behavior (Ayllon & Azrin, 1968). An accumulation of case studies and institutional experience continues to support its effectiveness in suppressing inappropriate behavior (including "symptoms"), increasing adaptive behavior, and increasing participation in treatment and rehabilitation (e.g., Paul & Menditto, 1992; Wong, Massel, Mosk, & Liberman, 1986). There are no controlled trials that specifically demonstrate the unique contribution of contingency management, within a broader social-learning based rehabilitation program, to outcome. In addition to general effects on maladaptive and adaptive behavior, when combined with other social-learning modalities contingency management has been shown to be effective with two of the most troublesome and drug-resistant problems encountered in inpatient settings: aggression (Beck, Menditto, Baldwin, Angelone, & Maddox, 1991) and polydipsia (Baldwin, Beck, Menditto, Arms, & Cormier, 1992).

A contingency management program or contract can be a vehicle for operationalizing and implementing the resolutions that derive from the new approach of therapeutic jurisprudence (Elbogen & Tomkins, 1999). So far there have been no controlled-outcome trials of this approach to contingency management. However, the approach should be expected to get considerable attention in the near future, as issues of voluntary and involuntary treatment are increasingly discussed and debated in national mental health forums.

Cognitive–Behavioral Therapy (CBT)

Some patients who take antipsychotic medications still have troublesome symptoms, such as hallucinations or delusions. A controlled trial (Drury, Birchwood, Cochrane, & MacMillan, 1996) showed that people with acute psychosis in acute inpatient settings, receiving standard pharmacological and psychosocial treatment, experienced a faster and more complete remission if they received a specialized version of CBT in addition to pharmacotherapy. Similar results were obtained by Sensky et al. (2000); Kuipers et al. (1997); Tarrier et al. (1998); and Buchremer, Klingberg, Holle, Schulze, and Hornung (1997), with patients who had been ill for a longer time. In these studies, CBT has also been shown efficacious in the residual phase of schizophrenia for improving psychophysiological self-regulation and stress tolerance, reducing drug-resistant symptoms (positive and negative), improving problem-solving skills, increasing medication adherence, and reducing relapse. Wykes, Parr, and Landau (1999) obtained positive results with a group form of CBT. In addition, Lecompte and Pelc (1996) found CBT effective in enlisting patients into the treatment process and improving medication adherence.

Hogarty's personal therapy (Hogarty, Greenwald, et al., 1997; Hogarty, Kornblith, et al., 1997) includes CBT elements but focuses on helping the patient identify and manage affective dysregulation. For patients who had supportive-living arrangements, personal therapy reduced relapse, eased symptoms, and improved social adjustment.

Neurocognitive Treatment and Environmental Engineering

Pharmacotherapy can reduce the cognitive disorganization of acute psychosis, but stabilized and optimally medicated individuals often have significant residual neuropsychological impairment. As previously mentioned, such impairment is a strong limiting factor in rehabilitation success. There is mounting evidence that some neurocognitive impairments in schizophrenia can be reduced by specialized therapy techniques that apply principles of experimental psychopathology, neuropsychology, and CBT (Brenner, 1987; Flesher, 1990; Spaulding, Storms, Goodrich, & Sullivan, 1986).

Two large-scale controlled trials have established that such techniques contribute uniquely to overall rehabilitation outcome (Hogarty & Flesher, 1999; Spaulding, Reed, Sullivan, Richardson, & Weiler, 1999). In both studies, the participants were clinically stable and optimally medicated with antipsychotics. Both studies showed that neurocognitive modalities made unique contributions to functional improvement, in the context of comprehensive rehabilitation. A third controlled trial of neurocognitive treatment (Wykes, Reeder, Corner, Williams, & Everitt, 1999) showed improvements in cognitive flexibility and memory. This study found that participants who received the neurocognitive treatment showed differential improvement in self-esteem, suggesting it has subjective as well as objective benefits.

A similar approach, but one based on operant learning principles, has proven effective in helping people with severe impairments achieve a level of functioning that allows them to participate in conventional skill training (Menditto, Baldwin, O'Neal, & Beck, 1991). In this approach, individuals are systematically reinforced with tokens as they successively approximate motor behaviors prerequisite to group participation, such as appropriate motor orientation, disregard of ambient distraction, and performance of elemental group-related tasks.

Acute Treatment, Crisis Intervention, and Related Milieu-Based Services

There is general agreement that the availability of acute inpatient services, crisis/respite services, or both, is a necessary component of a mental health service system for people with schizophrenia. However, there is some room for debate about the precise nature of crisis intervention services.

One view that has been dominant since the 1960s is that crises in schizophrenia are predominantly the result of psychotic relapse, and the best setting in which to evaluate and treat psychotic relapse is in an inpatient psychiatric unit. Psychiatric inpatient units do provide necessary safety and medical care, but they are not always necessarily the most cost-effective alternative. Crises in schizophrenia may be driven by a host of factors other than psychotic relapse, and in such cases addressing those factors in a timely way may be more important than removing the person to a protected environment and administering drugs. As a result, alternative crisis services and 24-hour respite facilities are increasingly included in mental health systems. Often, these are incorporated in a comprehensive case management system.

Another predominant view has been that however useful psychosocial treatment may be in the residual phase, pharmacotherapy is the sole treatment of choice for acute psychosis. This presumption is challenged by a 12-year study of drug-free treatment, the Soteria Project (Mosher, 1999). In a series of controlled studies, the drug-free condition proved comparable to conventional hospital-and-medication treatment, for a large majority of recipients. The drug-free treatment was considerably less expensive. It is interesting that the interpersonal therapeutic-community model of the Soteria Project is similar to one of the psychosocial treatment conditions previously validated by Paul and Lentz (1977). Although the social-learning condition produced the best outcome in Paul and Lentz's (1977) trial, the therapeutic-community condition was superior to conventional "medical model" treatment, and both social-learning and therapeutic-community treatments produced dramatic reductions in use of antipsychotic drugs. Strauss and Carpenter (1977) also reported successful treatment of acute schizophrenia without drugs.

Despite these findings, drug-free treatment of schizophrenia, especially in the acute phase, remains outside generally accepted standards of practice. Although caution about drug-free treatment is clearly indicated, the available data exacerbate suspicions that treatment of schizophrenia has become overly dependent on psychopharmacotherapy, even in the acute phase.

Case Management

The diversity and complexity of the rehabilitation technology require systematic coordination for cost-effective delivery. Multidisciplinary treatment teams operating within a case management model are typically used for this purpose (Holloway, Oliver, Collins, & Carson, 1995; Mueser, Bond, Drake, & Resnick, 1998).

Case management is closely associated with programs for assertive community treatment (PACT, also known as ACT). PACT is a comprehensive approach to services for people with severe and disabling psychiatric disorders. In addition to case management, PACT programs include conventional psychiatric services and varying amounts of rehabilitative services, delivered in an outreach mode that takes the services to the recipient when necessary. PACT has been manualized (Allness & Knoedler, 1998), to the degree that most relevant therapist skills, including case management, can be acquired by following the manual under experienced supervision. There has been much research on the efficacy and cost effectiveness of PACT programs, but the results have been inconsistent (see reviews by Mueser et al., 1998, and Latimer, 1999). PACT programs that include more living skills training and higher staff–client ratios appear to be more effective. Similarly, the transition from institution to community is enhanced by inclusion of focused skill training with case management (MacKain, Smith, Wallace, & Kopelowicz, 1998).

Role of Pharmacotherapy in the Treatment and Rehabilitation of People With Schizophrenia

The pharmacological agents most primarily associated with treatment of schizophrenia are grouped in a large and heterogeneous family, the antipsychotics. Recently, this family has been subdivided into the *typicals*, or neuroleptics, and the *atypicals* (see Tables 7.1 and 7.2). The neuroleptics are so named because they all produce side effects suggestive of neurotoxicity. Until the late 1980s there was only one known antipsychotic that was not a neuroleptic: clozapine. In early trials, clozapine was observed to cause a potentially lethal side effect—agranulocytosis, a suppression of white blood cell (WBC) production—in an unacceptably high proportion of individuals (see Meltzer, 1995). For that reason, clozapine was not approved for use in the United States until 1990. However, clinical use in Europe increasingly suggested that clozapine has important advantages over neuroleptics, and it was eventually made available in the United States, under a strict regimen of continuous monitoring. Shortly thereafter, additional atypical antipsychotics began to appear, and they continue to proliferate. They have little in common, except that whereas the neuroleptics all appear to work through strong blockade effects on the D_2 receptor of the neurotransmitter dopamine, the new ones affect other neurotransmitter systems and some show little or no D_2 blockade (see Table 7.3). This inspired the categorical distinction between the "typical" neuroleptic D_2 blockers and the atypicals. Today the development and marketing of ever safer and more effective atypical antipsychotic agents has become a major activity in the pharmaceutical industry.

Changing Views of Schizophrenia and Antipsychotic Agents

In the years following the introduction of the first antipsychotic drugs (the mid-1950s), their most clinically salient effect was suppression of the

Table 7.1. Selected Typical Antipsychotic Medications and Their Characteristics

Chemical name	Trade name	Dose (mg), usual range	Potency[a]
Phenothiazines			
Aliphatic			
Chlorpromazine	Thorazine	400–800	100
Piperazine			
Fluphenazine	Prolixin	4–20	
Trifluoperazine	Stelazine	6–20	5
Thioridazine	Mellaril	200–600	100
Butyrophenone			
Haloperidol	Haldol	8–32	2
Thioxanthene			
Thiothixene	Navane	15–30	5
Dihydroindolone			
Molindone	Moban	40–200	10
Dibenzoxazepine			
Loxapine	Loxitane	20–250	15

Note. From "Atypical Antipsychotics: A Practical Review" by D. A. Wirshing, W. C. Wirshing, S. R. Marder, C. S. Saunders, E. H. Rossotto, and S. M. Erhart, 1997, *Medscape Mental Health, 2*(10). Copyright 1997 by the Hatherleigh Company, Ltd. Adapted by permission.
[a]Potency is expressed as the proportionate dosage required for an antipsychotic effect, with chlorpromazine set at 100. Thus a potency of 50 indicates a drug is twice as potent as chlorpromazine.

symptoms of acute psychosis, including delusions, hallucinations, thought disorder, agitation, and gross disorganization (Davis & Casper, 1977). The past several years of research on the outcome of pharmacotherapy for schizophrenia have seen an emphasis on the domains of functioning where the neuroleptics fall short, most particularly, negative symptoms, deficit states, and cognitive and neuropsychological impairments. In addition,

Table 7.2. Atypical Antipsychotics: Relative Potencies and Side Effects

Drug	Potency (mg/day)	Sedation	Side effects autonomic	EPS	Relative clinical dose (CPZ equivalent)
Clozapine	200–600	+++	+++	(+)	1
Quetiapine	300–900	++	++	+	1
Risperidone	2–8	+	++	++	80
Olanzapine	10–25	++	+	(+)	20
Ziprasidone	80–200	++	++	++	2

Note. Plus signs represent semiquantitative estimates of the degree of side effects based on the available, relatively limited literature. Parentheses indicate very minimal effect. CPZ = chlorpromazine; EPS = extrapyramidal symptoms. From "Atypical Antipsychotics: A Practical Review" by D. A. Wirshing, W. C. Wirshing, S. R. Marder, C. S. Saunders, E. H. Rossotto, and S. M. Erhart, 1997, *Medscape Mental Health, 2*(10). Copyright 1997 by the Hatherleigh Company, Ltd. Adapted by permission.

Table 7.3. Atypical Antipsychotic Receptor-Binding Profiles

Drug	D1	D2	5-HT2	Alpha 1	Chol.	Hist.
Clozapine	++	+	+++	+++	+++	++
Quetiapine	(+)	+	+	++		++
Risperidone		+++	+++	+++		
Olanzapine	++	++	+++	++	+++	++
Sertindole		+	+++	++		
Ziprasidone	+	+++	+++	++		

Note. Plus signs represent semiquantitative estimates of the degree of side effects based on the available, relatively limited literature. Parentheses indicate very minimal effect. D = dopamine; 5-HT = 5-hydroxytryptamine; Chol. = cholinergic; Hist. = histaminergic. From "Atypical Antipsychotics" by D. A. Wirshing, W. C. Wirshing, S. R. Marder, C. S. Saunders, E. H. Rossotto, and S. M. Erhart, 1997, *Medscape Mental Health, 2*(10). Copyright 1997 by the Hatherleigh Company, Ltd. Adapted by permission.

there has been much study of response to atypicals by people who are known to be unresponsive to typicals. As of this writing, most of the published studies contrast clozapine (Clozaril), the first widely available atypical, with haloperidol (Haldol), a first-generation typical. There is a considerable amount of information on risperidone (Risperdal), the second widely available atypical, and on olanzapine (Zyprexa). Data on the remaining approved atypicals—quetiapine (Seroquel) and ziprasidone (Geodon)—are just beginning to appear.

There is broad agreement that about half of the people diagnosed with schizophrenia who are unresponsive to typicals show a fair to good response to clozapine and that clozapine produces substantially fewer side effects at standard therapeutic dose levels (Buchanan, 1995; Lieberman et al., 1994; Meltzer, 1995; Skelton, Pepe, & Pineo, 1995). There is controversy as to whether clozapine has differentially greater effects on negative symptoms (Breier, Buchanan, Kirkpatrick, Davis, et al., 1994; Carpenter, Conley, Buchanan, & Breier, 1995; Kane, 1996; Meltzer, 1992; Miller, Perry, Cadoret, & Andreasen, 1994; Rosenheck et al., 1999). The problem appears to be that the term *negative symptoms* represents a heterogeneous category of clinical expressions, probably linked to different neurophysiological and developmental mechanisms. Some may be primary, directly linked to the etiology of the disorder, whereas others are secondary, arising from incidental factors such as drug side effects or individuals' responses to the primary expressions. For example, some of the differential effectiveness of atypicals for negative symptoms (lack of motivation or feeling) may be attributable to their lower levels of extrapyramidal side effects (Kane et al., 1994). There is some evidence that secondary negative symptoms show more differential response than primary negative symptoms (Buchanan, 1995).

Both clozapine and risperidone are superior to typicals in reducing the degree of neurocognitive impairment that remains in the severe and persistent residual phase of the disorder, after the recipient has been determined to be medicated optimally (Keefe, Silva, Perkins, & Liebermann, 1999; Kern et al., 1999; Meltzer & McGurk, 1999). There is some preliminary evidence that olanzapine also improves cognitive functioning (Meltzer & McGurk, 1999). However, no atypical returns cognition to premorbid or normal levels, and the impact of the atypicals' superior cognitive effects on overall outcome is not clearly established.

It is not obvious why atypicals benefit neurocognition. One possibility is that they are simply more effective at resolving acute psychosis and the severe cognitive impairments attendant to that condition. Another possibility is that typical antipsychotics have detrimental effects on cognition during the residual phase, whereas atypicals lack these effects. Residual-phase impairments could be partly caused by the typicals' anticholinergic (interference with the action of acetylcholine in the brain) properties, as is suspected for some negative symptoms (it is noteworthy in this regard that, as discussed above, neurocognitive impairments are associated with negative symptoms). A third possibility is that, in addition to their antipsychotic action, atypicals affect other neurochemical systems that produce cognitive impairments in the residual phase of the disorder. In this regard, candidate mechanisms include selective acetylcholine agonism, downregulation of 5-hydroxytryptamine Type 2a receptors, and enhanced glycine modulation of the N-methyl-D-aspartate receptor, a component of the glutamate transmitter system (Goff & Evins, 1998; Goff, Henderson, Evins, & Amico, 1999; Meltzer & McGurk, 1999). It is entirely possible that different atypicals affect neurocognition in different ways.

Clozapine appears to moderate some dimensions of affective dysregulation, in the domains of hostility and irritability (Buchanan, 1995). This may prove an important advantage for managing aggression, mania, and depression when they co-occur with the more pathognomic characteristics of schizophrenia. Clozapine has been found to reduce aggression in particularly violent and treatment-resistant individuals (Menditto et al., 1996). Risperidone was found to be no more effective than typicals (Beck et al., 1997) in this regard.

The atypicals are considerably more expensive than the typicals. However, cost-effectiveness analyses indicate that the greater cost is more than offset by the reduced costs consequent to atypicals' greater clinical efficacy (Davies et al., 1998; Rivicki, 1999).

Strategies for Optimal Use of Antipsychotics

As awareness of the phasic nature of schizophrenia has increased, tactical principles for use of antipsychotics have evolved. For example, it was recognized early in the history of antipsychotic pharmacotherapy that dosages can be reduced to maintenance levels after resolution of the acute episode. Lower doses incur fewer side effects, thus enhancing regimen adherence. Lower doses are also thought to incur less risk for tardive dyskinesia (TD). However, titration to the lowest necessary dose is not without risks. Ironically, the development of high-intensity rehabilitation programs may increase stress levels, necessitating a higher dose than would otherwise be necessary, at least temporarily. Because rehabilitation tends to increase in intensity as acute psychosis is resolved, premature titration could promote relapse (Schooler & Spohn, 1982).

Systematic protocols for optimizing maintenance have been developed and are part of the aforementioned practice guidelines. However, there is little in any of those guidelines concerning integrating pharmacological and psychosocial treatment in the context of comprehensive psychiatric rehabilitation. This appears to be an important issue for current research. Collaboration among pharmacotherapists, neuropsychologists, behavior analysts, and rehabilitation therapists appears to be a key part of the solution.

The issue of polypharmacy (a regimen of more than one antipsychotic) has been hotly debated. For a long time, experimental studies showed no differences between specific typicals, other than differences in potency (dosage required for an antipsychotic effect). Nevertheless, clinicians were compelled by their experience to suspect that, in some individuals, combinations of antipsychotics can achieve better results than any single antipsychotic. As neuropharmacological knowledge and technology progressed, it became apparent that in fact each antipsychotic, typical and atypical, has a unique profile of histochemical activity. This converged with a growing realization that the D_2 receptor, and dopamine activity in general, is probably just one component of a complex biochemical system involved with psychosis (Weinberger, 1994; Weinberger & Lipska, 1995). As a result, pronouncements about polypharmacy have grown more circumspect (e.g., see Goff & Evins, 1998). In the end, these developments converge on the general principle that pharmacotherapy of schizophrenia should be driven by systematic trials, evaluated with cognitive and behavioral data, whether the intervention is a single drug or a combination.

The question of when to stop a medication trial can be as important as the choice of agent. Too often, regimens are continued long after they have demonstrated ineffectiveness. This is often because the targets for treatment are vaguely or incompletely specified. In the risk management decisions involved in controlling potentially dangerous behavior, discontinuing an agent intended to prevent harmful consequences is difficult to justify without clear and quantitative clinical data. The result is sometimes an accumulation of improbably complex regimens that do not contribute to stability or rehabilitation progress. This can be prevented by identifying targets precisely and inclusively before a medication trial begins, collecting reliable measurements over the course of the trial, and systematically analyzing the data before making the next treatment decisions.

For example, if a pharmacological intervention is chosen to eliminate assaultive behavior in a person with severe and persistent psychosis, the intervention should be preceded by a thorough functional behavioral analysis (FBA) of the assaultive behavior. The FBA should precisely and reliably identify the target behavior. It should reveal no antecedents or consequences associated with the behavior that could be easily controlled (control of such stimuli would be a compelling first-choice treatment option). If the selection of the pharmacological option is based on hypothesized relations between the target behavior and other typical targets for antipsychotic medication (e.g., the assaults are hypothesized to be associated with paranoid hallucinations, delusions, or both), then that hypothesis should be supported, or at least not disconfirmed, by FBA data. No other interventions potentially affecting assaultive behavior should be introduced during the period required to exert an effect. Restraint and seclusion are not typically expected to reduce assaultive behavior over time, but a properly executed "time out from reinforcement" program may have such an effect while also managing the risk of injury. For this reason, such behavioral interventions should often be tested for effectiveness before a pharmacological option is exercised.

If after 6 weeks the continuing FBA shows no decrease in assaultive behavior, the intervention should be stopped, the FBA data reanalyzed, and new hypotheses and interventions entertained. If the FBA data show some, but not sufficient, effect, further decisions must be made to try a different pharmacological intervention, continue the present medication but add additional interventions (e.g., a contingency management program selectively reinforcing assault-free periods), or abandon the pharmacological option altogether. In any case, the FBA must be continued until effective controlling factors, pharmacological or otherwise, are identified.

An absolute minimum time frame for determining antipsychotic pharmacotherapy to be ineffective is about 2 weeks. Full evaluation of antipsychotic effects on personal and social functioning may require more than a year, especially for the atypicals.

Considerations in the Choice of an Antipsychotic Agent

Ultimately, the best choice of antipsychotic agent must be determined empirically for each individual. Little is currently known about factors that may facilitate the choice of a candidate before the empirical trial. The choice of drug is influenced as much by side-effects considerations and circumstantial factors as by antipsychotic efficacy. Generally, the lower potency antipsychotics have more sedating action, so these get earlier consideration when agitation is part of the clinical picture. Sedation is often aversive, especially to individuals who do not need it, so the higher potency antipsychotics are preferred when sedation is not needed. However, the higher potency antipsychotics are more likely to produce extrapyramidal side effects (the high-potency atypicals are an exception to this). Two agents, haloperidol (Haldol) and fluphenazine (Prolixin), are available in an injectable slow-release medium that eliminates the need for daily dosing (see Glazer & Kane, 1992). This is advantageous when psychoeducation and skill training are insufficient to establish adherence to a regimen (or until those modalities have time to work).

Also, new understanding about subtypes of schizophrenia may influence medication choices. For example, it may be that the hypothesized neurodevelopmental subtype of schizophrenia (Knoll et al., 1999) responds best to atypicals because the multiple actions of the atypicals address the pervasive dysregulation of brain systems that inspired the neurodevelopmental model. In other subtypes, symptoms and other impairments may be more focally influenced by dopamine systems and consequently more responsive to specific dopamine blockade.

As the atypicals have proliferated, there has been increasing discussion of whether there is now an antipsychotic drug of first recourse. Clozapine would not be a candidate, despite its superior antipsychotic properties, because of the problems associated with agranulocytosis (discussed later). On the basis of lower risk of side effects and greater antipsychotic efficacy, any of the three recently introduced atypicals—olanzapine, quetiapine, and risperidone—should be given priority over any typical. Within the next few years, one atypical, or perhaps more than one, may emerge as the first choice for different subtypes or clinical pictures. Of course, even after a first-recourse agent is identified on safety and efficacy grounds, cost and other factors could further influence its use.

Adjunctive Pharmacotherapy and Related Issues

Managing antipsychotic side effects. Antipsychotic drugs produce problematic side effects in many individuals (see Table 7.4). A major category of side effects results from neurotransmitter dysregulation of the extrapyramidal motor system. It is thought that these side effects are the result of an imbalance of dopaminergic and acetylcholinergic activity in subcortical motor control systems, brought about by the selective blockade of dopamine. Simultaneous blockade of acetylcholine can relieve these symptoms in most cases. The anticholinergic agents trihexyphenidyl (Artane) and benztropine (Cogentin) are most commonly used for this purpose.

Table 7.4. Side Effects of Typical Antipsychotic Medications

| Drug | Type of symptom | | |
	Sedating	Autonomic	Extrapyramidal
Fluphenazine	+	+	+++
Perphenazine	++	+	++/+++
Trifluoperazine	++	+	+++
Mesoridazine	+++	++	+
Thioridazine	+++	+++	+
Acetophenazine	++	+	++/+++
Chlorpromazine	+++	+++	++
Triflupromazine	+++	++/+++	++
Haloperidol	+	+	+++
Thiothixene	+	+	+++
Chlorprothixene	+++	+++	+/+++
Molindone	++	+	+
Loxapine	++	+/++	++/+++

Note. Plus signs represent semiquantitative estimates of the degree of side effects based on the available, relatively limited literature. Slashes represent ambiguity.

A subcategory of side effects are Parkinsonian, so named because they mimic the symptoms of Parkinson's disease. These include suppression of facial motility (fixed facies), disruption of postural reflexes resulting in a shuffling gait and loss of balance, tremor, and muscle stiffness.

Other extrapyramidal side effects of neuroleptics include torticollis and oculogyrus, spasmlike contractions of the neck and eye muscles, respectively. These can be particularly frightening but are readily observable and usually respond quickly to anticholinergic treatment or change of antipsychotic. A related side effect is akathisia. Unlike the motor side effects, akathisia is primarily a subjective experience of agitation and restlessness, sometimes observable as motor restlessness or persistent irritability. It is often difficult to detect, partly because it is primarily subjective (and people with schizophrenia may have particular difficulty in reporting a purely subjective experience) and partly because it tends to appear several days to 2 weeks after initiating neuroleptics, after clinical vigilance for side effects has dissipated. Akathisia is extremely aversive and thought to be a major cause of medication nonadherence. It can usually be controlled adequately with anticholinergics. Its incidence with atypicals appears to be low, but this is not a reason for relaxing vigilance.

There is substantial evidence that anticholinergic agents can themselves produce cognitive impairments, especially in memory (Blanchard & Neale, 1992). For this reason, it is considered desirable to keep anticholinergic treatment to a minimum (and antipsychotics themselves have anticholinergic properties, to varying degrees). An alternative to anticholinergic treatment of side effects is the selective dopamine agonist amantadine (Symmetril). Amantadine increases dopamine activity in motor systems without necessarily affecting the other dopamine systems, allowing effective control of Parkinsonian symptoms in some individuals. However, it is considerably more costly than anticholinergics, and in many individuals its dopamine agonism is not selective enough to avoid exacerbation of psychotic symptoms. Most of the atypical antipsychotics produce fewer side effects, requiring little or no adjunctive treatment.

The D_2 blocking properties of neuroleptics cause an increase in blood prolactin levels, by way of a hypothalamic dopaminergic pathway that normally inhibits lactation. This sometimes produces gynecomastia (swelling of breast tissue, predominantly in males) and galactorrhea (expression of breast milk, predominantly in females). This is usually managed by switching to another antipsychotic. The atypicals, with less D_2 blocking activity, are less likely to cause this problem (see "Hyperprolactinaemia associated," 1999).

Neuroleptic malignant syndrome (NMS) is a rare but potentially lethal side effect involving the disruption of hypothalamic mechanisms that regulate body temperature. Symptoms include fever, diaphoresis, autonomic instability (fluctuations in blood pressure and heart rate), elevated WBC count, and compromised kidney function (indicated by elevated blood levels of serum creatinine). There is some evidence that as many as 12% of people on neuroleptics experience a mild, subclinical form of this syndrome. The malignant form is associated with high doses, high-potency agents, and intramuscular administration. It usually appears within 2 weeks of starting treatment, but it can appear at any time. It is managed by carefully observing recipients when they are started on a new antipsychotic and discontinuing it immediately if the symptoms occur. Dopamine blockade is thought to be a proximal cause of NMS, and dopamine agonists such as bromocriptine are sometimes recommended for acute treatment. NMS is a medical emergency and is generally managed in intensive care settings.

Side effects that are encountered with both typicals and atypicals include significant weight gain and a lowered seizure threshold. Management of these side effects must be based on case-by-case assessment of the relative advantages of switching antipsychotic versus adjunctive treatment. Weight gain is less likely when administering clozapine when quetiapine is also taken (Reinstein, Sirtovskaya, Jones, Mohan, & Cahasanov, 1999).

TD is a serious, potentially irreversible side effect of protracted use of antipsychotics. Its symptoms are spasmodic contraction of muscle groups: mostly oral, facial, and lingual muscles in the early stages, and the entire torso in later stages. It can be reliably detected in its early stages by physical examination. Dangerously common for typicals, it is thought to be rare for atypicals and thought not to occur at all with clozapine. The American Psychiatric Association has acknowledged that TD is an iatrogenic condition caused by antipsychotic drug treatment and has published a detailed protocol for early detection of and response to TD (Tardive Dyskinesia Task Force, 1980). Management of TD may involve a difficult choice between control of psychosis and TD symptoms, but early detection preserves some degrees of freedom in the decision process. As with all such decisions, the involvement of the identified patient and family is of paramount importance.

As previously mentioned, agranulocytosis is a potentially lethal side effect, extremely rare but thought to be less rare for clozapine, affecting 1%–2% of the recipients of that drug (Krupp & Barnes, 1992). This risk has been a major factor in weighing the advantages of clozapine's superior antipsychotic capabilities and lack of risk for TD. Use of clozapine requires strict adherence to a regimen of WBC counts, weekly at first and biweekly after 6 months (80% of cases occur within the first 18 weeks). A sudden drop in the WBC counts demands immediate discontinuation of the drug.[3]

Adjunctive treatment of affective and psychophysiological dysregulation. There is some evidence that agents normally used to enhance affective regulation and control seizures, including clonazepam (Klonopin), carbamazepine (Tegretol), and valproic acid (divalproex sodium, Depakote), among others, can enhance the effects of antipsychotics (Meltzer, 1992;

---

[3]Agranulocytosis is not to be confused with benign leukopenia, a milder suppression of WBCs that is occasionally related to use of low-potency agents such as chlorpromazine. Clozapine also may also produce benign leukopenia, so WBC counts must be carefully interpreted.

Schulz, Kahn, & Baker, 1990). It would be logical to expect that this enhancement is best when the clinical picture includes affective dysregulation closely associated with psychotic symptomatology, as in schizoaffective disorder and borderline personality disorder co-occurring with schizophrenia. However, there is insufficient experimental evidence to allow a confident conclusion about this. For an individual case, there may be sufficient evidence to justify a controlled clinical trial of an adjunctive affective regulation agent when satisfactory symptom control and stabilization cannot be achieved with antipsychotics alone. However, psychosocial interventions may also contribute to affective stabilization, and this should be weighed against the disadvantages of a more complex medication regimen. The implicit message to the recipient often is that drugs are preferable to skills as a means of managing one's emotional life. It is necessary to provide an educational intervention that will counteract this message.

Extreme caution is indicated in using anticonvulsants with antipsychotics. Carbamazepine and possibly also clonazepam may suppress bone marrow function, exacerbating the potential effects of neuroleptics and clozapine. Lithium is sometimes used in conjunction with neuroleptics (the evidence that lithium enhances antipsychotic effects on schizophrenic symptoms is weak, but it may be used for co-occurring manic symptoms), and this may increase the risk of NMS.

Adjunctive treatment of negative and deficit symptoms. Negative and deficit symptoms are still a persistent problem in treatment and rehabilitation of schizophrenia, even though the atypicals may be more effective in this regard. The discovery that D_2 blockade is not the sole mechanism of the antipsychotic effect, and the realization that people with schizophrenia may also have other psychiatric problems, such as depression, has spurred exploration of alternative pharmacological approaches.

Nontricyclic antidepressants appear to have some efficacy in reducing negative symptoms (Goff, Midha, & Brotman, 1991; Silver & Nassar, 1992), which is not surprising, considering the similarity between negative symptoms and depressive symptoms. The efficacy of atypicals for negative symptoms is probably related to their efficacy for neurocognitive impairments. The same might be logically expected of antidepressants, but that has not been experimentally demonstrated. Research in this domain has only just begun, and the next few years may see some significant advances.

Treatment of depression co-occurring with schizophrenia. Depressive signs sometimes occur with schizophrenia and can be effectively treated with antidepressant medications (Siris, 1994). CBT or interpersonal psychotherapy are logical alternatives, but there has not been systematic study of this possibility. Considering the greater safety of the nontricyclic antidepressants and their efficacy for reducing negative symptoms, they are probably the best first choice for treating depression in schizophrenia pharmacologically. One of the newer atypical antipsychotics, olanzapine, appears to be effective in treating depressive symptoms (Tollefson, Sanger, Lu, & Thieme, 1998).

Adjunctive treatment of anxiety and agitation. Anxiety often accompanies schizophrenic symptomatology, and this causes an understandable desire among many clinicians to treat the anxiety directly with pharmacotherapy. In addition, psychotic relapses are usually preceded by increases in anxious and depressive symptoms, before the appearance of acute schizophrenic symptoms (Jorgensen, 1998). Anxiolytics have been recommended as an adjunct to antipsychotics for emergency treatment of extreme agitation in schizophrenia, although the potential disinhibiting effects of anxiolytics demand caution (Corrigan, Yudofsky, & Silver, 1993; Wolkowitz & Pickar, 1991). The efficacy of chronic anxiolytic treatment has never been supported. As with affective regulation, the value of pharmacological treatment of problems that may be more effectively addressed with psychosocial treatment should be carefully weighed.

Coordinated Use of Pharmacotherapy and Psychosocial Therapy in the Treatment and Rehabilitation of People With Schizophrenia

All the foregoing considerations reduce to a fairly straightforward algorithm for coordinating pharmacotherapy and psychosocial treatment. Although simple in concept, implementation is, of course, much more complex.

The steps in the algorithm reflect a logical sequence of assessments and decisions. Refinement and further specification of algorithms such as this will be a primary focus in research and development of rehabilitation technology in the coming years.

An Algorithm for Treatment and Rehabilitation of Schizophrenia

In a preliminary differential diagnosis, rule out the presence of other conditions as possible causes of psychotic behavior.

- intoxication
- febrile delirium
- acute neuropathy
- known chronic or progressive neurological conditions
- bipolar disorder
- psychotic depression
- factitious report of symptoms
- malingering
- transient periods of psychoticlike behavior associated with extreme stress, anxiety, depression, or severe personality disorder

- psychotic-like behavior associated with cultural or sociological circumstances (e.g., spiritual, religious, or political beliefs associated with identifiable groups or ideologies that appear bizarre to other groups).

Proceed with the algorithm if, after ruling out or resolving these causes, a clinical picture of schizophrenia or other severe, adult-onset psychiatric condition persists, including continuous or episodic psychotic symptoms when untreated and significant compromise of personal and social functioning (the functional deficits need not be attributable to the psychotic symptoms).

1. Begin functional assessment and rehabilitation counseling to identify problems and treatment goals.
2. Does historical or current behavioral–observational data indicate problems in adherence to treatment and rehabilitation regimens or an inability to give informed consent to treatment? If yes, assess thoroughly and take action as indicated to protect individuals at risk and engage treatment (these actions must be continuously re-evaluated as recovery permits greater participation and less restriction and restores legal competence).
    - Establish means of appropriate substitute decision making (e.g., appointment of guardian, civil commitment, judicial supervision of treatment) when necessary.
    - Provide environmental structure sufficient to ensure safety at lowest possible level of restriction (e.g., hospitalization, crisis respite, supervised residential services).
    - Negotiate contingency management programs sufficient to establish engagement in treatment and rehabilitation at the lowest possible level of restriction.
3. (Under most circumstances, this step is conducted simultaneously with Step 2.) Do history and presentation suggest that the affected individual is currently experiencing an acute psychotic episode? If yes, take action to resolve acute episode.
    - Provide crisis intervention as circumstances demand.
    - Begin clinical trial of antipsychotic medication, beginning with first-recourse selection; titrate dose upward or select alternative as indicated by treatment response.
    - Administer adjunctive medication to control side effects as necessary.
    - Provide psychosocial interventions to enhance resolution of acute psychosis (e.g., specialized CBT) and suppress dangerous or unacceptable behaviors (e.g., time-out-from-reinforcement contingency management programs).
4. (When the antipsychotic used in resolving acute psychosis is a neuroleptic) is there evidence of residual negative symptoms, def-

icit states, side effects, or psychophysiological or affective dysregulation for which an atypical antipsychotic would be more beneficial? If yes, begin controlled trial of an atypical antipsychotic (under most circumstances, the switch should be gradual and staggered). Proceed to the next step when data indicate that the acute episode is stabilized as much as possible, that is, psychotic symptoms, related behaviors, and acute cognitive impairments are not expected to respond to further adjustments in medication or more time in the therapeutic milieu.

5. Is there evidence of residual negative symptoms, deficit states, or psychophysiological or affective dysregulation for which adjunctive pharmacotherapy may be beneficial? If yes, begin controlled trial of adjunctive pharmacotherapy targeting specific residual problems (e.g., antidepressant medication if residual state is suspected to be depression related, anticonvulsant for agitation or aggression).

6. Does assessment reveal residual neurocognitive impairments sufficient to compromise personal or social functioning or response to rehabilitation? If yes, provide neuropsychological intervention.
   - Begin trial of cognitive–rehabilitative intervention (e.g. Integrated Psychological Therapy, Cognitive Enhancement Therapy).
   - Provide supportive and prosthetic environmental conditions for residual impairments that limit functioning and are not eliminated by treatment.

7. Is there evidence of residual symptoms, affective dysregulation, or other persistent condition for which psychosocial treatment may be effective? If yes, begin trial of psychosocial treatment targeting specific problem (e.g., CBT for symptom control or depression, relapse prevention for substance abuse).

8. (This step is usually conducted simultaneously with Step 7.) Does functional assessment reveal deficits in key skill areas needed to achieve the affected individual's full potential, live in the least restrictive possible environment, and enjoy a satisfactory quality of life? If yes, begin psychosocial rehabilitation targeting specific skill deficits.

9. Does progress in rehabilitation allow titration of antipsychotic dose to maintenance level, discontinuation of adjunctive pharmacotherapy, reduction or discontinuation of restrictive environmental supports, or contingency management programs? If yes, adjust regimen accordingly.

10. Is recovery proceeding as expected, toward measurable goals identified by the entire treatment team (including identified patient and relevant family)? If no, identify barriers to progress, reformulate the treatment and rehabilitation plan, and recycle the entire algorithm.

Conclusion: The Role of the Psychologist in Treatment and Rehabilitation

The complexity and variety of the assessment and treatment technologies needed for effective rehabilitation make it clear why people with severe and disabling disorders usually receive services from an interdisciplinary team. Team members usually have overlapping as well as unique areas of expertise and clinical skills. Particular areas of expertise vary, even within disciplines, including psychology. The role of a particular psychologist may vary across different teams, complementing the other resources among the team members. Nevertheless, the background and perspective of psychologists usually give them a unique and especially useful role in identifying and resolving the key decisions to be made in the course of providing services. The algorithm for treatment and rehabilitation described in this chapter identifies those key decisions. Psychological assessment and functional behavioral analysis often emerge as the technologies most important in informing the key decisions. Whatever other resources the psychologist may bring—for example, special knowledge in social skills training, cognitive therapy, or psychopharmacology—systematic application of behavioral and psychological assessment data to key clinical decisions is their sine qua non. Such a central function in selecting and guiding treatment inevitably constitutes a leadership role. Psychologists who provide services to people with severe and disabling disorders should accept and prepare themselves for such a role.

References

Abramowitz, L. A., & Coursey, R. D. (1989). Impact of an educational support group of family participants who take care of their schizophrenic relatives. *Journal of Consulting and Clinical Psychology, 57*, 232–236.

Allness, D., & Knoedler, W. (1998). *The PACT model of community-based treatment for persons with severe and persistent mental illnesses: A manual for PACT start-up*. Arlington, VA: National Alliance for the Mentally Ill.

American Psychiatric Association. (1997). Practice guidelines for the treatment of patients with schizophrenia. *American Journal of Psychiatry, 154*(Suppl. 4), 1–63.

Anthony, W. A., Cohen, M., & Farkas, M. (1990). *Psychiatric rehabilitation*. Boston: Center for Psychiatric Rehabilitation.

Ayllon, T., & Azrin, N. (1968). *The token economy: A motivational system for therapy and rehabilitation*. New York: Appleton-Century-Crofts.

Baldwin, L., Beck, N., Menditto, A., Arms, T., & Cormier, J. F. (1992). Decreasing excessive water drinking by severe and persistent mentally ill forensic patients. *Hospital and Community Psychiatry, 43*, 507–509.

Beck, N., Greenfield, S., Gotham, H., Menditto, A., Stuve, P., & Hemme, C. (1997). Risperidone in the management of violent, treatment-resistant schizophrenics hospitalized in a maximum security forensic facility. *Journal of the American Academy of Psychiatry and the Law, 25*, 461–468.

Beck, N., Menditto, A., Baldwin, L., Angelone, E., & Maddox, M. (1991). Reduced frequency of aggressive behavior in forensic patients in a social learning program. *Hospital and Community Psychiatry, 42*, 750–752.

Benton, M., & Schroeder, H. (1998). Social skills training with schizophrenics: A meta-analytic evaluation. *Journal of Consulting and Clinical Psychology, 58*, 741–747.

Birchwood, M. (1995). Early intervention in psychotic relapse: Cognitive approaches to detection and management. *Behaviour Change, 12,* 2–19.

Blanchard, J. J., & Neale, J. M. (1992). Medication effects: Conceptual and methodological issues in schizophrenia research. *Clinical Psychology Review, 12,* 345–361.

Bradshaw, W. (1996). Structured group work for individuals with schizophrenia: A coping approach. *Research on Social Work Practice, 6,* 139–154.

Braginsky, B., Braginsky, D., & Ring, K. (1969). *Methods of madness: The mental hospital as a last resort.* New York: Holt, Rhinehart & Winston.

Breier, A., Buchanan, R., Kirkpatrick, B., Davis, O., et al. (1994). Effects of clozapine on positive and negative symptoms in outpatients with schizophrenia. *American Journal of Psychiatry, 151,* 20–26.

Brenner, H. D. (1987). On the importance of cognitive disorders in treatment and rehabilitation. In J. S. Strauss, W. Boker, & H. D. Brenner (Eds.), *Psychosocial treatment of schizophrenia.* Toronto, Ontario, Canada: Huber.

Buchanan, R. (1995). Clozapine: Efficacy and safety. *Schizophrenia Bulletin, 21,* 579–591.

Buchremer, G., Klingberg, S., Holle, R., Schulze, M. M., & Hornung, W. P. (1997). Psychoeducational psychotherapy for schizophrenic patients and their key relatives or caregivers: Results of a two-year follow-up. *Acta Psychiatrica Scandinavica, 95,* 483–491.

Carpenter, W., Conley, R., Buchanan, R., & Breier, A., (1995). Patient response and resource management: Another view of clozapine treatment of schizophrenia. *American Journal of Psychiatry, 152,* 827–832.

Corrigan, P., & Liberman, R. (Eds.). (1994). *Behavior therapy in psychiatric hospitals.* New York: Springer.

Corrigan, P., Yudofsky, S., & Silver, J. (1993). Pharmacological and behavioral treatments for aggressive psychiatric inpatients. *Hospital and Community Psychiatry, 44,* 125–133.

Davies, A., Adena, M., Keks, A., Catts, S., Lambert, T., & Schweitzer, I. (1998). Risperidone vs haloperidol: I. Meta-analysis of efficacy and safety. *Clinical Therapeutics, 20,* 58–71.

Davis, J., & Casper, R. (1977). Antipsychotic drugs: Clinical pharmacology and therapeutic use. *Drugs, 14,* 260–282.

Drury, V., Birchwood, M., Cochrane, R., & MacMillan, F. (1996). Cognitive therapy and recovery from acute psychosis: A controlled trial. I: Impact on psychotic symptoms. *British Journal of Psychiatry, 169,* 593–601.

Eckman, T. A., Liberman, R. P., Phipps, C. C., & Blair, K. E. (1990). Teaching medication management skills to schizophrenic patients. *Journal of Clinical Psychopharmacology, 10,* 33–38.

Elbogen, E., & Tomkins, A. (1999). The psychiatric hospital and therapeutic jurisprudence: Applying the law to promote mental health. In W. Spaulding (Ed.), *The role of the state hospital in the 21st century. New directions for mental health services,* No. 84 (pp. 71–84). San Francisco: Jossey Bass.

Falloon, I. R. H., & Liberman, R. P. (1983). Interactions between drug and psychosocial therapy in schizophrenia. *Schizophrenia Bulletin, 9,* 543–554.

Falloon, I. R. H., McGill, C. W., Boyd, J. L., & Pederson, J. (1987). Family management in the prevention of morbidity of schizophrenia: Social outcome of a two-year longitudinal study. *Psychological Medicine, 17,* 59–66.

Flesher, S. (1990). Cognitive habilitation in schizophrenia: A theoretical review and model of treatment. *Neuropsychology Review, 1,* 223–246.

Francis, A., Docherty, J. P., & Kahn, D. A. (1996). The expert consensus series: Treatment of schizophrenia. *Journal of Clinical Psychiatry, 57*(Suppl. 12B), 3–59.

Glazer, W., & Kane, J. (1992). Depot neuroleptic therapy: An underutilized treatment option. *Journal of Clinical Psychiatry, 53,* 426–433.

Goff, D., & Evins, E. (1998). Negative symptoms in schizophrenia: Neurobiological models and treatment response. *Harvard Review of Psychiatry, 6,* 59–77.

Goff, D., Henderson, D., Evins, A., & Amico, E. (1999). A placebo-controlled crossover trial of D-cycloserine added to clozapine in patients with schizophrenia. *Biological Psychiatry, 45,* 512–514.

Goff, D., Midha, K., & Brotman, A. (1991). An open trial of buspirone added to neuroleptics in schizophrenic patients. *Journal of Clinical Psychopharmacology, 11,* 193–197.

Goffman, E. (1961). *Asylums.* Garden City, NY: Doubleday.

Hogarty, G. E., Anderson, C. M., Reiss, D. J., Kornblith, S. J., Greenwald, D. P., Ulrich, R. F., & Carter, M. (1991). Family, psychoeducation, social skills training, and maintenance chemotherapy in the aftercare treatment of schizophrenia: II. Two-year effects of a controlled study on relapse and adjustment. *Archives of General Psychiatry, 48*, 340–347.

Hogarty, G. E., & Flesher, S. (1999). Practice principles of cognitive enhancement therapy for schizophrenia. *Schizophrenia Bulletin, 25*, 693–708.

Hogarty, G. E., Greenwald, D., Ulrich, R., Kornblith, S., DiBarry, A., Cooley, S., Carter, M., & Flesher, S. (1997). Three-year trials of personal therapy among schizophrenic patients living with or independent of family: II. Effects of adjustment of patients. *American Journal of Psychiatry, 154*, 1514–1524.

Hogarty, G. E., Kornblith, S., Greenwald, D., DeBarry, A., Cooley, S., Ulrich, R., Carter, M., & Flesher, S. (1997). Three-year trials of personal therapy among schizophrenic patients living with or independent of family: I. Description of study and effects of relapse rates. *American Journal of Psychiatry, 154*, 1504–1513.

Holloway, F., Oliver, N., Collins, E., & Carson, J. (1995). Case management: A critical review of the outcome literature. *European Psychiatry, 10*, 113–128.

Hyperprolactinaemia associated with effective antipsychotic treatment no longer inevitable. (1999). *Drug and Therapy Perspectives, 14*, 11–14.

Johnson, D. L. (Ed.). (1990). *Service needs of the seriously mentally ill: Training implications for psychology*. Washington, DC: American Psychological Association.

Johnson, D. L. (1995). Families and psychiatric rehabilitation. *International Journal of Mental Health, 24*, 47–58.

Jorgensen, P. (1998). Early signs of psychotic relapse in schizophrenia. *British Journal of Psychiatry, 172*, 327–330.

Kane, J. (1996). Commentary on the clozapine conflict. *American Journal of Psychiatry, 153*, 1507–1508.

Kane, J., Safferman, A., Pollack, S., Johns, C., Szymanski, S., Konig, M., & Lieberman, J. A. (1994). Clozapine, negative symptoms and extrapyramidal side effects. *Journal of Clinical Psychiatry, 55*(Suppl. B), 74–77.

Kavanagh, D. (1992). Schizophrenia. In P. Wilson (Ed.), *Principles and practice of relapse prevention* (pp. 157–190). New York: Guilford Press.

Keefe, R., Silva, S., Perkins, D., & Liebermann, J. (1999). The effects of atypical antipsychotic drugs on neurocognitive impairment in schizophrenia: A review and meta-analysis. *Schizophrenia Bulletin, 25*, 201–222.

Kendall, P. C. (1998). Empirically supported psychological therapies. *Journal of Consulting and Clinical Psychology, 66*, 3–6.

Kern, R., Green, M., Marshal, B., Wirshing, W., Wirshing, D., McGurk, S., Marder, S., & Mintz, J. (1999). Risperidone versus haloperidol on secondary memory: Can newer medications aid learning? *Schizophrenia Bulletin, 25*, 223–232.

Klein, D. (1980). Psychosocial treatment of schizophrenia, or psychosocial help for people with schizophrenia? *Schizophrenia Bulletin, 6*, 122–130.

Knoll, J., Garner, D., Ramberg, J., Kingsbury, S., Croissant, D., & McDermott, B. (1999). Heterogeneity of the psychoses: Is there a neurodegenerative psychosis? *Schizophrenia Bulletin, 24*, 365–380.

Krupp, P., & Barnes, P. (1992). Clozapine-associated aggranulocytosis: Risk and aetiology. *British Journal of Psychiatry, 160*(Suppl. 17), 38–40.

Kuipers, E., Garety, P., Fowler, D., Dunn, G., Bebbington, P., Freeman, D., & Hadley, C. (1997). London–East Anglia randomized controlled trial of cognitive behavioural therapy for psychosis. *British Journal of Psychiatry, 171*, 319–327.

Lam, D. (1991). Psychosocial family intervention in schizophrenia: A review of empirical studies. *Psychological Medicine, 21*, 423–441.

Latimer, E. A. (1999). Economic impacts of assertive community treatment: A review of the literature. *Canadian Journal of Psychiatry, 44*, 443–454.

Lecompte, D., & Pelc, C. (1996). A cognitive–behavioral program to improve compliance with medication in patients with schizophrenia. *International Journal of Mental Health, 25*, 51–56.

Leff, J., Kuipers, L., Berkowitz, R., & Sturgeon, D. (1985). A controlled trial of social intervention in the families of schizophrenic patients: Two year follow-up. *British Journal of Psychiatry, 146,* 594–600.

Lehman, A. F., Thompson, J. W., Dixon, L. B., & Scott, J. E. (1995). Introduction. Schizophrenia: Treatment outcomes research. *Schizophrenia Bulletin, 21,* 561–566.

Liberman, R. P. (Ed.). (1992). *Handbook of psychiatric rehabilitation.* New York: Macmillan.

Liberman, R. P., Corrigan, P., & Schade, M. (1989). Drug and psychosocial treatment interactions in schizophrenia. *International Review of Psychiatry, 1,* 283–295.

Liberman, R. P., Falloon, I. R. H., & Wallace, C. J. (1984). Drug–psychosocial interactions in the treatment of schizophrenia. In M. Mirabi (Ed.), *The severe and persistently mentally ill: Research and services.* New York: SP Medical & Scientific Books.

Lieberman, J., Safferman, A., Pollack, S., Szymanski, S., Johns, C., Howard, A., Kronig, M., Bookstein, P., & Kane, J. (1994). Clinical effects of clozapine in severe and persistent schizophrenia: Response to treatment and predictors of outcome. *American Journal of Psychiatry, 151,* 1744–1752.

MacKain, S., Smith, T., Wallace, C., & Kopelowicz, A. (1998). Evaluation of a community re-entry program. *International Review of Psychiatry, 10,* 76–83.

McEvoy, J., Scheifler, P., & Frances, A. (Eds.). (1999). Treatment of schizophrenia. *Journal of Clinical Psychiatry, 60*(Suppl. 11), 4–80.

McFarlane, W., & Cunningham, K. (1996). Multiple-family groups and psychoeducation: Creating therapeutic social networks. In J. Vaccaro & G. Clark (Eds.), *Practicing psychiatry in the community: A manual* (pp. 387–406). Washington DC: American Psychiatric Press.

McFarlane, W., Link, B., Dushay, R., Marchal, J., & Crilly, J. (1995). Psychoeducational multiple family groups: Four-year relapse outcome in schizophrenia. *Family Process, 34,* 127–144.

McFarlane, W., Lukens, E., Link, B., Dushay, R., Deakins, S. A., Newmark, M., Dunne, E. J., Horen, B., & Toran, J. (1995). Multiple-family groups and psychoeducation in the treatment of schizophrenia. *Archives of General Psychiatry, 52,* 679–687.

Meltzer, H. (1992). Treatment of the neuroleptic–nonresponsive schizophrenic patients. *Schizophrenia Bulletin, 18,* 515–542.

Meltzer, H. (1995). Treatment-resistant schizophrenia: The role of clozapine. *Current Medical Research and Opinion, 14,* 1–20.

Meltzer, H., & McGurk, S. (1999). The effects of clozapine, risperidone and olanzapine on cognitive functioning in schizophrenia. *Schizophrenia Bulletin, 25,* 233–255.

Menditto, A., Baldwin, L., O'Neal, L., & Beck, N. (1991). Social learning procedures for increasing attention and improving basic skills in severely regressed institutionalized patients. *Journal of Behavior Therapy and Experimental Psychiatry, 22,* 265–269.

Menditto, A. A., Beck, N. C., Stuve, P., Fisher, J. A., Stacy, M., Logue, M. B., & Baldwin, L. J. (1996). Effectiveness of clozapine and a social learning program for severely disabled psychiatric inpatients. *Psychiatric Services, 47,* 46–51.

Miller, D., Perry, P., Cadoret, R., & Andreasen, N. (1994). Clozapine's effect on negative symptoms in treatment-refractory schizophrenics. *Comprehensive Psychiatry, 35,* 8–15.

Mosher, L. R. (1999). Soteria and other alternatives to acute psychiatric hospitalization: A personal and professional review. *Journal of Nervous and Mental Disease, 187,* 142–149.

Mueser, K., Bond, G., Drake, R., & Resnick, S. (1998). Models of community care for severe mental illness: A review of research on case management. *Schizophrenia Bulletin, 24,* 37–73.

Mueser, K., & Gingrich, S. (1995). *Coping with schizophrenia: A guide for families.* Oakland, CA: New Harbinger Press.

Mueser, T., & Glynn, S. (2000). *Behavioral family therapy for psychiatric disorders* (2nd ed.). Oakland, CA: New Harbinger Press.

O'Connor, F. (1991). Symptom monitoring for relapse prevention in schizophrenia. *Archives of Psychiatric Nursing, 5,* 193–201.

Paul, G. L., & Lentz, R. J. (1977). *Psychosocial treatment of severe and persistent mental patients: Milieu versus social-learning programs.* Cambridge, MA: Harvard University Press.

Paul, G., & Menditto, A. (1992). Effectiveness of inpatient treatment programs for mentally ill adults in public psychiatric facilities. *Applied and Preventive Psychology*, *1*, 41–63.

Posner, C., Wilson, K., Kral, M., Lander, S., & McIlraith, J. (1992). Family psychoeducational support groups in schizophrenia. *American Journal of Orthopsychiatry*, *62*, 206–218.

Reinstein, M. J., Sirtovskaya, L. A., Jones, L. E., Mohan, S., & Cahasanov, M. A. (1999). *Clinical Drug Investigator*, *18*, 99–104.

Rivicki, D. (1999). Pharmacoeconomic evaluation of treatments for refractory schizophrenia: Clozapine-related studies. *Journal of Clinical Psychiatry*, *60*(Suppl. 1), 7–11.

Rosenheck, R., Dunn, L., Peszke, M., Cramer, J., Xu, W., Thomas, J., & Charney, D. (1999). Impact of clozapine on negative symptoms and on the deficit syndrome in refractory schizophrenia. *American Journal of Psychiatry*, *156*, 88–93.

Schooler, C., & Spohn, H. (1982). Social dysfunction and treatment failure in schizophrenia. *Schizophrenia Bulletin*, *8*, 85–98.

Schulz, C., Kahn, E., & Baker, R. (1990). Lithium and carbamazipine augmentation in treatment refractory schizophrenia. In B. Angrist & C. Schulz (Eds.), *The neuroleptic nonresponsive patient: Characterization and treatment* (pp. 109–136). Washington, DC: American Psychiatric Press.

Sensky, T., Turkington, D., Kingdon, D., Scott, J. L., Scott, J., Siddle, R., O'Carroll, M., & Barnes, T. R. (2000). A randomised controlled trial of cognitive–behavioral therapy for persistent symptoms in schizophrenia resistant to medication. *Archives of General Psychiatry*, *57*, 165–172.

Silver, H., & Nassar, A. (1992). Fluvoxamine improves negative symptoms in treated severe and persistent schizophrenia. *Biological Psychiatry*, *31*, 698–704.

Siris, S. (1994). Assessment and treatment of depression in schizophrenia. *Psychiatric Annals*, *24*, 463–467.

Skelton, J., Pepe, M., & Pineo, T. (1995). How much better is clozapine? A meta-analytic review and critical appraisal. *Experimental and Clinical Psychopharmacology*, *3*, 270–279.

Smith, T., & Docherty, J. (1998). Standards of care and clinical algorithms for treating schizophrenia. *Psychiatric Clinics of North America*, *21*, 203–220.

Spaulding, W. (1992). Some methodological prerequisites for outcome studies of cognitive treatment of schizophrenia. *Schizophrenia Bulletin*, *18*, 39–42.

Spaulding, W. D., Reed, D., Sullivan, M., Richardson, C., & Weiler, M. (1999). Effects of cognitive treatment in psychiatric rehabilitation. *Schizophrenia Bulletin*, *25*, 657–676.

Spaulding, W. D., Storms, L., Goodrich, V., & Sullivan, M. (1986). Applications of experimental psychopathology in psychiatric rehabilitation. *Schizophrenia Bulletin*, *12*, 560–577.

Strauss, J. S., & Carpenter, W. T., Jr. (1977). Prediction of outcome in schizophrenia: III. Five-year outcome and its predictors. *Archives of General Psychiatry*, *34*, 169–163.

Tardive Dyskinesia Task Force. (1980). Tardive dyskinesia: Summary of a task force report of the American Psychiatric Association. *American Journal of Psychiatry*, *137*, 163–172.

Tarrier, N., Yusupoff, L., Kinney, C., McCarthy, E., Gledhill, A., Haddock, G., & Morris, J. (1998). Randomised controlled trial of intensive cognitive behaviour therapy for patients with chronic schizophrenia. *British Medical Journal*, *317*, 303–307.

Tollefson, G. D., Sanger, T. M., Lu, Y., & Thieme, M. E. (1998). Depressive signs and symptoms in schizophrenia: A prospective blinded trial of olanzapine and haloperidol. *Archives of General Psychiatry*, *55*, 250–258.

Weinberger, D. (1994). Biological basis of schizophrenia: Structural/functional considerations relevant to potential for antipsychotic drug response. *Journal of Clinical Psychiatry Monograph Series*, *12*, 4–9.

Weinberger, D., & Lipska, B. (1995). Cortical maldevelopment, antipsychotic drugs and schizophrenia: A search for common ground. *Schizophrenia Research*, *16*, 87–110.

Wirshing, D. A., Wirshing, W. C., Marder, S. R., Saunders, C. S., Rossotto, E. H., & Erhart, S. M. (1997). Atypical antipsychotics: A practical review. *Medscape Mental Health*, *2*(10).

Wolkowitz, O., & Pickar, D. (1991). Benzodiazipines in the treatment of schizophrenia: A review and reappraisal. *American Journal of Psychiatry*, *48*, 714–726.

Wong, S., Massel, H., Mosk, M., & Liberman, R. (1986). Behavioral approaches to the treatment of schizophrenia. In G. Burroughs, T. Norman, & G. Rubenstein (Eds.), *Handbook of studies on schizophrenia* (pp. 79–100). Amsterdam: Elsevier.

Wykes, T., Parr, A. M., & Landau, S. (1999). Group treatment of auditory hallucinations. *British Journal of Psychiatry, 175,* 180–185.

Wykes, T., Reeder, C., Corner, J., Williams, C., & Everitt, B. (1999). The effects of neurocognitive remediation on executive processing in patients with schizophrenia. *Schizophrenia Bulletin, 25,* 291–307.

8

Combined Treatments for Smoking Cessation

*Marc E. Mooney and
Dorothy K. Hatsukami*

Despite impressive reductions in smoking in the United States over the past 40 years (Slade, 1992), smoking and nicotine dependence remain an immense public health problem in this country, with an estimated 27.7% of the population still smoking and with even higher prevalence among 18- to 34-year-olds (U.S. Department of Health and Human Services [USDHHS], 1999). Although nearly 80% of smokers indicate a desire to quit, and 35% of smokers attempt quitting annually (American Psychiatric Association, 1994), only 2.5% are successful annually. Indeed, smoking cessation may be best characterized as an ongoing process rather than a single quitting event, and the average person who succeeds in quitting will quit and relapse several times before achieving long-term abstinence. A full complement of health care providers, including clinical psychologists, primary care physicians, psychiatrists, and nurses, is needed to address this problem.

Beyond the recognition that nicotine dependence is a chronic relapsing disorder, it has become increasingly evident that smokers are not a homogenous population. Smokers differ in degree of nicotine dependence, in level of motivation to quit, and by comorbid mental disorders (Hughes, 1993; Prochaska & DiClemente, 1983; Swan, Jack, & Ward, 1997). In general, the overall population of smokers is likely to be weighted toward inclusion of the less educated and poor, those with mental disorders, and those more heavily dependent on nicotine (Hughes, 1996). Subtyping of patients on the basis of these dimensions for specialized care and more intensive treatment will become ever more important.

Recently, both the American Psychiatric Association (1996) and the Agency for Healthcare Research and Quality (AHRQ; Fiore et al., 2000) have produced summary documents providing guidelines and recommen-

This chapter was supported by National Institute of Drug Abuse Grants P50-DA09259 and 2T32-DA07097.

dations for smoking cessation. In this chapter we make frequent use of these documents, and readers interested in more detailed clinical recommendations are encouraged to read these guidelines. The American Psychiatric Association document *Practice Guideline for the Treatment of Patients With Nicotine Dependence* offers concrete recommendations on the assessment of nicotine dependence, the treatment of nicotine withdrawal, and special issues relating to comorbid diagnoses. In an equally accessible form is the AHRQ report *Treating Tobacco Use and Dependence* which examined multiple treatment dimensions including pharmacotherapy, behavioral therapy (BT; i.e., session length, total contact time, and number of sessions), setting of therapy, and the content of behavioral interventions.

Cigarette smoking is a psychopharmacological phenomenon, and the dual contributions of physiology and psychology must both be considered in the treatment of nicotine dependence. In this chapter we restrict the discussion primarily to pharmacotherapies currently approved by the Food and Drug Administration (FDA) and to behavioral therapies with broad empirical support (Fiore et al., 2000). We provide an overview of behavioral treatments and pharmacotherapies for smoking cessation, detailing dosing, side effects, contraindications, and effectiveness. With a knowledge of basic interventions thus established, we then discuss appropriate combinations, with emphasis on general treatment.

Assessment in Nicotine Dependence Treatment

In assessing patients for treatment of nicotine dependence, three key areas require attention: (a) degree of motivation, especially in regards to the *Stages of Change* (see Table 8.1); (b) level of nicotine dependence; and (c) comorbid mental disorders.

The Stages of Change, as developed and described by Prochaska and DiClemente (1983), reflect the various stages of motivational readiness through which smokers progress before quitting. These stages include (a) *precontemplation*, a period in which during the next 6 months the smoker is not considering quitting; (b) *contemplation*, a period during which a smoker is seriously thinking of quitting in the next 6 months; (c) *preparation*, a period during which a smoker who tried quitting in the previous year thinks about quitting in the next month; and (d) *action*, a 6-month period after the smoker makes overt changes to stop smoking (Prochaska, DiClemente, & Norcross, 1992). A fifth stage, *maintenance*, follows action and is of indeterminate duration, ending when relapse to smoking is no longer a problem (Prochaska et al., 1992).

Assessment of the Stages of Change is important, because certain interventions optimally suit the particular stages, and an instrument, the University of Rhode Island Change Assessment Scale (URICA; McConnaughy, Prochaska, & Velicer, 1983) can be used to assess the smoker's readiness to quit.

The URICA is a 32-item self-report questionnaire that assesses four of the Stages of Change—precontemplation, contemplation, action, and

Table 8.1. Sample Items From the University of Rhode Island
Assessment Scale

Stage of change	Sample questions
Precontemplation	1. As far as I'm concerned, I don't have any problem that needs changing.
	2. I'm not the one with the problem. It doesn't make much sense for me to be here.
Contemplation	1. I have a problem, and I really think I should work on it.
	2. I'm hoping this place will help me better understand myself.
Action	1. I am doing something about the problems that had been bothering me.
	2. Anyone can talk about changing; I'm actually doing something about it.
Maintenance	1. It worries me that I might slip back on a problem I had already changed, so I am here to seek help.
	2. I thought once I had resolved the problem I would be free of it, but sometimes I still find myself struggling with it.

Note. From "Stages of Change in Psychotherapy: Measurement and Sample Profiles" by
E. A. McConnaughy, J. O. Prochaska, and W. F. Velicer, 1983, *Psychotherapy: Theory,
Research, and Practice, 20*, p. 371. Copyright 1983 by Division of Psychotherapy (29) of
the American Psychological Association. Reprinted by permission.

maintenance—using 5-point Likert scales (McConnaughy et al., 1983).
The scale can be quickly completed and informs the clinician about which
interventions are most appropriate to the individual smoker. For instance,
a smoker identified as being in precontemplation will probably require
considerable encouragement and follow-up, because he or she may not
recognize the problem (see Figure 8.1). Interventions at this stage should
include informing the smoker about the many benefits of quitting (e.g.,
reduced risk of cancer and heart disease) and, possibly, *motivational interviewing* (Miller, 1996), a directive counseling technique intended to help
clients resolve ambivalence about quitting smoking. Important elements
of this technique include expression of empathy, avoidance of argumentation, and supporting self-efficacy (Miller, 1996). In motivational interviewing the counselor elicits reasons for quitting smoking, reinforces the
smoker for providing reasons for quitting smoking, and avoids confrontation (Miller, 1996). Use of motivational-interviewing techniques are not
exclusive to the precontemplation phase and can be used in other stages
to increase motivation to quit. Subsequent transitions through the Stages
of Change will bring a smoker to the action stage, when motivation to quit
is high. A treatment plan can be developed that includes a quit date, behavioral support, and pharmacotherapy. It is important to note that perhaps only 10%–15% of smokers are prepared for action (Prochaska, DiClemente, & Norcross, 1992) at any given time. Accordingly, uniform
application of action-oriented interventions are not indicated for most
smokers, and consistent effort to move them to the action stage remains
important.

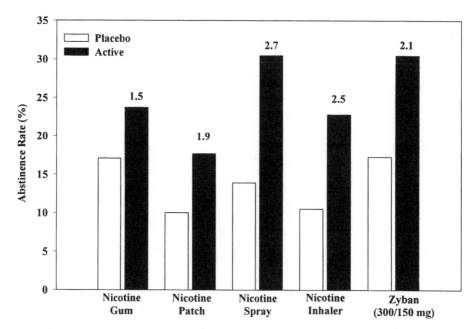

Figure 8.1. Average abstinence rates and odds ratios for the five Food and Drug Administration–approved smoking cessation treatments (Fiore et al., 2000). *Note.* Odds ratios are presented above each pharmacotherapy.

Another key area is the degree of nicotine dependence. Higher levels of dependence are associated with reduced rates of successful long-term abstinence (Hurt et al., 1992), and individuals who are highly dependent may require pharmacological as well as intensive behavioral treatment. The Fagerstrom Tolerance Questionnaire (FTQ; Fagerstrom & Schneider, 1989) provides a simple, quantitative score by which to gauge dependence (see Table 8.2). The FTQ provides a score from 0 to 11 and addresses the frequency and situational needs for cigarettes that are most related to strong nicotine dependence. A score of 7 or greater indicates notable nicotine dependence, and studies have shown that people who score high on the FTQ may require more intensive pharmacotherapy and are more prone to relapse (Fagerstrom & Schneider, 1989). As an alternative to the FTQ, the Fagerstrom Test for Nicotine Dependence (FTND; Heatherton, Kozlowski, Frecker, & Fagerstrom, 1991) was been developed and may be a more reliable and valid measure of nicotine dependence.[1]

Finally, existence of comorbid mental conditions must be assessed in

---

[1]The original FTQ was rationally constructed with no empirical assurance that all items measured the unitary construct of nicotine dependence. Subsequent studies (e.g., Heatherton et al., 1991) found a multifactorial structure as well as low internal-consistency reliability. Heatherton et al. (1991) developed a revised scale, the FTND, by excluding two items from the original FTQ and by altering scoring for two remaining items. The FTND showed improved internal consistency reliability, a unifactorial structure, and better agreement with the standard biochemical measure of nicotine dependence: plasma cotinine level. Both the FTQ and the FTND are at presently used in research.

Table 8.2. Fagerstrom Tolerance Questionnaire

Question	Answer/points
1. How soon after you wake up do you smoke your first cigarette?	Within 30 min/1 After 30 min/0
2. Do you find it difficult to refrain from smoking in places where it is forbidden, e.g., church, at the library, in cinema, etc.?	Yes/1 No/0
3. Which cigarette would you hate most to give up?	The first one in the morning/1 Any other/0
4. How many cigarettes/day do you smoke?	15 or less/0 16–25/1 26 or more/2
5. Do you smoke more frequently during the first hours after awakening than during the rest of the day?	Yes/1 No/0
6. Do you smoke if you are so ill that you are in bed most of the day?	Yes/1 No/0
7. What is the nicotine level of your usual brand of cigarettes?	0.9 mg or less/0 1.0–1.2 mg/1 1.3 mg or more/2
8. Do you inhale?	Never/0 Sometimes/1 Always/2

Note. From "Measuring Nicotine Dependence: A Review of the Fagerstrom Tolerance Questionnaire" by K. O. Fagerstrom and N. G. Schneider, 1989, *Journal of Behavioral Medicine, 12*, p. 164. Copyright 1989 by Plenum Press. Reprinted with permission.

light of the markedly elevated prevalence of cigarette smoking that has been observed among people with the major mental disorders. In particular, two common disorders, depression and schizophrenia, are associated with elevated levels of smoking; other examples include bulimia, the anxiety disorders, and attention deficit hyperactivity disorder (Breslau, 1995; Pomerleau, 1997). In one review, smoking prevalence among the major mental disorders varied from 50% to 80% (Hughes, 1993), with rates as high as 65% among individuals with histories of major depressive disorder (MDD) and 80% in people with schizophrenia. The rate of smoking among those with substance abuse disorders is also high; between 80% and 95% smoke (Hughes, 1994a).

Individuals with a previous history of mental illness may experience a recurrence of their disorders when attempting to quit. For example, given a history of MDD, a smoker attempting to quit is more likely to experience depressive mood (Covey, Glassman, & Stetner, 1990), and in some cases major depression can follow attempted cessation (Glassman et al., 1990). Epidemiological treatment studies of individuals with depressive histories have found substantially lower cessation rates compared to people who have never been affected by depression (Anda et al., 1990; Covey et al., 1990; Glassman et al., 1990). On the other hand, judging from the limited available literature, it seems that recovering alcoholics who quit smoking relapse to drinking at a rate no greater than those who continue to smoke (Breslau, Peterson, Schultz, Andreski, & Chilcoat, 1996; Hughes, 1993). All of these factors indicate that more frequent observation and intensive treatment may be required for smokers with comorbid disorders.

As a final consideration, nicotine withdrawal has been observed to lead to increased blood levels of some psychotropic medications, possibly worsening the side effects from these drugs (American Psychiatric Association, 1996). Treatment providers should be aware of such adverse events and monitor patients carefully.

Overview of Psychological and Pharmacological Strategies

Psychological Treatments

Pharmacological interventions for cigarette smoking cessation have dominated recent research and treatment efforts, but work in behavioral and cognitive techniques, which generally predate pharmacotherapeutic developments, also demands attention. In the following discussion we use BT generally to describe therapeutic techniques that may include both cognitive and behavioral elements. In a broad multimodal formulation, BT has been shown to produce abstinence rates in the 20%–25% range at 6 months and at rates twice that in control participants (American Psychiatric Association, 1996).

Description. The American Psychiatric Association (1996) guideline discusses several of the more common types of behavioral interventions, including skills training and relapse prevention, stimulus control, aversive therapy, social support, cue exposure, nicotine fading, and relaxation therapy (see Table 8.3). Despite the ostensible variety of behavioral techniques, few have received consistent empirical support. In addition, a lack of innovation in BTs for smoking in the past 15 years reflects a need for both renewed theoretical and practical efforts (Hajek, 1996; Shiffman, 1993).

Effectiveness. The AHRQ guideline took a more quantitative approach and examined a variety of treatment techniques to determine which were most effective and the optimal setting, number of sessions, session length, and total duration for BT. Guidelines from both the American Psychiatric Association (1996) and the AHRQ (Fiore et al., 2000) included similar recommendations concerning the effectiveness of the various BTs. The types of behavioral techniques that have been found to be significantly more effective than a reference control group include (a) *aversive cigarette smoking,* (b) *problem-solving and skills training,* and (c) *intratreatment social support.* Aversive cigarette smoking involves making smoking unpleasant by promoting nicotine intoxication; this is accomplished by methods of increased smoke exposure, such as rapid puffing, that lead to unpleasant

Table 8.3. Major Behavioral Therapies for Smoking Cessation

Technique	Brief description
Problem-solving/skills training	Smoker learns coping skills for situations likely to promote relapse; for example, oral substitutes (e.g., carrots or gum) may be used in place of cigarettes.
Stimulus control	Smoker identifies stimuli associated with smoking prior to quitting and avoids or removes them during the quit attempt.
Aversive smoking	Smoking is made aversive and less reinforcing to the smoker by promoting slight nicotine intoxication, by puffing rapidly or other methods of increased smoke exposure and its unpleasant side effects (e.g., nausea, dizziness).
Nicotine fading	Nicotine yield per cigarette is gradually reduced while the absolute number of cigarettes smoked remains the same or even increasing. Daily nicotine consumption, however, is reduced.
Social support	Smoker attempting to quit receives enhanced support and encouragement from a spouse or from other smokers attempting to quit.
Cue exposure	Smoker is repeatedly exposed to real or imaginary situations that elicit a strong desire to smoke in order to promote extinction of the association.
Relaxation	Smoker uses relaxation techniques to manage relapse situations associated with anxiety.

Note. From "Practice Guideline for the Treatment of Patients With Nicotine Dependence" by American Psychiatric Association, 1996, *American Journal of Psychiatry, 153*, pp. 10–11. Copyright 1996 by the American Psychiatric Association. Reprinted by permission.

side effects (e.g., nausea, dizziness). Although effective, aversive-smoking procedures have fallen into disfavor because of concerns about effects on health and the unpalatability of the approach. However, for healthy, motivated smokers, aversive techniques may be indicated (American Psychiatric Association, 1996; Fiore et al., 2000).

Problem-solving and skills training involve several key elements: (a) recognizing danger situations that activate or increase the desire to smoke (e.g., being around other smokers), (b) developing coping skills to stave off the urge to smoke (e.g., learning to avoid being around other smokers), and (c) providing basic information about smoking (e.g., the difficulties of nicotine withdrawal; Fiore et al., 2000). Intratreatment support involves a consistent policy of supporting the decision to quit and frequent follow-up visits or telephone calls during the initial quitting period. The AHRQ guideline emphasizes several points, including (a) encouraging the patient to consider quitting (moving a patient from the precontemplation stage to contemplation); (b) communicating empathy and concern (patients need to know you care); (c) encouraging a discussion about quitting (preparation for a quit attempt); and (d) providing information about withdrawal, addiction, and relapse (Fiore et al., 2000). In general, a multimodal behavioral therapeutic package is recommended that uses skills and relapse prevention training and intratreatment social support. Extratreatment social support involves both arranging for support outside of the clinic (e.g. supportive phone calls) and training the patient how to obtain support and encouragement from family, friends, and coworkers. Practical questions for any BT for smoking cessation include which mode produces the highest abstinence rates (i.e., group vs. individual vs. self-help vs. proactive telephone counseling) as well as the optimal length, total contact time, and number of therapeutic sessions (Fiore et al., 2000). BT techniques prove most effective within an individual or group counseling setting, whereas self-help materials and proactive telephone counseling provide smaller benefits compared to a control reference group. However, self-help interventions, although they have a low success rate, may be hindered by a lack of adherence, and some limited contact (even by telephone or mail) could improve their usefulness (Curry, 1993). On the other hand, the majority of smokers quit without individual or group counseling (Lichtenstein & Glasgow, 1992), and effective therapies requiring limited interaction with a clinician are needed (e.g., computerized interactive systems, e.g., Strecher et al., 1994). For more nicotine dependent smokers and those with comorbid diagnoses, such a minimal approach will generally prove insufficient.

Moreover, beyond the findings on treatment setting, significant positive relations were observed between abstinence rates and the number of minutes of treatment, total contact time, and number of treatment sessions. The highest quit rates were observed for those behavioral treatment programs offering 30 or more minutes of total contact time provided in 4 or more sessions, each 10 minutes or longer. The apparent dose–response relationship (i.e., time in therapy by abstinence rates) argues strongly for a behavioral treatment regimen that provides adequate time and attention to effectively provide therapy.

Summary. BT techniques—especially coping skills and relapse prevention training, intratreatment social support, and aversion therapy— have been shown to significantly improve abstinence rates above those of reference control groups. The AHRQ guideline suggests that an intensive treatment program should include (a) sessions at least 10 minutes long; (b) at least 4 sessions; and (c) total contact of 30 minutes or more (Fiore et al., 2000).

Pharmacotherapies

Although the effectiveness of BT for smoking cessation has been established, pharmacotherapy has become the dominant strategy in smoking cessation research and treatment during the 1990s. The primary pharmacotherapies available to smokers are the nicotine replacement therapies (NRTs; Hughes, 1994b), which include nicotine gum, the nicotine patch, nicotine nasal spray, and the nicotine inhaler. In a departure from NRT, the FDA approved bupropion (Zyban), an atypical antidepressant, for the treatment of smoking cessation. Furthermore, the AHRQ guideline has recommended that nortriptyline (marketed as the antidepressant Pamelor) and clonidine (the alpha-adrenergic agonist) may be used as second-line treatments if first-line treatments have proven ineffective. Although numerous agents have been tested for smoking cessation (e.g., anxiolytics, antihypertensives, and antidepressants; Hughes, 1994b), we discuss at length only FDA-approved agents.

NRTs

Description and mechanism of action. Four types of NRTs are currently approved by the FDA: nicotine gum, the nicotine patch, nicotine nasal spray, and the nicotine inhaler. Smokers can purchase nicotine gum (Nicorette, 2 and 4 mg) and the nicotine patch (Nicotrol, 15 mg, and Nicoderm, 21, 14, and 7 mg) over the counter. In addition, the products formerly labeled Habitrol (21, 14, and 7 mg) and Prostep (22 and 11 mg) are currently being marketed as generic, over the counter products through chain drug stores. The two most recently approved NRTs, nicotine nasal spray (Nicotrol NS, 10 mg/ml) and the nicotine inhaler (Nicotrol, 4 mg/cartridge), require a prescription. Clinicians should advise the smoker of the several substantial benefits of all the NRTs, including reduced nicotine withdrawal symptoms associated with smoking cessation, a reduced level of nicotine in the body, and significantly lower toxicity compared to cigarette smoking. Nicotine use per se has not been associated with cancer but has been primarily associated with fetal toxicity and increased risk for cardiovascular disease. However, the ill health effects resulting from nicotine are not as extensive as those resulting from cigarette smoking (Benowitz, 1988). Despite differences in route of administration, side effects, and contraindications, all the NRTs show nearly equal effectiveness (see Figure 8.1). Smokers attempting to quit have alternatives among the NRTs and should consider the ease and route of administration, the immediacy of effect, and the specific side effects and contraindications unique to each NRT (see Table 8.4).

Pharmacokinetics and dosing. The NRTs have differing time courses and effects in the body (see Table 8.4). The method of NRT administration is directly related to the respective pharmacokinetic differences (e.g., time to peak blood concentration of nicotine). For example, nicotine gum provides only temporary nicotine dosing and, to be optimally effective, must be used on a fixed schedule (e.g., every 1–2 hours; maximum use twenty-four 2-mg pieces per day or twenty-four 4-mg pieces per day), although smokers are also encouraged to use nicotine gum ad libitum when craving occurs. In contrast, the nicotine patch is administered once a day for either 16 hours (Nicotrol) or 24 hours (Nicoderm): Nicotine emanates from the patch throughout the day and, for some patches, at night. Nicotine nasal spray and inhalers are administered on an ad libitum basis. Nicotine spray

Table 8.4. Profile of Nicotine Replacement Products

Administration and immediacy of effect	Side effects	Contraindications
Nicotine gum		
Ad libitum or fixed schedule (2-mg piece = 1 mg; 4-mg piece = 2 mg), 20–30 min	GI distress, jaw soreness, burning in throat, hiccups	Temporo–mandibular joint diseases, dentures
Nicotine patch		
Once a day for 16 or 24 hr (15–22 mg), 6–12 hours	Topical skin reactions, abnormal dreams, joint or muscle pain	Skin disorders
Nicotine nasal spray		
Ad libitum (0.5 mg/spray, 1 mg/dose), 11–13 min	Nose and throat irritation, coughing, sneezing, nose running, eyes watering	Chronic nasal problems, respiratory problems
Nicotine inhaler		
Ad libitum (13 mg/puff), 15–20 min	Throat irritation, coughing, headaches	Allergy to menthol

Note. GI = gastrointestinal. From "Pharmacological and Behavioral Strategies for Smoking Cessation" by D. K. Hatsukami and M. E. Mooney, 1999, *Journal of Clinical Psychology in Medical Settings,* 6(1), 11–38. Copyright 1999 by Plenum Press. Reprinted with permission.

is provided in metered doses (one spray for each nostril) providing 1 mg of nicotine, and the maximum daily recommended dose is 40 mg (80 sprays). In the case of the nicotine inhaler, doses are administered in nicotine cartridges, and the recommended number of cartridges used is between 6 and 16 per day.

The NRTs need to be used for weeks after smoking cessation to provide maximum protection from the effects of nicotine withdrawal, to deal with episodes of craving, and possibly to provide some positive reinforcing effects from nicotine. The recommended use of nicotine gum is not to exceed 3 months, and gradual reduction in the use should begin about 6 weeks after quitting. The recommended use of the nicotine patch varies, with patch products being used from 6 weeks (e.g., Nicotrol) to up to 10 weeks (e.g, Nicoderm), followed by discontinuation. Furthermore, some patch treatments (e.g., Nicoderm, 21, 14, and 7 mg) allow for a gradual reduction in nicotine use (e.g., 21 mg in Weeks 1–6, 14 mg in Weeks 7–8, 7 mg in Weeks 9–10). However, no evidence exists that gradual reduction is more effective than a no-weaning condition (i.e., abrupt cessation from 21 mg; Stapleton et al., 1995). The nicotine patch is not recommended for use beyond 3 months. The nicotine nasal spray may be used up to 12 weeks, whereas the nicotine inhaler may be used for up to 6 months. It is recommended that patients should not smoke and use nicotine replacement, although there is little evidence of adverse effects from occasional lapses to smoking during NRT (Joseph et al., 1996).

There has been recent discussion over whether nicotine replacements should be used on a long-term basis. It is clear that nicotine dependence, for many smokers, is a chronic, relapsing disorder. Therefore, use of nicotine replacement over longer periods of time may be in order (Warner, Slade, & Sweanor, 1997).

Side effects and contraindications. Minimization of adverse side effects is important in optimizing treatment adherence. The side-effect profiles of the various NRTs are closely related to their respective routes of administration. Use of nicotine gum may produce such side effects as gastrointestinal distress, jaw soreness, burning in the throat, and hiccups. Nicotine patch side effects can include topical skin reactions, abnormal dreams, and joint and muscle pain. The nicotine inhaler can produce such side effects as throat irritation, coughing, and a running nose. Nicotine nasal spray side effects may include mouth and throat irritation, sneezing, coughing, running nose, and watery eyes.

Some general contraindications or conditions that require cautious use of each of the NRTs include unstable coronary artery disease, serious cardiac arrhythmia, vasospastic disease, uncontrolled hypertension, diabetes, insulin dependence, and peptic ulcers. Pregnancy is a conditional contraindication; however, depending on circumstances, physicians may prescribe NRT. It is important to remember that few contraindications are absolute, and the risk–benefit ratio must be carefully considered for each smoker.

Effectiveness. Considerably more outcome research is available for the long-term effectiveness of the nicotine patch and nicotine gum compared to the nicotine inhaler or nicotine spray. Long-term follow-up in nicotine gum and patch studies has typically occurred between 6 and 12 months, with the majority of observations being reported at 1 year. Similarly, almost all treatment studies of the nicotine inhaler and nicotine spray report abstinence rates at 1 year. Treatment has been conducted in a variety of settings, from a physician's office to smoking cessation treatment facilities. Mean long-term mean abstinence rates across the NRTs (generally point prevalence) range from 17.7% (patch) to 30.5% (spray), with fewer studies available for nicotine spray and inhaler and those restricted to self-selected, motivated smokers (Fiore et al., 2000; see Figure 8.1 and Table 8.5).

Research has addressed whether heavily dependent smokers may benefit from greater doses of nicotine or whether certain smokers may find a particular type of medication more effective. Earlier studies of nicotine gum used 2-mg gum doses, but later studies with 4-mg gum doses have been found to be more effective among more heavily dependent smokers (Herrera et al., 1995; Tonnensen et al., 1988). For smokers who smoke 25 cigarettes or more per day, 4 mg nicotine gum is especially indicated. The use of high-dose nicotine patch (e.g., 44 mg) therapy has not received clear support and is definitely not indicated for light smokers (Dale et al., 1995; Jorenby et al., 1995). Hughes et al. (1999) examined the effects of the nicotine patch across a range of doses (0, 21, 35, and 42 mg) in a multicenter study of heavy smokers (≥30 cigarettes/day). Although a trend toward increased 1-year quit rates was noted (7%, 13%, 9%, and 19%,

Table 8.5.   Treatment Outcomes for Nicotine Replacement Products

Nicotine replacement	Time of follow-up (months)	% Abstinent, active	% Abstinent, placebo	Odds ratios (95% C.I.[a])
Nicotine patch	6–12 months	16.0–19.5	10.0	1.7–2.2
Nicotine gum	6–12 months	20.6–26.7	17.1	1.3–1.8
Nicotine nasal spray	12 months	21.8–39.2	13.9	1.8–4.1
Nicotine inhaler	12 months	16.4–29.2	10.5	1.7–3.6

Note. From "Treating Tobacco Use and Dependence. Clinical Practice Guideline." Fiore et al. (2000). Rockville, MD: U.S. Department of Health and Human Services. Public Health Service. AHRQ Publication No. 00-0032. June 2000.
[a]95% C.I. = 95% confidence interval.

respectively), no differences were statistically significant. Last, nicotine nasal spray may be particularly helpful for heavily dependent smokers (Sutherland et al., 1992).

Non-nicotine pharmacotherapy

Description. Although a number of non-nicotine smoking cessation agents have been tested, bupropion is the only one so far approved by the FDA. Bupropion is available by prescription for smoking cessation under the proprietary name Zyban. (Bupropion is also marketed as Wellbutrin for the treatment of depression.) Zyban is bupropion in a sustained-release formulation (i.e., bupropion SR) that allows for less frequent dosing and a better safety profile than immediate-release formulations of the drug (Hsyu et al., 1997). The neurophysiological mechanisms by which bupropion helps some to quit smoking cigarettes are not clearly known but likely involve the dopaminergic pathways (Hurt et al., 1997).

Dosing. On average, bupropion must be taken for 8 days to achieve steady-state plasma levels (Ferris & Cooper, 1993); accordingly, 1–2 weeks before quitting smoking the patient begins Zyban treatment. During the first 3 days of treatment, the patient takes 150 mg every morning. The dose is subsequently increased to 300 mg/day (150 mg twice a day), with each dose taken at least 8 hours apart. Total treatment duration varies from 7 to 12 weeks but continues on a 300 mg/day schedule. Although Hurt et al.'s (1997) study demonstrated the highest abstinence rate for the 300-mg dose, it should be noted that at 1 year both the 150-mg and 300-mg dose conditions were not statistically significant from one another, although both were superior to placebo. Accordingly, for individuals who cannot tolerate a 300-mg dose there is some room to lower the dose and still maintain therapeutic effects.

Side effects and contraindications. Dry mouth and insomnia are the most common side effects of Zyban. Agitation, nausea, and tremor occur less frequently. Zyban lowers the seizure threshold in a dose-dependent fashion. Above 450 mg/day, risk of seizure increases substantially; hence, such doses are not recommended. Contraindications to use of Zyban include concurrent use of other forms of bupropion (Wellbutrin or Wellbutrin SR). Monoamine oxidase inhibitors should be discontinued at least 14 days before initiating treatment with Zyban, and a waiting period of at least 14 days after stopping Zyban should be observed before starting these medications again. Patients should be cautioned not to take other prescribed antidepressants while taking Zyban. Seizure disorder or any clinical situation that might increase risk for seizures (e.g., use or withdrawal from some drugs of abuse) is a contraindication to Zyban use. Last, Zyban is contraindicated when a current or prior diagnosis of bulimia or anorexia nervosa exists, again because of the possibility of increased seizure risk.

Effectiveness. Two controlled trials demonstrate the success of Zyban as a treatment in smoking cessation, both alone and combined with the nicotine patch (Hurt et al., 1997; Jorenby et al., 1999). Hurt et al. (1997) found that at 1-year follow-up both 150- and 300-mg doses produced significantly higher abstinence rates than the placebo group (see Table 8.6).

Jorenby et al. (1999) examined the combined use of Zyban and the nicotine patch. At long-term follow-up (52 weeks), participants who were treated with Zyban and the nicotine patch had the highest abstinence rate (35.5%) but were not significantly different from those who received Zyban alone (31.1%). Both the Zyban–nicotine patch and Zyban treatment produced abstinence rates that were significantly higher than the nicotine patch (16.4%) or the placebo patch treatment (15.6%). The lack of treatment effect observed with the nicotine patch is unusual.

Summary. An effective set of pharmacotherapies exists for smoking cessation: the NRTs and Zyban. In selecting a treatment, the specific benefits, side effects, and contraindications should be matched to the needs

Table 8.6. Cessation Rates for Bupropion in a Controlled Clinical Trial

Treatment condition	End of treatment (%)	12 months (%)	Odds ratios
Placebo (n = 153)	19.0	12.4	
Bupropion			
100 mg/day (n = 153)	28.8*	19.6	1.72
150 mg/day (n = 153)	38.6*	22.9*	2.09*
300 mg/day (n = 156)	44.2*†	23.1*	2.12*

Note. From "Pharmacological and Behavioral Strategies for Smoking Cessation" by D. K. Hatsukami and M. E. Mooney, 1999, Journal of Clinical Psychology in Medical Settings. Copyright 1999 by Plenum Press. Reprinted with permission. Table values are from "A Comparison of Sustained-Release Bupropion and Placebo for Smoking Cessation" by R. D. Hurt et al., 1997, New England Journal of Medicine, 337, p. 1198. Copyright 1997 by the Massachusetts Medical Society. All rights reserved. Adapted with permission.
*p < .05 from placebo.   †p < .05 from 100 mg/day.

and tolerances of the patient. For instance, the nicotine patch is most suitable to smokers who require an easily administered product and a sustained level of nicotine. On the other hand, many smokers have concerns about weight gain and desire an oral substitute for cigarettes: Nicotine gum has been observed to minimize smoking cessation related weight gain (Gross, Stitzer, & Maldonado, 1989; Leischow, Sachs, Bostrom, & Hansen, 1992). Furthermore, the nicotine inhaler may prove suitable to individuals who desire a treatment that mimics smoking behavior. Among the NRTs, nicotine nasal spray provides the more dependent smokers the most rapid relief. Although the nicotine patch provides a fixed dose, the other three NRTs allow for individual dosing. The last FDA-approved product, Zyban, is a convenient non-nicotine agent that has also been observed to reduce weight gain that follows smoking cessation (Hurt et al., 1997; Jorenby et al., 1999).

Combined Pharmacological–Behavioral Treatments

The joint use of pharmacotherapy and behavioral treatments has a strong logical basis in the dual physical and psychological determinants of nicotine dependence. Most research on this interaction has involved BT and either nicotine gum or the nicotine patch. Reviews have shown that adding NRTs to BT increases abstinence (i.e., NRT + BT > BT) and that adding behavioral treatments to NRT (i.e., NRT + BT > NRT) also augments the success rates, although this effect is less clear with the nicotine patch (Hughes, 1995; Law & Tang, 1995). At this point, no studies have examined the effects of adding behavioral treatment to other pharmacotherapies. The focus of this review is an examination of the effects of adding behavioral treatment to nicotine replacements and, where possible, the effects of level of behavioral treatment.

Nicotine gum and BT. Three meta-analyses examining nicotine gum provide important evidence as to the adjunctive benefits of BT. First, Cepeda-Benito (1993) demonstrated that more intensive BT (i.e., 3 or more hours of therapy within 4 weeks compared to less than this standard) combined with nicotine gum can yield higher abstinence rates at end of treatment and at long-term follow-up (34% vs. 11%).[2] A second meta-analysis examined the effects of nicotine gum in different contexts (i.e., a primary care setting, a hospital, a community volunteer program, or a smoking cessation clinic) of behavioral treatment (Silagy, Mant, Fowler, & Lodge, 1994a, 1994b). The greatest success rates were observed in the smoking cessation clinic (36%), whereas the primary care setting showed the lowest abstinence rates (11%; Silagy et al., 1994b). In addition, Silagy et al. (1994b) found that higher behavioral intensity (i.e., one or more consultations ≥30 minutes or two or more follow-ups compared to routine physician care) produced nearly double the long-term abstinence rate (25%

---

[2]Interpolated from Figure 8.1 (Cepeda-Benito, 1993, p. 826).

vs. 13%). Finally, Law and Tang (1995) compared two groups (across studies) in which 2-mg gum was prescribed. In some studies, gum was dispensed in a general practice or hospital setting, whereas in others patients received care in a smoking cessation clinic. The latter group had an appreciably higher abstinence rate (11% vs. 3%). As mentioned earlier, successful use of nicotine gum requires its consistent administration: Adjunctive BT may provide motivation to use the gum and insight into the withdrawal process as well as motivation and tools to stay abstinent.

Nicotine patch and BT. As assessed by several meta-analyses on the topic, adjunctive BT for the nicotine patch has produced a mixed picture. Fiore, Smith, Jorenby, and Baker (1994) found that more intensive BT[3] produced higher abstinence rates than less intensive BT (27% vs. 20%; Fiore et al., 1994). In agreement, Law and Tang (1995) observed that individuals who used the patch in smoking cessation clinics achieved abstinence rates three times better than individuals observed in a family practice milieu who used the nicotine patch with minimal psychosocial support (13% vs. 4%; outcomes at 6 months or longer). In contrast, Silagy et al. (1994a, 1994b), examining different contexts and intensities of treatment (as they did for nicotine gum), found no significant differences in abstinence rates. The less than robust findings observed for the nicotine patch may be explained by different definitions of intensity of treatment, or possibly because the patch may facilitate the dissociation between stimuli and smoking behavior or nicotine dosing, whereas with nicotine gum these associations continue. Thus, although the smoker is learning new skills to deal with situations associated with smoking, the user of nicotine gum still relies on nicotine as a coping tool. At this point, clarification of these findings is not possible given incomplete descriptions of the BT regimens used and how they were united with nicotine patch use.

Summary. The logical basis for combining NRT with BT remains appealing. NRT helps to diminish craving and the withdrawal syndrome, whereas BT may promote enhanced compliance with NRT, improved coping and problem-solving skills for relapse prevention, and enhanced motivation to remain abstinent. Nicotine spray and inhalers, like nicotine gum, require frequent use to maintain therapeutic plasma nicotine levels, and BT may prove a useful and essential adjunct to these modes. Models for the treatment of other substance abuse disorders (such as alcoholism and drug dependence) do not use brief interventions but instead provide intensive behavioral support (Hughes, 1995). Given the tremendous economic and social tolls of smoking, it seems that more thorough and com-

---

[3] In Fiore et al.'s (1994) study a numerical definition of high- versus low-intensity BT was used so four treatment parameters could be assessed (0 = negative response, 1 = positive response). The parameters were (a) was counseling the primary goal of the session? (yes = 1), (b) frequency of meetings for first 4 weeks of patch therapy ≥1/week? (yes = 1), (c) ≥7 meetings over 12 weeks? (yes = 1), and (d) length of consultations ≥40 minutes? (yes = 1). A score of 3 or 4 indicated high-intensity BT, whereas a score of 2, 1, or 0 indicated low-intensity treatment.

prehensive treatment regimens may also be indicated for nicotine dependence and should be made accessible to all smokers.

Treatment

Algorithms

Clinicians, especially general practitioners, see a wide variety of cigarette smokers, and the selection of the best treatment plan can be facilitated by the use of an *algorithm*. Algorithms, best illustrated in schematic flowcharts, enable complex step-by-step decisions to be made, somewhat mechanically, while allowing for clinician discretion. Elaborate smoking cessation algorithms have been prepared (Cox, 1993; Hughes, 1994a; Orleans, 1993; Fiore et al., 2000). Practical treatment, at least implicitly, involves algorithmic thinking, and readers are encouraged to review the algorithms cited.

Basic Treatment

Initial assessment should provide information on degree of nicotine dependence as well as on current or historical medical and mental health problems. Irrespective of motivational status, the clinician should provide a basic level of care to each smoker and promote readiness to quit (Fiore et al., 2000). First, the health care provider should ask about tobacco use and encourage the smoker to quit, communicating empathy and concern about the smoker's well-being. Enhancing motivation can involve discussing the so-called five "R's." The message must be *relevant* to the smoker (e.g. discussion of a smoking-related ailment), communiate the *risks* of smoking (e.g., life expectancy), the *rewards* of quitting (e.g. financial savings), and the *roadblocks* experienced in quitting (e.g., withdrawal symptoms). Additionally, these messages should be *repeated* at each clinic visit. The techniques used in this phase of the intervention can be those used in motivational interviewing (Miller, 1996). For those ready to quit, pharmacological treatments, provision of intratreatment support, and educational materials are appropriate. NRT and Zyban have been recommended as the first line treatments for all quitting smokers, unless they are contraindicated (American Psychiatric Association, 1996; Fiore et al., 2000). Moreover, relapse prevention strategies should be discussed, including the development of replacement behaviors for smoking (e.g., oral substitutes, relaxation exercises), the recognition of environmental situations (e.g., psychosocial stressors) that threaten relapse to smoking, and the tools to deal with these situations. The clinician must provide some follow-up to determine the smoker's efforts to quit and provide support. The amount of time spent on providing the basic level of support may be minimal, graduating or referring to more intensive measures if indicated.

The average smoker who does quit permanently usually makes several attempts, and follow-up is always indicated to determine if additional help is required. Treatment of the quitting smoker may use the concept of *re-cycling*, which automatically provides for continued treatment and booster therapy after relapse (Lando, Pirie, Roski, McGovern, & Schmid, 1996; Tonnensen, Norregaard, Sawe, & Simonsen, 1993). After failed quit attempts, increasingly intensive treatment needs to be applied. Furthermore, comorbid mental illness, substance abuse, and excessive withdrawal-related symptoms mark special populations especially in need of more aggressive care as a first line of treatment. These intensive treatments may require individual or group behavioral support that spans several sessions. In the following sections we examine the needs of special populations.

Intensive or Specialized Treatment

For smokers who have been unable to quit with less intensive regimens, involving brief advice and pharmacotherapy, certain complicating factors or comorbid diagnoses may be at work. For instance, highly dependent smokers have great concerns about withdrawal and craving. Smokers, especially females, worry about excessive weight gain following cessation. Comorbid diagnoses, including depression and alcoholism, are associated with markedly higher rates of smoking. These populations need to be identified and their special needs integrated into a treatment plan. These groups are neither exhaustive nor independent, and it would be possible to find individuals who fall into all of the broad categories listed.

High Nicotine Dependence

High nicotine dependence is often defined by a score of 7 or higher on the FTQ. In addition, smokers who smoke 25 or more cigarettes per day are often classified as heavy smokers and are generally considered more nicotine dependent. However, those who smoke fewer cigarettes daily may achieve similar plasma levels of nicotine. The nicotine withdrawal syndrome may prove especially difficult for these smokers, and NRT at higher doses (i.e., 4-mg nicotine gum or combination therapies; Herrera et al., 1995; Tonnensen et al., 1988) or with a quicker onset of effect (e.g., nicotine inhaler) may prove essential to a successful quit attempt. In addition, adjunctive behavioral treatment can also enhance long-term abstinence among this group of smokers. In a study of combined NRT (gum) and behavioral support, Hall, Tunstall, Rugg, Jones, and Benowitz (1985) compared smokers with high and low cotinine levels at the beginning of treatment (higher cotinine levels indicate more nicotine exposure). The high-cotinine smokers showed appreciably higher abstinence rates when provided combined nicotine gum and behavioral treatment compared to gum or behavioral treatment alone. In contrast, low-cotinine smokers showed similar abstinence rates across conditions. Therefore, the more dependent a smoker is, the greater the likelihood the individual will benefit from more intensive behavioral treatment.

Weight Gain

An additional symptomatic concern of smokers attempting to quit is weight gain. Perhaps because of a smoking-related lowering of the body's weight set point (the weight the body seeks to maintain by means of metabolic processes), smokers on average weigh about 8 lbs less than nonsmokers (Klesges, Meyers, Klesges, & LaVasque, 1989). The mean weight gain that follows smoking cessation is about 8 pounds and may be more a function of the body's set point rebounding, which may secondarily lead to temporarily increased eating (Klesges et al., 1989; Perkins, 1993) and decreased metabolic rate, particularly during activity (Perkins, 1992). Studies that have included behavioral interventions specific to weight control, although they have led to decreased weight gain (Hall, Tunstall, Vila, & Duffy, 1992; Pirie et al., 1992, have not shown better long-term cessation rates. Although smokers, especially women, may be concerned about weight gain and may forego quitting smoking because of this concern, emphasis must be placed on the greater benefit of smoking cessation. Nevertheless, for smokers with serious concerns about weight gain, nicotine gum and Zyban have been observed to minimize weight gain related to smoking cessation (Gross et al., 1989; Hurt et al., 1997; Leischow et al., 1992) while the person is on the medication.

Comorbid Conditions

The general issues relating to comorbid mental illness and nicotine dependence were already discussed. Because of the lack of research on the special treatment needs of these diagnostic groups, specific recommendations cannot be made. For example, although a high prevalence of smoking exists in populations of active and recovering alcoholics, to date no research has examined the combination of BT and pharmacological treatment for these populations. One study (Hurt et al., 1995) showed that nonalcoholic smokers experienced a higher rate of abstinence than recovering alcoholics (31% vs. 0%, respectively, at 1 year). This study demonstrates a need for comprehensive treatment beyond pharmacotherapy. Moreover, limited treatment data exist to recommend a specific course of treatment for individuals with major depressive disorder (MDD; Hall, Munoz, & Reus, 1994; Hall et al., 1998). Generally, more intensive behavioral support may be indicated with careful monitoring of depressive symptomatology. With regard to pharmacotherapy, the antidepressant nortriptyline has yielded superior quit rates (as compared to placebo) in both individuals with and without histories of MDD (Hall et al., 1998). The general need of individuals with mental illness for psychotherapeutic support and for structured treatment certainly applies with respect to smoking cessation interventions for them.

Summary

Smoking cessation treatments include a variety of both pharmacotherapeutic and behavioral interventions. Through their combination, an approach can be adopted in which all smokers receive initial care that involves brief advice and support as well as an appropriate NRT or Zyban. However, some smokers who experience a higher degree of dependence; a comorbid disorder; or who have special issues that require attention, such as weight gain, may need more intensive or specialized therapy at the outset. Furthermore, because nicotine dependence is a chronic relapsing disorder, the clinician and patient must be prepared for repeated efforts to quit. Failure to quit may reflect lack of motivation or the occurrence of unexpected psychosocial stressors, or it may indicate the effects of greater dependence or comorbid disorders that are thwarting efforts to stop smoking. The clinician can be an important force in continuing to motivate smokers to quit, providing them the means as well as the encouragement to overcome the challenges of nicotine cessation.

Conclusion

This chapter has overviewed pharmacological, behavioral, and combined therapies for smoking cessation. At this point, the clinician should have guidelines for combining pharmacological and psychological treatments as well as for selecting a single or combined therapy. Some general conclusions are available for the treatment of smokers.

1. Smokers should be assessed for Stages of Change, degree of motivation to quit, degree of nicotine dependence, and comorbid mental disorders that might present obstacles to treatment.
2. All smokers should receive nicotine replacement, except when contraindicated (American Psychiatric Association, 1996; Fiore et al., 2000).
3. The choice of pharmacological agents should take into consideration the profile of their effects and the needs of each smoker. Factors that should be taken into consideration include side effects, contraindications, ease of administration, the need for oral substitutes, speed of relief, and degree of physical dependence on nicotine.
4. *Intensive* behavioral treatment should include (a) 4 or more sessions; (b) sessions lasting at least 10 minutes; and (c) a total contact time longer than 30 minutes (Fiore et al., 2000). The most *minimal* behavioral treatment should include sessions 1 to 3 minutes in length and include at least 2 sessions.
5. Four behavioral treatments have received empirical support: problem-solving and skills training, aversive therapy, intratreatment social support, and extratreatment social support.
6. The extent of behavioral treatment may depend on the needs of

the individual smoker. All smokers should be provided a basic level of care, which includes advice to quit, assistance in quitting (pharmacotherapy, self-help materials), and arrangement for follow-up (Fiore et al., 2000). This intervention could be brief. More intensive treatment may be necessary for smokers who are highly dependent on nicotine or who have a comorbid mental disorder, and special attention may need to be paid to weight gain. Furthermore, individuals who have failed with brief interventions may require more intensive treatment.

7. Nicotine dependence is a chronic relapsing disorder. Long-term treatment and repeated efforts at cessation may be needed.

If one rule might be given for smoking cessation treatment, it would be persistence. Nicotine dependence is a highly entrained psychopharmacological disorder, and smokers experience an environment that at any turn might elicit craving for the use of nicotine. Unlike other substance dependencies, tobacco use does not pose immediate catastrophic risks: Its costs are steady and pervasive, and the toll will likely come only after years of use. Smokers need reassurance that they can eventually quit, the tools to do so, and to be aware of the numerous benefits of going smoke free.

References

American Psychiatric Association. (1994). *Diagnostic and statistical manual of mental disorders* (4th ed.). Washington, DC: Author.

American Psychiatric Association. (1996). Practice guideline for the treatment of patients with nicotine dependence. *American Journal of Psychiatry, 153*(Suppl. 10), 1–31.

Anda, R. F., Williamson, D. F., Escobedo, L. G., Mast, M. E., Giovino, G. A., & Remington, P. L. (1990). Depression and the dynamics of smoking. *Journal of the American Medical Association, 264*, 1541–1545.

Benowitz, N. L. (1988). Pharmacological aspects of cigarette smoking and nicotine addiction. *New England Journal of Medicine, 319*, 1318–1330.

Breslau, N. (1995). Psychiatric co-morbidity of smoking and nicotine dependence. *Behavior Genetics, 25*, 95–101.

Breslau, N., Peterson, E., Schultz, L., Andreski, P., & Chilcoat, H. (1996). Are smokers with alcohol disorders less likely to quit? *American Journal of Public Health, 86*, 985–990.

Cepeda-Benito, A. (1993). Meta-analytical review of the efficacy of nicotine chewing gum in smoking treatment programs. *Journal of Consulting and Clinical Psychology, 61*, 822–830.

Covey, L. S., Glassman, A. H., & Stetner, F. (1990). Depression and depressive symptoms in smoking cessation. *Comprehensive Psychiatry, 31*, 350–354.

Cox, J. L. (1993). Algorithms for nicotine withdrawal therapy. *Health Values, 17*, 41–50.

Curry, S. J. (1993). Self-help interventions for smoking cessation. *Journal of Consulting and Clinical Psychology, 61*, 790–803.

Dale, L. C., Hurt, R. D., Offord, K. P., Lawson, G. M., Croghan, I. T., & Schroeder, D. R. (1995). High dose nicotine patch therapy: Percentage of replacement and smoking cessation. *Journal of the American Medical Association, 274*, 1353–1358.

Fagerstrom, K. O., & Schneider, N. G. (1989). Measuring nicotine dependence: A review of the Fagerstrom Tolerance Questionnaire. *Journal of Behavioral Medicine, 12*, 159–182.

Ferris, R. M., & Cooper, B. R. (1993). Mechanism of antidepressant activity of bupropion. *Journal of Clinical Psychiatry Monographs, 11*, 2–14.

Fiore, M. C., Bailey, W. C., Cohen, S. J., Dorfman, S. F., Goldstein, M. G., Gritz, E. R., Heyman, R. B., Jaen, C. R., Kottke, T. E., Lando, H. A., Mecklenburg, R. E., Mullen P. D., Nett, L. M., Robinson, L., Stitzer, M. L., Tommasello, A.C., Villejo, L., Wewers, M. E. (2000). Treating tobacco use and dependence. Clinical practice guideline. Rockville, MD: U.S. Department of Health and Human Services. Public Health Service.

Fiore, M. C., Smith, S. S., Jorenby, D. E., & Baker, T. B. (1994). The effectiveness of the nicotine patch for smoking cessation. *Journal of the American Medical Association, 271*, 1940–1947.

Glassman, A. H., Helzer, J. E., Covey, L. S., Cottler, L. B., Stetner, F., Tipp, J. E., & Johnson, J. (1990). Smoking, smoking cessation, and major depression. *Journal of the American Medical Association, 264*, 1546–1549.

Gross, J., Stitzer, M. L., & Maldonado, J. (1989). Nicotine replacement: Effects on post-cessation weight gain. *Journal of Consulting and Clinical Psychology, 57*, 87–92.

Hajek, P. (1996). Current issues in behavioral and pharmacological approaches to smoking cessation. *Addictive Behaviors, 21*, 699–707.

Hall, S. M., Munoz, R. F., & Reus, V. I. (1994). Cognitive–behavioral intervention increases abstinence rates for depressive-history smokers. *Journal of Consulting and Clinical Psychology, 62*, 141–146.

Hall, S. M., Reus, V. I., Munoz, R. F., Sees, K. L., Humfleet, G., Hatzy, D. T., Frederick, S., & Triffleman, E. (1998). Nortriptyline and cognitive–behavioral therapy in the treatment of cigarette smoking. *Archives of General Psychiatry, 55*, 683–690.

Hall, S. M., Tunstall, C., Rugg, D., Jones, R. T., & Benowitz, N. (1985). Nicotine gum and behavioral treatment in smoking cessation. *Journal of Consulting and Clinical Psychology, 53*, 256–258.

Hall, S. M., Tunstall, C. D., Vila, K. L., & Duffy, J. (1992). Weight gain prevention and smoking cessation: Cautionary findings. *American Journal of Public Health, 82*, 799–803.

Hatsukami, D. K., & Mooney, M. E. (1999). Pharmacological and behavioral strategies for smoking cessation. *Journal of Clinical Psychology in Medical Settings, 6*(1), 11–38.

Heatherton, T. F., Kozlowski, L. T., Frecker, R. C., & Fagerstrom, K. O. (1991). The Fagerstrom Test for Nicotine Dependence: A revision of the Fagerstrom Tolerance Questionnaire. *British Journal of Addiction, 86*, 1119–1127.

Herrera, N., Franco, R., Herrera, L., Partidas, A., Rolando, R., & Fagerstrom, K. O. (1995). Nicotine gum, 2 and 4 mg, for nicotine dependence: A double-blind placebo controlled trial within a behavior modification support program. *Chest, 108*, 447–451.

Hsyu, P., Singh, A., Giargiari, T. D., Dunn, J. A., Ascher, J. A., & Johnston, J. A. (1997). Pharmacokinetics of bupropion and its metabolites in cigarette smokers versus non-smokers. *Journal of Clinical Pharmacology, 37*, 737–743.

Hughes, J. R. (1993). Possible effects of smoke-free inpatient units on psychiatric diagnosis and treatment. *Journal of Clinical Psychiatry, 54*, 109–114.

Hughes, J. R. (1994a). An algorithm for smoking cessation. *Archives of Family Medicine, 3*, 280–285.

Hughes, J. R. (1994b). Non-nicotine pharmacotherapies for smoking cessation. *Journal of Drug Development, 6*, 197–203.

Hughes, J. R. (1995). Combining behavioral therapy and pharmacotherapy for smoking cessation: An update. In L. Onken, J. Blaine, & J. Boren (Eds.), *Integrating behavior therapies with medication in the treatment of drug dependence* (NIH Publication No. 95-3899, pp. 92–109). Washington, DC: U.S. Government Printing Office.

Hughes, J. R. (1996). The future of smoking cessation therapy in the United States. *Addiction, 91*, 1792–1802.

Hughes, J. R., Lesmes, G. R., Hatsukami, D. K., Richmond, R. L., Lichtenstein, E., Jorenby, D. E., Broughton, J. O., Fortmann, S. P., Leischow, S. J., McKenna, J. P., Rennard, S. I., Wadland, W. C., & Heatley, S. A. (1999). Are higher doses of nicotine replacement more effective for smoking cessation? *Nicotine and Tobacco Research, 1*, 169–174.

Hurt, R. D., Dale, L. C., Offord, K. P., Bruce, B. K., McClain, F. L., & Eberman, K. M. (1992). Inpatient treatment of severe nicotine dependence. *Mayo Clinic Proceedings, 67*(9), 823–828.

Hurt, R. D., Dale, L. C., Offord, K. P., Croghan, I. T., Hays, J. T., & Gomez-Dahl, L. (1995).

Nicotine patch therapy for smoking cessation in recovering alcoholics. *Addiction, 90,* 1541–1546.

Hurt, R. D., Sachs, D. P. L., Glover, E. D., Offord, K. P., Johnston, J. A., Dale, L. C., Khayrallah, M. A., Schroeder, D. R., Glover, P. N., Sullivan, C. R., Croghan, I. T., & Sullivan, P. M. (1997). A comparison of sustained-release bupropion and placebo for smoking cessation. *New England Journal of Medicine, 337,* 1195–2002.

Jorenby, D. E., Leischow, S. J., Nides, M. A., Rennard, S. I., Johnston, J. J., Hughes, A. R., Smith, S. S., Muramoto, M. L., Daughton, D. M., Doan, K., Fiore, M. C., & Baker, T. B. (1999). A controlled trial of sustained-release bupropion, a nicotine patch, or both for smoking cessation. *New England Journal of Medicine, 340,* 685–691.

Jorenby, D. E., Smith, S. S., Fiore, M. C., Hurt, R. D., Offord, K. P., Croghan, I. T., Hays, J. T., Lewis, S. F., & Baker, T. B. (1995). Varying nicotine patch dose and type of smoking cessation counseling. *Journal of the American Medical Association, 274,* 1347–1352.

Joseph, A. M., Norman, S. M., Ferry, L. H., Prochazka, A. V., Westman, E. C., Steele, B. G., Sherman, S. E., Cleveland, M., Antonnucio, D. O., Hartman, N., & McGovern, P. G. (1996). The safety of transdermal nicotine as an aid to smoking cessation in patients with cardiac disease. *New England Journal of Medicine, 335,* 1792–1798.

Klesges, R. C., Meyers, A. W., Klesges, L. M., & LaVasque, M. E. (1989). Smoking, body weight, and their effects on smoking behavior: A comprehensive review of the literature. *Psychological Bulletin, 106,* 204–230.

Lando, H. A., Pirie, P. L., Roski, J., McGovern, P. G., & Schmid, L. A. (1996). Promoting abstinence among relapsed smokers: The effect of telephone support. *American Journal of Public Health, 86,* 1786–1790.

Law, M., & Tang, J. L. (1995). An analysis of the effectiveness of interventions intended to help people stop smoking. *Archives of Internal Medicine, 155,* 1933–1941.

Leischow, S. J., Sachs, D. P. L., Bostrom, A. G., & Hansen, M. D. (1992). Effects of differing nicotine-replacement doses on weight gain after smoking cessation. *Archives of Family Medicine, 1,* 233–237.

Lichtenstein, E., & Glasgow, R. E. (1992). Smoking cessation: What have we learned over the past decade? *Journal of Consulting and Clinical Psychology, 60,* 518–527.

McConnaughy, E. A., Prochaska, J. O., & Velicer, W. F. (1983). Stages of change in psychotherapy: Measurement and sample profiles. *Psychotherapy: Theory, Research, and Practice, 20,* 368–375.

Miller, W. R. (1996). Motivational interviewing: Research, practice, and puzzles. *Addictive Behaviors, 21,* 835–842.

Orleans, C. J. (1993). Treating nicotine dependence in medical settings: A stepped-care model. In C. F. Orleans & J. Slade (Eds.), *Nicotine addiction: Principles and management* (pp. 145–161). New York: Oxford University Press.

Perkins, K. A. (1992). Effects of tobacco smoking on caloric intake. *British Journal of Addiction, 87,* 193–205.

Perkins, K. A. (1993). Weight gain following smoking cessation. *Journal of Consulting & Clinical Psychology, 61*(5), 768–777.

Pirie, P. L., McBride, C. M., Hellerstedt, W., Jeffery, R. W., Hatsukami, D., Allen, S., & Lando, H. (1992). Smoking cessation in women concerned about weight. *American Journal of Public Health, 82,* 1238–1243.

Pomerleau, C. S. (1997). Cofactors for smoking and evolutionary psychobiology. *Addiction, 92,* 397–408.

Prochaska, J. O., & DiClemente, C. C. (1983). Stages and processes of self-change of smoking: Toward an integrative model of change. *Journal of Consulting and Clinical Psychology, 51,* 390–395.

Prochaska, J. O., DiClemente, C. C., & Norcross, J. C. (1992). In search of how people change: Application to addictive behavior. *American Psychologist, 47,* 1102–1114.

Shiffman, S. (1993). Smoking cessation treatment: Any progress? *Journal of Consulting and Clinical Psychology, 61,* 718–722.

Silagy, C., Mant, D., Fowler, G., & Lodge, M. (1994a). The effectiveness of nicotine replacement therapies in smoking cessation. *Online Journal of Current Clinical Trials* [On-line serial]. Available: Doc. No. 940114, January 14.

Silagy, C., Mant, D., Fowler, G., & Lodge, M. (1994b). Meta-analysis on efficacy of nicotine replacement therapies in smoking cessation. *The Lancet, 343*, 139–142.

Slade, J. (1992). The tobacco epidemic: Lessons from history. *Journal of Psychoactive Drugs, 24*, 99–109.

Stapleton, J. A., Russell, M. A. H., Feyerabend, C., Wiseman, S. M., Gustavsson, G., Sawe, U., & Wiseman, D. (1995). Dose effects and predictors of outcome in a randomized trial of transdermal nicotine patches in general practice. *Addiction, 90*, 31–42.

Strecher, V. J., Kreuter, M., Jan Den Boer, D., Kobrin, S., Hospers, H. J., & Skinner, C. S. (1994). The effects of computer-tailored smoking cessation messages in family practice settings. *Journal of Family Practice, 39*, 262–270.

Sutherland, G., Stapleton, J. A., Russell, M. A. H., Jarvis, M. J., Hajek, P., Belcher, M., & Feyerabend, C. (1992). Randomised controlled trial of nasal nicotine spray in smoking cessation. *The Lancet, 340*, 324–329.

Swan, G. E., Jack, L. M., & Ward, M. M. (1997). Subgroups of smokers with different success rates after use of transdermal nicotine. *Addiction, 92*, 207–218.

Tonnensen, P., Fryd, V., Hansen, M., Helsted, J., Gunnersen, A. B., Forchammer, H., & Stockner, M. (1988). Two and four mg nicotine chewing gum and group counseling in smoking cessation: An open, randomized, controlled trial with 22 month follow-up. *Addictive Behaviors, 13*, 17–27.

Tonnensen, P., Norregaard, J., Sawe, U., & Simonsen, K. (1993). Recycling with nicotine patches in smoking cessation. *Addiction, 88*, 533–539.

U. S. Department of Health and Human Services. (1999). *Summary of findings from the 1998 National Household Survey of Drug Abuse.* (DHHS Publication No. 99-3328). Washington, DC: U.S. Government Printing Office.

Warner, K. E., Slade, J., & Sweanor, D. T. (1997). The emerging market for long-term nicotine maintenance. *Journal of the American Medical Association, 278*, 1087–1092.

9

Combined Treatments for Substance Dependence

Kathleen M. Carroll

The area of combined pharmacological–behavioral approaches for the treatment of substance use disorders is fraught with ironies. For example, the recent development of effective pharmacotherapies for a range of substance use disorders (e.g., naltrexone, buprenorphine, L-alpha-acetyl-methadol [LAAM]) has dramatically increased the repertoire of clinicians who treat individuals with substance use disorders (O'Brien, 1997). At the same time, few of these novel, science-based therapies have been implemented in clinical practice (Institute of Medicine, 1998). Second, although substance use represents a complex mix of behavioral and physiological factors, a number of clinicians who treat individuals with substance use disorders strongly resist the use of pharmacological treatments that target physical aspects of substance use and dependence (e.g., craving, tolerance, comorbid disorders). This is largely due to philosophical and ideological resistance that is rare in the treatment of other disorders, essentially maintaining "it's wrong to treat drug dependence with drugs." Third, despite broad acknowledgment of the enormous societal costs of untreated substance abuse, many effective pharmacological treatments for substance use disorders, particularly methadone maintenance, are heavily restricted (and even prohibited in some states), sharply reducing the availability of treatment. Finally, despite compelling evidence that demonstrates that combined pharmacological–behavioral approaches represent in many cases the optimal strategy for substance use disorders, effective combined approaches are rarely seen in clinical practice. This in part reflects the many practical difficulties associated with both the multidimensional nature of substance abusers' problems (e.g., need for assessment and treatment of myriad concurrent medical, legal, family, psychological, employment, and other problems) as well as the complexities and risks associated with providing combined treatment for substance use disorders in office and other outpatient settings (e.g., availability of medical personnel and resources, need to monitor substance use closely through urine and breathalyzer tests).

Support for this chapter was provided by National Institute on Drug Abuse Grants P50-DA09241 and K05-DA00457.

This chapter focuses on two areas: (a) the complementary roles of pharmacological and behavioral approaches in the treatment of substance use disorders and (b) an overview of current pharmacological approaches for substance dependence disorders, with an emphasis on the evidence supporting combined approaches for these complex disorders.

Description and Assessment of Substance Abuse

Although there are important differences across substances of abuse in terms of use patterns, abuse liability, tolerance and withdrawal syndromes, half-lives, nature of the clinical population, and so on, in recent years both research and clinical conceptions of substance use have moved toward recognizing broad similarities in pathological patterns of use across various psychoactive substances (Donovan & Marlatt, 1988; Edwards, Arif, & Hodgson, 1981; Kosten, Rounsaville, Babor, Spitzer, & Williams, 1987). This broader conception of substance use disorders, stressing commonalities across addictive behaviors and substances of abuse, has been codified by the adoption of a uniform set of dependence criteria across substances in both the *Diagnostic and Statistical Manual of Mental Disorders* (3rd ed., rev.; *DSM–III–R*; American Psychiatric Association, 1987; Rounsaville, Spitzer, & Williams, 1986) and *DSM–IV* (American Psychiatric Association, 1994; Cottler et al., 1995; Nathan, 1989).

This broader conception of substance use has also been reinforced by research that has pointed to consistencies, across types of substance dependence, in factors associated with the development of substance use disorders (Glantz & Pickens, 1992; Kandel & Logan, 1984), comorbid disorders and co-occurring problems (Kessler et al., 1994; McLellan, Luborsky, Woody, & O'Brien, 1980), predictors of outcome (McLellan et al., 1994), the nature of relapse (Hunt, Barnett, & Branch, 1971; Marlatt & Gordon, 1985), and processes of behavior change (Miller & Heather, 1986; Prochaska, DiClemente, & Norcross, 1992). This is paralleled by the growing development of assessment instruments that can be used across a variety of substance use disorders (reviewed in Donovan & Marlatt, 1988; Rounsaville, Tims, Horton, & Sowder, 1993).

Roles of Pharmacological Versus Behavioral Treatments

In the treatment of substance use disorders, the development of behavioral and pharmacological treatments have tended to progress along separate lines. Recent years have seen the introduction of powerful new pharmacotherapies, such as buprenorphine and naltrexone, but comparatively little work on how to maximize treatment outcomes by also focusing on the context in which these novel pharmacotherapies are delivered. Similarly, a range of innovative behavioral strategies have been specified and evaluated, but often without including a pharmacotherapy component, even for treatments targeted for types of substance use in which effective pharmacotherapies are available. Thus, before specific pharmacological approaches and strategies for effective combined approaches are reviewed, it is important to understand the complementary often nonoverlapping roles of pharmacotherapy and psychotherapy.

The target symptoms addressed and roles typically played by pharmacotherapies differ from those of behavioral treatments in their course of action, time to effect, target symptoms, and durability of benefits (Elkin, Pilkonis, Docherty, & Sotsky, 1988). In general, pharmacotherapies have a much more narrow application than do most behavioral treatments for substance use disorders; that is, most behavioral therapies are applicable across a range of treatment settings (e.g., inpatient, outpatient, residential), modalities (e.g., group, individual, family) and to a wide variety of substance-using populations. For example, it is possible to apply a disease-model, behavioral, or motivational approach, with comparatively minor modifications, regardless of whether the patient is an opiate, alcohol, or cocaine user. On the other hand, most available pharmacotherapies are applicable only to a single class of substance use and exert their effects over a comparatively narrow band of symptoms. For example, methadone produces cross-tolerance for opioids but has little effect on concurrent cocaine abuse. Similarly, disulfiram produces nausea after alcohol ingestion but not after ingestion of illicit substances. A notable exception is naltrexone, which can be an effective treatment for either opioid or alcohol dependence (O'Malley et al., 1992; Volpicelli, Alterman, Hayashida, & O'Brien, 1992).

Roles of Pharmacotherapy

Common roles and indications for pharmacotherapy in the treatment of substance dependence disorders include the following.

Detoxification

For those classes of substances that produce substantial physical withdrawal syndromes (e.g., alcohol, opioids, sedative–hypnotics), medications are often needed to reduce or control the often-dangerous symptoms associated with withdrawal. Benzodiazepenes are often used to manage symptoms of alcohol withdrawal (see Barber & O'Brien, 1999; Mayo-Smith, 1998, for detailed descriptions). Agents such as methadone, clonidine, naltrexone, and buprenorphine are typically used for the management of opioid withdrawal (see Barber & O'Brien, 1999; O'Connor & Kosten, 1998). In contrast, the role of behavioral treatments during detoxification is typically extremely limited because of the level of discomfort, agitation, and confusion the patient may experience. However, recent studies have suggested the effectiveness of behavioral strategies in increasing retention and abstinence in the context of longer term outpatient detoxification protocols (Bickel, Amass, Higgins, Badger, & Esch, 1997).

Stabilization and Maintenance

A widely used example of the use of a medication for long-term stabilization of substance-dependent individuals is methadone maintenance for opioid dependence, a treatment strategy that involves the daily administration of a long-acting opioid (methadone) as a substitute for the illicit use of short-acting opioids (typically heroin). Methadone maintenance permits the patient to function normally without experiencing withdrawal symptoms, craving, or side effects. The large body of research on methadone maintenance confirms its importance in fostering treatment retention, providing the opportunity to evaluate and treat other problems and disorders that often coexist with opioid dependence (e.g., medical, legal, and occupational problems), reducing the risk of HIV infection and other complications through reducing intravenous drug use, and providing a level of stabilization that permits the inception of psychotherapy and other aspects of treatment (see Lowinson, Marion, Joseph, & Dole, 1992; Payte & Zweben, 1998). Another example are nicotine replacement therapies, which effectively provide nicotine while minimizing other harmful aspects of smoking (Hughes, 1995; Schmitz, Henningfield, & Jarvik, 1998) and which are described in chapter 8 of this volume.

Antagonist and Other Behaviorally Oriented Pharmacotherapies

A more novel pharmacological strategy is the use of antagonist treatment, that is, the use of medications that block the effects of specific drugs. An example of this approach is naltrexone, an effective, long-acting opioid antagonist. Naltrexone is nonaddicting, does not have the reinforcing properties of opioids, has few side effects and, most important, effectively blocks the effects of opioids (Barber & O'Brien, 1999; Stine, Meandzija, & Kosten, 1998). Therefore, naltrexone treatment represents a potent behavioral strategy: Because opioid ingestion will not be reinforced while the patient is taking naltrexone, unreinforced opioid use allows extinction of relationships between conditioned drug cues and drug use. For example, a naltrexone-maintained patient, anticipating that opioid use will not result in desired drug effects, may be more likely to learn to live in an environment full of drug cues and high-risk situations without resorting to drug use.

Treatment of Coexisting Disorders

An important role of pharmacotherapy in the treatment of substance use disorders is as treatment for coexisting psychiatric syndromes that may precede or play a role in the maintenance or complications of drug dependence. The frequent co-occurrence of other mental disorders, particularly affective and anxiety disorders, with substance use disorders is well documented in a variety of populations and settings (Kessler et al., 1994; Regier et al., 1990). Given that psychiatric disorders often precede development of substance use disorders, several researchers and clinicians have hypothesized that individuals with primary psychiatric disorders may be attempting to self-medicate their psychiatric symptoms with drugs and alcohol (Khantzian, 1975; Wurmser, 1978). Thus, effective pharmacological treatment of the underlying psychiatric disorder may improve not only the psychiatric disorder but also the perceived need for and therefore the use of illicit drugs (Rosenthal & Westreich, 1999). Examples of this type of approach include the use of antidepressant treatment for depressed alcohol- (Cornelius et al., 1997; Mason, Kocsis, Ritvo, & Cutler, 1996; McGrath et al., 1996), opioid- (Nunes, Quitkin, Brady, & Stewart, 1991), and cocaine-dependent (Margolin, Avants, & Kosten, 1995) individuals.

Roles of Behavioral Treatments

Most behavioral approaches for substance abuse address several common issues and tasks. Although different approaches vary in the degree to which emphasis is placed on these common tasks, some attention to these issues is likely to be involved in any successful treatment (Rounsaville & Carroll, 1997). Moreover, it should be noted that currently available pharmacotherapies for drug dependence would be expected to have little or no effect in these areas commonly addressed by behavioral therapies.

Setting the Resolve to Stop

Rare is the substance abuser who seeks treatment without some degree of ambivalence regarding cessation of drug use. Even at the time of treatment seeking, which usually occurs only after substance-related problems have become severe, substance abusers usually can identify many ways in which they want or feel the need for drugs and have difficulty developing a clear picture of what life without drugs might be like (Rounsaville & Carroll, 1997). Moreover, given the substantial external pressures that may precipitate application for treatment, many patients are highly ambivalent about treatment itself. Ambivalence must be addressed if the patient is to experience him- or herself as an active participant in treatment; if the patient perceives treatment as wholly imposed upon him or her by external forces and does not have a clear sense of personal goals for treatment, it is likely that any form of treatment will be of limited usefulness. Treatments based on principles of motivational psychology, such as motivational interviewing (Miller & Rollnick, 1991) or motivation enhancement therapy (Miller, Zweben, DiClemente, & Rychtarik, 1992), concentrate almost exclusively on strategies intended to bolster the patient's own motivational resources. However, most behavioral treatments include some exploration of what the patient stands to lose or gain through continued substance use as a means to enhance motivation for treatment and abstinence.

Teaching Coping Skills

Social learning theory posits that substance abuse may represent a means of coping with difficult situations, positive and negative affects, invitations by peers to use substances, and so on. By the time substance use is severe enough for treatment, use of substances may represent the individual's single, overgeneralized means of coping with a variety of situations, settings, and states. If stable abstinence is to be achieved, treatment must help the patient recognize the high-risk situations in which he or she is most likely to use substances and develop other, more effective means of coping with such situations. Although cognitive–behavioral approaches concentrate almost exclusively on skills training as a means of preventing relapse to substance use (e.g., Carroll, 1998; Marlatt & Gordon, 1985; Monti, Abrams, Kadden, & Cooney, 1989), most treatment approaches touch on the relationship between high-risk situations and substance use to some extent. Another example is the innovative work by Childress and her colleagues (Childress et al., 1993; Childress, McLellan, & O'Brien, 1984), on cue exposure and reactivity, which may enhance patients' capacity to cope effectively with craving for substances.

Changing Reinforcement Contingencies

By the time treatment is sought, many substance abusers spend the preponderance of their time involved in acquiring, using, and recovering from substance use, to the exclusion of other endeavors and rewards. The abuser may be estranged from friends and family and have few social contacts who do not use drugs. If the patient is still working, employment often becomes only a means of acquiring money to buy drugs, and the fulfilling or challenging aspects of work have faded. Few other activities, such as hobbies, athletics, or involvement with community or church groups, can stand up to the demands of substance dependence. Typically, rewards available in daily life are narrowed progressively to those derived from drug use, and other diversions may be neither available nor perceived as enjoyable. When drug use is stopped, its absence may leave the patient with the need to fill the time that had been spent using drugs and to find rewards that can substitute for those derived from drug use. Thus, most behavioral treatments encourage patients to identify and develop fulfilling alternatives to substance use, as exemplified by the community reinforcement approach (CRA; Azrin, 1976) or contingency management (Budney & Higgins, 1998).

Fostering Management of Painful Affect

The most commonly cited reasons for relapse are powerful negative affects (Marlatt & Gordon, 1985), and some clinicians have suggested that failure of affect regulation is a critical dynamic underlying the development of compulsive drug use (Khantzian, 1975; Wurmser, 1978). Moreover, the difficulty many substance abusers have in recognizing and articulating their affect states has been noted in several populations (Keller, Carroll, Nich, & Rounsaville, 1995; Taylor, Parker, & Bagby, 1990). Thus, an important common task in substance abuse treatment is to help the patient develop ways of coping with powerful dysphoric affects and to learn to recognize and identify the probable cause of these feelings (Rounsaville & Carroll, 1997). Again, although psychodynamically oriented treatments, such as supportive–expressive (SE) therapy (Luborsky, 1984), emphasize the role of affect, virtually all forms of psychotherapy for substance abuse include a variety of techniques for coping with strong affect.

Improving Interpersonal Functioning and Enhancing Social Supports

A consistent finding in the literature on relapse to drug abuse is the protective influence of an adequate network of social supports (Longabaugh, Beattie, Noel, Stout, & Malloy, 1993; Marlatt & Gordon, 1985). Typical issues presented by drug abusers are loss of or damage to valued relationships occurring when using drugs was the principal priority, failure to have achieved satisfactory relationships even prior to having initiated drug use, and inability to identify friends or intimates who are not themselves drug users (Rounsaville & Carroll, 1997). Many forms of treatment, including family therapy (McCrady & Epstein, 1995), 12-step approaches (Nowinski, Baker, & Carroll, 1992), interpersonal therapy (Rounsaville, Gawin, & Kleber, 1985), and network therapy (Galanter, 1993), make building and maintaining a network of social supports for abstinence a central focus of treatment.

Fostering Compliance With Pharmacotherapy

When pharmacotherapies are used in the treatment of substance abuse, high rates of noncompliance are not uncommon. Thus, a major role that behavioral treatments play when pharmacotherapies are used in the treatment of substance use is in fostering compliance, as most strategies to improve compliance are inherently psychosocial (Carroll, 1997b). These include, for example, regular monitoring of medication compliance; encouragement of patient self-monitoring of compliance (e.g., through medication logs or diaries); clear communication between patient and staff about the study medication, its expected effects, side effects, and benefits; repeatedly stressing the importance of compliance; contracting with the patients for adherence; directly reinforcing compliance through incentives or rewards; providing telephone calls or other prompts; and frequent contact and the provision of extensive support and encouragement to the patient and his or her family (see Haynes, Taylor, & Sackett, 1979; Meichenbaum & Turk, 1987).

Pharmacological Treatments for Substance Dependence: An Overview

As noted above, enormous progress has been made in the development of effective pharmacotherapies for several substance use disorders. Before moving to a review of specific pharmacotherapies, their indications, and how their effectiveness can be enhanced through combining them with behavioral approaches, three major issues regarding pharmacological approaches to substance use disorders should be noted. First, behavioral treatments continue to constitute the bulk of substance abuse treatment in the United States. Numerous uncontrolled studies as well as randomized trials consistently point to the benefits of purely behavioral approaches for many substance use disorders (Higgins, 1999; Hubbard, Craddock, Flynn, Anderson, & Etheridge, 1997; McLellan & McKay, 1998). In most cases, pharmacotherapies (other than those used for detoxification, stabilization, or treatment of comorbid disorders) are typically seen as adjunctive strategies, to be used when behavioral treatment alone has been demonstrated to be insufficient for a particular individual.

Second, as shown in Table 9.1, for most types of illicit drug use no effective pharmacotherapies exist. Classes of drug use for which no effective pharmacotherapies have been identified include cocaine, marijuana and other hallucinogens, amphetamines, inhalants, phencyclidine, and sedatives/hypnotics/anxiolytics. Although major advances have been made in identifying physiologic mechanisms of action for many of these substances and, in a few cases (such as marijuana), specific receptors have been identified that should accelerate progress in identifying pharmacological treatments, behavioral therapies remain the sole available treatment for most classes of drug dependence (see O'Brien, 1996, for a review).

Third, there is a general consensus that even for the most potent pharmacotherapies for drug use purely pharmacological approaches are insufficient for most substance abusers, and the best outcomes are seen for combined treatments. Pharmacotherapeutic treatments for substance abusers delivered alone, without psychotherapeutic support, are usually seen as insufficient as a means of promoting stable abstinence in drug abusers. As described above, most pharmacotherapies are comparatively

Table 9.1. Summary of Available Pharmacotherapies for Substance Dependence

	Alcohol	Opioids	Cocaine	Marijuana	Benzodiazepenes	Hallucinogens
Withdrawal	X	X	NA	NA	X	NA
Agonists		X				
Antagonists		X				
Aversive	X					
Anticraving	X					
Comorbid	X	X	X	X	X	X

Note. NA = not applicable.
From "Integrating Psychotherapy and Pharmacology to Improve Drug Abuse Outcomes," by K. M. Carroll, 1997, *Journal of Addictive Behaviors, 22,* 233–245. Copyright 1997 by Elsevier Science. Reprinted with permission.

specific and narrow in their actions and thus rarely considered "adequate treatments" in and of themselves. Furthermore, because few patients will persist or comply with a purely pharmacotherapeutic approach, pharmacotherapies delivered alone, without any supportive or compliance-enhancing elements, are usually not considered feasible.

Even where pharmacotherapy is seen as the primary component of treatment (as in the case of methadone maintenance), some form of psychosocial treatment is needed to provide a minimal supportive structure within which pharmacotherapeutic treatment can be conducted effectively. Furthermore, it is widely recognized that drug effects can be enhanced or diminished with respect to the context in which the drug is delivered; that is, a drug administered in the context of a supportive clinician–patient relationship, with clear expectations of possible drug benefits and side effects, close monitoring of drug compliance, and encouragement for abstinence, is likely to be more effective than a drug delivered without such elements. Thus, even for primarily pharmacotherapeutic treatments a psychotherapeutic component is almost always included to foster patients' retention in treatment and compliance with pharmacotherapy and to address the numerous comorbid psychosocial problems that occur so frequently among individuals with substance use disorders (O'Brien, 1996; Rounsaville & Carroll, 1997; Schuckit, 1996).

Pharmacotherapy of Alcohol Dependence

Disulfiram. The most commonly used pharmacological adjunct for the treatment of alcohol dependence and abuse is disulfiram, or Antabuse. Disulfiram interferes with normal metabolism of alcohol, which results in an accumulation of acetaldhyde, and hence drinking following ingestion of disulfiram results in an intense physiologic reaction, characterized by flushing, rapid or irregular heartbeat, dizziness, nausea, and headache (see Fuller, 1989; Schuckit, 1996). Thus, disulfiram treatment is intended to work as a deterrent to drinking.

Despite the sustained popularity and widespread use of disulfiram, a landmark multicenter randomized clinical trial found that disulfiram was no more effective than inactive doses of disulfiram or no medication in terms of rates of abstinence, time to first drink, unemployment, or social stability (Fuller et al., 1986). However, for participants who did drink, disulfiram treatment was associated with significantly fewer total drinking days. Rates of compliance with disulfiram in the study were low (20% of all participants), but abstinence rates were reasonably good (43%) among compliant participants. This study highlights several important problems with the use of disulfiram: (a) compliance is a major problem and must be monitored closely and (b) many patients are unwilling to take disulfiram (62% of those eligible for the study refused to participate).

Thus, several investigators have evaluated the effectiveness of behavioral treatments to improve retention and compliance with disulfiram. One of the most promising strategies is disulfiram contracts, in which the patient's spouse or a significant other agrees to observe the patient take disulfiram each day and reward the patient for compliance with disulfiram (O'Farrell & Bayog, 1986). Azrin, Sisson, Meyers, and Godley (1982) reported positive and durable results from a randomized clinical trial that compared unmonitored disulfiram with disulfiram contracts in which disulfiram ingestion was monitored by the patient's spouse or administered as part of a multifaceted behavioral program (CRA). CRA, a broad-spectrum approach developed by Azrin (1976), incorporates skills training, behavioral family therapy, and job-finding training, as well as a disulfiram component. Combined disulfiram–behavioral treatment for alcohol dependence illustrates how a pharmacotherapy that may be marginally effective when used alone can be highly effective when used with in combinations with treatments that foster compliance and target other aspects of substance abuse (Allen & Litten, 1992).

Naltrexone. A major development in the treatment of alcohol dependence was the Food and Drug Administration (FDA)'s recent approval of naltrexone. The strategy of using naltrexone, an opioid antagonist, in the treatment of alcoholism derives from findings that suggest that naltrexone reduces alcohol consumption in animals (Volpicelli, Davis, & Olgin, 1986) and alcohol craving and use in humans (Volpicelli, O'Brien, Alterman, et al., 1990). In randomized clinical trials, naltrexone has been shown to be more effective than placebo in reducing alcohol use and craving (O'Malley et al., 1992; Volpicelli et al., 1992). As with disulfiram, best responses were seen among patients who were compliant with naltrexone (Volpicelli et al., 1997). This underscores the importance of delivering naltrexone in conjunction with an effective behavioral approach that addresses compliance.

Thus, it is not surprising that naltrexone's effects have been found to differ somewhat with respect to the nature of the behavioral treatment with which it is delivered; for example, in O'Malley's (1992) study, the highest rates of abstinence were found when the patient received naltrexone plus a supportive clinical management psychotherapy condition that encouraged complete abstinence from alcohol and other substances. However, for patients who drank, the combination of a cognitive–behavioral coping skills approach and naltrexone was superior in terms of rates of relapse and drinks per occasion. It should be noted that naltrexone should be administered only in the context of a comprehensive treatment program, including some form of behavioral treatment plus regular monitoring of alcohol and other substance use. Several evaluations of naltrexone's effectiveness, including trials in nontraditional substance abuse treatment settings, such as primary care offices, are ongoing (O'Connor, Farren, Rounsaville, & O'Malley, 1997).

Other new alcohol pharmacotherapies. There is a small body of clinical research suggesting that GABA-ergic agents (i.e., acamprosate, available for use in Europe and the United Kingdom; Smith, 1999) or serotonergic agents, such as ondansetron (Johnson et al., 2000), may be of benefit in the treatment of alcohol dependence. Like other, better investigated agents, these drugs may have a role in a multifaceted treatment regimen but will not present stand-alone solutions to complex behavioral problems.

Pharmacotherapy of Opioid Dependence

Methadone maintenance. The inception of methadone maintenance treatment revolutionized the treatment of opioid addiction as it displayed the previously unseen ability to keep addicts in treatment and to reduce their illicit opioid use, outcomes with which nonpharmacological treatments had fared comparatively poorly (Brill, 1977; Nyswander, Winick, Bernstein, Brill, & Kaufer, 1958; O'Malley, Anderson, & Lazare, 1972). Beyond its ability to retain opioid addicts in treatment and help control opioid use, methadone maintenance also reduces the risk of HIV infection and other medical complications by reducing intravenous drug use (Ball, Lange, Myers, & Friedman, 1988; Metzger et al., 1993) and provides the opportunity to evaluate and treat concurrent disorders, including medical, family, and psychiatric problems (Lowinson et al., 1992). The bulk of the large body of literature on the effectiveness of methadone maintenance points to the success of methadone maintenance in retaining opioid addicts in treatment and reducing their illicit opioid use and illegal activity (Ball & Ross, 1991). Methadone maintenance treatment, especially when provided at adequate doses and combined with drug counseling, substantially decreases illicit opioid use, injection drug use, criminal activity, and morbidity and mortality risk (O'Brien, 1996). However, there is a great deal of variability in the success across different methadone maintenance programs, which appears to be largely associated with variability in delivery of adequate dosing of methadone as well as variability in provision and quality of psychosocial services (Ball & Ross, 1991; Corty & Ball, 1987).

Moreover, there are several problems with methadone maintenance, including illicit diversion of take-home methadone doses; difficulties with detoxification from methadone maintenance to a drug-free state; and the concurrent use of other substances, particularly alcohol and cocaine, among methadone-maintained patients (Kosten & McCance, 1996). Thus, a range of psychosocial treatments have been evaluated for their ability to address these drawbacks of methadone maintenance as well as to enhance and extend the benefits of methadone maintenance. Several types of behavioral approaches have been identified as effective in enhancing and extending the benefits of methadone maintenance treatment; these are summarized below.

Behavioral treatments in the context of maintenance therapies. Before a description is offered of specific approaches that have been demonstrated to be effective in enhancing the effectiveness of opioid maintenance therapies, the importance for such approaches should be highlighted by a brief review of a study that authoritatively established the significance of psychosocial treatments even in the context of a pharmacotherapy as potent as methadone. McLellan, Arndt, Metzger, Woody, and O'Brien (1993) randomly assigned 92 opiate-dependent individuals to either (a) methadone maintenance alone, without psychosocial services; (b) methadone maintenance with standard services, which included regular meetings with a counselor; and (c) enhanced methadone maintenance, which included regular counseling plus on-site medical care psychiatric evaluation, employment counseling, and family therapy, in a 24-week trial. Although some patients did reasonably well in the methadone alone condition, 69% of this group had to be transferred out of this condition within 3 months of treatment inception because their substance use did not improve, or even worsened, or because they experienced significant medical or psychiatric problems that required a more intensive level of care. In terms of drug use and psychosocial outcomes, the best outcomes were seen in the enhanced methadone maintenance condition, with intermediate outcomes for the standard methadone services condition and poorest outcomes for the methadone alone condition. This study underlines that although methadone maintenance treatment has powerful effects in terms of keeping addicts in treatment and making them available for psychosocial treatments, a purely pharmacological approach will not be sufficient for the large majority of patients, and that better outcomes are closely associated with higher levels of psychosocial treatments.

Contingency management approaches. Several studies have evaluated the use of contingency management to reduce the use of illicit drugs in addicts who are maintained on methadone. In these studies, a reinforcer is provided to patients who demonstrate specified target behaviors, such as providing drug-free urine specimens, accomplishing specific treatment goals, or attending treatment sessions. For example, methadone take-home privileges contingent on reduced drug use is an approach that capitalizes on an inexpensive reinforcer that is potentially available in all methadone maintenance programs. Stitzer and her colleagues (see Stitzer, Iguchi, Kidorf, & Bigelow, 1993) have done extensive work in evaluating methadone take-home privileges as a reward for decreased illicit drug use. In a series of well-controlled trials, this group of researchers has demonstrated (a) the relative benefits of positive over negative contingencies (Stitzer, Bickel, Bigelow, & Liebson, 1986); (b) the attractiveness of take-home privileges over other incentives available within methadone maintenance clinics (Stitzer & Bigelow, 1978); (c) the effectiveness of targeting and rewarding drug-free urines over other, more distal behaviors, such as group attendance (Iguchi et al., 1996); and (d) the benefits of using take-home privileges contingent on drug-free urines over noncontingent take-home privileges (Stitzer, Iguchi, & Felch, 1992).

Silverman, Higgins, et al. (1996), drawing on the compelling work of Steve Higgins and his colleagues (see Budney & Higgins, 1998), evaluated a voucher-based contingency management system to address concurrent illicit drug use (typically cocaine) among methadone-maintained opioid addicts. In this approach, urine specimens are required three times weekly in order to systematically detect all episodes of drug use. Abstinence, verified through drug-free urine screens, is reinforced through a voucher system in which patients receive points redeemable for items consistent with a drug-free lifestyle that are intended to help the patient develop alternate reinforcers to drug use (e.g., movie tickets, sporting goods). Patients do not receive money directly. To encourage longer periods of consecutive abstinence, the value of the points earned by the patients increases with each successive clean urine specimen, and the value of the points is reset when the patient produces a drug-positive urine screen. In a very elegant series of studies, Silverman and his colleagues (Silverman, Higgins, et al., 1996; Silverman, Wong, et al., 1996; Silverman et al., 1998) have demonstrated the efficacy of this approach in reducing illicit opioid and cocaine use and producing a number of treatment benefits among this very difficult population.

Although contingency management procedures appear quite promising in modifying previously intractable problems in methadone maintenance programs, particularly continued illicit drug use among clients, they have rarely been implemented in clinical practice. A major obstacle to the implementation of contingency management voucher approaches in regular clinical settings may be their cost (up to $1,200 over 12 weeks). However, a number of investigators are evaluating less expensive contingency management approaches among other populations (Petry, Martin, Cooney, & Kranzler, 2000). Moreover, the positive effects associated with management procedures may diminish substantially when the contingencies are no longer in effect. This may suggest that in methadone maintenance treatment specific reinforcers may grow weaker with time, be replaced by other reinforcers, or both. For example, for clients entering a methadone program from the street, contingency payments or dose increases may be highly motivating, whereas for clients who have been stabilized and are working and who may have less free time, other reinforcers, such as take-home doses or permission to omit counseling sessions, may be more attractive later in treatment. Although the effects of contingency management procedures may diminish to some extent over time, they may still be highly valuable in that they may provide an interruption in illicit drug use (or other undesirable behaviors), and this may serve as an opportunity for other interventions to take effect (Higgins, Wong, Badger, Haug-Ogden, & Dantona, 2000).

Other psychotherapies. Only a few studies have evaluated other forms of psychotherapy as strategies to enhance outcome from opioid maintenance therapies. The landmark study in this area was conducted by Woody, Luborsky, McLellan, O'Brien, and their colleagues (1983) and was recently replicated in community settings by this group (Woody, McLellan, Luborsky, & O'Brien, 1995). Although the original study is now more than 15 years old, it remains the most impressive demonstration of the benefits and role of psychotherapy in the context of methadone maintenance programs. Moreover, it has generated several substudies that have added greatly to an understanding of the types of patients who may benefit from psychotherapy in the context of methadone maintenance programs.

One hundred ten opiate addicts entering a methadone maintenance program were randomly assigned to one of three treatments: drug counseling alone, drug counseling plus SE psychotherapy, or drug counseling plus cognitive psychotherapy (CT). After a 6-month course of treatment, although the SE and CT groups did not differ significantly from each other on most measures of outcome, patients who received either form of professional psychotherapy evidenced greater improvement in more outcome domains than those who received drug counseling alone (Woody et al., 1983). Furthermore, gains made by the patients who received professional psychotherapy were sustained over a 12-month follow-up, whereas patients who received drug counseling alone evidenced some attrition of gains (Woody, McLellan, Luborsky, & O'Brien, 1987). This study also demonstrated differential response to psychotherapy as a function of patient characteristics, which may point to the best use of psychotherapy (relative to drug counseling) when resources are scarce: Although methadone-maintained opiate addicts with lower levels of psychopathology tended to improve regardless of whether they received professional psychotherapy or drug counseling, those with higher levels of psychopathology tended to improve only if they received psychotherapy.

New maintenance therapies. In addition, two new maintenance therapies have recently been developed for opioid dependence that also promise to make effective maintenance therapies more broadly available. This is significant, because access to methadone treatment is limited in many areas, and currently fewer than 1 in 5 heroin users receives treatment for drug dependence (National Institutes of Health, 1997). Barriers to access to methadone maintenance include limited patient and community acceptance of methadone as well as regulatory restrictions and the lack of availability in many areas of the country (Stine & Kosten, 1997).

Thus, the advent of two new maintenance agents in recent years is particularly significant, as both LAAM and buprenorphine may make effective pharmacotherapies for opioid dependent individuals much more widely available. LAAM has recently gained FDA approval as the first alternative to methadone as a maintenance treatment for opioid dependence. Although similar to methadone in terms of the level of physical dependence it produces (Fraser & Isbell, 1952), LAAM is much longer-acting than methadone, and it can suppress symptoms of opiate withdrawal for more than 72 hours (Fraser & Isbell, 1952; Jaffe, Schuster, Smith, & Blachley, 1970; Kosten & McCance, 1996). Thus, relative to methadone, LAAM has the advantages of offering less-frequent dosing (for example, it can be effectively administered with a thrice-weekly dosing schedule), potentially reducing program costs and increasing availability. However, it does share with methadone the disadvantages of difficulties with withdrawal, the potential for diversion, and potential for overdose (Greenstein, Fudala, & O'Brien, 1992). Furthermore, despite FDA approval, LAAM is rarely available in the U.S., either within or outside of traditional methadone programs. Among the reasons for its limited use include somewhat reduced efficacy for reducing illicit opioid use and greater attrition, compared to methadone, as well as patient preference (Stine et al., 1998).

Buprenorphine, a partial mu agonist and kappa antagonist, represents a promising alternative to either methadone or LAAM (Blaine, 1992). Because of its unique pharmacological properties, there may be a number of advantages to its use, compared to either methadone or LAAM, as a maintenance agent for the treatment of opioid dependent individuals. Compared with methadone, its mixed agonist–agonist properties result in a lower risk of overdose (Walsh, Preston, Stitzer, Cone, & Bigelow, 1994; Walsh, Preston, Bigelow, & Stitzer, 1995). Moreover, buprenorphine may also have a reduced abuse liability in opiate-dependent individuals (and thus less likelihood for diversion) because its use may precipitate withdrawal symptoms (Strain, Preston, Liebson, & Bigelow, 1995; Walsh et al., 1995). Compared with methadone, withdrawal from buprenorphine is typically more mild (Amass, Bickel, Higgins, & Hughes, 1994; Fudala, Jaffe, Dax, & Johnson, 1990; Negus & Woods, 1995). Its safety and efficacy have been demonstrated in a number of trials (Kosten, Schottenfeld, Ziedonis, & Falcioni, 1993; Ling, Wesson, Charavastra, & Klett, 1996; Schottenfeld, Pakes, Oliveto, Ziedonis, & Kosten, 1997). Because of buprenorphine's comparatively lower abuse liability, once approved, it is likely to be much more widely available and less stringently regulated, compared with methadone and LAAM.

Because LAAM and buprenorphine have been made available only recently, very few studies have attempted to identify the minimal or optimal intensity of behavioral treatment to be administered in conjunction with these agents. However, it is likely that the same principles will emerge over time regarding these agents as have with methadone. That is, while these agents may be sufficient treatment when used alone for a small number of opioid-dependent individuals, best outcomes for the majority will be seen when LAAM or buprenorphine are delivered with comprehensive psychosocial treatments.

Naltrexone/agonist treatment. Opioid antagonist treatment (naltrexone) offers many advantages over methadone maintenance, including that it is nonaddicting and can be prescribed without concerns about diversion; has a benign side-effect profile; and may be less costly, in terms of demands on professional time and of patient time, than the daily or near-daily clinic visits required for methadone maintenance (Rounsaville, 1995). Most important are behavioral aspects of the treatment, as unreinforced opiate use allows extinction of relations between cues and drug use. Although naltrexone treatment is likely to be attractive only to a minority of opioid addicts (Greenstein, Arndt, McLellan, O'Brien, & Evans, 1984), its unique properties make it an important alternative to methadone maintenance.

However, naltrexone has not, despite its many advantages, fulfilled its promise. Naltrexone treatment programs remain comparatively rare and underutilized with respect to methadone maintenance programs (Rounsaville, 1995). This is in large part due to problems with retention, particularly during the induction phase, where, on average, 40% of patients drop out during the first month of treatment, and 60% drop out by 3 months (Greenstein et al., 1992). Naltrexone treatment has other disadvantages that may play a role in its characteristically poor levels of retention, including (a) discomfort associated with detoxification and protracted withdrawal symptoms, (b) lack of negative consequences for abrupt discontinuation, and (c) no reinforcement for ingestion, all of which may lead to inconsistent compliance with naltrexone treatment and high rates of attrition.

Preliminary evaluations of behavioral interventions targeted to address naltrexone's weaknesses have been encouraging. Several investigators (Grabowski et al., 1979; Meyer, Mirin, Altman, & McNamee, 1976) have reported success using contingency payments as reinforcements for naltrexone consumption. Family therapy and counseling have also been used to enhance retention in naltrexone programs (Anton, Hogan, Jalali, Riordan, & Kleber, 1981). More recently, some of the most promising data regarding strategies to enhance outcome in naltrexone treatment have come from investigators evaluating contingency management approaches. Preston et al. (1999) reported improved retention and naltrexone compliance when patients were provided voucher incentives for naltrexone compliance compared with groups receiving noncontingent or no vouchers. Again, however, it is not clear the extent to which these procedures will be implemented outside of research settings or how durable they are after the termination of the incentive program.

Summary

For classes of substance use disorders for which effective pharmacotherapies have been developed, the availability of methadone, naltrexone, and Antabuse has vastly extended clinicians' ability to treat these disorders, but they have by no means cured substance dependence. These powerful agents tend to work primarily on the symptoms of substance dependence that are time limited and autonomous, but they have little influence on the enduring behavioral characteristics of substance use. Moreover, the data consistently suggest that (a) compliance with (and thus effectiveness of) these agents is often poor if the medication is not delivered in conjunction with a potent behavioral therapy and (b) the best outcomes are seen for combined treatments.

In short, pharmacotherapies work only if substance abusers see the value of stopping substance use, and substance abusers have consistently found ways to circumvent pharmacological interventions. It is unlikely that a pharmacological intervention will be developed that gives addicts the motivation to stop using drugs, helps them see the value in renouncing substance use, improves their ability to cope with the day-to-day frustrations in living, or provides alternatives to the reinforcements drugs and drug-using lifestyles provide. The bulk of the evidence suggests that pharmacotherapies can be very effective treatment adjuncts, but in most cases the effects of pharmacotherapies can be broadened, enhanced, and extended by the addition of behavioral treatments (Carroll & Rounsaville, 1993).

Behavioral therapies and pharmacotherapies work through different mechanisms and address different problems, and neither is completely effective by itself. Because the bulk of the evidence in the treatment of substance abuse suggests that the two forms of treatment tend to work better in combination than alone, integrated treatments, targeted to the specific needs of each patient, may be the optimal strategy for helping patients whose lives have been disturbed by substance abuse (Carroll, 1997a).

References

Allen, J. P., & Litten, R. Z. (1992). Techniques to enhance compliance with disulfiram. *Alcoholism: Clinical and Experimental Research, 16*, 1035–1041.

Amass, L., Bickel, W. K., Higgins, S. T., & Hughes, J. R. (1994). A preliminary investigation of outcome following gradual or rapid buprenorphine detoxification. *Journal of Addictive Disease, 13*, 33–45.

American Psychiatric Association. (1987). *Diagnostic and statistical manual of mental disorders* (3rd ed., rev.). Washington, DC: Author.

American Psychiatric Association. (1994). *Diagnostic and statistical manual of mental disorders* (4th ed.). Washington, DC: Author.

Anton, R. F., Hogan, I., Jalali, B., Riordan, C. E., & Kleber, H. D. (1981). Multiple family therapy and naltrexone in the treatment of opiate dependence. *Drug and Alcohol Dependence, 8*, 157–168.

Azrin, N. H. (1976). Improvements in the community-reinforcement approach to alcoholism. *Behavior Research and Therapy, 14*, 339–348.

Azrin, N. H., Sisson, R. W., Meyers, R., & Godley, M. (1982). Alcoholism treatment by disulfiram and community reinforcement therapy. *Journal of Behavior Therapy and Experimental Psychiatry, 13*, 105–112.

Ball, J., Lange, W. R., Myers, C. P., & Friedman, S. R. (1988). Reducing the risk of AIDS through methadone maintenance treatment. *Journal of Health and Social Behavior, 29*, 214–216.

Ball, J. C., & Ross, A. (1991). *The effectiveness of methadone maintenance treatment*. New York: Springer-Verlag.

Barber, W. S., & O'Brien, C. P. (1999). Pharmacotherapies. In B. S. McCrady & E. E. Epstein (Eds.), *Addictions: A comprehensive guidebook* (pp. 347–369). New York: Oxford University Press.

Bickel, W. K., Amass, L., Higgins, S. T., Badger, G. J., & Esch, R. A. (1997). Effects of adding behavioral treatment to opioid detoxification with buprenorphine. *Journal of Consulting and Clinical Psychology, 65*, 803–810.

Blaine, J. D. (Ed.). (1992). *Buprenorphine: An alternative treatment for opioid dependence* (NIDA Research Monograph Series No. 121). Rockville, MD: National Institute on Drug Abuse.

Brill, L. (1977). The treatment of drug abuse: Evolution of a perspective. *American Journal of Psychiatry, 134*, 157–160.

Budney, A. J., & Higgins, S. T. (1998). *A community reinforcement plus vouchers approach: Treating cocaine addiction*. Rockville, MD: National Institute on Drug Abuse.

Carroll, K. M. (1997a). Integrating psychotherapy and pharmacotherapy to improve drug abuse outcomes. *Journal of Addictive Behaviors, 22*, 233–245.

Carroll, K. M. (1997b). Manual guided psychosocial treatment: A new virtual requirement for pharmacotherapy trials? *Archives of General Psychiatry, 54*, 923–928.

Carroll, K. M. (1998). *A cognitive–behavioral approach: Treating cocaine addiction* (NIH Publication No. 98-4308). Rockville, MD: National Institute on Drug Abuse.

Carroll, K. M., & Rounsaville, B. J. (1993). Implications of recent research on psychotherapy for drug abuse. In G. Edwards, J. Strang, & J. H. Jaffe (Eds.), *Drugs, alcohol, and tobacco: Making the science and policy connections* (pp. 211–221). New York: Oxford University Press.

Childress, A. R., Hole, A. V., Ehrman, R. N., Robbins, S. J., McLellan, A. T., & O'Brien, C. P. (1993). Cue reactivity and cue reactivity interventions in drug dependence. In L. S. Onken, J. D. Blaine, & J. J. Boren (Eds.), *Behavioral treatments for drug abuse and dependence* (NIDA Research Monograph Series No. 137, pp. 73–95). Rockville, MD: National Institute on Drug Abuse.

Childress, A. R., McLellan, A. T., & O'Brien, C. P. (1984). Assessment and extinction of conditioned withdrawal-like responses in an integrated treatment for opiate dependence. In L. S. Harris (Ed.), *Problems of drug dependence, 1984* (NIDA Research Monograph Series No. 55, pp. 202–210). Rockville, MD: National Institute on Drug Abuse.

Cornelius, J. R., Salloum, I. M., Ehler, J. G., Jarrett, P. J., Cornelius, M. D., Perel, J. M., Thase, M. E., & Black, A. (1997). Fluoxetine in depressed alcoholics: A double-blind, placebo-controlled trial. *Archives of General Psychiatry, 54*, 700–705.

Corty, E., & Ball, J. C. (1987). Admissions to methadone maintenance: Comparisions between programs and implications for treatment. *Journal of Substance Abuse Treatment, 4*, 181–187.

Cottler, L. B., Schuckit, M. A., Helzer, J. E., Crowley, T., Woody, G., & Nathan, P. (1995). The *DSM–IV* field trial for substance use disorders: Major results. *Drug and Alcohol Dependence, 38*, 59–69.

Donovan, D. M., & Marlatt, G. A. (Eds.). (1988). *Assessment of addictive behaviors*. New York: Guilford Press.

Edwards, G., Arif, A., & Hodgson, R. (1981). Nomenclature and classification of drug and alcohol-related problems: A WHO memorandum. *Bulletin of the World Health Organization, 59*, 225–242.

Elkin, I., Pilkonis, P. A., Docherty, J. P., & Sotsky, S. M. (1988). Conceptual and methodological issues in comparative studies of psychotherapy and pharmacotherapy, II: Nature and timing of treatment effects. *American Journal of Psychiatry, 145*, 1070–1076.

Fraser, H. F., & Isbell, H. (1952). Actions and addiction liabilities of alpha acetylmethadols in man. *Journal of Pharmacology & Experimental Therapeutics, 105*, 458–465.

Fudala, P. J., Jaffe, J. H., Dax, E. M., & Johnson, R. E. (1990). Use of buprenorphine in the treatment of opioid addiction II: Physiologic and behavioral effects of daily and alternate-day administration and abrupt withdrawal. *Clinical Pharmacology and Therapeutics, 47*, 525–534.

Fuller, R. K. (1989). Antidipsotropic medications. In W. R. Miller & R. K. Hester (Eds.), *Handbook of alcoholism treatment approaches: Effective alternatives* (pp. 117–127). New York: Pergamon Press.

Fuller, R. K., Branchey, L., Brightwell, D. R., Derman, R. M., Emrick, C. D., Iber, F. L., James, K. E., Lacoursiere, R. B., Lee, K. K., & Lowenstam, I. (1986). Disulfiram treatment for alcoholism: A Veterans Administration cooperative study. *Journal of the American Medical Association, 256*, 1449–1455.

Galanter, M. (1993). *Network therapy for alcohol and drug abuse: A new approach in practice*. New York: Basic Books.

Glantz, M., & Pickens, R. W. (Eds.). (1992). *Vulnerability to drug abuse*. Washington, DC: American Psychological Association.

Grabowski, J., O'Brien, C. P., Greenstein, R., Long, M., Steinberg-Donato, S., & Ternes, J. (1979). Effects of contingent payments on compliance with a naltrexone regimen. *American Journal of Drug and Alcohol Abuse, 6*, 355–365.

Greenstein, R. A., Arndt, I. C., McLellan, A. T., O'Brien, C. P., & Evans, B. (1984). Naltrexone: A clinical perspective. *Journal of Clinical Psychiatry, 45*, 25–28.

Greenstein, R. A., Fudala, P. J., & O'Brien, C. P. (1992). Alternative pharmacotherapies for opiate addiction. In J. H. Lowinsohn, P. Ruiz, & R. B. Millman (Eds.), *Comprehensive textbook of substance abuse* (2nd ed., pp. 562–573). New York: Williams & Wilkins.

Haynes, R. B., Taylor, D. W., & Sackett, D. L. (Eds.). (1979). *Compliance in health care*. Baltimore: Johns Hopkins University Press.

Higgins, S. T. (1999). We've come a long way: Comments on cocaine treatment outcome research. *Archives of General Psychiatry, 56*, 516–518.

Higgins, S. T., Wong, C. J., Badger, G. J., Haug-Ogden, D. E., & Dantona, R. L. (2000). Contingent reinforcement increases cocaine abstinence during outpatient treatment and one year follow-up. *Journal of Consulting and Clinical Psychology, 68*, 64–72.

Hubbard, R. L., Craddock, S. G., Flynn, P. M., Anderson, J., & Etheridge, R. M. (1997). Overview of 1-year follow-up outcomes in the Drug Abuse Treatment Outcome Study (DATOS). *Psychology of Addictive Behaviors, 11*, 261–278.

Hughes, J. R. (1995). Combining behavioral therapy and pharmacotherapy for smoking cessation: An update. In L. S. Onken & J. D. Blaine (Eds.), *Integrating psychosocial therapies with pharmacotherapies in the treatment of drug dependence* (NIDA Research Monograph Series No. 105, NIH Publication No. 95-3899, pp. 92–109). Rockville, MD: National Institute on Drug Abuse.

Hunt, W. A., Barnett, L. W., & Branch, L. G. (1971). Relapse rates in addiction programs. *Journal of Clinical Psychology, 27*, 455–456.

Iguchi, M. Y., Lamb, R. J., Belding, M. A., Platt, J. J., Husband, S. D., & Morral, A. R. (1996). Contingent reinforcement of group participation versus abstinence in a methadone maintenance program. *Experimental and Clinical Psychopharmacology, 4*, 1–7.

Institute of Medicine. (1998). *Bridging the gap between practice and research: Forging partnerships with community-based drug and alcohol treatment*. Washington, DC: National Academy Press.

Jaffe, J. H., Schuster, C. R., Smith, B. B., & Blachley, P. H. (1970). Comparison of acetylmethadol and methadone in the treatment of long-term heroin users: A pilot study. *Journal of the American Medical Association, 211*, 1834–1836.

Johnson, B. A., Roache, J. D., Javors, M. A., DiClemente, C. C., Cloninger, C. R., Prihoda, T. J., Bordnick, P. S., Ait-Daoud, N., & Hensler, J. (2000). Ondansetron for reduction of drinking among biologically predisposed alcoholic patients: A randomized controlled trial. *Journal of the American Medical Association, 284*, 963–971.

Kandel, D. B., & Logan, J. A. (1984). Patterns of drug use from adolescence to young adulthood: I. Periods of risk for initiation, continued use, and discontinuation. *American Journal of Public Health, 74*, 660–666.

Keller, D. S., Carroll, K. M., Nich, C., & Rounsaville, B. J. (1995). Differential treatment response in alexithymic cocaine abusers: Findings from a randomized clinical trial of psychotherapy and pharmacotherapy. *American Journal on Addictions, 4*, 234–244.

Kessler, R. C., McGonagle, K. A., Zhao, S., Nelson, C. B., Hughes, M., Eshlemen, S., Wittchen, H., & Kendler, K. S. (1994). Lifetime and 12-month prevalence of *DSM–III–R* psychiatric disorders in the United States: Results from the National Comorbidity Survey. *Archives of General Psychiatry, 51*, 8–19.

Khantzian, E. J. (1975). Self-selection and progression in drug dependence. *Psychiatry Digest, 10*, 19–22.

Kosten, T. R., & McCance, E. F. (1996). A review of pharmacotherapies for substance abuse. *American Journal on Addictions, 5*, 58–64.

Kosten, T. R., Rounsaville, B. J., Babor, T. F., Spitzer, R. L., & Williams, J. B. W. (1987). Substance use disorders in *DSM–III–R*: Evidence for the dependence syndrome across different psychoactive substances. *British Journal of Psychiatry, 151*, 834–843.

Kosten, T. R., Schottenfeld R., Ziedonis, D., & Falcioni, J. (1993). Buprenorphine versus methadone maintenance for opioid dependence. *Journal of Nervous and Mental Disease, 181*, 358–364.

Ling, W., Wesson, D. R., Charavastra, C., & Klett, C. J. (1996). A controlled trial comparing buprenorphine and methadone maintenance in opioid dependence. *Archives of General Psychiatry 53*, 401–407.

Longabaugh, R., Beattie, M., Noel, R., Stout, R., & Malloy, P. (1993). The effect of social support on treatment outcome. *Journal of Studies on Alcohol, 54*, 465–478.

Lowinson, J. H., Marion, I. J., Joseph, H., & Dole, V. P. (1992). Methadone maintenance. In J. H. Lowinsohn, P. Ruiz, & R. B. Millman (Eds.), *Comprehensive textbook of substance abuse*, (2nd ed., pp. 550–561). New York: Williams & Wilkins.

Luborsky, L. (1984). *Principles of psychoanalytic psychotherapy: A manual for supportive-expressive treatment*. New York: Basic Books.

Margolin, A., Avants, S. K., & Kosten, T. R. (1995). Mazindol for relapse prevention to cocaine abuse in methadone-maintained patients. *American Journal of Drug & Alcohol Abuse, 21*, 469–481.

Marlatt, G. A., & Gordon, J. R. (Eds.). (1985). *Relapse prevention: Maintenance strategies in the treatment of addictive behaviors*. New York: Guilford Press.

Mason, B. J., Kocsis, J. H., Ritvo, E. C., & Cutler, R. B. (1996). A double-blind, placebo-controlled trial of desipramine for primary alcohol dependence stratified on the presence or absence of major depression. *Journal of the American Medical Association, 275*, 761–767.

Mayo-Smith, M. (1998). Management of alcohol intoxication and withdrawal. In A. W. Graham & T. K. Schultz (Eds.), *Principles of addiction medicine* (2nd ed., pp. 431–441). Chevy Chase, MD: American Society of Addiction Medicine.

McCrady, B. S., & Epstein, E. E. (1995). Marital therapy in the treatment of alcohol problems. In N. S. Jacobson & A. S Gurman (Eds.), *Clinical handbook of couple therapy* (pp. 369–393). New York: Guilford Press.

McGrath, P. J., Nunes, E. V., Stewart, J. W., Goldman, D., Agosti, V., Ocepek-Welikson, K., & Quitkin, F. M. (1996). Imipramine treatment of alcoholics with primary depression: A placebo controlled clinical trial. *Archives of General Psychiatry, 53*, 232–240.

McLellan, A. T., Alterman, A. I., Metzger, D. S., Grissom, G. R., Woody, G. E., Luborsky, L., & O'Brien, C. P. (1994). Similarity of outcome predictors across opiate, cocaine, and alcohol treatments: Role of treatment services. *Journal of Consulting and Clinical Psychology, 62*, 1141–1158.

McLellan, A. T., Arndt, I. O., Metzger, D. S., Woody, G. E., O'Brien, C. P. (1993). The effects of psychosocial services in substance abuse treatment. *Journal of the American Medical Association, 269*, 1953–1959.

McLellan, A. T., Luborsky, L., Woody, G. E., & O'Brien, C. P. (1980). An improved diagnostic evaluation instrument for substance abuse patients: The Addiction Severity Index. *Journal of Nervous and Mental Disease, 168*, 26–33.

McLellan, A. T., & McKay, J. R. (1998). The treatment of addiction: What can research offer practice? In S. Lamb, M. R. Greenlick, & D. McCarty (Eds.), *Bridging the gap between practice and research: Forging partnerships with community based drug and alcohol treatment* (pp. 147–185). Washington, DC: National Academy Press.

Meichenbaum, D., & Turk, D. C. (1987). *Facilitating treatment adherence*. New York: Plenum.

Metzger, D. S., Woody, G. E., McLellan, A. T., O'Brien, C. P., Druley, P., Navaline, H., Dephilippis, D., Stolley, P., & Abrutyn, E. (1993). Human immunodeficiency virus seroconversion among in and out-of-treatment drug users: An 18-month prospective follow-up. *Journal of AIDS, 6*, 1049–1056.

Meyer, R. E., Mirin, S. M., Altman, J. L., & McNamee, B. (1976). A behavioral paradigm for the evaluation of narcotic antagonists. *Archives of General Psychiatry, 33*, 371–377.

Miller, W. R., & Heather, N. (Eds.). (1986). *Treating addictive behaviors: Processes of change*. New York: Plenum.

Miller, W. R., & Rollnick, S. (1991). *Motivational interviewing: Preparing people to change addictive behavior*. New York: Guilford Press.

Miller, W. R., Zweben, A., DiClemente, C. C., & Rychtarik, R. G. (1992). *Motivational enhancement therapy manual: A clinical research guide for therapists treating individuals with alcohol abuse and dependence* (NIAAA Project MATCH Monograph Series, Vol. 2, DHHS Publication No. ADM 92-1894). Rockville, MD: National Institute on Alcohol Abuse and Alcoholism.

Monti, P. M., Abrams, D. B., Kadden, R. M., & Cooney, N. L. (1989). *Treating alcohol dependence: A coping skills training guide in the treatment of alcoholism*. New York: Guilford Press.

Nathan, P. E. (1989). Substance use disorders in the *DSM–IV*. *Journal of Abnormal Psychology, 100*, 356–361.

National Institutes of Health. (1997, November). *Effective medical treatment of heroin addiction* (NIH Consensus Statement 15).

Negus, S. S., & Woods, J. H. (1995). Reinforcing effects, discriminative stimulus effects, and physical dependence liability of buprenorphine. In A. Cowan & J. W. Lewis (Eds.), *Buprenorphine: Combating drug abuse with a unique opioid* (pp. 71–101). New York: Wiley-Liss.

Nowinski, J., Baker, S., & Carroll, K. M. (1992). *Twelve-step facilitation therapy manual: A clinical research guide for therapists treating individuals with alcohol abuse and dependence* (NIAAA Project MATCH Monograph Series, Vol. 1, DHHS Publication No. ADM 92-1893). Rockville, MD: National Institute on Alcohol Abuse and Alcoholism.

Nunes, E. V., Quitkin, F. M., Brady, R., & Stewart, J. W. (1991). Imipramine treatment of methadone maintenance patients with affective disorder and illicit drug use. *American Journal of Psychiatry, 148*, 667–669.

Nyswander, M., Winick, C., Bernstein, A., Brill, I., & Kaufer, G. (1958). The treatment of drug addicts as voluntary outpatients: A progress report. *American Journal of Orthopsychiatry, 28*, 714–727.

O'Brien, C. P. (1996). Recent developments in the pharmacotherapy of substance abuse. *Journal of Consulting and Clinical Psychology, 64*, 677–686.

O'Brien, C. P. (1997). A range of research-based pharmacotherapies for addiction. *Science, 278*, 66–70.

O'Connor, P. G., Farren, C. K., Rounsaville, B. J., & O'Malley, S. S. (1997). A preliminary investigation of the management of alcohol dependence with naltrexone by primary care providers. *American Journal of Medicine, 103*, 477–482.

O'Connor, P. G., & Kosten, T. R. (1998). Management of opioid intoxication and withdrawal. In A. W. Graham & T. K. Schultz (Eds.), *Principles of addiction medicine* (2nd ed., pp. 457–464). Chevy Chase, MD: American Society of Addiction Medicine.

O'Farrell, T. J., & Bayog, R. D. (1986). Antabuse contracts for married alcoholics and their spouses: A method to insure Antabuse taking and decrease conflict about alcohol. *Journal of Substance Abuse Treatment, 3*, 1–8.

O'Malley, J. E., Anderson, W. H., & Lazare, A. (1972). Failure of outpatient treatment of drug abuse: I. Heroin. *American Journal of Psychiatry, 128*, 865–868.

O'Malley, S. S., Jaffe, A. J., Chang, G., Schottenfeld, R. S., Meyer, R. E., & Rounsaville, B. J. (1992). Naltrexone and coping skills therapy for alcohol dependence: A controlled study. *Archives of General Psychiatry, 49*, 881–887.

Payte, J. T., & Zweben, J. E. (1998). Opioid maintenance therapies. In A. W. Graham & T. K. Schultz (Eds.), *Principles of addiction medicine* (2nd ed., pp. 557–570). Chevy Chase, MD: American Society of Addiction Medicine.

Petry, N. M., Martin, B., Cooney, J. L., & Kranzler, H. R. (2000). Give them prizes and they will come: Contingency management treatment of alcohol dependence. *Journal of Consulting and Clinical Psychology, 68*, 250–257.

Preston, K. L., Silverman, K., Umbricht, A., DeJusus, A., Montoya, I. D., & Schuster, C. R. (1999). Improvement in naltrexone treatment compliance with contingency management. *Drug and Alcohol Dependence, 54*, 127–135.

Prochaska, J. O., DiClemente, C. C., & Norcross, J. C. (1992). In search of how people change: Applications to addictive behaviors. *American Psychologist, 47*, 1102–1114.

Regier, D. A., Farmer, M. E., Rae, D. S., Locke, B. Z., Keith, S. J., Judd, L. L., & Goodwin, F. K. (1990). Comorbidity of mental disorders with alcohol and other drug use. *Journal of the American Medical Association, 264*, 2511–2518.

Rosenthal, R. N., & Westreich, L. (1999). Treatment of persons with dual diagnoses of substance use disorder and other psychological therapies. In B. S. McCrady & E. E. Epstein (Eds.), *Addictions: A comprehensive textbook* (pp. 439–476). New York: Oxford University Press.

Rounsaville, B. J. (1995). Can psychotherapy rescue naltrexone treatment of opioid addiction? In L. S. Onken & J. D. Blaine (Eds.), *Potentiating the efficacy of medications: Integrating psychosocial therapies with pharmacotherapies in the treatment of drug dependence* (NIDA Research Monograph Series No. 105, NIH Publication No. 95-3899, pp. 37–52). Rockville, MD: National Institute on Drug Abuse.

Rounsaville, B. J., & Carroll, K. M. (1997). Individual psychotherapy for drug abusers. In J. H. Lowinsohn, P. Ruiz, & R. B. Millman (Eds.), *Comprehensive textbook of substance abuse* (3rd ed., pp. 430–439). New York: Williams & Wilkins.

Rounsaville, B. J., Gawin, F. H., & Kleber, H. D. (1985). Interpersonal psychotherapy adapted for ambulatory cocaine abusers. *American Journal of Drug and Alcohol Abuse, 11*, 171–191.

Rounsaville, B. J., Spitzer, R. L., & Williams, J. B. W. (1986). Proposed changes in *DSM–III* substance use disorders: Description and rationale. *American Journal of Psychiatry, 143*, 463–468.

Rounsaville, B. J., Tims, F. M., Horton, A. M., & Sowder, B. J. (Eds.). (1993). *A diagnostic sourcebook on drug abuse research and treatment* (NIH Publication No. 93-3508). Rockville, MD: National Institute on Drug Abuse.

Schmitz, J. M., Henningfield, J. E., & Jarvik, M. E. (1998). Pharmacologic therapies for nicotine dependence. In A. W. Graham & T. K. Schultz (Eds.), *Principles of addiction medicine* (2nd ed., pp. 571–582). Chevy Chase, MD: American Society of Addiction Medicine.

Schottenfeld, R. S., Pakes, J. R., Oliveto, A., Ziedonis, D., & Kosten, T. R. (1997). Buprenorphine vs. methadone maintenance treatment for concurrent opioid dependence and cocaine abuse. *Archives of General Psychiatry, 54*, 713–720.

Schuckit, M. A. (1996). Recent developments in the pharmacotherapy of alcohol dependence. *Journal of Consulting and Clinical Psychology, 64*, 669–676.

Silverman, K., Higgins, S. T., Brooner, R. K., Montoya, I. D., Cone, E. J., Schuster, C. R., & Preston, K. L. (1996). Sustained cocaine abstinence in methadone maintenance patients through voucher-based reinforcement therapy. *Archives of General Psychiatry, 53*, 409–415.

Silverman K., Wong, C. J., Higgins, S. T., Brooner, R. K., Montoya, I. D., Contoreggi, C., Umbricht-Schneiter, D., Schuster, C. R., & Preston, K. L. (1996). Increasing opiate abstinence through voucher-based reinforcement therapy. *Drug and Alcohol Dependence, 41*, 157–165.

Silverman, K., Wong, C. J., Umbricht-Schneiter, A., Montoya, I. D., Schuster, C. R., & Preston, K. L. (1998). Broad beneficial effects of cocaine abstinence reinforcement among methadone patients. *Journal of Consulting and Clinical Psychology, 66*, 811–824.

Smith, R. M. (1999). Medications and alcohol craving. *Alcohol Research and Health, 23*, 207–213.

Stine, S. M., & Kosten, T. R. (1997). *New treatments for opiate dependence*. New York: Guilford.

Stine, S. M., Meandzija, B., & Kosten, T. R. (1998). Pharmacologic therapies for opioid addiction. In A. W. Graham & T. K. Schultz (Eds.), *Principles of addiction medicine* (2nd ed., pp. 545–555). Chevy Chase, MD: American Society of Addiction Medicine.

Stitzer, M. L., Bickel, W. K., Bigelow, G. E, & Liebson, I. A. (1986). Effect of methadone dose contingencies on urinalysis test results of polydrug-abusing methadone maintenance patients. *Drug and Alcohol Dependence, 18*, 341–348.

Stitzer, M. L., & Bigelow, G. E. (1978). Contingency management in a methadone maintenance program: Availability of reinforcers. *International Journal of the Addictions, 13*, 737–746.

Stitzer, M. L., Iguchi, M. Y., & Felch, L. J. (1992). Contingent take-home incentive: Effects on drug use of methadone maintenance patients. *Journal of Consulting and Clinical Psychology, 60*, 927–934.

Stitzer, M. L., Iguchi, M. Y., Kidorf, M., & Bigelow, G. E. (1993). Contingency management in methadone treatment: The case for positive incentives. In L. S. Onken, J. D. Blaine, & J. J. Boren (Eds.), *Behavioral treatments for drug abuse and dependence* (NIDA Research Monograph Series No. 137, pp. 19–36). Rockville, MD: National Institute on Drug Abuse.

Strain, E. C., Preston, K. L., Liebson, I. A., & Bigelow, G. E. (1995). Buprenorphine effects in methadone-maintained volunteers: Effects at two hours after methadone. *Journal of Pharmacology & Experimental Therapeutics, 272*, 628–638.

Taylor, G. J., Parker, J. D., & Bagby, R. M. (1990). A preliminary investigation of alexithymia in men with psychoactive substance dependence. *American Journal of Psychiatry, 147*, 1228–1230.

Volpicelli, J. R., Alterman, A. I., Hayashida, M., & O'Brien, C. P. (1992). Naltrexone and the treatment of alcohol dependence. *Archives of General Psychiatry, 49*, 876–880.

Volpicelli, J. R., Davis, M. A., Olgin, J. E. (1986). Naltrexone blocks the post-shock increase of ethanol consumption. *Life Sciences, 38,* 841–847.

Volpicelli, J. R., O'Brien, C. P., Alterman A. I., et al. (1990). Naltrexone and the treatment of alcohol dependence. In L. D. Reid (Ed.), *Opioids, bulimia, and alcohol abuse and alcoholism.* New York: Springer-Verlag.

Volpicelli, J. R., Rhines, K. C., Rhines, J. S., Volpicelli, L. A., Alterman, A. I., & O'Brien, C. P. (1997). Naltrexone and alcohol dependence: Role of subject compliance. *Archives of General Psychiatry, 54,* 737–742.

Walsh, S. L., Preston, K. L., Bigelow, G. E., & Stitzer, M. L (1995). Acute administration of buprenorphine in humans: Partial agonist and blockade effects. *Journal of Pharmacology & Experimental Therapeutics, 274,* 361–372.

Walsh, S. L., Preston, K. L., Stitzer, M. L., Cone, E. J., Bigelow, G. E. (1994). Clinical pharmacology of buprenorphine: Ceiling effects at high doses. *Clinical Pharmacology & Therapeutics, 55,* 569–580.

Woody, G. E., Luborsky, L., McLellan, A. T., O'Brien, C. P., Beck, A. T., Blaine, J., Herman, I., & Hole, A. (1983). Psychotherapy for opiate addicts: Does it help? *Archives of General Psychiatry, 40,* 639–645.

Woody, G. E., McLellan, A. T., Luborsky, L., & O'Brien, C. P. (1987). Twelve-month follow-up of psychotherapy for opiate dependence. *American Journal of Psychiatry, 144,* 590–596.

Woody, G. E., McLellan, A. T., Luborsky, L., & O'Brien, C. P. (1995). Psychotherapy in community methadone programs: A validation study. *American Journal of Psychiatry, 152,* 1302–1308.

Wurmser, L. (1978). *The hidden dimension.* New York: Jason Aronson.

10

Pharmacological and Psychological Treatments of Obesity and Binge Eating Disorder

Carlos M. Grilo

Obesity is a major public health problem (Bray, 1998). Despite pervasive sociocultural pressures to be thin (Brownell & Rodin, 1994), more than 34 million Americans are overweight (Kuczmarski, 1992), and the prevalence of obesity continues to increase (Flegal, Carroll, Kuczmarski, & Johnson, 1998; Kuczmarski, Carroll, Flegal, & Troiano, 1997), especially in women and certain ethnic and racial groups (Williamson, Kahn, Remington, & Anda, 1990). Obesity is associated with substantial morbidity and mortality (Eckel, 1997; Eckel & Kraus, 1998; Manson et al., 1990, 1995; National Task Force on the Prevention and Treatment of Obesity, 2000), social stigma (Wadden & Stunkard, 1985), and staggering economic health costs that continue to rise (Wolf & Colditz, 1998).

The past 35 years have witnessed the development of a variety of treatment programs for obesity (see Wilson, 1994, for a history of the progression of interventions for obesity). Overall, the treatment literature is characterized by two general findings: (a) Significant short-term weight loss can be achieved by a number of treatment approaches but (b) for many patients, weight loss is difficult to maintain over time.

The 1990s have witnessed several important developments that represent the impetus for this chapter. First, there has been a paradigmatic shift toward viewing obesity as a chronic biological problem of energy regulation (Bray, 1992; Wilson, 1994). Second, after 20 years without a major pharmacological advance (or at least no new medications approved for obesity), recent years witnessed the approval of three new obesity medications: fenfluramine (in 1996), sibutramine (in 1997), and orlistat (in 1999), and the abrupt withdrawal of one of them (fenfluramine and dexfenfluramine) from the market after the identification of major associated health risks (Abenhaim et al., 1996). Third, emerging evidence suggests that weight losses as little as 10%—although cosmetically disappointing to many—may result in significant health benefits (Blackburn, 1995).

Preparation of this chapter was supported in part by National Institutes of Health Grant DK49587 and a Donaghue Medical Research Foundation Investigator award.

Fourth, there is growing evidence suggesting the special role of physical activity and fitness in weight control and improving health (Lee, Jackson, & Blair, 1998).

In this chapter I provide a brief overview of the treatment literature with a special emphasis on emerging findings regarding pharmacological approaches for obesity. By way of introduction to this chapter, there is currently no accepted role for pharmacotherapy alone for the treatment of obesity (U.S. Department of Health and Human Services [USDHHS], 1998). The National Heart Lung and Blood Institute, together with the National Institute of Diabetes and Digestive and Kidney Diseases, in the first federal obesity clinical guidelines (USDHHS, 1998), stated that the most effective approach to weight loss includes caloric reduction, increased physical activity, and behavior therapy to enhance eating and activity changes. The federal guidelines promulgated by the USDHHS (1998) were reviewed by 115 health experts and endorsed by representatives from 54 organizations. These guidelines recommended that professionals prescribe a lifestyle behavioral approach for at least 6 months before attempting an obesity medication trial.

These federal guidelines have been widely echoed by leading obesity experts. The North American Association for the Study of Obesity, in a press release dated April 26, 1999, in response to the Food and Drug Administration (FDA) approval of orlistat, noted that

> orlistat (Xenical) and other pharmacological agents can be used as additional tools to help selected patients achieve successful long-term weight management. However, pharmacotherapy should only be used as part of a comprehensive weight management program, which includes a medical examination, diet counseling, physical activity education, and behavior modification.

Because pharmacotherapy for obesity needs to be considered and—if indicated—applied as one component of an ongoing comprehensive treatment plan, a brief overview of the voluminous literature pertaining to the major components of treatment is provided here. Attention is paid to recent emerging findings from research on morbidity and mortality and from the exercise literature. These two literatures have new findings with significant implications for treatment formulation and implementation. Last, obesity is associated with a plethora of medical and psychiatric morbidities. The morbidities (most notably heart disease, high blood pressure, and diabetes) often require additional medical follow-up and various adaptations of the treatments that I describe here. Detailed consideration of the management of these varied comorbid conditions is beyond the scope of this chapter. I will, however, review a specific subgroup of obese patients with a coexisting mental disorder—binge eating disorder (BED; American Psychiatric Association, 1994). The literature—especially pharmacotherapy—for BED is somewhat distinct from the obesity treatment and pharmacotherapy literature and thus warrants a particular focus.

The goal of this chapter is to present empirically supported recommendations for comprehensive treatments of obesity and BED. Practical issues for implementation of rational pharmacotherapy for obesity will be noted. Last, limitations in the research literature as well as the limitations of available treatments will be highlighted. An understanding of these limitations is essential for implementing treatments as well as for stimulating future research.

Description and Assessment of Obesity

Obesity is defined as excess adipose tissue that results from excess energy intake relative to energy expenditure (Grilo & Brownell, 1998). *Overweight* is defined as excess deviation in body weight above a certain standard ("ideal") for height. The points at which excess fat or excess weight are used to define overweight or obesity are relatively arbitrary and are frequently and hotly debated.

The most frequently used weight standard has historically been the Metropolitan Life Insurance (1983) tables, and many researchers have adopted the standard that body weight 20% above ideal weight equals "overweight." It is important to note that excess weight does not always reflect excess fat (e.g., some extremely muscular athletes may be overweight but not overly fat). Nonetheless, the various measures of weight by height (percent overweight, weight–height ratio, or body mass index (BMI) correlate roughly 0.7 with direct measurements of body fat (Grilo & Brownell, 1998).

At present researchers in the field of obesity most frequently use BMI rather than the Metropolitan Life tables as the standard measurement. BMI is defined as weight in kilograms divided by height (in m^2). A BMI ≥ 27 is generally thought to be associated with substantially increased health risks. Figure 10.1a shows the widely used Bray (1978) nomogram for BMI and recommendations for assessment and treatment. On June 17, 1998, the National Institutes of Health (NIH), in its *Clinical Guidelines on the Identification, Evaluation, and Treatment of Overweight and Obesity* (USDHHS, 1998), adopted a lower threshold for overweight (i.e., BMI ≥ 25) and retained the standard of BMI ≥ 30 as signifying obesity.

In addition to excess fat, it is important to consider the distribution of fat. Abdominal fat distribution (upper-body or android-type obesity) is associated with greater morbidity and mortality than is lower body (gynoid-type) obesity. Although abdominal fat distribution is found more frequently in men than in women, its presence in both sexes is associated with increased health risks. Thus, although in general a BMI ≥ 30 is associated with sharp increase in health risks, waist-to-hip ratio (WHR) is a stronger predictor of health risk (especially for cardiovascular disease) than is body weight, body fat, or BMI (National Task Force on Prevention and Treatment of Obesity, 2000; USDHHS, 1998). WHR is generally considered an adequate estimate for intra-abdominal obesity that would otherwise require sophisticated and expensive methods (Lichtenbelt & Fo-

KNOW YOUR BODY MASS INDEX

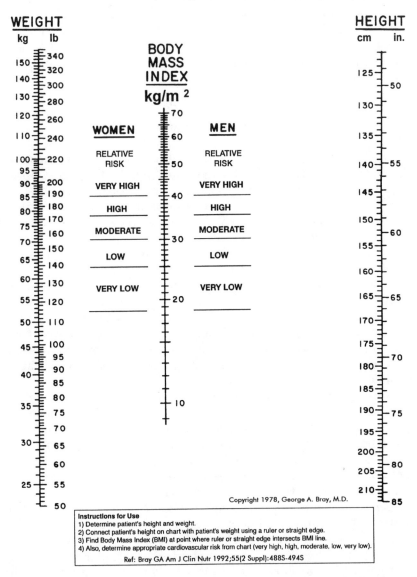

Figure 10.1(a). Know Your Body Mass Index. *Note.* From "Definitions, Measurements, and Classification of the Syndrome of Obesity," by G. A. Bray, 1978, *International Journal of Obesity, 2*, p. 99. Copyright 1978 by G. A. Bray. Reprinted with permission of the author.

gelholm, 1999). Figure 10.1b also shows the widely used Bray (1988) nomogram for WHR and recommendations for intervention. USDHHS (1998) guidelines note that a WHR over 40 in men and over 35 in women indicates increased medical risk in people with BMIs >25.

BMI, waist circumference, and WHR measures are generally adequate

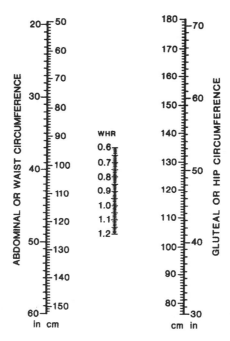

Figure 10.1(b).   Nomogram for Waist-to-Hip Ratio. *Note.* From "Obesity: Part I —Pathogenesis," by G. A. Bray & D. S. Gray, 1988, *Western Journal of Medicine, 149,* p. 429. Copyright 1988 by G. A. Bray. Reprinted with permission of the authors.

measurements for most obesity programs. Sophisticated technologies are available for determining precise levels of obesity, fat distribution, and energy expenditure (see Lichtenbelt & Fogelholm, 1999). At present, these technologies contribute to improved research but have limited utility for standard practice.

Medical Assessment

Medical assessment of obesity represents a broad and potentially complex process. As a general rule, increasing obesity—especially increasing WHR —is associated with greater risk for morbidity and mortality. In addition, a family history of illnesses associated with obesity (e.g., diabetes, heart disease, high cholesterol) should be considered (Blackwell & Kanders, 1987). Exhibit 10.1 summarizes general factors to consider when performing a medical history assessment of patients with obesity. (See Weinsier, 1995, and USDHHS, 1998, for further details.)

Psychological Assessment

Psychological assessment of obesity also represents a broad and complex area. Excellent reviews of the psychological aspects of obesity are available

Exhibit 10.1.   Factors to Consider During Medical History of Obese Patients

---

Factors associated with obesity
  Family history of obesity
  Age of onset (childhood, adolescence, adulthood)
  Potential endocrine abnormalities (e.g., hypothyroidism, Cushing syndrome)
  Life stressors or significant development changes
  Dietary and physical activity patterns
  Binge eating patterns
History of medical complications of obesity
  Glucose intolerance and diabetes mellitus
  Hypertension, hyperlipidemia, coronary artery disease
  Cancer
  Respiratory disease (e.g., sleep apnea)
  Osteoarthritis
  Hepatobiliary disease
Previous treatment
  Past nutritional, behavioral, psychosocial therapies
  Past pharmacological and surgical therapies for obesity
  Successes, failures, patterns, weight-cycles, complications (adverse reactions)
Factors suggesting precaution regarding weight reduction
  <20 or >65 years of age
  History of anorexia nervosa
  Pregnancy or lactation

Note. Exhibit based in part on Weinsier (1995) and USDHHS (1998).

elsewhere (Friedman & Brownell, 1995), as are detailed discussions of assessment protocols (Grilo, 1996). In brief, obese and nonobese people show few differences in psychological functioning. If the two extremes of weight (i.e., anorexia and morbid obesity) are excluded, obese and non-obese groups generally show similar rates of psychological disorders. This psychological literature has, however, pointed to two areas that might be of particular concern. Some research has suggested that obese people may have lower self-esteem, although most studies have observed higher body image dissatisfaction (see Friedman & Brownell, 1995; Grilo, 1996). Obese people who binge eat (see below), however, represent a subgroup of obese patients characterized by high rates of psychological problems (Grilo, 1998). In assessing psychological problems associated with obesity, a par-ticularly useful self-report instrument is the Questionnaire on Eating and Weight Patterns–Revised (Yanovski, 1993), a psychometrically established measure used in the *Diagnostic and Statistical Manual of Mental Disor-ders* (4th ed.; *DSM–IV*; American Psychiatric Association, 1994) field trials (Spitzer et al., 1993) that produces valuable data regarding weight and dieting history, weight cycling, body image, and binge eating. It produces the necessary information for generating two specific eating disorder di-agnoses: BED and bulimia nervosa. The presence of problems with binge eating may signal the need for a more comprehensive psychological as-sessment (see Grilo, 1998). The Eating Disorder Examination (Fairburn

& Cooper, 1993), a semistructured interview that also has a self-report version (Fairburn & Beglin, 1994), is widely used in the field (Grilo, Masheb, & Wilson, in press). The presence of binge eating also signals the need to consider additional pharmacological and psychological interventions (see below).

Overview of Treatment

A plethora of nonpharmacological treatments exist for obesity. These include, for example, self-help programs, self-help groups, numerous commercial programs, dietary programs, behavioral treatments, very-low-calorie diet (VLCD) programs, residential programs, and surgery. VLCD approaches were extensively studied (and used) in the 1980s and early 1990s (Wadden, Van Itallie, & Blackburn, 1990) but eventually received limited empirical support (Foster, Wadden, Peterson, Letizia, Bartlett, & Conill, 1992; Wadden & Bartlett, 1992; Wadden, Foster, & Letizia, 1994; Wadden, Sternberg, Letizia, Stunkard, & Foster, 1989; Wadden, Stunkard, & Liebschutz, 1988). Regarding surgical interventions, a variety of procedures have been developed for obesity and have been shown to produce impressive weight losses and significant improvements in both health and quality-of-life indexes (Benotti & Forse, 1995; Hsu et al., 1998; Sjostrom, Lissner, Wedel, & Sjostrom, 1999; Sugarman, Starkey, & Birkenhauer, 1987). Beyond noting that bariatric surgery (i.e., the surgical management of obesity) continues to be used for severe obesity, surgical interventions are not discussed further in this chapter. The following brief review focuses selectively on interventions that have received the most study (behavioral treatments and exercise) with a view toward recommending a comprehensive approach that may also include pharmacotherapy.

Behavioral Treatment

Ferster, Nurnberger, and Levitt's (1962) application of behavioral principles to eating behaviors is generally credited as the formal beginning of behavioral treatments for obesity (Wilson, 1994). Behavioral treatments —based initially on the premise that learning principles can be applied to correct excessive eating that leads to excess weight—have evolved considerably (Stunkard, 1992; Stunkard & Berthold, 1985; Wilson, 1994).

Behavior therapy is based on functional analyses of behavior (Wilson, 1994). This, in the case of obesity, has generally targeted eating and exercise behaviors, with a particular focus on identifying the antecedents and consequences of problematic behaviors. The early application of behavior therapy focused primarily on modifying specific eating behaviors and developed in parallel with dietary and exercise interventions. Over the years, the different approaches have been integrated, and today the application of behavioral therapies generally occurs in combination with dietary–nutritional interventions, exercise interventions, or both (e.g.,

Wadden, Vogt, Foster, & Anderson, 1998; Wilson, 1994). Indeed, the LEARN Program (Brownell, 2000)—which is generally regarded as a leading behavioral weight control program, given its widespread use at leading obesity centers (e.g., Anderson et al., 1999; Goodrick, Poston, Kimball, Reeves, & Foreyt, 1998)—is an acronym for *l*ifestyle, *e*xercise, *a*ttitudes, *r*elationships, and *n*utrition.

The efficacy of behavioral obesity treatments has been studied extensively and has been the subject of numerous reviews (e.g., Brownell & Jeffery, 1987; Brownell & Kramer, 1989; Brownell & Wadden, 1992; Grilo, 1996; USDHHS, 1998; Wilson, 1994). Overall, most behavioral treatments produce significant short-term weight losses but are characterized by substantial posttreatment weight regain (Wilson, 1994). Studies generally find that patients, on average, regain one third to one half of their weight loss during the first year posttreatment and that most patients regain their entire weight loss by 5 years (Kramer, Jeffery, Forster, & Snell, 1989; Wadden et al., 1989).

Increased concerns regarding the inability to produce lasting weight loss (Brownell & Wadden, 1992) led to investigations of relapse (Grilo, Shiffman, & Wing, 1989, 1993; Schlundt, Sbrocco, & Bell, 1989) and numerous approaches to better maintenance of weight loss (e.g., Perri, McAllister, Gange, Jordan, McAdoo, & Nezu, 1988; see also Marlatt & Gordon, 1985; Perri, Nezu, & Viegener, 1992). Treatments became longer, relapse prevention techniques became standard components, and a plethora of maintenance components was added. These enhanced treatments showed slight trends toward greater weight losses; however, these generally plateaued for most patients regardless of the type of treatment. Wilson (1994) noted that the observed increases in weight losses appeared to be primarily a function of the increased length of treatments and not due to increased potency of any specific treatment.

Pharmacotherapy

Until the 1990s, pharmacotherapy played a relatively minor role in the treatment of obesity. Available medications were approved only for very short-term use. Difficulties in performing longer term studies, concerns regarding the safety and abuse of medications, and consistent findings showing rapid weight regain following medication discontinuation contributed to the fact that no new obesity medications were approved for use over a period of 20 years.

Several forces converged to result in vigorous development and testing of obesity medications. Rapid advances in behavioral and molecular genetics (e.g., Zhang et al., 1994; see also Chagnon, Perusse, & Bouchard, 1998) and energy regulation research (Westerterp-Plantenga, Steffens, & Tremblay, 1999) supported the emerging view that obesity is not an acute problem but instead a chronic problem of energy regulation (Weintraub, 1992; Wilson, 1994). In addition, an elaborate long-term study that tested a combination pharmacotherapy regimen with behavioral treatment

(Weintraub, 1992; Weintraub, Sundaresan, Madan, et al., 1992; Weintraub, Sundaresan, Schuster, et al., 1992; Weintraub, Sundaresan, Schuster, Ginsberg, et al., 1992) provided an innovative model for sequencing and combining treatments and placed obesity treatment within a model of a chronic condition requiring ongoing management. This research strongly suggested the potential of pharmacotherapy to help obese patients achieve improved weight control.

Today, there is a general consensus among obesity experts and regulatory health agencies, such as the FDA, that obesity medications are recommended for use only in individuals who have BMIs ≥30 or have BMIs ≥27 with at least two obesity-related morbidities (USDDHS, 1998). As noted above, instituting a comprehensive lifestyle behavioral approach for at least 6 months without success is recommended before attempting an obesity medication regimen (USDDHS, 1998).

Common contraindications to obesity medications include pregnancy or lactation, severe systemic illness, cardiac-related conditions, medication regimens that might interact (especially notable here is treatment with monoamine oxidase inhibitor (MAOI antidepressants), and uncontrolled high blood pressure. Obesity medications also are not recommended for individuals younger than age 18 or older than 65. Additional (less absolute) contraindications include a history of certain severe mental illnesses, such as psychosis, bipolar disorder, anorexia nervosa, or any current severe mental disorders, such as severe depression, anxiety, or substance use problems that require immediate intervention. Currently, there are approximately 12 FDA-approved medications for weight control in the United States (Allison & Saunders, 1999; Atkinson, 1997; Dhurandhar & Atkinson, 1998). Ten medications are centrally active adrenergic drugs. One medication (sibutramine, marketed as Meridia) is a centrally active combined adrenergic and serotenergic drug. Another agent (orlistat) is the first locally active medication approved that works by altering absorption of dietary fat calories. Characteristic features of these agents are briefly reviewed later.

Adrenergic medications. Of the centrally active adrenergic drugs, three (amphetamine, methamphetamine, and phenmetrazine) are classified as Drug Enforcement Agency (DEA) Schedule II, four (benzphetamine, chlorphentermine, chlortermine, and phendimetrazine) as DEA Schedule III, and three (diethylpropion, mazindol, and phentermine) as DEA Schedule IV. DEA Schedule II and III drugs (reflecting high potential and some potential for abuse) are generally not recommended and are no longer in routine clinical use.

The three DEA Schedule IV adrenergic drugs are recommended and approved for only very short use (Bray, 1992). Scoville's (1975) early review of more than 200 studies with more than 10,000 patients with adrenergic drugs noted that in approximately 40% of the controlled studies the active drug produced significantly more weight loss than placebo, which across studies averaged 0.5 lb (0.22 kg)/week more weight loss. More recent reviews of adrenergic obesity medications have produced similar findings (Bray, 1992, 1995; Galloway, Farquhar, & Munro, 1984).

Of the adrenergic drugs, the most carefully studied is phentermine, which is approved by the FDA for short-term treatment (i.e., 3 months or less). Phentermine is currently distributed by seven pharmaceutical companies and is available in either resin (Brand name Ionamine) or hydrochloride forms (e.g., brand names: Adipex-P, Banobese, Fastin, Obenix). Current manufacturers' recommended doses (similar to those used in most controlled trials) are 15–30 mg/day for the resin form and 18.75–37.5 mg/day for the hydrochloride. Phentermine used alone generally results in short-term weight losses of 4 kg (Weintraub, 1984). (Longer term use of phentermine has been studied but within the context of concurrent use with another obesity medication and behavior therapy [Weintraub, Sundaresan, Madan, Schuster, Balder, Lasagna, & Cox, 1992; Weintraub, Sundaresan, Schuster, Averbuch, Stein, & Byrne, 1992; Weintraub, Sundaresan, Schuster, Ginsberg, Madan, Balder, Stein, & Byrne, 1992], so loss figures are not comparable.)

Phentermine is commonly associated with side effects of rapid heart rate, increased blood pressure, restlessness, constipation, and diminished sexual arousal. Because of phentermine's sympathomimetic properties it is essential to avoid concomitant use of MAOIs (or to initiate treatment within 3 weeks of discontinuing MAOIs).

Serotonergic drugs. Particular attention has been paid to three serotonergic medications: fenfluramines, fluoxetine, and sibutramine (an inhibitor of both serotonin and noradrenaline reuptake). The fenfluramines were approved by the FDA and subsequently withdrawn from the market; fluoxetine has not been approved for weight loss indications, and sibutramine was only recently approved.

Fenfluramine and dexfenfluramine. For a decade, intensive research focused on a number of agents that affected serotonergic systems, most notably fenfluramine (brand name Pondimin) and dexfenfluramine (brand name Redux; Bray, 1992, 1995; Brownell & Stunkard, 1981; Guy-Grand, Apfelbaum, Crepaldi, Gries, Lefebvre, & Turner, 1989). The fenfluramines inhibit serotonin reuptake and simultaneously stimulate serotonin release, and they have produced significant weight losses in numerous trials (Brownell & Stunkard, 1981; Douglas et al., 1983; Guy-Grand et al., 1989). Fenfluramine (optimal dosing at 60 mg/day) and dexfenfluramine (optimal dosing at 15 mg twice per day) produced weight losses comparable to those reported in studies with the noradrenergic drugs.

Brownell and Stunkard (1981), in an early classic study, found that the addition of fenfluramine to behavior therapy produced greater weight loss than behavior therapy alone (10.8 kg vs. 7.1 kg). Unfortunately, patients who received fenfluramine regained weight faster than patients who received behavior therapy alone; hence by 1-year follow-up the medication-plus-behavior-therapy condition versus the behavior-therapy condition were similar. Craighead, Stunkard, and O'Brien (1981) reported a nearly identical pattern: Fenfluramine plus behavior therapy and fenfluramine alone produced greater weight loss than behavior therapy alone, but the pharmacotherapy conditions were found to have significantly greater weight regain following treatment.

In a particularly impressive study, Weintraub and colleagues (Weintraub, Sundaresan, Madan, et al., 1992; Weintraub, Sundaresan, Schuster, Averbuch et al., 1992; Weintraub, Sundaresan, Schuster, Ginsberg, et al., 1992) examined the effectiveness of the combination of fenfluramine and phentermine in a long-term study involving a complex design with multiple treatment components, including behavior therapy. This study found that an active drug treatment produced significantly greater weight loss than placebo in obese patients receiving comprehensive dietary interventions and behavior therapy. The observed weight losses were superior at short- and long-term follow-up periods of up to 3.5 years. Discontinuation from the drug treatment (after 190 weeks) resulted in a regain of most of the weight loss, despite ongoing behavior therapy (Weintraub, Sundaresan, Madan, et al., 1992; Weintraub, Sundaresan, Schuster, Averbuch, et al., 1992; Weintraub, Sundaresan, Schuster, Ginsberg, et al., 1992). These results received support from another large study (Atkinson, Blank, Loper, Schumacher, & Lutes, 1995).

More recently, following increasingly widespread use, fenfluramine and dexfenfluramine were abruptly removed from the market following a number of reports of two potential major medical problems associated with their use (primary pulmonary hypertension and heart valve abnormalities; Abenhaim et al., 1996; Kurz & Van Ermen, 1997; McCann, Seiden, Rubin, & Ricaurte, 1997). This raised serious questions for the field of pharmaceutical treatment of obesity, including the adequacy of safety trials, the appropriate selection of patients, and more careful consideration of potential cost–benefit ratios.

In part as a result, the FDA and NIH have take cautious stances on the long-term use of obesity medications and have required greater rigor in trials testing efficacy and safety. Because of widespread concern that many average-weight people were obtaining weight loss medications for cosmetic reasons, the new federal guidelines (USDHHS, 1998) included clear recommendations that obesity medications not be prescribed for non-obese individuals. There is nonetheless increasing appreciation that obesity itself is associated with increased risk for morbidity and mortality and that potential risks associated with obesity medication treatment must be balanced against the health risks of obesity (Eckel & Kraus, 1998).

Fluoxetine. Fluoxetine, an inhibitor of serotonin reuptake, is a widely prescribed antidepressant. Fluoxetine is approved by the FDA for the treatment of bulimia nervosa but is not approved as an obesity medication. Fluoxetine, in contrast to fenfluramine, does not stimulate release of serotonin and has not been linked to the medical problems found with the fenfluramines. Fluoxetine, used at 60 mg/day dosing (higher than typical for depression but similar to dosing for bulimia nervosa; Fluoxetine Bulimia Nervosa Collaborative Study Group, 1992), was at one time thought to be a useful agent in producing some weight loss (Goldstein & Potvin, 1994). Clinical experience and further reports suggesting that weight regain occurs after 6 months of chronic dosing (Goldstein et al., 1995) have diminished interest in the use of fluoxetine as a weight-loss agent.

Sibutramine. Sibutramine (brand name Meridia), an inhibitor of serotonin and noradrenaline reuptake (Knoll Pharmaceuticals, 1997), was approved by the FDA in 1998 for the treatment of obesity. Sibutramine has demonstrated efficacy for acute weight loss in several randomized placebo-controlled trials (Bray et al., 1996, 1999; Drouin, Hanotin, Courcier, & Leutenegger, 1994; Hanotin, Thomas, Jones, Leutenegger, & Drouin, 1998; Jones, Newman, & Romanec, 1994; Jones, Smith, Kelly, & Gray, 1995; Lean, 1997; Seagle, Bessesen, & Hill, 1998).

Several controlled trials have reported that, compared to weight losses of <1 kg on pill placebo, that 10- and 15-mg dosing of sibutramine produce roughly 6 kg of weight loss, with most of the weight loss occurring within the first 12 weeks (see Lean, 1997). Hanotin et al. (1998) reported that 10 mg/day sibutramine produced a weight loss of 5.1 kg ± 0.5 kg (n = 59) and that 15 mg/day sibutramine produced a weight loss of 4.9 kg ± 0.5 kg (n = 62); both doses were superior to placebo (1.4 kg ± 0.5 kg). Roughly 50% of participants who received sibutramine lost more than 5% of their initial body weight. The attrition rate was roughly 17%. Controlled trials have revealed a relatively mild side-effect profile. The most common side effects include mild degrees of dry mouth, constipation, and insomnia. Of greater note are reports of increased heart rate. Ten- and 15-mg dosing of sibutramine produce increases of roughly 2 mm/Hg of systolic and diastolic blood pressure in patients with normal blood pressure. Roughly 12% of patients experience clinically significant rises in blood pressure. It is interesting that, in patients with high blood pressure, sibutramine seems to produce slight decreases (Lean, 1997). The incidence of valvular heart disease (like that seen with the fenfluramines) has been 2.3% of patients treated with sibutramine versus 2.6% of patients treated with placebo.

Noncentrally acting drugs that influence nutrition partitioning: orlistat. The FDA approved orlistat (brand name Xenical) for the treatment of obesity in April 1999. Orlistat represents a novel pharmacological approach: It is the first noncentrally acting medication approved for obesity. Orlistat is a lipase inhibitor, that is, it inhibits the activity of pancreatic and gastric lipases and thereby the digestion and absorption of dietary fat calories (Hoffman-LaRoche, 1998). Orlistat produces a dose-dependent reduction in dietary fat absorption (Hauptman, Jeunet, & Hartmann, 1992); studies have generally reported a maximum 30% reduction in the absorption of fat on a regimen of 120 mg three times daily (Drent & Van der Veen, 1993).

Orlistat has demonstrated efficacy for acute weight loss in randomized placebo-controlled trials (Tonstad et al., 1994) and for longer term weight control (i.e., over a 2-year period; Davidson, Hauptman, DiGirolamo et al., 1999; Sjostrom, Rissanen, Andersen, et al., 1998). In a large U.S. multisite, double-blind, placebo-controlled study with 1,187 obese patients, Davidson et al. (1999) reported that patients treated with orlistat 120 mg three times daily plus dietary intervention and behavior therapy lost significantly more weight (an average of 5.8 kg more) than patients who received placebo plus the diet and behavior therapy during the first year of treatment. In this study all patients received a weight-maintenance dietary intervention for the first year, then were randomized to receive either placebo, orlistat 60 mg three times daily, or orlistat 120 mg three times daily. High-dose orlistat (120-mg three times daily dosing) resulted in significantly less weight regain (35% regain) than the 60-mg three times daily dosing (51%) and the placebo (63% regain). The European Multicentre Orlistat Study Group (Sjostrom et al., 1998) found that obese patients treated with orlistat (120 mg three times daily) plus diet lost significantly more weight than patients who received placebo plus diet during the first year of treatment. During the second year, in which patients were reassigned in double-blind fashion either orlistat plus a weight maintenance diet or placebo plus diet, the 120-mg three times daily orlistat dosing resulted in approximately 50% less weight regain. Thus, two large multisite studies (Davidson et al., 1999; Sjostrom et al., 1998) found that the addition of orlistat to dietary intervention produced significantly greater weight loss during the first year of treatment and lessened the amount of weight regain during the second year of weight maintenance therapy.

In addition to augmenting weight loss and weight loss maintenance, the addition of orlistat to dietary interventions was associated with significantly greater improvements in some obesity-related disease risk factors. Both the U.S. (Davidson et al., 1999) and European (Sjostrom et al., 1998) multisite studies reported that the addition of orlistat was associated with significantly greater improvements in lipid profiles and insulin levels. Similarly, Hollander and colleagues (1998)—in a multicenter 1-year randomized, double-blind, placebo-controlled trial—found that orlistat (120 mg three times daily) plus diet was significantly superior to placebo plus diet in the treatment of obese men and women with Type II diabetes. The addition of orlistat produced significantly greater weight loss and weight maintenance as well as greater improvements in lipid profiles and blood glucose control.

Orlistat is associated with certain common side effects, although the available follow-up data generally support its safety (Harp, 1998). Because orlistat works locally by blocking digestion and absorption of dietary fat calories, the most common side effects are gastrointestinal in nature. Because considerable fat passes through the intestines, stool softening, oily stools and spotting, and increased stool size are not uncommon. It is also possible that some percentage of important nutrients, such as fat-soluble vitamins, are lost, so it is recommended that patients take a vitamin supplement while taking orlistat.

Behavior Therapy, Medication, or Both

There are surprisingly few controlled studies that speak to the question of whether behavior therapy (or any psychosocial intervention) adds to the efficacy of pharmacotherapy alone. This is doubly surprising given the near-universal rapid regain of weight following discontinuation of medication-only treatment. Adding to this uncertainty is the fact that the controlled trials reviewed above generally addressed the issue of pharmacotherapy versus placebo only within the context of clinical research. These studies involved conditions that are difficult to replicate in clinical practice, such as careful monitoring, the prescription of calorie restriction, dietary counseling, and some form of behavior therapy.

Two earlier studies by Craighead and her colleagues (Craighead, 1984; Craighead, Stunkard, & O'Brien, 1981) suggested that behavior therapy alone is superior to pharmacotherapy alone and provide support for the view that the addition of some type of psychosocial intervention augments the efficacy of obesity pharmacotherapy alone. Craighead et al. (1981) found that weekly group behavior therapy plus pharmacotherapy with fenfluramine (120 mg/day) and weekly group social support plus pharmacotherapy (fenfluramine 120 mg/day) both produced significantly greater weight loss (15.3 kg and 14.5 kg, respectively) than pharmacotherapy plus once-monthly routine office visits (6.0 kg) during the 26-week study.

A more recent study by Wadden et al. (1997) of obese patients being treated by pharmacotherapy (fenfluramine–phentermine combination) found that brief structured physician visits coupled with good manualized protocols produced comparable results to those achieved by traditional group behavior therapy provided by a nutritionist plus the patient manual. The generalizability of this study is limited by its small sample size and the use of a combination medication regimen that no longer has FDA approval. Thus, these results need to be replicated in other primary care settings and with different pharmacotherapies. Nonetheless, these preliminary findings suggest the potential of a way to augment the typical busy primary care practice. This seems required given Craighead's (1984; Craighead et al., 1981) findings noted earlier. It is worth noting that the use of such minimal intervention and guided self-help strategies using detailed patient manuals has received impressive support in a number of controlled trials with bulimia nervosa and BED (Carter & Fairburn, 1998).

In sum, prescription of obesity treatment is complex, and the appropriateness of any treatment depends on a number of factors. Obesity is a heterogeneous disorder (Brownell & Wadden, 1991), and patients vary greatly in their needs. Although recent years have seen attempts to provide guidelines (e.g., Brownell & Wadden, 1991; USDHHS, 1998), continued research is needed to develop even better guidelines. In general, risk–benefit ratios should be considered first in matching patients and available treatments. A moderately obese patient with significant medical comorbidities would warrant consideration of more aggressive and comprehensive treatment (including, possibly, medication) than would a slightly overweight person.

Binge Eating Disorder

Binge eating, originally recognized as a problem in obese people by Stunkard (1959), has recently been identified as an important clinical problem with significant implication for treatment prescription (Grilo, 1998; Stunkard, 1994; Yanovski, 1993). BED, defined as recurrent binge eating without extreme weight compensatory practices, coupled with distress regarding the binges (Grilo, in press), was added as a research diagnostic category to the *DSM–IV* following two multisite field trials (Spitzer et al., 1992, 1993).

BED may be present in as many as one fourth to one third of obese patients who present to university-based weight control programs (Spitzer et al., 1992). BED is associated with increased BMI and obesity (Telch, Agras, & Rossiter, 1988), and BED may represent a risk factor for subsequent weight gain (Agras, Telch, Arnow, Eldredge, & Marnell, 1997). Research has consistently found that overweight BED patients have higher levels of psychopathology (e.g., Kuehnel & Wadden, 1994; Yanovski, Nelson, Dubbert, & Spitzer, 1993), greater body image dissatisfaction, and poorer psychological functioning (e.g., Grilo, 1998, in press; Grilo, Wilfley, Jones, Brownell, & Rodin, 1994; Telch & Agras, 1994; Yanovski, 1993) than other overweight patients. BED patients are characterized by cognitive symptomatology (i.e., dysfunctional attitudes regarding eating and overvalued ideas regarding weight and shape) comparable to those of bulimia nervosa patients (Hay & Fairburn, 1998; Masheb & Grilo, 2000; Wilfley, Schwartz, Spurrell, & Fairburn, 1997).

In the first comprehensive literature review of binge eating and obesity and of emerging BED research, Yanovski (1993) compared the treatment responses of obese binge eaters and non-binge eaters with different types of weight control programs. Some studies found that obese binge eaters benefited less than nonbingers from weight control programs (e.g., Marcus, Wing, & Hopkins, 1988), although contrary evidence also exists (e.g., Wadden, Foster, & Letizia, 1992). More recent treatment outcome research (e.g., Gladis et al., 1998; Marcus, Wing, & Fairburn, 1995; Porzelius, Houston, Smith, Arfken, & Fisher, 1995) has rekindled this debate.

Nonetheless, these initial trends in the obesity treatment literature for binge eaters opened the door for well-established pharmacological and psychological interventions for bulimia nervosa (an eating disorder also characterized by binge eating) to be tested. In particular, antidepressant pharmacotherapy and cognitive–behavioral therapy (CBT) have been found to be efficacious in a large number of controlled trials for bulimia (see Wilson & Fairburn, 1993). Thus, pharmacological approaches to BED have generally followed bulimia rather than obesity medication strategies.

Pharmacotherapy

Pharmacotherapy versus placebo for BED has been compared in five studies (Alger, Schwalberg, Bigaouette, Michalek, & Howard, 1991; Hudson et al., 1998; McCann & Agras, 1990; McElroy et al., 2000; Stunkard, Berk-owitz, Tanrikut, Reiss, & Young, 1996), and pharmacotherapy in combination with either CBT or behavioral weight loss has been tested in three studies (Agras et al., 1994, de Zwann, Nutzinger, & Schnoenbeck, 1992; Marcus et al., 1990). Overall, these first-generation pharmacotherapy trials have been of short duration, with short follow-ups, have used varied assessment methods, have operationalized BED differently, and have used relatively narrow outcome measures (see Grilo, 1998; Grilo & Devlin, 1997). Most notable is that, although BED patients are characterized by problems in three domains—(a) binge eating and associated dysfunctional behaviors and attitudes about eating and overvalued ideas regarding weight and shape, (b) elevated psychological symptomatology, and (c) obesity and associated physical morbidities—few pharmacotherapy studies have reported data across domains.

McCann and Agras (1990), in a 12-week randomized double-blind trial, found that desipramine 100–300 mg daily was significantly superior than placebo in reducing binge eating (63% reduction and 60% abstinence rates vs. 16% and 15%, respectively). Unfortunately, relapse to baseline levels of binge eating occurred within 4 weeks of discontinuation of medication. Alger et al. (1991) found that two different medications—the tricyclic antidepressant imipramine, used at up to 200 mg/day, and the opioid antagonist naltrexone, used at up to 150 mg/day—produced substantial reductions in binge eating but that the reductions were not greater than observed with placebo (all three conditions produced roughly 70% reductions). No weight loss was observed in the three conditions.

Hudson et al. (1998), in a 9-week randomized double-blind trial found that fluvoxamine in doses of 50–300 mg produced significantly greater reductions in binge eating than placebo did. Of the patients who received fluvoxamine and completed the 9 weeks of treatment, 45% stopped binge eating, and an additional 28% improved at least moderately (vs. 24% plus 24%, respectively, on placebo). Patients had little weight change. Those who received fluvoxamine lost an average of 2.7 lbs (1.22 kg), and those who received placebo lost 0.3 lbs (0.13 kg). Although Hudson et al. concluded that their findings supported the efficacy of fluvoxamine for BED, it is worth noting that if their analyses had considered patients randomized to all treatments, then the efficacy of fluvoxamine versus placebo became less certain. McElroy and colleagues (2000), in a 6-week randomized double-blind trial comparing sertraline and placebo in 34 BED patients, found that a 6-week trial of sertraline (flexible dosing from 50 mg to 200 mg) produced significantly greater reductions in binge eating and reduction in BMI (mean difference of 0.6 units) than placebo. The relatively small sample size and brevity of the trial limit the generalizability of this study, as does the fact that a majority (61%) of the patients treated with sertraline had a previous diagnosis of major depression.

To date, only one trial has tested an obesity medication (albeit one subsequently withdrawn from the market) in the management of BED. Stunkard and colleagues (1996) examined the efficacy of d-fenfluramine versus placebo. A single-blind placebo 4-week lead-in period with 50 severely obese women with BED produced substantial reductions in binge eating in 22 participants. The remaining 28 symptomatic obese BED patients were randomly assigned to either d-fenfluramine or placebo (double blind) for 8 weeks. Fifteen mg to 30 mg of d-fenfluramine daily produced a significantly greater reduction in binge eating than placebo, but no weight loss was observed. Relapse to baseline levels occurred within 4 weeks of medication discontinuation.

Thus, the few controlled medication trials performed to date with BED have generally found that antidepressants and appetite suppressants (one study) produce significantly greater acute reductions in binge eating than placebo but that binge eating returns rapidly following medication discontinuation. Medications tested to date have not produced weight loss in BED patients, with the one notable exception of the small ($n = 34$ patients) 6-week trial with sertraline (McElroy et al., 2000).

CBT and Behavioral Weight Loss

Variants of CBT adapted from well-established interventions for bulimia nervosa (Fairburn, Marcus, & Wilson, 1993; Wilson & Fairburn, 1993) have been tested in several controlled trials with BED. In what can be regarded as the first generation of controlled trials in BED, the specifics of the CBT have varied somewhat (see Agras et al., 1994; Fairburn et al., 1993; Marcus, 1997). For example, some treatment manuals have been modified to include additional weight control interventions (e.g., prescription of walking 30 min/day three times/week, psychoeducation regarding heart-healthy nutrition and decreasing dietary fat intake, weekly weigh-ins). CBT has been applied using individual, group, and guided self-help methods and has varied in length from 8 weeks to 6 months. These variations notwithstanding, the CBT protocols have generally followed the published CBT manual for bulimia nervosa (Fairburn et al., 1993).

CBT has been compared with wait-list controls in four studies (Marcus et al., 1995; Peterson et al., 1998; Telch, Agras, Rossiter, Wilfley, & Kenardy, 1990; Wilfley et al., 1993), with behavioral weight control in three studies (Agras et al., 1994; Marcus et al., 1995; Porzelius et al., 1995), and with interpersonal psychotherapy in one study (Wilfley et al., 1993). CBT applied by means of either guided or self-help formats has been tested in three controlled trials (Carter & Fairburn, 1998; Loeb, Wilson, Gilbert, & Labouvie, 2000; Peterson et al., 1998). Overall, attrition rates for CBT have tended to be lower (range: 17%–35%, with an average of roughly 25%) than those observed in pharmacological trials (range: 14%–54%, with an average of roughly 30%).

All controlled trials of CBT for BED reported to date have observed significantly superior reductions and abstinence rates in binge eating and greater improvements in psychological measures than wait-list controls. Moreover, available follow-up data suggest that the improvements are robust and well sustained for at least 6 months posttreatment (Carter & Fairburn, 1998; Marcus et al., 1995; Wilfley et al., 1993). Marcus et al.

(1995), for example, reported that individual CBT reduced binge eating from an average of 22 binges/month to 0.7 binges/month and that the improvements were sustained at a 12-month follow-up. Wilfley et al. (1993) reported that group CBT produced a 48% reduction and a 28% abstinence rate in binge eating versus 28% and 0%, respectively, observed in the wait-list control condition. Carter and Fairburn (1998), in a 12-week "effectiveness" trial of a CBT manual applied in primary care settings, observed abstinence rates of 50% for guided self-help and 43% for pure self-help, versus 8% in the wait-list control condition.

Marcus et al. (1995) reported that individual behavioral weight loss therapy (moderate calorie reduction plus nutrition and exercise components) was comparable to CBT in reducing binge eating. However, the behavioral weight loss treatment resulted in an average weight loss of 21.6 lbs (9.79 kg), the majority of which was maintained during the posttreatment year, whereas the CBT produced no weight loss. A second (smaller) study (Porzelius et al., 1995) reported that obese patients with BED lost more weight in CBT than in behavioral weight loss regimens. Obese patients who did not binge benefited equally from the two approaches.

Combined or Sequenced Treatments

Controlled trials that have directly compared pharmacological and psychological treatments jointly and in combination are ongoing and await completion. To date, three studies have examined the benefit of adding antidepressants to either CBT or to behavioral weight loss treatments. Fluvoxamine (de Zwann et al., 1992), fluoxetine (Marcus et al., 1990), and desipramine (Agras et al., 1994) did not seem to contribute much added effect to either CBT or weight control treatments for reducing binge eating, although a slight advantage for producing short-term weight loss was observed. Further research is needed to determine the optimal combination or sequence of treatments for obese binge eaters to reduce binge eating, improve psychological functioning, and to produce lasting weight loss.

In evaluating either pharmacological or behavioral studies, however, it is particularly important to stress that most investigations have not found that reduced frequency of binging leads to significant weight loss. Only one controlled trial with *DSM–IV*-defined BED—an unpublished study by Marcus et al. (1995)—has reported significant weight loss as a benefit of reduction in binging. Marcus et al. (1995) reported that BED patients who received 6-month behavioral weight loss treatment lost an average of 21.6 lbs (9.79 kg), whereas patients who received CBT showed no weight change (the two treatments produced comparable and impressive reductions in binge eating). None of the pharmacotherapy trials and none of the CBT trials reported weight loss. The lack of efficacy in reducing weight is particularly striking for the CBT trials because these are characterized by impressive effect sizes of reduced binge eating.

Weight loss represents an important clinical need for obese patients with BED. As noted earlier, the initial findings from pre-*DSM–IV* BED research, and the initial promise of CBT and pharmacological interventions adapted from bulimia nervosa, have led clinical researchers, including myself (Wilfley et al., 1993; Wilfley, Grilo, & Rodin, 1997), to suggest that addressing the binge eating first rather than making weight loss the focus might represent a prudent clinical strategy. Recent findings, however, have reopened this issue, and the ideal sequence and treatments remain empirically unanswered questions.

Gladis et al. (1998) found no evidence that obese patients who binge eat fare less well in behavioral weight loss treatments than those who do not binge eat. Porzelius et al. (1995) reported that obese patients who were binge eaters had comparable reductions in binge eating in either a behavioral weight loss treatment or a behavioral weight loss treatment augmented with CBT components. It is interesting that Porzelius et al.—in contrast to Marcus et al. (1995)—found that obese binge eaters lost more weight in the CBT treatment than in the behavioral weight loss treatment. Limited sample size, uncertainty whether the obese binge eaters met BED criteria, and the "hybrid CBT" used make comparison of Porzelius et al.'s study with those of others difficult. Continued research in this area is clearly needed.

Agras et al. (1997) performed a 1-year follow-up of 93 obese female patients with BED who were treated with CBT. The reductions in binge eating and the remission rates were well sustained during the year following treatment, but weight regain was not uncommon. Agras et al. (1997) determined that patients who achieved complete abstinence from binge eating during treatment were likely to lose weight posttreatment. Indeed, patients who were completely abstinent from binge eating lost 8.81 lb (4.0 kg), whereas patients who did not achieve abstinence (even if substantially improved) from binge eating gained 7.93 lb (3.6 kg) by the 1-year follow-up. Seventy-four percent of patients who completely ceased binge eating lost weight following treatment.

The important role of exercise for weight control may also be critical for obese BED patients. One study (Levine, Marcus, & Moulton, 1996) reported that the addition of programmed exercise to behavioral weight loss treatment significantly enhanced the effect on binge eating and weight loss. This supports Marcus's (1997) clinical recommendation regarding the adaptation of CBT to the special needs of obese patients.

It remains unclear if medication or psychological intervention as single modalities represent optimum interventions as single modalities. Although comparison across studies with different designs is difficult, overall it seems that CBT trials tend to have lower attrition, more robust short-term outcomes, and are especially superior in terms of maintenance (whereas relapse tends to be rapid and nearly universal following medication discontinuation). Studies of combined pharmacological and psychological treatments have produced less than impressive results to date, but the outcome of well-designed ongoing combined treatment studies has yet to be determined.

General Treatment Issues and Interventions

Number of Calories and Type of Meal Plan

Substantial variation exists in the nutritional and caloric recommendations of different behavioral weight loss programs. Except for the case of VLCDs, most university-affiliated programs recommend a general goal of 1,200 kcal/day for producing weight loss. Given gender and individual differences in metabolic processes and energy expenditure, Grilo and Brownell (1998) recommended the following general approach to estimate calorie goals for a patient. First, begin with a 1,500 kcal/day goal for men and a 1,200 kcal/day goal for women and carefully monitor all food intake in a food diary. This information will allow for the calculation of the caloric intake necessary to accomplish weekly weight loss goals. This approach assumes intraperson variability over time because of changes in water loss, metabolic shifts, lean tissue loss, and changes in activity levels and thus will produce a more individualized caloric estimate. In addition to total caloric expenditure, any weight control program must consider balanced nutrition practices. The U.S. Department of Agriculture (1992) published the Food Guide Pyramid, which is now widely disseminated on many food packages. The Food Guide Pyramid schematically shows recommended dietary guidelines with clearly specified daily servings for all five food groups.

Research during the 1990s, using techniques such as doubly labeled water (Schoeller, 1988), has documented limitations in the reliability of dietary self-report and called into question claims that certain obese people do not eat substantially more than lean people do. Although both lean and obese people tend to underestimate their caloric intake, the underestimation by obese people has been found to be approximately 35%, which is substantially greater than underestimates by lean people (Bandini, Schoeller, Cyr, & Dietz, 1990; Lichtman et al., 1992; Prentice et al., 1986). Lichtman et al. (1992), for example, found that a sample of "diet-resistant" obese patients underestimated the amount of food they ate during a 2-week period by 47% and overestimated their level of physical activity by 51%.

These findings suggest that the failure to lose weight (or sustain weight loss) is due, to a considerable degree, to overeating and underactivity (i.e., noncompliance). A striking example of this is found in a study by Smith and Wing (1991), who found that the frequently observed pattern of less weight loss during a second trial of a VLCD versus the first trial was due to behavioral nonadherence rather than to hypothesized metabolic alterations due to caloric restriction. The important clinical implication is that professionals must devote time to the detailed description of caloric values and measurement and focus repeatedly on the value of careful ongoing self-monitoring (Wilson & Vitousek, 1999). Moreover, it may be particularly useful to have periodic reviews of caloric estimation to prevent "drift."

Exercise

Research strongly suggests that increased physical activity is a critical component of any program for weight loss (Bouchard, Despres, & Tremblay, 1993; Grilo, 1994; Grilo, Brownell, & Stunkard, 1993). Exercise alone, without dietary changes, is usually insufficient to produce significant weight loss in many obese people. The combination of exercise and diet, although not consistently associated with short-term weight loss, is usually associated with successful weight loss maintenance across different obese patient groups (Bryner, Toffle, Ulrich, & Yeater, 1997; Epstein, Wing, Koeske, Ossip, & Beck, 1982; Epstein, Wing, Koeske, & Valoski, 1984; Hill, Sparling, Shields, & Heller, 1987; Kayman, Bruvold, & Stern, 1990; Pavlou, Krey, & Steffee, 1989; Perri et al., 1988). Moreover, exercise predicts weight maintenance across different forms of dietary interventions (Pavlou et al., 1989).

Physical activity and fitness are associated with decreased morbidity and mortality by means of a number of possible mechanisms (Blair, Goodyear, Gibbons, & Cooper, 1984; Leon, Connett, Jacobs, & Rauramaa, 1987; Paffenbarger, Hyde, Wing, & Hsieh, 1986; Powell, Caspersen, Koplan, & Ford, 1989). The benefits of exercise may be especially salient in obese patients with poor health-risk factor profiles (Helmrich, Ragland, Leung, & Paffenbarger, 1991; Kanaley, Andresen-Reid, Oenning, Kottke, & Jensen, 1993). Wood et al. (1988) found that the combination of moderate exercise and the National Cholesterol Education Program Diet was necessary for improving lipoprotein and apolipoprotein ratios in moderately overweight sedentary people. It appears that exercise can result in health improvement even with only minimal weight loss (Powell et al., 1989; Wood et al., 1988). Moreover, studies from the Cooper Institute have provided impressive evidence that fitness protects against health risks even in overweight people (Barlow, Kohl, Gibbons, & Blair, 1995; Lee et al., 1998). Recent convergent findings from well-controlled studies suggest that modest levels of physical activity may be sufficient to produce improvements in health (Barlow et al., 1995; Blair et al., 1989; DeBusk, Stenestrand, Sheehan, & Haskell, 1990; Duncan, Gordon, & Scott, 1991; Helmrich et al., 1991; Rippe, Ward, Porcari, & Freedson, 1988). Two recent randomized controlled clinical trials suggested that lifestyle physical activity interventions may be as effective as structured exercise programs. Dunn et al. (1999) reported that in previously sedentary healthy adults lifestyle exercise was similar in efficacy to a structured exercise program in improving physical activity, cardiorespiratory fitness, and blood pressure. Anderson et al. (1999) reported that the addition of lifestyle exercise or structured exercise to a behavior therapy program produced similar improvements in obese women.

Weight Loss Goals

Emerging evidence suggests that weight losses as little as 10% may result in significant health benefits (Blackburn, 1995). Such weight losses are cosmetically and psychologically disappointing to the majority of obese patients entering treatment (Foster, Wadden, Vogt, & Brewer, 1997). The so-called 10% solution has increasingly been voiced by obesity experts given emerging—albeit uncertain—evidence (Yanovski, Bain, & Williamson, 1999) for the beneficial effects of weight loss as little as 10% (Blackburn, 1995; Foster & Kendall, 1994; Goldstein, 1991; Wadden, Steen, Wingate, & Foster, 1996; Wing et al., 1987).

The important implication is that professionals work sensitively with obese patients to establish goals that can be reasonably attained and maintained. Research shows that most obese patients hold unrealistic and unattainable weight loss goals (Foster et al., 1997) that may contribute to frustration with their programs or with themselves. Discussing weight loss goals and expectations is an important step early in treatment. Sharing with patients the important health benefits that can potentially be achieved with modest weight losses is one step.

Summary and Conclusions

In this chapter I have provided an overview of some of the major issues relevant to the assessment and treatment of obesity. While maintaining a view toward presenting issues relevant for rational pharmacological treatment for obesity, I have attempted to rely most heavily on empirically supported approaches. The following represent the major treatment issues that follow from this review:

1. There currently exists no established patient–treatment matching algorithm, although significant advances have been made in recent years to provide guidelines for comprehensive treatment. In general, the greater the obesity, and the greater the medical morbidities (or risk) present, the greater the justification for considering the addition of pharmacotherapy (Manson & Faich, 1996).
2. On the basis of current knowledge, a comprehensive program involving improved nutrition (eating less and eating better), increased physical activity, and behavior and lifestyle change is likely to be continuously required for successful weight loss maintenance. There currently exists no established role for medication-only treatment for obesity.
3. Given the complexities of obesity and energy regulation, further enhancement of long-term outcome, as least for some patients, may be accomplished by means of the integration of pharmacological approaches into the comprehensive treatment package.
4. There currently exists no established long-term medication treatment approach or algorithm for obesity. This represents one of the greatest challenges facing the field. Obesity is increasingly viewed as a long-term chronic physical problem that requires (in many cases) ongoing attention. Future research needs to consider how best to safely integrate medication treatments (e.g., sequentially

using both medication monotherapies or combined medication therapies) with other energy-balance (diet and exercise) and psychological (behavioral, cognitive–behavioral) approaches (Grilo, Devlin, Cachelin, & Yanouski, 1997).

5. Certain medication approaches may be indicated for certain subgroups of obese patients. For instance, the presence of BED may indicate the need for antidepressant medication either alone or in combination with specific psychological therapies, such as CBT.

6. The presence of medical conditions that are either independent from or associated with the obesity may require ongoing medication management. Careful consideration is required of the medication regimens and potential interactions with potential medications for obesity, binge eating, or associated problems.

7. Greater attention needs to be paid to the multiple benefits (e.g., health profile, fitness, psychological benefits) of behavioral and lifestyle change, instead of the traditional focus on weight loss per se.

References

Abenhaim, L., Moride, Y., Brenot, F., Rich, S., Benichou, J., Kurz, X., Higgenbottam, T., Oakley, C., Wouters, E., Aubler, M., Simonneau, G., & Begaud, B. (1996). Appetite-suppressant drugs and the risk of primary pulmonary hypertension. *New England Journal of Medicine, 336,* 609–616.

Agras, W. S., Telch, C. F., Arnow, B., Eldredge, K., & Marnell, M. (1997). One year followup of cognitive behavioral therapy for obese individuals with binge eating disorder. *Journal of Consulting and Clinical Psychology, 65,* 343–347.

Agras, W. S., Telch, C. F., Arnow, B., Eldredge, K., Wilfley, D. E., Raeburn, S. D., Henderson, J., & Marnell, M. (1994). Weight loss, cognitive–behavioral, and desipramine treatments in binge eating disorder: An additive design. *Behavior Therapy, 25,* 225–238.

Alger, S. A., Schwalberg, M. D., Bigaouette, J. M., Michalek, A. V., & Howard, L. J. (1991). Effect of a tricyclic antidepressant and opiate antagonist on binge-eating behavior in normal weight bulimic and obese binge-eating subjects. *American Journal of Clinical Nutrition, 53,* 865–871.

Allison, D. B., & Saunders, S. (1999). Three prescription weight loss medications—A review. *Weight Control Digest, 9,* 829–832.

American Psychiatric Association. (1994). *Diagnostic and statistical manual of mental disorders* (4th ed.). Washington, DC: Author.

Anderson, R. E., Wadden, T. A., Bartlett, S. J., Zemel, B., Verde, T. J., & Franckowiak, S. C. (1999). Effects of lifestyle activity vs structured aerobic exercise in obese women. *Journal of the American Medical Association, 281,* 335–340.

Atkinson, R. L. (1997). Use of drugs in the treatment of obesity. *Annual Review of Nutrition, 17,* 383–403.

Atkinson, R. L., Blank, R. C., Loper, J. F., Schumacher, D., & Lutes, R. A. (1995). Combined drug treatment of obesity. *Obesity Research, 3,* 497S–500S.

Bandini, L. G., Schoeller, D., Cyr, H. N., & Dietz, W. H. (1990). Validity of reported energy intake in obese and nonobese adolescents. *American Journal of Clinical Nutrition, 52,* 421–425.

Barlow, C. E., Kohl, H. W., Gibbons, L. W., & Blair, S. N. (1995). Physical fitness, mortality and obesity. *International Journal of Obesity, 19,* S41–S44.

Benotti, P. N., & Forse, R. A. (1995). The role of gastric surgery in the multidisciplinary management of severe obesity. *American Journal of Surgery, 169,* 361–367.

Blackburn, G. L. (1995). Effect of degree of weight loss on health benefits. *Obesity Research*, *3*, 211S–216S.

Blackwell, G. L., & Kanders, B. S. (1987). Medical evaluation and treatment of the obese patient with cardiovascular disease. *American Journal of Cardiology*, *60*, 55–58.

Blair, S. N., Goodyear, N. N., Gibbons, L. W., & Cooper, K. H. (1984). Physical activity and incidence of hypertension in healthy normotensive men and women. *Journal of the American Medical Association*, *252*, 487–490.

Blair, S. N., Kohl, H. W., Paffenberger, R. S., Clark, D. G., Cooper, K. H., & Gibbons, L. W. (1989). Physical fitness and all-cause mortality: A prospective study of healthy men and women. *Journal of the American Medical Association*, *262*, 2395–2401.

Bouchard, C., Despres, J. P., & Tremblay, A. (1993). Exercise and obesity. *Obesity Research*, *1*, 133–147.

Bray, G. A. (1978). Definitions, measurements, and classification of the syndrome of obesity. *International Journal of Obesity*, *2*, 99.

Bray, G. A. (1992). Drug treatment of obesity. *American Journal of Clinical Nutrition*, *55*, 538–544.

Bray, G. A. (1995). Evaluation of drugs for treating obesity. *Obesity Research*, *3*(Suppl. 4), 425S–434S.

Bray, G. A. (1998). Obesity: A time bomb to be defused. *The Lancet*, *352*, 160–161.

Bray, G. A., Blackburn, G. L., Ferguson, J. M., Greenway, F. L., Jain, A. K., Mendel, C. M., Ryan, D. H., Schwartz, S. L., Scheinbaum, M. L., & Seaton, T. B. (1999). Sibutramine-dose response and long-term efficacy in weight loss, a double-blind study. *International Journal of Obesity*, *18*, 60.

Bray, G. A., & Gray, D. S. (1988). Obesity: Part I—Pathogenesis. *Western Journal of Medicine*, *149*, 429–441.

Bray, G. A., Ryan, D. H., Gordon, D., Heidingsfelder, S., Cerise, F., & Wilson, K. (1996). A double-blind randomized placebo-controlled trial of sibutramine. *Obesity Research*, *5*, 578–586.

Brownell, K. D. (2000). *The LEARN 2000 program for weight control*. Dallas, TX: American Health.

Brownell, K. D., & Jeffery, R. W. (1987). Improving long-term weight loss: Pushing the limits of treatment. *Behavior Therapy*, *18*, 353–374.

Brownell, K. D., & Kramer, F. M. (1989). Behavioral management of obesity. *Medical Clinics of North America*, *73*, 185–201.

Brownell, K. D., & Rodin, J. (1994). The dieting maelstrom: Is it possible and advisable to lose weight? *American Psychologist*, *49*, 781–791.

Brownell, K. D., & Stunkard, A. J. (1981). Couples training, pharmocotherapy, and behavior therapy in the treatment of obesity. *Archives of General Psychiatry*, *38*, 1224–1229.

Brownell, K. D., & Wadden, T. A. (1991). The heterogeneity of obesity: Fitting treatments to individuals. *Behavior Therapy*, *22*, 153–177.

Brownell, K. D., & Wadden, T. A. (1992). Etiology and treatment of obesity: Toward understanding a serious, prevalent, and refractory disorder. *Journal of Consulting and Clinical Psychology*, *60*, 505–517.

Bryner, R. W., Toffle, R. C., Ulrich, I. H., & Yeater, R. A. (1997). The effects of exercise intensity on body composition, weight loss, and dietary composition in women. *Journal of the American College of Nutrition*, *16*, 68–73.

Carter, J. C., & Fairburn, C. G. (1998). Cognitive–behavioral self-help for binge eating disorder: A controlled effectiveness study. *Journal of Consulting and Clinical Psychology*, *66*, 616–623.

Chagnon, Y. C., Perusse, L., & Bouchard, C. (1998). The human obesity gene map: The 1997 updates. *Obesity Research*, *6*, 76–92.

Craighead, L. W. (1984). Sequencing of behavior therapy and pharmacotherapy for obesity. *Journal of Consulting and Clinical Psychology*, *52*, 190–199.

Craighead, L. W., Stunkard, A. J., & O'Brien, R. (1981). Behavioral therapy and pharmacotherapy of obesity. *Archives of General Psychiatry*, *38*, 763–768.

Davidson, M. H., Hauptman, J., DiGirolamo, M., Foreyt, J. P., Halsted, C. H., Heber, D., Heimburger, D. C., Lucas, C. P., Robbins, D. C., Chung, J., & Heymsfield, S. B. (1999). Weight control and risk factor reduction in obese subjects treated for 2 years with or-listat: A randomized controlled trial. *Journal of the American Medical Association, 281,* 235–242.

DeBusk, R. F., Stenestrand, U., Sheehan, M., & Haskell, W. L. (1990). Training effects of long versus short bouts of exercise in healthy subjects. *American Journal of Cardiology, 65,* 1010–1013.

de Zwann, M., Nutzinger, D. O., & Schnoenbeck, G. (1992). Binge eating in overweight women. *Comprehensive Psychiatry, 33,* 256–261.

Dhurandhar, N. V., & Atkinson, R. L. (1998). Drug treatment of obesity: A status report. *Weight Control Digest, 8,* S1–S11.

Douglas, J. G., Preston, P. G., Haslett, C., Gough, J., Frasier, I., Chalmers, S. R., & Munro, J. F. (1983). Long-term efficacy of fenfluramine in treatment of obesity. *The Lancet, 1*(8321), 384–386.

Drent, M. L., & Van der Veen, E. A. (1993). Lipase inhibition: A novel concept in the treatment of obesity. *International Journal of Obesity, 17,* 241–244.

Drouin, P., Hanotin, C., Courcier, S., & Leutenegger, E. (1994). A dose ranging study: Efficacy and tolerability of sibutramine in weight loss. *International Journal of Obesity, 18,* 60.

Duncan, J. J., Gordon, N. F., & Scott, C. B. (1991). Women walking for health and fitness: How much is enough? *Journal of the American Medical Association, 266,* 3295–3299.

Dunn, A. L., Marcus, S. H., Kampert, J. B., Garcia, M. E., Kohl, H. W., & Blair, S. N. (1999). Comparison of lifestyle and structured interventions to increase physical activity and cardiorespiratory fitness: A randomized trial. *Journal of the American Medical Association, 281,* 327–334.

Eckel, R. H. (1997). Obesity in heart disease. *Circulation, 96,* 3248–3250.

Eckel, R. H., & Kraus, R. H. (1998). American Heart Association call to action: Obesity as a major risk factor for coronary heart disease. *Circulation, 97,* 2099–2100.

Epstein, L. H., Wing, R. R., Koeske, R., Ossip, D. J., & Beck, S. (1982). A comparison of lifestyle change and programmed aerobic exercise on weight and fitness changes in obese children. *Behavior Therapy, 13,* 651–665.

Epstein, L. H., Wing, R. R., Koeske, R., & Valoski, A. (1984). The effects of diet plus exercise on weight change in parents and children. *Journal of Consulting and Clinical Psychology, 52,* 429–437.

Fairburn, C. G., & Beglin, S. J. (1994). Assessment of eating disorders: Interview or self-report questionnaire? *International Journal of Eating Disorders, 16,* 363–370.

Fairburn, C. G., & Cooper, Z. (1993). The Eating Disorder Examination (12th ed.), In C. G. Fairburn & G. T. Wilson (Eds.), *Binge eating: Nature, assessment and treatment* (pp. 317–360). New York: Guilford Press.

Fairburn, C. G., Marcus, M., & Wilson, G. T. (1993). Cognitive behavioral therapy for binge eating and bulimia nervosa: A comprehensive treatment manual. In C. Fairburn & G. T. Wilson (Eds.), *Binge eating: Nature, assessment, and treatment* (pp. 361–404). New York: Guilford Press.

Ferster, C. B., Nurnberger, J. I., & Levitt, E. E. (1962). The control of eating. *Journal of Mathetics, 1,* 87–109.

Flegal, K. M., Carroll, M. D., Kuczmarski, R., & Johnson, C. L. (1998). Overweight and obesity in the United States: Prevalence and trends, 1960–1994. *International Journal of Obesity and Related Metabolic Disorders, 22,* 39–47.

Fluoxetine Bulimia Nervosa Collaborative Study Group. (1992). Fluoxetine in the treatment of bulimia nervosa. *Archives of General Psychiatry, 49,* 139–147.

Foster, G. D., & Kendall, P. C. (1994). The realistic treatment of obesity: Changing the scales of success. *Clinical Psychology Review, 14,* 701–736.

Foster, G. D., Wadden, T. A., Peterson, F. J., Letizia, K. A., Bartlett, S. J., & Conill, A. M. (1992). A controlled comparison of three very-low-calorie diets: Effects on weight, body composition, and symptoms. *American Journal of Clinical Nutrition, 55,* 811–817.

Foster, G. D., Wadden, T. A., Vogt, R. A., & Brewer, G. (1997). What is a reasonable weight? Patient expectations and evaluations of obesity treatment outcomes. *Journal of Consulting and Clinical Psychology, 65*, 79–85.

Friedman, M. A., & Brownell, K. D. (1995). Psychological correlates of obesity: Moving to the next research generation. *Psychological Bulletin, 117*, 3–17.

Galloway, S. M., Farquhar, D. L., & Munro, J. F. (1984). The current status of anti-obesity drugs. *Postgraduate Medical Journal, 60*, 19–26.

Gladis, M. M., Wadden, T. A., Vogt, R., Foster, G., Kuehnel, R. H., & Bartlett, S. J. (1998). Behavioral treatment of obese binge eaters: Do they need different care? *Journal of Psychosomatic Research, 44*, 375–384.

Goldstein, D. J. (1991). Beneficial effects of modest weight loss. *International Journal of Obesity, 16*, 397–416.

Goldstein, D., & Potvin, J. (1994). Long-term weight loss: The effects of pharmacologic agents. *American Journal of Clinical Nutrition, 60*, 647–657.

Goldstein, D. J., Rampey, A. H., Roback, P. J., Wilson, M. G., Hamilton, S. H., Sayler, M. E., & Tollefson, G. D. (1995). Efficacy and safety of long-term fluoxetine for obesity —Maximizing success. *Obesity Research, 3*(Suppl. 4), 481S–490S.

Goodrick, G. K., Poston II, W. S. C., Kimball, K. T., Reeves, R. S., & Foreyt, J. P. (1998). Nondieting versus dieting treatment for overweight binge-eating women. *Journal of Consulting and Clinical Psychology, 66*, 363–368.

Grilo, C. M. (1994). Physical activity and obesity. *Biomedicine and Pharmacotherapy, 48*, 127–136.

Grilo, C. M. (1996). Treatment of obesity: An integrative model. In J. K. Thompson (Ed.), *Body image, eating disorders, and obesity: An integrative guide for assessment and treatment* (pp. 389–423). Washington, DC: American Psychological Association.

Grilo, C. M. (1998). The assessment and treatment of binge eating disorder. *Journal of Practical Psychiatry and Behavioral Health, 4*, 191–201.

Grilo, C. M. (in press). Binge eating disorder. In C. G. Fairburn & K. D. Brownell (Eds.), *Comprehensive textbook of obesity and eating disorders*. New York: Guilford Press.

Grilo, C. M., & Brownell, K. D. (1998). Interventions for weight management. In *ACSM resource manual for guidelines for exercise testing and prescription* (3rd ed.). Philadelphia: Lea & Fibiger.

Grilo, C. M., Brownell, K. D., & Stunkard, A. J. (1993). The metabolic and psychological importance of exercise in weight control. In A. J. Stunkard & T. A. Wadden (Eds.), *Obesity: Theory and therapy* (pp. 253–273). New York: Raven Press.

Grilo, C. M., & Devlin, M. J. (1997). Medication treatments for binge eating disorder. *Weight Control Digest, 7*, 633–639.

Grilo, C. M., Devlin, M. J., Cachelin, F. M., & Yanovski, S. (1997). Report of the NIH workshop on the development of research priorities in eating disorders. *Psychopharmacology Bulletin, 33*, 321–333.

Grilo, C. M., Masheb, R. M., & Wilson, G. T. (in press). A comparison of different methods for assessing the features of eating disorders in patients with binge eating disorder. *Journal of Consulting and Clinical Psychology.*

Grilo, C. M., Shiffman, S., & Wing, R. R. (1989). Relapse crises and coping among dieters. *Journal of Consulting and Clinical Psychology, 57*, 488–495.

Grilo, C. M., Shiffman, S., & Wing, R. R. (1993). Coping with dietary relapse crises and their aftermath. *Addictive Behaviors, 18*, 89–102.

Grilo, C. M., Wilfley, D. E., Jones, A., Brownell, K. D., & Rodin, J. (1994). The social self, body dissatisfaction, and binge eating in obese females. *Obesity Research, 2*, 24–27.

Guy-Grand, B., Apfelbaum, M., Crepaldi, G., Greis, A., Lefebvre, P., & Turner, P. (1989). International trial of long-term dexfenfluramine in obesity. *The Lancet, 2*(8672), 1142–1145.

Hanotin, C., Thomas, F., Jones, S. P., Leutenegger, E., & Drouin, P. (1998). Efficacy and tolerability of sibutramine in obese patients: A dose-ranging study. *International Journal of Obesity, 22*, 32–38.

Harp, J. B. (1998). An assessment of the efficacy and safety of orlistat for the long-term management of obesity. *Journal of Nutrition and Biochemistry, 9*, 516–521.

Hauptman, J. B., Jeunet, F. S., & Hartmann, D. (1992). Initial studies in humans with the novel gastrointestinal lipase inhibitor Ro 18-0647 (tetrahydrolipstatin). *American Journal of Clinical Nutrition, 55*(Suppl. 1), 309S–313S.

Hay, P. J., & Fairburn, C. G. (1998). The validity of the *DSM–IV* scheme for classifying bulimic eating disorders. *International Journal of Eating Disorders, 23*, 7–15.

Helmrich, S. P., Ragland, D. R., Leung, R. W., & Paffenbarger, R. S. (1991). Physical activity and reduced occurrence of non-insulin-dependent diabetes mellitus. *New England Journal of Medicine, 325*, 147–152.

Hill, J. O., Sparling, P. B., Shields, T. W., & Heller, P. A. (1987). Effects of exercise and food restriction on body composition and metabolic rate in obese women. *American Journal of Clinical Nutrition, 46*, 622–630.

Hoffman-La Roche (1998). Orlistat monograph. Basel, Switzerland.

Hollander, P. A., Elbein, S. C., Hirsch, I. B., Kelley, O., McGill, J., Taylor, T., Weiss, S. R., Crockett, S. E., Kaplan, R. A., Comstock, J., Lucas, C. P., Lodewick, P. A., Canovatchel, W., Chung, J., & Hauptman, J. (1998). Role of orlistat in the treatment of obese patients with type 2 diabetes. *Diabetes Care, 21*, 1288–1294.

Hsu, G. L. K., Benotti, P. N., Dwyer, J., Roberts, S., Saltzman, E., Shikora, S., Rolls, B. J., & Rand, W. (1998). Nonsurgical factors that influence the outcome of bariatric surgery: A review. *Psychosomatic Medicine, 60*, 338–346.

Hudson, J. I., McElroy, S. L., Raymond, N. C., Crow, S., Keck, P. E., Carter, W. P., Michell, J. E., Strakowski, S. M., Pope, H. G., Coleman, B. S., & Jonas, J. M. (1998). Fluvoxamine treatment of binge eating disorder: A multicenter, placebo-controlled trial. *American Journal of Psychiatry, 155*, 1756–1762.

Jones, S. P., Newman, B. M., & Romanec, F. M. (1994). Sibutramine hydrochloride: Weight loss in overweight subjects. *International Journal of Obesity and Related Metabolic Disorders, 18*, 61.

Jones, S. P., Smith, I. G., Kelly, F., & Gray, J. A. (1995). Long term weight loss with sibutramine [Abstract]. *International Journal of Obesity, 19*(Suppl. 2), 41.

Kanaley, J. A., Andresen-Reid, M. L., Oenning, L., Kottke, B. A., & Jensen, M. D. (1993). Differential health benefits of weight loss in upper-body and lower-body obese women. *American Journal of Clinical Nutrition, 57*, 20–26.

Kayman, S., Bruvold, W., & Stern, J. S. (1990). Maintenance and relapse after weight loss in women: Behavioral aspects. *American Journal of Clinical Nutrition, 52*, 800–807.

Knoll Pharmaceuticals. (1997). *Meridia monograph*. Mt. Olive, NJ: Author.

Kramer, F. M., Jeffery, R. W., Forster, J. L., & Snell, M. K. (1989). Long-term follow-up of behavioral treatment for obesity: Patterns of weight regain in men and women. *International Journal of Obesity, 13*, 123–136.

Kuczmarski, R. J. (1992). Prevalence of overweight and weight gain in the United States. *American Journal of Clinical Nutrition, 55*, 495S–502S.

Kuczmarski, R. J., Carroll, M. D., Flegal, K. M., & Troiano, R. P. (1997). Varying body mass index cutoff points to describe overweight prevalence among U.S. adults: NHANES III (1998 to 1994). *Obesity Research, 5*, 542–548.

Kuehnel, R. H., & Wadden, T. A. (1994). Binge eating disorder, weight cycling, and psychopathology. *International Journal of Eating Disorders, 15*, 321–329.

Kurz, X., & Van Ermen, A. (1997). Valvular heart disease associated with fenfluramine-phentermine. *New England Journal of Medicine, 337*, 1772–1773.

Lean, M. E. J. (1997). Sibutramine—A review of clinical efficacy. *International Journal of Obesity, 21*, S30–36.

Lee, C. D., Jackson, A. S., & Blair, S. N. (1998). US weight guidelines: Is it also important to consider cardiorespiratory fitness? *International Journal of Obesity, 22*, S2–S7.

Leon, A. S., Connett, J., Jacobs, D. R., & Rauramaa, R. (1987). Leisure-time physical activity levels and risk of coronary heart disease and death. *Journal of the American Medical Association, 258*, 2388–2395.

Levine, M., Marcus, M. D., & Moulton, P. (1996). Exercise in the treatment of binge eating disorder. *International Journal of Eating Disorders, 19*, 171–177.

Lichtenbelt, W. V. M., & Fogelholm, M. (1999). Body composition. In M. S. Westerterp-Plantenga, A. B. Steffens, & A. Tremblay (Eds.), *Regulation of food intake and energy expenditure* (pp. 383–404). Milano, Italy: Medical Publishing and New Media.

Lichtman, S. W., Pisarska, K., Berman, E. R., Pestone, M., Dowling, H., Offenbacher, E., Weisel, H., Heshka, S., Matthews, D. W., & Heymsfield, S. B. (1992). Discrepancy between self-reported and actual caloric intake and exercise in obese subjects. *New England Journal of Medicine, 327,* 1893–1898.

Loeb, K. L., Wilson, G. T., Gilbert, J. S., & Labouvie, E. (2000). Guided and unguided self-help for binge eating. *Behaviour Research and Therapy, 38,* 259–272.

Manson, J. E., Colditz, G. A., Stampfer, M. J., Willet, W. C., Rosner, B., Monson, R. R., Speizer, F. E., & Hennekens, C. H. (1990). A prospective study of obesity and risk of coronary heart disease in women. *New England Journal of Medicine, 322,* 882–889.

Manson, J. E., & Faich, G. A. (1996). Pharmacotherapy for obesity—Do the benefits outweigh the risk? *New England Journal of Medicine, 335,* 659–660.

Manson, J. E., Willett, W. C., Stampfer, M., Colditz, G. A., Hunter, D. J., Hankinson, S. E., Hennekens, C. H., & Speizer, F. E. (1995). Body weight and mortality among women. *New England Journal of Medicine, 333,* 677–685.

Marcus, M. D. (1997). Adapting treatment for patients with binge eating disorder. In D. M. Garner & P. Garfinkel (Eds.), *Handbook of treatment for binge eating disorders* (2nd ed., pp. 484–493). New York: Guilford Press.

Marcus, M. D., Wing, R. R., Ewing, L., Kern, E., McDermott, M., & Gooding, W. (1990). A double-blind, placebo-controlled trial of fluoxetine plus behavior modification in the treatment of obese binge eaters. *American Journal of Psychiatry, 147,* 876–881.

Marcus, M. D., Wing, R., & Fairburn, C. (1995). Cognitive treatment of binge eating versus behavioral weight control in the treatment of binge eating disorder. *Annals of Behavioral Medicine, 17,* S090.

Marcus, M. D., Wing, R. R., & Hopkins, J. (1988). Obese binge eaters: Affect, cognitions, and response to behavioral weight control treatment. *Journal of Consulting and Clinical Psychology, 56,* 433–439.

Marlatt, G. A., & Gordon, J. R. (1985). (Eds.). *Relapse prevention: Maintenance strategies in the treatment of addictive behaviors.* New York: Guilford Press.

Masheb, R. M., & Grilo, C. M. (2000). Binge eating disorder: The need for additional diagnostic criteria. *Comprehensive Psychiatry, 41,* 159–162.

McCann, U. D., & Agras, W. S. (1990). Successful treatment of nonpurging bulimia nervosa with desipramine: A double-blind, placebo-controlled study. *American Journal of Psychiatry, 147,* 1509–1513.

McCann, U., Seiden, L., Rubin, L., & Ricaurte, G. (1997). Brain serotonin neurotoxicity and primary pulmonary hypertension from fenfluramine and dexfenfluramine. *Journal of the American Medical Association, 278,* 666–672.

McElroy, S. L., Casuto, L. S., Nelson, E. B., Lake, K. A., Soutullo, C. A., Keck, P. E., & Hudson, J. I. (2000). Placebo-controlled trial of sertraline in the treatment of binge eating disorder. *American Journal of Psychiatry, 157,* 1004–1006.

Metropolitan Life Insurance Company. (1983). 1983 metropolitan height and weight tables. *Statistical Bulletin of the Metropolitan Life Insurance Company, 64,* 2.

National Task Force on the Prevention and Treatment of Obesity. (2000). Overweight, obesity, and health risk. *Archives of Internal Medicine, 160,* 898–904.

Paffenbarger, R. S., Hyde, R. T., Wing, A. L., & Hsieh, C. C. (1986). Physical activity, all cause mortality, and longevity of college alumni. *New England Journal of Medicine, 314,* 605–613.

Pavlou, K. N., Krey, S., & Steffee, W. P. (1989). Exercise as an adjunct to weight loss and maintenance in moderately obese subjects. *American Journal of Clinical Nutrition, 49,* 1115–1123.

Perri, M. G., McAllister, D. A., Gange, J. J., Jordan, R. C., McAdoo, W. G., & Nezu, A. M. (1988). Effects of four maintenance programs on the long-term management of obesity. *Journal of Consulting and Clinical Psychology, 56,* 529–534.

Perri, M. G., Nezu, A. M., & Viegener, B. J. (1992). *Improving the long-term management of obesity: Theory, research, and clinical guidelines.* New York: Wiley.

Peterson, C. B., Mitchell, J. E., Engbloom, S., Nugent, S., Mussell, M. P., & Miller, J. P. (1998). Group cognitive–behavioral treatment of binge eating disorder: A comparison of therapist-led versus self-help formats. *International Journal of Eating Disorders, 24,* 125–136.

Porzelius, L. K., Houston, C., Smith, M., Arfken, C., & Fisher, E. (1995). Comparison of a standard behavioral weight loss treatment and a binge eating weight loss treatment. *Behavioral Therapy, 26*, 119–134.

Powell, K. E., Caspersen, C. J., Koplan, J. P., & Ford, E. S. (1989). Physical activity and chronic disease. *American Journal of Clinical Nutrition, 49*, 999–1006.

Prentice, A. M., Black, A. E., Coward, W. A., Davies, H. L., Goldberg, G. R., Murgatroyd, P. R., Ashford, J., Sawyer, M., & Whitehead, R. G. (1986). High levels of energy expenditure in obese women. *British Medical Journal, 292*, 983–987.

Rippe, J. M., Ward, A., Porcari J. P., & Freedson, P. S. (1988). Walking for health and fitness. *Journal of the American Medical Association, 259*, 2720–2724.

Schlundt, D. G., Sbrocco, T., & Bell, C. (1989). Identification of high risk situations in a behavioral weight loss program: Application of the relapse prevention model. *International Journal of Obesity, 13*, 223–234.

Schoeller, D. A. (1988). Measurement of energy expenditure in free-living humans by using doubly-labeled water. *Journal of Nutrition, 118*, 1278–1289.

Scoville, B. A. (1975). Review of amphetamine-like drugs by the Food and Drug Administration: Clinical data and value judgements. In G. A. Bray (Ed.), *Obesity in perspective* (DHEW [NIH] Publication No. 75-708). Washington, DC: U.S. Government Printing Office.

Seagle, H. M., Bessesen, D. H., & Hill, J. O. (1998). Effects of sibutramine on resting metabolic rate and weight loss in overweight women. *Obesity Research, 6*, 115–121.

Sjostrom, C. D., Lissner, L., Wedel, H., & Sjostrom, L. (1999). Reduction in incidence of diabetes, hypertension, and lipid disturbances after intentional weight loss induced by bariatric surgery: The SOS Intervention Study. *Obesity Research, 7*, 477–484.

Sjostrom, L., Rissanen, A., Andersen, T., Boldrin, M., Golay, A., Koppeschaar, H. P. F., Krempf, M., for the European Multicentre Orlistat Study Group. (1998). Randomized placebo-controlled trial of orlistat for weight loss and prevention of weight regain in obese patients. *The Lancet, 352*, 167–172.

Smith, D. E., & Wing, R. R. (1991). Diminished weight loss and behavioral compliance during repeated diets in obese patients with Type II diabetes. *Health Psychology, 10*, 378–383.

Spitzer, R. L., Devlin, M., Walsh, B. T., Hasin, D., Wing, R. R., Marcus, M. D., Stunkard, A. J., Wadden, T. A., Yanovski, S., Agras, W. S., Mitchell, J., & Nonas, C. (1992). Binge eating disorder: A multi-site field trial of the diagnostic criteria. *International Journal of Eating Disorders, 11*, 191–203.

Spitzer, R. L., Yanovski, S., Wadden, T., Wing, R., Marcus, M., Stunkard, A., Devlin, M., Mitchell, J., & Hasin, D. (1993). Binge eating disorder: Its further validation in a multisite study. *International Journal of Eating Disorders, 13*, 137–153.

Stunkard, A. J. (1959). Eating patterns and obesity. *Psychiatric Quarterly, 33*, 284–295.

Stunkard, A. J. (1992). An overview of current treatments for obesity. In T. A. Wadden & T. B. Van Itallie (Eds.), *Treatment of the seriously obese patient* (pp. 33–43). New York: Guilford Press.

Stunkard, A. J. (1994). Binge eating disorder and the treatment of obesity. *Obesity Research, 2*, 279–280.

Stunkard, A. J., Berkowitz, R., Tanrikut, C., Reiss, E., & Young, L. (1996). d-Fenfluramine treatment of binge eating disorder. *American Journal of Psychiatry, 153*, 1455–1459.

Stunkard, A. J., & Berthold, H. C. (1985). What is behavior therapy: A very short description of behavioral weight control. *American Journal of Clinical Nutrition, 41*, 821–823.

Sugarman, H. J., Starkey, J. V., & Birkenhauer, R. (1987). A randomized prospective trial of gastric bypass versus vertical banded gastroplasty for morbid obesity and their effects on sweets versus non-sweets eaters. *American Surgery, 205*, 613–624.

Telch, C. F., & Agras, W. S. (1994). Obesity, binge eating, and psychopathology: Are they related? *International Journal of Eating Disorders, 15*, 53–61.

Telch, C. F., Agras, W. S., & Rossiter, E. M. (1988). Binge eating increases with increasing adiposity. *International Journal of Eating Disorders, 7*, 115–119.

Telch, C. F., Agras, W. S., Rossiter, E., Wilfley, D., & Kenardy, J. (1990). Group cognitive–

behavioral treatment for the non-purging bulimic: An initial evaluation. *Journal of Consulting and Clinical Psychology, 58,* 629–635.

Tonstad, S., Pometta, D., Erkelens, D., Ose, L., Moccetti, T., Schouten, J., Golay, A., Reitsma, J., Del Bufalo, A., & Pasotti, E. (1994). The effect of the gastrointestinal lipase inhibitor, orlistat, on serum lipids and lipoprotiens in patients with primary hyperlipidaemia. *European Journal of Clinical Pharmacology, 46,* 405–410.

U.S. Department of Agriculture. (1992). Food guide pyramid. In *Home and Garden Bulletin,* No. 252, Human Nutrition Information Service, Washington, DC: Author.

U.S. Department of Health and Human Services, National Institutes of Health, and the National Heart, Lung and Blood Institute. (1998). *Clinical guidelines on the identification, evaluation and treatment of overweight and obesity in adults—The evidence report.* Rockville, MD: Author.

Wadden, T. A., & Bartlett, S. J. (1992). Very low calorie diets: An overview and appraisal. In T. A. Wadden & T. B. Van Itallie (Eds.), *Treatment of the seriously obese patient* (pp. 44–79). New York: Guilford Press.

Wadden, T. A., Berkowitz, R. I., Vogt, R. A., Steen, S. N., Stunkard, A. J., & Foster, G. D. (1997). Lifestyle modification in the pharmacologic treatment of obesity: A pilot investigation of a potential primary care approach. *Obesity Research, 5,* 218–226.

Wadden, T. A., Foster, G. D., & Letizia, K. A. (1992). Response of obese binge eaters to behavior therapy combined with very low calorie diet. *Journal of Consulting and Clinical Psychology, 60,* 808–811.

Wadden, T. A., Foster, G. D., & Letizia, K. A. (1994). One-year behavioral treatment of obesity: Comparison of moderate and severe caloric restriction and the effects of weight maintenance therapy. *Journal of Consulting and Clinical Psychology, 62,* 165–171.

Wadden, T. A., Steen, S. N., Wingate, B. J., & Foster, G. D. (1996). Psycho-social consequences of weight reduction: How much weight loss is enough? *American Journal of Clinical Nutrition, 63,* 461–465.

Wadden, T. A., Sternberg, J. A., Letizia, K. A., Stunkard, A. J., & Foster, G. D. (1989). Treatment of obesity by very low calorie diet, behavior therapy, and their combination: A five-year perspective. *International Journal of Obesity, 13,* 39–46.

Wadden, T. A., & Stunkard, A. J. (1985). Social and psychological consequences of obesity. *Annals of Internal Medicine, 103,* 1062–1067.

Wadden, T. A., Stunkard, A. J., & Liebschutz, J. (1988). Three-year follow-up of the treatment of obesity by very low calorie diet, behavior therapy, and their combination. *Journal of Consulting and Clinical Psychology, 56,* 925–928.

Wadden, T. A., Van Itallie, T. B., & Blackburn, G. L. (1990). Responsible and irresponsible use of very-low-calorie diets in the treatment of obesity. *Journal of the American Medical Association, 263,* 83–85.

Wadden, T. A., Vogt, R. A., Foster, G. D., & Anderson, D. A. (1998). Exercise and the maintenance of weight loss: 1-year follow-up of a controlled clinical trial. *Journal of Consulting and Clinical Psychology, 66,* 429–433.

Weinsier, R. L. (1995). Clinical assessment of obese patients. In K. D. Brownell & C. G. Fairburn (Eds.), *Eating disorders and obesity: A comprehensive handbook* (pp. 463–468). New York: Guilford Press.

Weintraub, M. (1984). A double blind clinical trial in weight control. *Archives of Internal Medicine, 144,* 1143–1148.

Weintraub, M. (1992). Long-term weight control: The National Heart, Lung, and Blood Institute funded multimodal intervention study. *Clinical Pharmacological Therapy, 51,* 581–646.

Weintraub, M., Sundaresan, P. R., Madan, M., Schuster, B., Balder, A., Lasagna, L., & Cox, C. (1992). Long-term weight control study I (weeks 0 to 34). *Clinical Pharmacological Therapy, 51,* 586–594.

Weintraub, M., Sundaresan, P. R., Schuster, B., Averbuch, M., Stein, E. C., & Byrne, L. (1992). Long-term weight control study V (weeks 190–210). *Clinical Pharmacological Therapy, 51,* 615–618.

Weintraub, M., Sundaresan, P. R., Schuster, B., Ginsberg, G., Madan, M., Balder, A., Stein, E. C., & Byrne, L. (1992). Long-term weight control study II (weeks 34 to 104). *Clinical Pharmacological Therapy, 51,* 595–601.

Westerterp-Plantenga, M. S., Steffens, A. B., & Tremblay, A. (1999). *Regulation of food intake and energy expenditure.* Milano, Italy: Medical Publishing and New Media.

Wilfley, D. E., Agras, W. S., Telch, C. F., Rossiter, E. M., Schneider, J. A., Cole, A. J., Sifford, L., & Raeburn, S. D. (1993). Group CBT and group interpersonal psychotherapy for nonpurging bulimics: A controlled comparison. *Journal of Consulting and Clinical Psychology, 61,* 296–305.

Wilfley, D. E., Grilo, C. M., & Rodin, J. (1997). Group psychotherapy for the treatment of bulimia nervosa and binge eating disorder: Research and clinical methods. In J. Spira (Ed.), *Group therapy for the medically ill* (pp. 225–295). New York: Guilford Press.

Wilfley, D. E., Schwartz, M. B., Spurrell, E. B., & Fairburn, C. G. (1997). Assessing the specific psychopathology of binge eating disorder patients: Interview or self-report? *Behavior Research and Therapy, 12,* 1151–1159.

Williamson, D. F., Kahn, H. S., Remington, P. L., & Anda, R. F. (1990). The 10-year incidence of overweight and major weight gain in U.S. adults. *Archives of Internal Medicine, 150,* 665–672.

Wilson, G. T. (1994). Behavioral treatment of obesity: Thirty years and counting. *Advances in Behaviour Research and Therapy, 16,* 31–75.

Wilson, G. T., & Fairburn, C. G. (1993). Cognitive treatments for eating disorders. *Journal of Consulting and Clinical Psychology, 61,* 261–269.

Wilson, G. T., & Vitousek, K. M. (1999). Self-monitoring in the assessment of eating disorders. *Psychological Assessment, 11,* 480–489.

Wing, R., Koeske, R., Epstein, L., Nowalk, M., Gooding, W., & Becker, D. (1987). Long-term effects of modest weight loss in type II diabetic patients. *Archives of Internal Medicine, 147,* 1749–1753.

Wolf, A. M., & Colditz, G. A. (1998). Current estimates of the economic cost of obesity in the United States. *Obesity Research, 6,* 97–106.

Wood, P. D., Stefanick, M. L., Dreon, D. M., Frey-Hewitt, B., Garay, S. C., Williams, P. T., Superko, H. R., Fortmann, S. P., Albers, J. J., Vranizan, K. M., Ellsworth, N. M., Terry, R. B., & Haskell, W. L. (1988). Changes in plasma lipids and lipoproteins in overweight men during weight loss through dieting as compared with exercise. *New England Journal of Medicine, 319,* 1173–1179.

Yanovski, S. Z. (1993). Binge eating disorder: Current knowledge and future directions. *Obesity Research, 1,* 306–324.

Yanovski, S. Z., Bain, R. P., & Williamson, D. F. (1999). Report of a National Institutes of Health—Centers for Disease Control and Prevention workshop on the feasibility of conducting a randomized clinical trial to estimate the long-term health effects of intentional weight loss in obese persons. *American Journal of Clinical Nutrition, 69,* 366–372.

Yanovski, S. Z., Nelson, J. E., Dubbert, B. K., & Spitzer, R. L. (1993). Association of binge eating disorder and psychiatric comorbidity in obese subjects. *American Journal of Psychiatry, 150,* 1472–1479.

Zhang, Y. Y., Proenca, R., Maffei, M., Barone, M., Leopold, L., & Friedman, J. M. (1994). Positional cloning of the mouse obese gene and its human homolog. *Nature, 372,* 425–432.

11

Clinical Outcomes Assessment for the Practicing Clinician

James M. Meredith, Michael J. Lambert, and John F. Drozd

Although a number of studies have questioned the value of combining medication and psychotherapy (Hollon, 1996; Hollon et al., 1992; Hollon, Shelton, & Loosen, 1991), new research hints that the combination of medication and cognitive–behavioral therapy (CBT) produces better results than either treatment alone for both anxiety and depression (Barlow, Gorman, Shear, & Woods, 2000; Keller et al., 2000). Considering the tremendous differences between controlled research and actual clinical practice, many practitioners may find this interesting but still scratch their heads wondering how they can replicate these results with their patients' in today's cost-conscious, managed care environment. For most, integrating CBT with medication means the addition of services and commitment of already-limited resources. It simply is not practical to offer combined treatment to all patients. So, what indicators should a clinician use to guide his or her decisions about which patients should receive medication alone, CBT alone, or a combination of the two? In this chapter we present one strategy to answer these questions based on clinical outcomes management practices and illustrate through case examples how we use data generated from this program to guide integrative (medication + CBT) treatments.

Clinical outcomes management (COM) refers to the practice of using standardized measures to systematically assess changes in patients' clinical status over time. Initially developed for clinical trials research of psychotherapy efficacy, over the past 10 years COM has been associated with efforts to contain costs by managed health care organizations. A parallel movement in professional psychology recognizes that the integration of research and practice is crucial to the economic viability of the mental health profession, because practitioners must demonstrate competence in delivering empirically validated "efficacious" treatments (Clement, 1996). The intensified efforts to measure the effectiveness of mental health ser-

The opinions of James M. Meredith are his as a private citizen and do not represent the official opinion of the United States Air Force or Department of Defense.

vices as they are actually practiced in the day-to-day clinical setting have
had two important consequences.

First, cost containment organizations now demand clinical outcomes
assessment to initially define and subsequently evaluate the attainment
of specific treatment goals (Lambert, 1983; Mirin & Namerow, 1991). Second, managed care organizations and practicing clinicians have demanded
outcome measures that are substantially different from those typically
used in research settings. Generally, outcome measures used in academic
research tend to take too much time to administer and are prohibitively
expensive for use in practice settings. The outcome measures used by managed care and the practicing clinician must be easy to score, have low cost
per administration, high sensitivity to changes in psychological distress
over short periods of time, and tap into key characteristics associated with
mental health functioning (Burlingame, Lambert, Reisinger, Neff, & Mosier, 1995; Lambert et al., 1996). The response to this need for valid, practical clinical outcome measures in managed care has resulted in the development of measures that are better suited to the needs of the practicing
clinician who wants to do the kind of effectiveness research advocated by
Seligman (1995).

However, the practicing clinician is faced with the question of what
measures to use. This is not an easy question to answer, because the selection and use of outcome measures is complicated by the incredible array
of immediately available measures. In the next section we describe our
choice of a set of measures that are well suited to the task of assessing
patient improvement and deterioration, and we illustrate, using case examples, the application of these measures to guide the selection and integration of psychopharmacology and psychotherapy.

Overview of Instrument Selection

Two years ago an Air Force psychology working group was formed to develop a COM system to facilitate improvements in effectiveness research
throughout the Air Force. The working group focused on identifying validated instruments that could be used at every session without undue expense and administrative burden. This resulted in the creation of the COM
assessment process outlined in Figure 11.1. This process provides one common measure to all patients and additional measures tailored to the specific problems for which the patient is being treated. The building blocks
for this program are a set of psychometrically sound outcome measures
that meet nearly all of 11 criteria suggested for outcome measures by a
panel of experts convened by the National Institute of Mental Health
(NIMH). Newman and Ciarlo (1994) provided an in-depth description of
the NIMH panel suggestions that are summarized below.

1. *Relevance to target group and independent of treatment provided.*
    The measures suggested are appropriate for adults age 17 or
    older who can read at a sixth-grade level. The contents of the

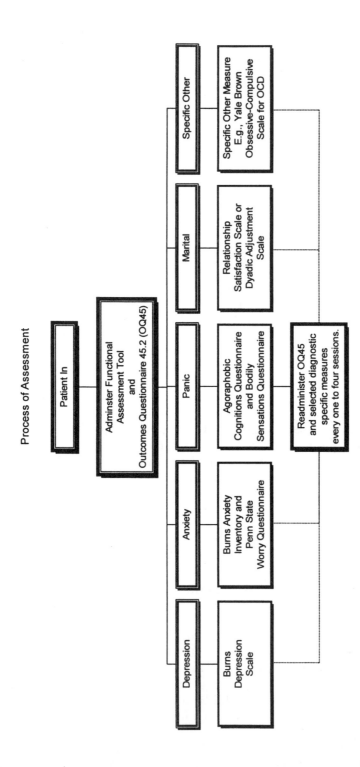

Figure 11.1. Air Force working group outcomes assessment process. *Note.* OQ45 = Outcomes Questionnaire 45.2; Q. = Questionnaire; Adj. = Adjective; YBOCS = Yale–Brown Obsessive–Compulsive Scale; OCD = obsessive–compulsive disorder.

measures are related to day-to-day functioning and are not based on or biased toward any particular treatment theory or modality. Thus, they are as appropriate for patients undergoing psycho-pharmacological treatments as for those undergoing various types of psychotherapy.

2. *Simple, teachable methods.* These instruments are designed for ease of administration. A wide range of service professionals, from clinic receptionists to clinicians themselves, can easily administer them. After several administrations, most patients can be instructed to access these measures from an established point in the reception area and complete them in the moments before the session. Instructions are straightforward and do not require a complex understanding of the instrument being used. Scoring is simple and quick, requiring only addition. Most can be self-scored by patients.

3. *Use of measures with objective referents.* The instruments selected contain objective constructs indicative of quality of life and psychological symptomatology. However, they are all self-report measures that require patients to establish a subjective understanding of their current condition and rate intensity of experience.

4. *Use of multiple respondents.* These measures are self-reports limited to the responses of the patients and thus do not make use of multiple respondents.

5. *Process-identifying outcome measures.* The selected measures are not intended to identify the process, course, or likely outcome of a pathological condition. If they were to do so, they would likely lose the desirable features of ease of administration, short administration time, and straightforward scoring and interpretation. The repeated administration of these instruments combined with meaningful diagnostic data and professional interpretation can provide valuable information leading to process identification.

6. *Psychometric strength.* These instruments are reliable, valid, and sensitive to treatment related change.

7. *Low costs.* Each of the instruments is very cost effective, with minimal cost per administration. Most are available for a minimal licensing fee that allows lifetime privilege to reproduce and administer the instrument on an unlimited basis. Cost per administration then becomes limited to reproduction and administration costs, which appear to average about 3 cents per administration. Practical considerations weighed by the working group included patients' ability to complete the measure in fewer than 10 minutes and the ability to reproduce each measure on one side of a single, standard 8.5 in. $\times$ 11 in. (21.6 cm $\times$ 28 cm) sheet of paper.

8. *Understanding by nonprofessional audiences.* The selected measures are all well suited to interdisciplinary settings and appear

to have been designed to be easily understood both conceptually and practically by people in many settings. This not only makes for ease of administration, but also patients and other nonprofessional observers easily understand the results. Most mental health patients understand the utility of regularly analyzing current symptom distress and social functioning, in the same way that they understand and accept the function of the blood pressure tests routinely used in primary care settings. For most of the measures, a high score represents some level of psychological distress, whereas a lower score indicates better functioning and less pathology.

9. *Easy feedback and uncomplicated interpretation.* All of the selected instruments are readily self-scored and easy to interpret. Interpretation begins with comparing the total score of one administration against established norms to determine the current level of distress and whether this level is considered normal or abnormal. Further information is derived from examining individual item responses, particularly responses related to the critical items about suicidality, violence, and substance abuse. Interpretations of an individual patient's progress are based on repeated measures across sessions. Interpretation can be expanded to examine score profiles of specific treatment providers, therapeutic interventions, or patient populations. Feedback is very easy, starting with a comparison of the total score to the normative data, including whether the score falls in a healthy or unhealthy range, and extending to graphs of progress and explanations of trends, patterns, and cycles.

10. *Useful in clinical services.* The selected measures can help establish levels of needed treatment, justify continuing or terminating treatment, track patient progress across time, and monitor treatment and provider effectiveness. The simplicity of use, low cost, and straightforward interpretation are features that make these very useful tools in a clinical setting.

11. *Compatibility with clinical theories and practices.* The selected instruments appear to be useful and meaningful for any clinician, regardless of clientele, theoretical perspective, or therapeutic style.

Overview of Selected Instruments

Outcome measurement is complex, and self-report measures represent only a beginning point on which to elaborate. Ogles, Lambert, and Masters (1996) and Sederer and Dickey (1996) have described a variety of possible outcome measures that go beyond self-report, including therapist ratings; other ratings; and behavioral observations, such as frequency counts. Many of these additional outcome measures are used in research and academic settings but are in many cases prohibitively time and cost intensive. Numerous self-report assessment instruments exist to measure patient problems. The Air Force working group screened many instruments and reached a consensus on the "best" instruments for clinical use. For each presenting problem we reviewed the existing literature (Fischer & Corcoran, 1994; Strupp, Horowitz, & Lambert, 1997) and consulted experts in specific problem areas (e.g., M. Craske, April 1997; A. Friedman, May 1997; & R. DeGuiseppe, July 1997, personal communications) to develop a list of the most frequently cited and commonly used measures. After acquiring these measures, the group met to evaluate each and selected those that closely matched the NIMH criteria. In outpatient settings the three problems seen most commonly are anxiety, depression, and relationship difficulties. In this section we examine the instrument that we selected to provide a broad measure of these most frequently presented problems: the Outcomes Questionnaire 45.2 (OQ45; Lambert et al., 1996; see Appendix 11.A). Limitations of time and space do not permit the full description of each of the additional instruments illustrated in Figure 11.1, but references are included for the interested reader.

The OQ45 (Lambert et al., 1996) is a 45-item self-report measure that requires the patient to rate each item on a 5-point Likert scale that ranges from *never* to *always*. It was designed to assess symptoms across a wide range of adult mental disorders and syndromes, including stress-related illness and V codes (a problem that is a focus of clinical attention but is not a diagnosis of a mental disorder, e.g. V61.1 Partner Relational Problem). Its uses include baseline screening, assignment to level of treatment, and monitoring of progress. It was not designed to be used as a diagnostic tool. The length of the OQ45 makes it tolerable to patients for repeated testing while providing clinicians with data that can be used for decision making. The items in the OQ45 were developed to sample three broad content areas that are of critical importance in measuring patient status and psychotherapy outcome. These content areas make up three subscales of *Symptom Distress (SD)*, *Interpersonal Relationships (IR)*, and *Social Role Functioning (SR)*.

The SD subscale is composed of 25 items, 23 of which relate to symptoms of anxiety and depression and 2 items that screen for substance abuse. The SD subscale does not separate out the anxiety and depressive symptoms into different subscales, because these symptoms tend to co-occur in a wide variety of patients (e.g., Feldman, 1993).

The IR subscale is composed of 11 items that measure satisfaction with and problems in interpersonal relationships. Items dealing with marriage, friendships, and family life attempt to measure conflict, isolation, and withdrawal in interpersonal relationships. The importance of including a measure of interpersonal satisfaction is borne out by research on life satisfaction and quality of life that indicates that positive connection to others is a key factor to happiness (Andrews & Witney, 1974; Beiser, 1983; Blau, 1977; Diener, 1984; Veit & Ware, 1983). In addition, interpersonal difficulties are related to psychopathology, either as cause or effect (Horowitz, Rosenberg, Baer, Ureno, & Villasenor, 1988).

The SR subscale consists of nine items that measure satisfaction with or problems in tasks related to employment, family life, and leisure. Satisfaction in these areas is highly correlated with overall life satisfaction (Beiser, 1983; Blau, 1977; Frisch, Cornell, Villanueva, & Retzlaff, 1992; Veit & Ware, 1983) and provides a strong rationale for inclusion of items related to performance in work and leisure tasks.

Normative data were drawn from undergraduate students, business workers, and community members across various geographical locations in the United States, resulting in a sample of 815 participants. Clinical samples were drawn from outpatient and inpatient mental health facilities (n = 342). Retest administrations were done 3 weeks after the initial testing and weekly thereafter for a 10-week period. Stability coefficients based on the Pearson product–moment coefficient provided estimates of reliability. Analysis of the nonpatient and patient samples revealed clear differences between the sample mean scores (Umphress, Lambert, Smart, Barlow, & Clouse, 1997). The OQ45 total score correlations to a variety of scales measuring symptom clusters of anxiety, depression, quality of life, social adjustment, and interpersonal functioning revealed high to moderately high concurrent validity. Pearson product–moment correlation coefficients between the OQ45 total score and a host of widely used instruments (Beck Depression Inventory, Global Severity Index of the Symptom Checklist–90–R, Zung Self-Rating Depression Scale, Zung Self-Rating Anxiety Scale, Taylor Manifest Anxiety Scale, and the State–Trait Anxiety Inventory) ranged from .64 to .88. These data indicate that clinicians could be confident that the OQ45 total score provides a valid index of mental health.

The OQ45 is self-administered and requires no instructions beyond those printed on the answer sheet. In most cases, patients will complete the scale in about 5 minutes. A few particularly careful patients may require as much as 18–20 minutes, whereas others may take as little as 3 minutes. If the patient is unable to read, or if the test is administered by telephone for follow-up data gathering, administration can be completed by reading items to the patient. This is accomplished by giving the patient a card with a 0–4 numerical scale corresponding to *never* to *almost always* or by asking him or her to write the scale out and refer to it while the administrator reads the items.

The OQ45 includes five critical items that should be queried whenever they are answered as greater than 0 (*never*). These items assess suicidal thinking and behavior, substance abuse, and threat of violence. Close attention to the responses to these items provides the obvious benefits of identifying key areas of critical importance to treatment success and preventing avoidable tragedy. In addition, the treatment provider's documentation of the patient's response to querying about these items and documentation of the provider thinking and planning regarding the patient status provides important risk management and legal protection.

Interpretation of the OQ45 is straightforward and easy for both the provider and patient to understand. Cutoff scores for the total score and for each subscale are used to distinguish between healthy and unhealthy levels of distress and function. A reliable change index (RCI) was derived between the community and community mental health samples to determine the level of change by an individual in treatment that can be considered reliable or clinically significant (Jacobson & Truax, 1991). The RCI value computed for the total score is 14 or more points. Descriptive labels for each successive 14-point interval above the cutoff score range from mild to extreme. Patient response to treatment is categorized on the basis of the 14-point RCI and the healthy–unhealthy cutoff score. Patients who improve by 14 points and fall below the cutoff are considered "recovered." Patients who improve by 14 or more points but still remain above the cutoff are "improved." Patients whose scores do not change by 14 or more points are "unchanged." Patients whose scores increase by 14 or more points have "deteriorated."

Outcomes Assessment Process

As illustrated in Figure 11.1, our approach to COM begins with the initial contact and proceeds routinely throughout treatment to termination. The assessment process begins with a triage interview based on responses to a self-administered patient information questionnaire (the Functional Assessment Tool [FAT]; see Appendix 11.B) and a global measure of symptom distress and interpersonal and work functioning (OQ45; see Appendix 11.A) and then becomes more tailored to target each patient's specific presenting problem. Immediately before their initial appointment, patients complete the 6-page FAT. This instrument was developed as a triage tool to document symptomatology and patient functioning within the major life domains. It takes most outpatients 20–30 minutes to complete and results in the specification of treatment goals and level-of-care recommendations. After completing the FAT, patients complete the OQ45.

Our initial assessment concludes with the administration of symptom-specific measures. These are selected on the basis of complaints and problem areas identified from the more general screening with the FAT and a clinical interview. For depressive symptoms, we recommend the Burns Depression Checklist (Burns, 1995). For anxiety, we recommend the Burns Anxiety Inventory (Burns, 1995) and the Penn State Worry Questionnaire (Meyer, Miller, Metzger, & Borkovec, 1990). For panic, we use the Body Sensations Questionnaire (Chambless, Caputo, Bright, & Gallagher, 1984). For obsessive–compulsive symptoms, we use the Yale–Brown Obsessive–Compulsive Scale (YBOCS; Goodman et al., 1989). For relationship problems, we use the Relationship Satisfaction Scale (Burns, 1995). We record patients' initial scores on these measures along with their initial OQ45 subscale and total scores, *Diagnostic and Statistical Manual of Mental Disorders* (4th ed., American Psychiatric Association, 1994) diagnosis, and relevant demographic and contact information on the Treatment Summary Form (see Figure 11.2). We maintain this form in the patient's record and use it to record each follow-up contact and associated assessment scores. We reassess with the OQ45 at regular intervals, which vary from every session to as long as every four sessions depending on the

TREATMENT SUMMARY FORM

PATIENT:		AGE:	WORK PHONE:		HOME PHONE:			
AXIS I:								
AXIS II:								
AXIS III:								
Current Medications:								
Drug Allergies:								

MEASURES OF CHANGE

Date / Provider	INTERVENTION				

Figure 11.2. The Treatment Summary Form. *Note.* WK = work; H = home.

inclination of the provider and the utility of the OQ45 for the particular patient and problem. For example, the normative data from the mental health patient sample revealed that 17% of mental health patients started in the normal range on the OQ45 but still had a specific problem area with which they requested assistance. With patients for whom the OQ45 is less useful, the symptom-specific measures pertinent to the patient's complaints become much more important and are typically administered at every session.

With rare exception, patients understand and readily adapt to this progress assessment process, coming a few minutes before their sessions to self-administer and self-score the assessment measures they regularly use. Each session then begins with the review of their outcome scores.

This is an opportunity for the therapist to underscore the importance of the assessment measures by using the results to discuss the effectiveness of, and adjust, treatment. If this opportunity is routinely overlooked, one likely result is that the patient will begin to see less reason to take the assessment measures in a serious fashion, and the validity of the assessment is likely to decline. With this in mind, we now examine some of the benefits of using standardized measures from intake and throughout treatment to help with the treatment decision-making process. Our use of the OQ45, our overall measure of outcome, illustrates these points.

Outcomes assessment in treatment planning

At intake, we examine the OQ45 for positive critical items, subscale scores, and total score. The critical items provide information on risk of harm and substance abuse. The subscale scores provide additional information on the targets for treatment, helping to focus interventions on specific aspects of patients' difficulties. The total score, when combined with other patient information, helps with treatment-level decisions. Low scores that fall in the healthy range provide support for low-intensity treatment options, such as referring a patient to a community support group, prevention and psychoeducational programs, or bibliotherapy. Lambert, Okiishi, Finch, and Johnson (1998) reported that "approximately 15% of patients in out-patient treatment, along with 5% in community mental health centers and 20–25% in employee assistance program setting, report functioning in the normal range on standardized tests at intake" (p. 69). On the other hand, highly elevated scores would indicate a need for more intensive treatment, with consideration of more immediate and frequent follow-up, medication treatment, or hospitalization. Thus the OQ45 provides an important contribution to the decision-making process at intake by clarifying the current level of distress.

Outcomes assessment in treatment monitoring

After intake, patients take the OQ45 at weekly or greater intervals just before sessions. This requires only a few moments of the patients' time, and they do not report it as being burdensome. The score at any individual session may be useful, but of more value is the ability to see the patterns and trends revealed by the patient's scores across the course of therapy. Progress in therapy is signaled by significant reductions in OQ45 scores. In the course of treatment, when the patient returns to the normal range on the OQ45 this would be a signal to begin spacing out sessions and discussing termination plans. With adequate duration of treatment, scores that fail to show improvement or even increase alert the therapist to the need for revision of the treatment plan, consultation, or both. Finally, scores that indicate progress but fail to reach normal range support continuation of treatment. A case example follows to illustrate how this actually plays out in treatment.

Case Example: Partial Response in a Patient With Obsessive–Compulsive Disorder

This case illustrates the benefit of more methodical outcomes assessment in both determining whether to add psychotherapy to the treatment mix and in helping the patient understand the need for a new type of treatment. Sara M., a 28-year-old full-time homemaker, presented with the desire to continue medication treatment for obsessive–compulsive disorder (OCD). She had originally sought treatment 3 years prior because of an inability to complete normal household tasks. Sara reported having been bothered by obsessions and compulsions for 10 years. However, she was able to function in spite of them until confronted with the increased responsibilities brought on by the birth of a child. Her obsessions consisted of fear that she would perform violent and horrible acts if she became addicted to drugs by someone putting them into her food or drink or if she allowed herself to think or do anything bad. Consequently, she developed an elaborate set of rituals to guard against drug contamination and bad behavior. These included never eating or drinking anything that had been out of her sight for any period of time, repeating anything during which she had an errant thought or uttered a curse word, avoiding any contact with anything that represented drugs, and carefully inspecting any items to be purchased. When she originally sought treatment, she was spending 4–8-hours daily maintaining her rituals. For example, she frequently returned to the shower five or six times if she had a negative thought while completing her morning self-care. She had to redo the laundry repeatedly if anything negative occurred during the wash cycle. Shopping for groceries could take several hours as she pulled a can off the shelves, inspected it, returned it to the shelf, selected another, turned it to the correct orientation, and so on.

For 3 years, Sara's treatment consisted of 60–80 mg fluoxetine daily. This resulted in more than 50% reduction in her symptoms. She accomplished most tasks with only three to four repetitions, as opposed to seven or eight repetitions before treatment. She reduced 3-hour shopping trips to 1.5 hours. Before her start of treatment with us, Sarah had received some psychoeducational material on OCD but no psychotherapy. Her OQ45 score at intake was 92, indicating a moderate level of distress. Her YBOCS score of 29 indicated severe OCD. At the maximum dosage of 80 mg fluoxetine per day, she was bothered by side effects of jitteriness and decreased libido. Because she experienced improvement with the medication, Sara resigned herself to the side effects and believed the best she outcome she could hope for was a maintenance of functioning in the moderate range of distress. In addition to the OQ45 and YBOCS, we agreed on individualized measures of outcome, including having Sara record the frequency of repetitive behaviors and making 0–10 ratings of anxiety when resisting compulsive behaviors.

Sara appeared surprised and motivated when her therapist stated his expectation for the outcome was that she would be in the healthy range on the OQ45 and YBOCS measures and would experience minimal re-

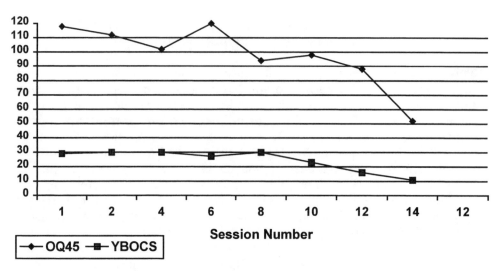

Figure 11.3. Outcomes Questionnaire 45.2 and Yale–Brown Obsessive–Compulsive Scale outcome scores for Sara M. (obsessive–compulsive disorder). *Note.* OQ45 = Outcomes Questionnaire 45.2; YBOCS = Yale–Brown Obsessive–Compulsive Scale.

peating and avoidant behaviors. She willingly agreed to engage in exposure and response prevention treatment based on the program outlined by Foa and Wilson (1991). Her score on the OQ45 dropped from 118 (extreme) to 52 (normal) and on the YBOCS dropped from 29 (severe) to 11 (mild). These results are illustrated in Figure 11.3.

With significant documented improvement in both standardized and individualized outcome measures, Sara agreed to begin to taper her fluoxetine. She easily tapered to 20 mg a day but then resisted further reduction. At this reduced dosage, she experienced no change in her symptoms and none of the side effects associated with the higher dosage.

The use of standardized outcome measures with Sara provided critical information regarding her actual progress. Sara's initial self-report of improvement and satisfaction while on medication alone indicated that she felt quite good about her status, reflecting her understanding that a 50% reduction in her symptoms was all that she should expect. A therapist could easily continue a medication-only treatment plan that left Sara with significant impairment and distress based on her subjective self-assessment. The use of standardized outcome measures provided critical motivation by giving her a healthier goal for her symptom levels.

Computer Database Outcome Scores in
Clinic Management/Quality Improvement

When providers compile outcome data in a database, significant benefits can accrue beyond directing and improving an individual patient's treatment. We see three opportunities for improvement offered by compiling standardized clinical-outcomes data across patients. First, pooled COM data provide therapists with direct feedback about their effectiveness and the effectiveness of their interventions with specific types of patients or across all their patients. Second, data generated from our COM program provides therapists or groups of therapists with comparative feedback (i.e., how they are doing with all or specific types of patients relative to other therapists). Finally, such data provide a method to identify and track problem or poorly responding patients for risk management and quality-improvement purposes. Before we examine the benefits of creating computer tracking of outcomes, we describe an easily managed system to enter and track outcomes in a database.

James M. Meredith has created a simple Microsoft Access database that includes the basic elements of outcome tracking. A patient data table includes all the relevant information for each patient: name; a unique identification number; age; gender; race; referral source; and diagnoses on Axes I, II, and III. Each patient has another table associated with his or her unique identifier that consists of appointment details. In the simplest form, this appointment detail table includes the date seen, the therapist seen, types of interventions, and the OQ45 score. Once the initial data entry is completed, it is relatively simple to add the basic appointment details after each appointment. Reports from this database provide therapist and clinic the feedback that creates the three benefits listed above.

First, each therapist in the database can get feedback on his or her overall effectiveness with all his or her patients or on differential effectiveness with different types of patients or interventions. A report on overall effectiveness would take all a particular therapist's patients and calculate change scores from the initial to final session. The feedback could take the form of an average change score as well as the percentage of patients who fall into the predefined groups of resolved, improved, unchanged, and deteriorated. Sorting by diagnosis and by type of intervention would yield change scores and resolution rates by diagnosis and type of intervention. Figure 11.4 illustrates the effectiveness of a particular form of treatment, a four-session cognitive–behavioral stress management program, with data compiled from 32 patients.

Report parameters could be modified to provide many different types of feedback to individual therapists or groups of therapists. For example, a therapist could have feedback on effectiveness at various stages of treatment, from early (two to three sessions) to complete (initial to last session), in reports defined by duration of treatment or by number of sessions. Alternatively, a therapist could have a report showing how he or she compares to the rest of the therapists in a treatment setting or to therapists using different interventions. Lambert et al. (1998) reported an example of this, contrasting a specialist in brief therapy with a group of trainee therapists. Figure 11.5 depicts this comparison using percentage of patients "recovered," that is, with a decrease in scores of at least 14 points and a final score in the healthy or normal zone. The brief-therapy specialist is an experienced psychologist whose practice is based on a solution-focused therapy (Johnson & Miller, 1994) that emphasizes the identifica-

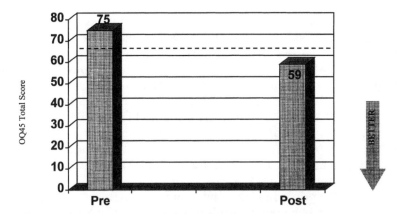

Figure 11.4. Average Outcomes Questionnaire 45.2 scores for stress program completers (*N* = 32). *Note.* OQ45 = Outcomes Questionnaire 45.2. The dotted line represents the Total Score cutoff, with scores above 63 representing clinically significant problems and scores below 63 representing normal functioning.

tion of a problem and collaborative efforts to keep focused on the problem while maintaining a positive working alliance. The data presented for the brief-therapy specialist were derived from 27 consecutive private-practice patients (14 men and 13 women) over the first few months of the therapist's implementation of the OQ45 for tracking patient progress. The pa-

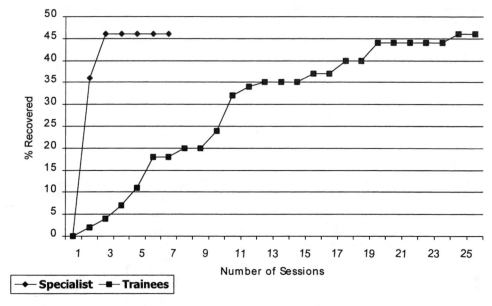

Figure 11.5. Comparison of brief therapy specialist (*n* = 22) and group of 36 trainee therapists (*n* = 45). From "Outcome Assessment: From Conceptualization to Implementation," by M. J. Lambert et al. 1998, *Professional Psychology: Research and Practice, 29,* 63–70. Copyright 1998 by the American Psychological Association. Reprinted with permission.

tients' diagnoses were of a wide variety, including dysthymia, anxiety disorders, adjustment disorders, major depression, and substance abuse. Patients received the OQ45 from the clinic secretary, who scored it and placed it in the patient's file before each session. Patients had a mean of 3.1 sessions and a mode of 2 sessions. The patients began therapy with a mean OQ45 of 82.1, which represents a moderate level of distress and is in the score range of the original normative clinical sample (M = 83.1; Lambert et al., 1996). They ended therapy with a mean score of 60.4. These data are contrasted with a larger sample of patients treated by 36 clinicians in their second or third year of training. The data reveal a striking difference between the rate at which the patients of the experienced specialist recovered and the rate at which the trainees' patients recovered. The trainees required 25 sessions to reach the recovery rate that the experienced clinician reached in 3 sessions. This dramatic difference raises many interesting questions about the relevance of experience and therapy style on treatment outcome. It is interesting that the data indicate that although the experienced clinician could produce a certain success rate much faster than the group of trainees, the final recovered rates were the same. This suggests that "experience of therapists may play a primary role in determining the 'efficiency' of the outcome rather than the ultimate success of treatment" (Lambert, Okiishi, Finch, & Johnson, 1998, p. 68). Lambert et al. (1998) pointed out the many valuable questions stimulated by these data, including the roles that differences in feedback, emphasis on immediate problem resolution, and commitment to brief treatment play in amount of time required for recovery.

Second, this type of database can provide comparative data for therapists, clinics, or both (Lambert & Brown, 1996). With data from multiple therapists included, any individual therapist can see how he or she compares to others or to the group of therapists as a whole in effectiveness and patient response rates. Figure 11.6 represents average change in OQ45 scores for a group of providers at a small Air Force outpatient mental health clinic. If a group of clinics such as exists in health maintenance organizations or government agencies such as the Veterans Administration or Department of Defense began to collect such data, the relative effectiveness of clinics could be compared. These data would raise questions about the source of differences and eventually allow the identification of master therapists and master clinics that can reliably deliver effective treatment in general or for specific disorders. In contrast to the rarefied atmosphere of efficacy studies, these data would represent effectiveness as measured by the way treatment is delivered in the real world. Finding therapists and treatment combinations that work in real settings could begin to marry research and practice in the effectiveness paradigm advocated by Seligman (1995).

Third, and finally, the accumulation of these data provides easy identification of patients who are failing to respond to treatment. A report identifying all patients who have remained unchanged or deteriorated, despite adequate trials of treatment, can be used to schedule these unresponsive patients for treatment team consultation. For example, of the 100

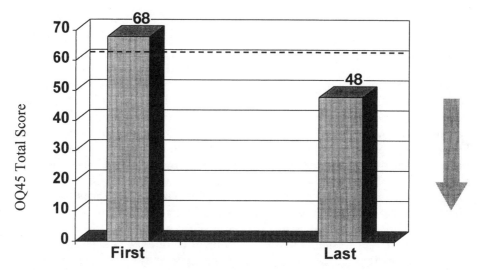

Figure 11.6. Average Outcomes Questionnaire 45.2 (OQ45) scores for outpatient clinic patients ($N = 100$). *Note.* OQ45 = Outcomes Questionnaire 45.2. This chart shows the clinical effectiveness of mental health care for patients who have attended more than one session during the first quarter of 1999 at a small Air Force mental health clinic. The dotted line represents the Total Score cutoff, with scores above 63 representing clinically significant problems and scores below 63 representing normal functioning.

patients entered into the database at the Air Force clinic, 10 were flagged as either failing to improve or deteriorating over the course of four or more sessions. These 10 patients were then scheduled for consultation and problem solving at regularly scheduled provider meetings. This is good for the consumers of mental health treatments, both at the patient and at the third-party payer levels. Knowing quickly when treatment is not producing the desired results will enable clinicians to be more responsive and thus meet risk-management demands.

Conclusion

The advantages of assessing initial patient status, change, and treatment outcome extend beyond pacifying the demands of managed care companies for data demonstrating the effectiveness of interventions. Using these tools, we can begin to explore the components of interventions that are most effective in producing clinically significant and sustained outcomes in settings that are representative of how therapy is actually delivered. The type of outcome measurement described here is the heart of Seligman's (1995) effectiveness research paradigm, in which the professional practitioner assumes a greater role in influencing both the theory and practice of psychotherapy.

Patients will also benefit from this practice. We intentionally selected quick, easy-to-score measures that can be used immediately in session to provide objective feedback to patients as evidence of change or lack thereof. The process of feedback alone can be an effective component of interventions.

For those who do not currently use routine assessments, we recognize the additional time and expense required to systematically track patient progress. However, we believe this cost will be easily recouped to the extent that the recommended assessment process results in improved interventions and patient care. As more and more research becomes available on how combined treatments affect the patient, our understanding of the process of change as it actually occurs in the clinical setting will improve. The process of continuous quality assessment promoted here will be a valuable mechanism through which clinicians can begin to shed light on the elusive process of change and the variables that affect it. By adopting the COM process providers can begin to collect data within and across clinics that can be used to better understand and serve patients, interventions and, ultimately, the discipline. Bringing these tools to bear on the combined therapies will naturally encourage additional research into ways that medication and psychosocial approaches can be best combined to benefit patients. At the very least, we hope this chapter will spark the use of assessment tools and processes within clinicians' practices that will contribute to the dialogue regarding the utility of combining medication and psychotherapy.

Appendix 11.A   Outcome Questionnaire

Instructions: Read each item carefully and circle the number under the category that best describes how you have been feeling over the *last week*. We are defining *work* as employment, school, housework, volunteer work, etc.

	Never	Rarely	Some-times	Freq-uently	Almost Always	SD	IR	SR
1. I get along well with others.	4	3	2	1	0			
2. I tire quickly.	0	1	2	3	4			
3. I feel no interest in things.	0	1	2	3	4			
4. I feel stressed at work/school.	0	1	2	3	4			
5. I blame myself for things.	0	1	2	3	4			
6. I feel irritated.	0	1	2	3	4			
7. I feel unhappy in my marriage/significant relationship.	0	1	2	3	4			
8. I have thoughts of ending my life.	0	1	2	3	4			
9. I feel weak.	0	1	2	3	4			
10. I feel fearful.	0	1	2	3	4			
11. After heavy drinking, I need a drink the next morning to get going. (If you do not drink, mark "never.")	0	1	2	3	4			
12. I find my work/school satisfying.	4	3	2	1	0			
13. I am a happy person.	4	3	2	1	0			
14. I work/study too much.	0	1	2	3	4			
15. I feel worthless.	0	1	2	3	4			
16. I am concerned about family troubles.	0	1	2	3	4			
17. I have an unfulfilling sex life.	0	1	2	3	4			
18. I feel lonely.	0	1	2	3	4			
19. I have frequent arguments.	0	1	2	3	4			
20. I feel loved and wanted.	4	3	2	1	0			
21. I enjoy my spare time.	4	3	2	1	0			
22. I have difficulty concentrating.	0	1	2	3	4			
23. I feel hopeless about the future.	0	1	2	3	4			
24. I like myself.	4	3	2	1	0			
25. Disturbing thoughts come into my mind that I can't get rid of.	0	1	2	3	4			
26. I feel annoyed by people who criticize my drinking (or drug use). (If not applicable, mark "never.")	0	1	2	3	4			
27. I have an upset stomach.	0	1	2	3	4			
28. I am not working/studying as well as I used to.	0	1	2	3	4			
29. My heart pounds too much.	0	1	2	3	4			
30. I have trouble getting along with friends and close acquaintances.	0	1	2	3	4			
31. I am satisfied with my life.	4	3	2	1	0			
32. I have trouble at work/school because of drinking or drug use. (If not applicable, mark "never.")	0	1	2	3	4			
33. I feel that something bad is going to happen.	0	1	2	3	4			
34. I have sore muscles.	0	1	2	3	4			
35. I feel afraid of open spaces, driving, or being on buses, subways, etc.	0	1	2	3	4			
36. I feel nervous.	0	1	2	3	4			
37. I feel my love relationships are full and complete.	4	3	2	1	0			
38. I feel that I am not doing well at work/school.	0	1	2	3	4			
39. I have too many disagreements at work/school.	0	1	2	3	4			
40. I feel something is wrong with my mind.	0	1	2	3	4			
41. I have trouble falling asleep or staying asleep.	0	1	2	3	4			
42. I feel blue.	0	1	2	3	4			
43. I am satisfied with my relationships with others.	4	3	2	1	0			
44. I feel angry enough at work/school to do something I may regret.	0	1	2	3	4			
45. I have headaches.	0	1	2	3	4			
Developed by Michael J. Lambert, PhD, and Gary M. Burlingame, PhD © 1996, American Professional Credentialing Services LLC				*Column Totals =*				
				Total =				

Note.   The Outcome Questionnaire 45.2 (OQ45), a brief 45-item self-report outcome/tracking instrument. The OQ45 is the result of a unique partnership among behavioral health care administrators, practitioners, and academic researchers in response to demands for cost containment, quality care, reliable monitoring, and accountability for services provided. It is used to assess patient change and measures patient functioning in the areas of major psychiatric symptoms, social role functioning, and interpersonal relations. In the Air Force Life Skills Centers, patients complete the OQ45 at intake and prior to each therapeutic contact (therapy session or class).

Patients are considered "recovered" when they meet two criteria for clinically significant change: (a) moving from the OQ dysfunctional distribution (OQ Total Score ≥ 63) into the OQ functional distribution (OQ Total ≤ 63) and (b) showing positive gains of sufficient magnitude to be considered statistically reliable (improvement from Class 1 to Class 4 of at least 15 OQ points). Patients are considered "improved" if they show positive gains of sufficient magnitude to be considered statistically reliable (improvement from Class 1 to Class 4 of at least 15 OQ points) but do not move from the OQ dysfunctional distribution into the OQ functional distribution. Patients are categorized as "no change" if the absolute value of the difference between their Class 1 and Class 4 OQ Total Scores is less than 15 points. Patients are considered deteriorated if their Class 4 OQ Total Scores is 15 points or greater than their Class 1 OQ Total Score. SD = Symptom Distress; IR = Interpersonal Relationships; SR = Social role functioning. From *Administration and Scoring Manual for the OQ452*, by M. J. Lambert et al., 1996, Wharton, NJ. Copyright 1996 by American Professional Credentialing Services, LLC, http://www.apcs@erols.com. Reprinted with permission.

Appendix 11.B   Functional Assessment Tool

FUNCTIONAL ASSESSMENT TOOL

The purpose of this questionnaire is to help your provider learn more about you. By completing these questions as fully and as accurately as you can, you'll speed the process of getting the treatment most in line with your reasons for coming to this clinic. If you do not want to answer a question, please write, "Do not care to answer."

General Information
Date: _____
Name:	Sponsor's SSN:
Age:	Date of Birth:	Gender (circle one): M F
Ethnic group (circle one): American Indian/Alaskan   White, Not of Hispanic Origin   Latino or Hispanic   Black, not of Hispanic Origin   Asian or Pacific Islander   Other: _____
Address:
City: State: Zip Code:
Telephone Numbers   (days):   (evenings):
Occupation: Who referred you?
Marital Status (circle one):   Single   Married   Separated   Divorced
Emergency Contact: Relation: Phone:
Where are your medical records kept?
MILITARY MEMBER INFORMATION: Branch of Service: USAF   USN   USA   USMC   USCG
Rank   Status of Military Member (circle one):   Active Duty   Retired   Deceased   TDRL
Flying Status: Yes   No   Sensitive Duty Program Clearance (circle any that apply): SCI   PRP   PS
Your relationship to military member (circle one):   self   spouse   child   parent
Present duty assignment of active duty member: Base: Squadron: Office Symbol:
Tricare Coverage Plan (circle one): Active Duty   Tricare Prime   Tricare Standard   Tricare Senior
Supplemental Insurance Company: ID Number:

Information About Your Concern or Problem

1. Please describe the primary problem/concern for which you have come to our clinic.

2. How long have you been experiencing this concern or problem?

3. What led to your decision to seek help now? What's different today?

4. Please describe any significant events occurring at that time, or since then, which may relate to the problem(s).

5. Have you had difficulties or troubles like this before? Yes/No. If "yes," please describe.

6. What solutions to your problems have been most helpful?

Stressors

7. Is there anything else, recent or long-standing, that has been very stressful for you? Yes/No. If "yes," circle all that apply. Financial, Work Related, Legal/Disciplinary, Physical Injury, Trauma/Abuse, Family/Interpersonal. Please describe.

Psychological Function

8. How would you describe your mood during the past week? Depressed, Irritable, Anxious, Good, Other_____

9. Has your appetite changed? Yes/No. If "yes," Up/Down? Weight change? (Up/Down) _____Lb.

10. Have you noticed a change in your sleep pattern? Yes/No. If "yes," how much more __ or less___?

11. Have you noticed a change in your normal amount of energy? Yes/No. If "yes," more or less?

12. Have you recently lost interest in pleasurable activities? Yes/No.

13. Are you feeling at the present time helpless or hopeless? Yes/No.

14. Do you find it difficult to concentrate? Yes/No.

15. Have you had any problems functioning normally at your job/at home/socially? Yes/No. If "yes," please describe.

16. Have you recently engaged in any dangerous or impulsive activities? Yes/No. If "yes," please explain.

17. Do you have any repetitive thoughts that don't seem to stop? Yes/No. If "yes," what are the thoughts?

18. Do your thoughts seem to be going so fast that you can't keep up with them? Yes/No.

19. Have you in the last 3 days had thoughts that don't make sense or seem unreal? Yes/No. If "yes," please describe.

20. Do you see, hear, feel or smell things that other people do not? Yes/No.

21. Do you feel others are against you, trying to harm you or control you? Yes/No.

Substance Use (Alcohol)

22. On average how much do you usually drink? Consider all beverage forms of alcohol (wine, beer, liquor) and circle one below.

   Don't Drink   Less than 1–2 drinks a day   1–2 drinks a day   3–6 drinks a day   7 or more drinks a day

If you do not drink and you've never had a problem with drinking, please skip to item 34. If you do drink or have ever had a problem with drinking, please continue with the next item.
23. When was the last time you drank and how much?

24. Has there been an increase in the amount of your drinking during the past six months? Yes/No.

25. Have you recently cut back or felt you should? Yes/No.

26. Have you recently felt annoyed by people criticizing your drinking? Yes/No.

27. Have you recently felt guilty or bad about your drinking? Yes/No.

28. Have you ever taken a drink to relieve a hangover or calm your nerves? Yes/No. (e.g., morning drinking)
If you answered "yes" to any of the last four questions (items 25–28), continue with remaining questions. If all answers were "no", go to item 34.

29. Have you recently had problems (work/social/legal) because of your drinking? Yes/No. Circle all that apply.

30. Have you recently experienced medical problems from your drinking? Yes/No. (e.g., stomach, high blood pressure, accidents, injuries, liver problems)

31. Have you recently been unable to remember events that occurred while you were drinking (i.e., blackouts)? Yes/No.

32. Have you recently been treated in an alcohol treatment program and then returned to drinking (last 24 months)? Yes/No.

33. Have you ever experienced shakes or tremors, seizures, hallucinations, increased sweating, insomnia, racing heart, increased irritability or restlessness when you tried to stop or decrease the amount of drinking? Yes/No. If "yes," circle all of the underlined symptoms that apply. Do you currently have any of the above symptoms? Yes/No.

Substance Use (Drugs)

34. Do you use any illicit or street drugs? Yes/No. If "yes," circle the ones used.

Cannabinoids (marijuana, hashish)	Crack/Cocaine	Inhalants (glue, paint, aerosol cans)
Opiates (heroin)	PCP, LSD	Amphetamines (uppers)
Steroids	Other:_____	

35. Do you use prescription medications in ways not prescribed for you? Yes/No. Please describe. (names of medications, amount, frequency)

If the answers to questions 34 and 35 are "no," go to item 46; if one or both are "yes," please continue with the next items.

36. How often do you use drugs? Daily/Weekly

37. When did you last use drugs?   How much did you use that time?

38. Has there been an increase in your drug use during the past six months? Yes/No.

39. Has your drug use caused any problems at work, at home, at school, or with the law? Yes/No. (circle all that apply)

40. Have you recently had any physical problems related to your drug use? Yes/No. If "yes," list problems.

41. Have you recently been treated for drug use and then returned to using drugs? Yes/No.

42. Have you ever been hospitalized for drug withdrawal and/or treatment? Yes/No.

43. What's the longest you have gone in the last 12 months without using drugs? (< day, < week, <month, >month)

44. Do you engage in risky behaviors to support your use of drugs? Yes/No. If "yes," please describe.

45. Are you currently experiencing any signs of withdrawal? Yes/No.

Risk of Harm to Self or Others

46. Have you gotten so distressed about your current situation that you wish you would not wake-up or not be around anymore? Yes/No

47. Has your situation made you so distressed that you wish you could end your own life? Yes/No. *(If "no," then skip to item 60)*

48. Are you thinking about hurting yourself right now? Yes/No.

49. Do you have a specific plan to hurt yourself? Yes/No.

50. Have you done anything recently to hurt yourself? Yes/No.

51. Do you engage in self-injurious behaviors (scratching, cutting, or burning yourself) to release pain or stress? Yes/No.

52. Are you now hearing voices telling you to hurt or kill yourself? Yes/No.

53. Have you heard voices telling you to hurt yourself? Yes/No.

54. If you have not hurt yourself, but have thought about it, what has stopped you?

55. Do you have access to any weapons/means to hurt yourself? Yes/No. If "yes," what kind?

56. Is your safety at risk if you are left alone? Yes/No.

57. What are some ways that you could keep yourself safe in the next 24 hours?

58. Would you call someone before hurting yourself? Yes/No.

59. Have you ever tried to hurt or kill yourself? Yes/No. If "yes," how so? _____

60. Has your current situation made you so distressed that you have thought about hurting or killing someone else? Yes/No. *(If "no," then go to item 67; if "yes," continue with the next item.)*

61. Have you considered any particular person? Yes/No. If "yes," what is the person's name: _____
Where do they live/work? _____ What is their phone number? _____

62. Have you considered any particular ways or plans to hurt someone else? Yes/No.
Please explain.

63. Do you have access to means/weapons? Yes/No.
If so, what kind?

64. If you were able to get help with your problems, would you still feel as though you would harm/kill others? Yes/No.

65. If you are having thoughts about hurting others, what are some ways you can keep yourself from acting on those thoughts?

66. Do you currently hear voices telling you to hurt other people? Yes/No.

67. Within the past six months, have you slapped, punched, pushed, or kicked anyone? Yes/No. (circle all that apply.)

68. Have you ever hurt anyone (including spouse or children) or destroyed property because you could not control your anger ? Yes/No. If "yes," please explain.

69. Have you ever been arrested for violent behavior? Yes/No.

70. Have you been to Family Advocacy because of physical conflicts with or abuse of family members? Yes/No.

Quality of Life

71. Do you live alone? Yes/No.

72. Are things at home going all right? Yes/No. If "no," please describe.

73. Are you geographically isolated from your family or friends? Yes/No.

74. Is there anyone you can confide in? Yes/No.

75. Have you recently experienced rejection by other people around you? Yes/No.

76. Do you feel as though your relationships with family and friends are in a state of conflict? Yes/No.

77. Have you recently withdrawn from friends and family and become isolated? Yes/No.

78. Do you belong to any groups or organizations that are supportive and helpful to you? Yes/No. If "yes," please describe.

79. What do you like to do for leisure?

80. Is spirituality a source of support in your life?
81. Do your spiritual beliefs affect your current problems? Yes/No. If "yes," please describe how.

82. Is it important to you to have a counselor who shares your spiritual beliefs? Yes/No.

Learning, Education, and Occupation

83. Is English your primary language? Yes/No. If "no," please explain.

84. Do you have any difficulty reading or writing? Yes/No. If "yes," please explain.

85. How many years of education have you completed? _____   Degrees:

86. Are you experiencing problems with your current occupation (occupation means your role in life, as worker, student, home caretaker)? Yes/No. If "yes," please describe.

87. Are you facing legal problems or administrative/disciplinary actions? Yes/No. If "yes," please describe.

Family and Childhood History

88. Did you experience any problems or difficulties in your upbringing that may be impacting your current problems? Yes/No. If "yes," please describe.

89. Did you experience any traumatic events during your childhood that may be impacting your current problems? Yes/No. If "yes," please describe.

90. Do any of your blood relatives (parents, siblings, or children) suffer from alcoholism/drug abuse or any other type of mental or emotional disorder? Yes/No. If "yes," please fill out information below regarding each relative with disorder.

Relationship:_____   Type of Problem: _____   Treatment: _____

Relationship:_____   Type of Problem: _____   Treatment: _____

Relationship:_____   Type of Problem: _____   Treatment: _____

Relationship:_____   Type of Problem: _____   Treatment: _____

Mental Health and Substance Abuse Treatment History

91. Have you received counseling or treatment for mental, emotional, alcohol, or substance use problems in the past? Yes/No. *(If "no," then go to item 96; if "yes," continue with next item.)*

92. In your previous mental health treatment, were you hospitalized? Yes/No.

93. Were you prescribed medications? If "yes," which medications?

94. Are you currently in treatment? Yes/No. If "yes," what is the name of the provider?

95. Have you ever been prescribed medications for anxiety, sleeplessness, depression, unusual thoughts? Yes/No. If " yes," which medications?

Health/Medical Status and History

96. How is your health? (excellent, good, fair, poor) If fair or poor, please explain.

97. Have you had any serious illnesses or operations in the past year?

98. Do you have any concerns about your eating or nutrition? Yes/No. If "yes," please describe.

99. Would you like to learn more about proper nutrition? Yes/No.

100. Do you have any concerns about your physical health and/or chronic health problems? Yes/No. If "yes," please describe.

101. Do you take any prescription medications? Please list.

102. Do you take any over-the-counter medications (e.g., ASA, sleep aids, diet pills, antacids, cough/cold/allergy)? Please describe, including amount and frequency of each medication.

Treatment Goals Checklist

In order to offer you the treatment opportunities most in line with your reasons for coming to this clinic, we would appreciate your circling the number of each goal you wish to address. Please read each item.

1.	Improving communication with _____	11.	Better managing physical pain
2.	Reducing family difficulties	12.	Better managing my anger or temper
3.	Improving my sleep	13.	Receiving medication help
4.	Controlling my drug/alcohol/tobacco use (circle any that apply)	14.	Thoughts of harm to self or others
5.	Controlling my eating or weight	15.	Military discharge or reassignment
6.	Dealing with purging (vomiting, laxatives)	16.	Better accepting a loss or death
7.	Reducing fears/worries about _____	17.	Learning how to relax
8.	Improving my sexual relationship	18.	Improving communication / assertiveness
9.	Reacting too emotionally	19.	Feeling less depressed or guilty
10.	Other (describe):		

Now please review your list and decide which 3 goals you *most* wish to discuss/change at this time.

My *three most important* goals are (write in the goal numbers):   **First** _____   **Second** _____   **Third** _____

How motivated are you to work on the goals you selected above?   Very   Somewhat   A little   Not at all

What strengths or resources do you have that will help you work on the goals you've selected?

What barriers or problems may prevent you from making progress on the goals you've selected?

References

American Psychiatric Association. (1994). *Diagnostic and statistical manual of mental disorders* (4th ed.). Washington, DC: Author.

Andrews, F. M., & Witney, S. B. (1974). Developing measures of perceived life quality: Results from several national surveys. *Social Indicators Research, 1*, 1–26.

Barlow, D. H., Gorman, J. M., Shear, M. K., & Woods, S. W. (2000). Cognitive–behavioral therapy, imipramine, or their combination for panic disorder: A randomized controlled trial. *Journal of the American Medical Association, 283*(19), 2529–2536.

Beiser, M. (1983). Components and correlates of mental well being. *Journal of Health and Social Behavior, 15*, 320–327.

Blau, T. H. (1977). Quality of life, social interaction, and criteria of change. *Professional Psychology, 8*, 464–473.

Burlingame, G. M., Lambert, M. J., Reisinger, C. W., Neff, J., & Mosier, J. (1995). Pragmatics of tracking mental health outcomes in a managed care setting. *Journal of Mental Health Administration, 22*, 226–236.

Burns, D. D. (1995). *Therapist's tool kit: Comprehensive assessment and treatment tools for the mental health professional.* Gladwyne, PA: David Burns.

Chambless, D. L., Caputo, G. C., Bright, P., & Gallagher, R. (1984). Assessment of fear in agoraphobics: The Body Sensations Questionnaire and the Agoraphobic Cognitions Questionnaire. *Journal of Consulting and Clinical Psychology, 52*, 1090–1097.

Clement, P. W. (1996). Evaluation in private practice. *Clinical Psychology: Science and Practice, 3*, 146–159.

Diener, E. (1984). Subjective well-being. *Psychological Bulletin, 95*, 542–575.

Feldman, L. A. (1993). Distinguishing depression and anxiety in self-report: Evidence from confirmatory factor analysis on nonclinical and clinical samples. *Journal of Consulting and Clinical Psychology, 61*, 631–638.

Fischer, J., & Corcoran, K. (1994). *Measures for clinical practice: A sourcebook* (2nd ed.). New York: Free Press.

Foa, E. B., & Wilson, R. (1991). *Stop obsessing: How to overcome your obsessions and compulsions.* New York: Bantam Books.

Frisch, M. B., Cornell, J., Villaneuva, M., & Retzlaff, P. J. (1992). Clinical validation of the Quality of Life Inventory: A measure of life satisfaction for use in treatment planning and outcome assessment. *Psychological Assessment, 4*, 92–101.

Goodman, W. K., Price, L. H, Rasmussen, S. A., Mazure, C., Fleischmann, R. L., Hill, C. L., Heninger, G. R., & Charney, D. S. (1989). The Yale–Brown Obsessive Compulsive Scale: Development, use, and reliability. *Archives of General Psychiatry, 46*, 1006–1011.

Hollon, S. D. (1996). The efficacy and effectiveness of psychotherapy relative to medications. *American Psychologist, 51*, 1025–1030.

Hollon, S. D., DeRubeis, R. J., Evans, M. D., Wiemer, M. J., Garvey, M. J., Grove, W. M., & Tuason, V. B. (1992). Cognitive therapy and pharmacotherapy for depression: Singly and in combination. *Archives of General Psychiatry, 49*, 774–781.

Hollon, S. D., Shelton, R. C., & Loosen, P. T. (1991). Cognitive therapy and pharmacotherapy for depression. *Journal of Consulting and Clinical Psychology, 59*, 88–99.

Horowitz, L. M., Rosenberg, S. E., Baer, B. A., Ureno, G., & Villasenor, V. S. (1988). Inventory of Interpersonal Problems: Psychometric properties and clinical applications. *Journal of Consulting and Clinical Psychology, 56*, 885–892.

Jacobson, N. S., & Truax, P. (1991). Clinical significance: A statistical approach to defining meaningful change in psychotherapy research. *Journal of Consulting and Clinical Psychology, 59*, 12–19.

Johnson, L. D., & Miller, S. D. (1994). Modification of depression risk factors: A solution focused approach. *Psychotherapy, 23*, 493–506.

Keller, M. B., McCullough, J. P., Klein, D. N., Arnow, B., Dunner, D. L., Gelenberg, A. J., Markowitz, J. C., Nemeroff, C. B., Russell, J. M., Thase, M. E., Trivedi, M. H., & Zajecka, J. (2000). A comparison of nefazodone, the cognitive behavioral-analysis system of psychotherapy, and their combination for the treatment of chronic depression. *New England Journal of Medicine, 342*(20), 1462–1470.

Lambert, M. J. (1983). Introduction to assessment of psychotherapy outcome: Historical perspective and current issues. In M. J. Lambert, E. R. Christensen, & S. S. DeJulio (Eds.) *The assessment of psychotherapy outcome* (pp. 3–32). New York: Wiley.

Lambert, M. J., & Brown, G. S. (1996). Databased management for tracking outcome in private practice. *Clinical Psychology, 32,* 172–178.

Lambert, M. J., Hansen, N. B., Umpress, V., Lunnen, K., Okiishi, J., Burlingame, G. M., & Reisinger, C. W. (1996). *Administration and scoring manual for the OQ45.2.* Stevenson, MD: American Professional Credentialing Services.

Lambert, M. J., Okiishi, J. C., Finch, A. E., & Johnson, L. D. (1998). Outcome assessment: From conceptualization to implementation. *Professional Psychology: Research and Practice, 29,* 63–70.

Meyer, E. C., Miller, S. M., Metzger, F., & Borkovec, T. D. (1990). Development and validation of the Penn State Worry Questionnaire. *Behavior Research and Therapy, 28,* 487–495.

Mirin, S., & Namerow, M. (1991). Why study treatment outcome? *Hospital and Community Psychiatry, 42,* 1007–1013.

Newman, F. L., & Ciarlo, J. A. (1994). Criteria for selecting psychological instruments for treatment outcome assessments. In M. E. Maruish (Ed.), *The use of psychological testing for treatment planning and outcome assessment* (pp. 98–110). Hillsdale, NJ: Erlbaum.

Ogles, B. M., Lambert, M. J., & Masters, K. (1996). *Assessing outcome in clinical practice.* New York: Allyn & Bacon.

Sederer, L. I., & Dickey, B. (1996). *Outcomes assessment in clinical practice.* Baltimore: Williams & Wilkins.

Seligman, M. E. P. (1995). The effectiveness of psychotherapy: The *Consumer Reports* study. *American Psychologist, 50,* 965–974.

Strupp, H. H., Horowitz, L. M., & Lambert, M. J. (1997). *Measuring patient changes in mood, anxiety, and personality disorders: Toward a core battery.* Washington, DC: American Psychological Association.

Umphress, V. J., Lambert, M. J., Smart, D. W., Barlow, S. H., & Clouse, G. (1997). Concurrent and construct validity of the Outcome Questionnaire. *Journal of Psychoeducational Assessment, 15,* 40–55.

Veit, C. T., & Ware, J. E. (1983). The structure of psychological distress and well-being in general populations. *Journal of Consulting and Clinical Psychology, 51,* 730–742.

Appendix

Generic and Trade Names of Drugs Cited in This Volume

Antipsychotic Agents

Typical antipsychotics

Generic Name	Trade Name
Acetophenazine	Tindal (withdrawn in the U.S.)
Chlorpromazine	Thorazine, Chlorpromanyl
Chlorprothixine	Taractan, Tarasan
Fluphenazine	Proxilin, Permetin
Fluphenazine enanthate	Moditen Enanthate
Fluphenazine decanoate	
Haloperidol	Haldol, Novoperidol, Peridol,
Haldol decanoate	Haldol LA
Loxapine	Loxitane; Loxapac
Molindone	Moban
Mesoridazine	Serentil
Perphenazine	Trilafon
Promazine	Sparine
Trifluoperazine	Stelazine, Suprazine
Trifluopromazine	Vesprin
Thioridazine	Mellaril, Mellaril-S
Thiothixene	Navane

Novel or atypical antipsychotics

Generic Name	Trade Name
Clozapine	Clozaril
Olanzapine	Zyprexa
Risperidone	Risperdal
Quetiapine	Seroquel
Ziprasidone	Geodon

Trade names are those commonly used in the United States and Canada, not all trade names may be listed.

Drugs used to treat side effects of antipsychotic agents

Generic Name	Trade Name
Amantadine	Symmetrel, Cerebramed, Endatadine, others
Benztropine	Cogentin
Diphenhydramine	Benadryl, others
Trihexyphenidyl	Artane, Trihexy, Trihexydyl

Drugs Used in the Treatment of Substance Abuse Disorders

Generic Name	Trade Name
Buprenorphine	Buprenex
Clonidine	Catapres
Disulfiram	Antabuse
Nalmefene	Cervene, Revex
Acamprosate	(not approved in U.S.)
Naloxone	Narcan
Naltrexone	Trexan, Revia, Depade
Nicotine	
Transdermal patches	Habitrol, ProStep
Nasal Spray	Nicotrol
Polacrilex	Nicorette gum
Ondansetron	Zofran
Levomethadyl acetate hydrochloride (LAAM)	Orlaam, Levo-alpha-acetyl-methadol

Drugs Used in the Treatment of Depression

Generic Name	Trade Name
Amitriptyline	Elavil, Endep
Amoxapine	Asendin
Brofaromine	(not available in the U.S.)
Bupropion	Wellbutrin
Sustained release	Wellbutrin SR, Zyban
Citalopram	Celexa
Clomipramine	Anafranil
Desipramine	Norpramin, Petrofrane
Dothiepin	(not available in the U.S.)
Doxepin	Sinequan, Adapin
Fluoxetine	Prozac, Sarafem
Fluvoxamine	Luvox
Imipramine	Tofranil, Antipress, Impril, Janimine, others
Isocarboxacid	Marplan*
Lofepramine	(not available in the U.S.)
Maprotiline	Ludiomil
Mianserin	(not available in the U.S.)
Mirtazapine	Remeron
Moclobemide	Manerix (not available in the U.S.)
Nefazodone	Serzone
Nortriptyline	Pamelor, Aventyl
Paroxetine	Paxil, Paxil CR (continuous release)
Protriptyline	Vivactyl
Reboxetine	Edronax (not available in the U.S.)
Sertraline	Zoloft
Trazodone	Desyrel
Tranylcypromine	Parnate
Trimipramine	Surmontil
Venlafaxine	Effexor, Effexor SR (sustained release)

*MAOI withdrawn from the general U.S. market, available by special request.

Additional indications for antidepressant agents

Enuresis: imipramine
Generalized anxiety disorder: amitriptyline, doxepin, venlafaxine
Obsessive–compulsive disorder: clomipramine, fluoxetine, fluvoxamine, paroxetine and sertraline
Panic disorder: sertraline, paroxetine
Posttraumatic stress disorder: sertraline
Pruritis: doxepin
Social anxiety disorder: paroxetine
Social phobia: paroxetine
Smoking cessation: bupropion

Benzodiazepines and Other Sedative Hypnotics

Generic Name	Trade Name
Alprazolam	Xanax, Alprazol
Buspirone	Buspar, Buspirex
Chlorazepate	Tranxene, Gen-Xene, Clopate
Chloral hydrate	Noctec
Chlordiazepoxide	Librium, A-Poxide, Mitran, others
Clonazepam	Klonopin, Rivotril
Diazepam	Valium, Valcaps, Rival, E-Meval, others
Estazolam	ProSom
Flurazepam	Dalmane, Durapam, Lupam, Somnol
Gabapentin	Neurontin
Lorazepam	Ativan, Alzapam
Nitrazepam	(Mogadon, not available in the U.S.)
Oxazepam	Serax, Novoxapam, Zapex
Quazepam	Doral
Temazepam	Restoril
Triazolam	Halcion, Apo-Triazo, Novatriolam
Zaleplon	Sonata
Zolpidem	Ambien
Zopiclone	Imovane, Rhovane (not available in the U.S.)

Beta Receptor Agonists (Beta Blockers)

Generic Name	Trade Name
Atenolol	Tenormin
Propranolol	Inderal, Betachron, Detensol
Pindolol	Visken, Novopindol

Mood Stabilizers

Generic Name	Trade Name
Valproic acid, Divalproex sodium	Depakote, others
Lithium	Lithobid, Eskalith, Carbolith

Stimulants and Agents Used to Control Obesity

Generic Name	Trade Name
Amphetamine	Benzedrine, Desoxyn
Benzphetamine	Didrex
Chlorphentermine	No information available
Chlortermine	No information available
Diethylpropion	Depletite, Nobesine, Tenuate, Tepamil
Dexfenfluramine	Redux
Fenfluramine	Pondimin
Mazindol	Mazanor, Sanorex
Orlistat	Xenical
Phentermine	Fastin, Adipex-P, Phentrol
Phentermine resin complex	Ionamin
Phenmetrazine	Discontinued in 1991
Phendimetrazine	Plegine, Anorex, Adipost, others
Sibutramine	Meridia

Glossary of Technical Terms

agonist A drug that changes the function of a receptor as a result of binding to it. Agonists may be partial, that is, they produce a lower response at full receptor occupancy than do full agonists. Inverse agonists exist; these bind to the same sites as agonists but produce opposite effects.

agranulocytosis A deficiency of neutrophils (a subtype of white blood cells), presumptively caused by an allergic-type response to administration of drugs. Initial symptoms may include fever, sore throat, and oral ulcerations. Severe immune response impairment may result, with high mortality in patients developing the condition. Often associated with the use of clozapine, seen less frequently with phenothiazine antipsychotics and other drugs.

akathisia An internal or subjective sense of muscular restlessness or agitation, manifested by a desire to move about, difficulty sitting still, or persistent irritability. It is presumptively related to a perturbation in dopaminergic neurotransmission. Most commonly associated with initiation or increased dose of traditional antipsychotics, it is occasionally observed with use of other psychotropics, such as the *selective serotonin reuptake inhibitors*.

antagonist A drug that has no change on receptor function as a result of binding to that receptor. Antagonists may be competitive, that is, they may compete with *agonists* for occupancy of the same receptor site, or they may be noncompetitive—that is, they bind to another portion of the target molecule so as to prevent agonist binding. They may also be reversible or irreversible, depending on their degree of affinity for a receptor site. Antagonists may reverse the effects of both agonists and inverse agonists.

bioavailability The fraction of an administered dose that reaches systemic circulation. Varies according to the chemical composition of drugs, route of administration, stability of compound in the gastrointestinal tract, and extent of a drug's *metabolism* prior to reaching systemic circulation.

clearance Rate of elimination of a drug from the system, measured as ratio of amount eliminated to plasma concentration of drug. Liver and kidneys are the major sites of elimination; blood flow, organ function, enzyme action, and many other factors are important in determining clearance.

cytochrome P450 enzyme family   A large group of proteins, mainly but not exclusively located in liver cells, that are responsible for transforming many drugs from nonpolar (nonwater soluble), nonexcretable forms to more polar (water soluble), excretable forms. The P450 family of enzymes is broken down into a number of different subgroups; of these, the 2D6, 2C9, 3A4, and 1A2 isozymes are most important in the metabolism of psychotropic drugs. Many of the serotonin reuptake inhibitors serve as substrates for certain cytochromes, that is, they are largely or exclusively metabolized by that cytochrome enzyme class. Drugs may also inhibit enzymes, meaning that their affinity for that enzyme is so great that other drugs utilizing the same enzyme system may be unable to be metabolized; this will cause increases in the serum concentrations of these other drugs and is the cause of many important drug interactions. Some drugs induce enzymes, that is, they cause the body to manufacture more. In these cases, chronic administration will require that higher doses of the drug be given in order to maintain the same plasma level.

dependence   A continuous concept, which refers to both physiological (e.g., receptor) and psychological variables. Dependence is multifactorial, and encompasses amount and frequency of use; development of *tolerance* and *withdrawal*; inability to abstain; and the degree of physical, social, and personal impairment caused by use of the substance.

dystonia   An abnormal alteration in muscle tone, often associated with the use of dopamingergic antipsychotics, such as the phenothiazines (e.g. Thorazine) or butyrophenones (e.g. Haldol). Often characterized by spasming or rigidity of the muscles of the face, neck, or truck.

extrapyramidal side effects   A cluster of symptoms characteristically associated with the use of high-potency, traditional antipsychotics, including *Parkinsonian symptoms*, dystonia, and *akathisia*. Evidently originates from dysregulation of the neurotransmitters dopamine and acetylcholine in the extrapyramidal motor system.

first-pass metabolism   Certain drugs are highly metabolized by the liver and may be extensively broken down or extracted on their first contact with that organ. Essentially all drugs absorbed through the stomach and much of the upper intestinal tract are filtered through the liver prior to reaching systemic circulation. Drugs are occasionally administered sublingually; this introduces the agent to systemic circulation via absorption through oral mucosa and thus avoids first-pass metabolism.

free fraction   Refers to that percentage of a drug in systemic circulation that is available to interact with target receptor sites. The portion of a drug that is bound to *plasma proteins* (see the definition of plasma protein binding) or other binding sites is therapeutically inert, that is, it is unable to attach to the target receptor and produce the desired treatment effect. Generally, most psychotropics have a very high protein binding ratio; often around 80%–95% of these drugs is bound to plasma proteins, leaving a free fraction of only 5%–20% of the drug in systemic circulation available to interact at the target site.

half-life (T 1/2)   The time required to eliminate one-half of the serum concentration of a drug. Many factors influence the elimination of drugs, and half-life therefore varies widely in different individuals and different disease states. Also, a distinction is made between distribution half-lives (the time it takes for a drug to be distributed to different body tissues) and elimination half-lives. See *steady state*.

metabolism   The biotransformation of drugs into forms that can be excreted by the body. Some drugs require numerous metabolic steps (often taking place in the liver, such as oxidation and glucuronization); others, such as lithium, undergo little or no metabolic transformation. Some drugs are prodrugs, that is, they must be partially metabolized before they reach an active form. Valium (diazepam) is one such drug; its active metabolite is oxazepam (serax).

neuroleptic malignant syndrome   A syndrome characterized by autonomic instability (tachycardia, labile blood pressure), fever, rigidity, and cognitive changes that may result from initiation of treatment with antipsychotics in susceptible individuals. Presumptively caused by the rapid blockade of postsynaptic dopamine receptors, it is largely associated with traditional, high-potency antipsychotics and is much more rarely observed with atypical agents. It is a potentially fatal condition requiring emergent medical care.

neutropenia   A benign reduction in white blood cells (often by 30%–60%) that may result from the administration of phenothiazines or carbamazepine. It must be distinguished from the more marked and clinically significant syndrome of *agranulocytosis*.

oulogyric crisis   A localized or focal dystonia of muscles controlling eye movement, resulting in inability to control eye movements.

Parkinsonian symptoms   A category of *extrapyramidal side effects* of antipsychotic medications, so named because they mimic the side effects of Parkinson's disease and are commonly characterized by gait disturbance (a shuffling gait), psychomotor retardation, postural rigidity and immobile facial features (masked facies), a resting hand tremor, and emotional blunting.

pharmacodynamics   The effects of drugs on the body and the mechanisms by which they produce those effects (i.e., "what the drug does to the body"). Pharmacodynamics includes drug–receptor interaction, duration of drug action, drug effects on neuronal transmission, drug effects on gene transcription, and other functions.

pharmacokinetics   Refers to the processes by which drugs are absorbed, distributed, metabolized, and eliminated from the body (i.e., "what the body does to the drug"). The pharmacokinetic profile of a particular drug will determine how much of the drug is required to produce the desired effect and how long the drug will remain at the target site in the body. Gender, age, health or disease states, and, in certain cases, ethnicity (heritable expression of metabolic enzymes) affect the pharmacokinetics of any particular drug. Co-administration of two or more drugs may result in interactions affecting the pharmacokinetic profile of one or more of those drugs, as may dietary factors or the ingestion of herbal preparations.

phases of treatment   Pharmacological treatment can be broadly divided into three phases. *Acute*: the initial period of treatment when presenting symptoms are addressed and initial response to treatment gauged, often 4–6 weeks in duration. *Continuation*: The period after initial, acute symptoms have resolved, often 4–6 months in duration. *Maintenance*: Long-term treatment with the general goal of preventing relapse of new episodes.

plasma protein binding   Plasma proteins are molecular components of plasma, the noncellular component of blood. Many drugs, and many psychotropic drugs in particular, bind avidly to plasma protein sites. The main plasma protein is albumin, which is manufactured in the liver and is a binding site for many drugs, especially acidic drugs. Several other plasma proteins exist in smaller quantity, such as Alpha1 acid glycoprotein, which tends to bind basic drugs. Many drugs will displace others from plasma protein binding sites if they have a higher affinity for that site. This may increase the *free fraction* of the displaced drug and is a potential source of drug interactions, though the clinical significance of such interactions is unclear.

rebound   One of a series of discontinuation phenomena occurring after the cessation of a pharmacological agent. It refers to a transient phase after cessation of drug use in which initial symptoms occur in more intense manifestations than originally. It may be followed by *recurrence*.

recurrence   A discontinuation phenomenon in which the symptoms of the underlying disorder being treated re-emerge when treatment is stopped, at roughly the same level seen prior to initiation of treatment.

SSRI   Selective serotonin reuptake inhibitor, also SRI (serotonin reuptake inhibitor), a class of drugs used primarily in the treatment of depression, obsessive–compulsive disorder, and social phobia, among others. So called because of their ability to relatively selectively inhibit the reuptake of the neurotransmitter serotonin from the synaptic cleft by blocking the action of a transporter located on the surface of the presynaptic neuron.

steady state   A state of equilibrium in which the amount of a drug administered equals the amount eliminated from plasma so that a constant plasma concentration is maintained. Time to steady state is a function of the elimination *half-life* of an agent. After one half-life, a drug reaches 50% steady state, after two, 75%, after three, 87.5%; etc. Time to steady state is generally calculated as 4–5 half-lives.

tardive dyskinesia   A syndrome consisting of the production of involuntary muscle movements, often associated with the long-term use of antipsychotics, particularly high-potency typical agents, such as haloperidol. Symptoms tend to develop after chronic use and may be masked by the administration of antipsychotics, thus becoming manifest only after the drug is discontinued or the dose lowered. Symptoms include the buccolingual masticatory movements (lip smacking, involuntary tongue and jaw movements) and slow, writhing (choreoathetoid) movements of the extremities or trunk.

tolerance   A phenomenon wherein greater doses of drug are required to achieve the same physiological or psychological effect. Tolerance develops at different rates for different processes; substance abusers tend to become more tolerant to the euphoric effects of a drug more rapidly than to other effects such as the respiratory depressant effects of opiates. Tolerance is an important concept with regard to the benzodiazepines, because individuals frequently become tolerant to the hypnotic effect of these drugs, and may begin to use higher does to achieve this effect.

torticollis   A localized or focal dystonia involving involuntary contraction of neck muscles, usually the sternocleidomastoid muscle, resulting in the head being pulled back or to one side. Often associated with high-potency antipsychotic use.

two-compartment modeling   This refers to the unequal distribution of some drugs in the body, first via wide distribution in blood or organs having high blood flow and then accumulating more slowly in tissue, with resultant differences in concentration and rates of elimination between the two compartments. The *pharmacokinetics* of lithium closely resemble a two-compartment model.

volume of distribution   A theoretical measure referring to the size of the body compartment necessary to account for the total amount of drug in the body if it were present throughout the body in the same concentration found in plasma. Body compartments are extracellular water, total body water, blood (including plasma), bone, and fat. Drugs are distributed into these compartments as a function of chemical properties (lipid solubility, protein binding); molecular size (large molecules tend to stay in plasma), and several other factors.

withdrawal   A time-limited, discontinuation phenomenon, marked by physical and psychological changes. Physical withdrawal occurs when cellular adaptations brought on by administration of a drug are reversed by drug cessation or by administration of an *antagonist*. Although usually associated with drugs of abuse (cocaine, heroin, benzodiazepines, alcohol), withdrawal may accompany cessation of many other compounds, including the serotonin reuptake inhibitors and other antidepressants.

Author Index

Numbers in italics refer to listings in reference sections.

Terzano, M. G., 115, *128*
Thase, M. E., 19, 20, *30, 31, 32,* 131, 133, 135, 138, 143, 147, 149, *154, 155, 157, 158, 159, 232, 298*
Thibodeau, N., *76*
Thiel, A., 57, *80*
Thieme, M. E., 182, *189*
Thomas, F., 250, *264*
Thomas, J., *31, 189*
Thomas, M., 131, *152*
Thompson, J. W., *31,* 164, *188*
Thornley, B., 13, *32*
Thorpy, M. J., 120, *127, 129*
Tiller, J. W. G., 83, *109*
Tims, F. M., 216, *236*
Tipp, J. E., *211*
Todaro, J., *80*
Toffle, R. C., 259, *262*
Tohen, M., 15, *30*
Toksoz, B. K., 143, *153*
Tollefson, G. D., 63, 68, *80,* 182, *189, 264*
Tomenson, B. M., 134, *152*
Tomkins, A., 169, *186*
Tommasello, A. C., *211*
Tonnenson, P., 201, 207, *213*
Tonstad, S., 250, *268*
Toran, J., *188*
Torgerson, D. J., 13, *31*
Totten, A. M., *51*
Trabert, W., *107*
Trachtenberg, A. I., 8, *9*
Trakowski, J. H., 85, 90, *108*
Tran, G. Q., 60, *80*
Tremblay, A., 246, 259, *262, 269*
Tricamo, E., *157*
Triffleman, E., *211*
Trivedi, M. H., 20, 21, 22, *32,* 133, *154, 155, 159, 298*
Troiano, R. P., 239, *265*
Trower, P., 92, 95, *109*
Truax, P. A., *30,* 278, *298*
Tsai, W., *51*
Tsuang, M. T., 55, *78*
Tuason, V. B., *154, 155, 298*
Tunstall, C. D., 207, 208, *211*
Turk, D. C., 221, *234*
Turkington, D., *189*
Turner, P., 248, *264*
Turner, R. M., 70, 71, *76*
Turner, S. M., 90, 91, 92, 93, 95, 96, *109*
Turtonen, J., *77*

Uhde, T. W., *105*
Uhlenhuth, E. H., 111, 116, *126, 127*
Ulrich, I. H., 259, *262*
Ulrich, R. F., *187*

Umbricht, A., *235*
Umphress, V. J., *9,* 277, *299*
Unutzer, J., *159*
Ureno, G., 276, *298*
U.S. Department of Agriculture, 258, *268*
U.S. Department of Health and Human Services, 191, *213,* 240, 241, 242, 243, 246, 247, 249, 252, *268*
U.S. General Accounting Office, 34, *52*

Valenstein, E. S., 22, *32*
Vallego, J., 83, *105*
Valoski, A., 259, *263*
van Balkom, A. J. L. M., 70, 71, 72, *80*
van der Helm, M., 70, *75*
Van der Veen, E. A., 250, *263*
van Dyck, R., 70, 71, *80*
Van Ermen, A., 249, *265*
Van Itallie, T. B., 245, *268*
van Kraanen, J., 71, *75*
van Oppen, P., 70, *80*
van Vleit, I., 93, 94, *109*
van Zanten, B. L., 70, *75*
VandenBos, G. R., 21, *31*
Vasey, M., 90, *108*
Vaught, J. L., *79*
Veit, C. T., 276, 277, *299*
Velicer, W. F., 192, 193, *212*
Verde, T. J., *261*
Vermeulen, A. W., 70, *80*
Versiani, M., 92, 93, 94, *109*
Viegener, B. J., 246, *266*
Vigontas, A., *127*
Vila, K. L., 208, *211*
Villaneuva, M., 276, *298*
Villasenor, V. S., 277, *298*
Villejo, L., *211*
Visser, S., 70, *75*
Viswanathan, R., 99, *106*
Vitale, A., *77*
Vittone, B. J., *105*
Vitousek, K. M., 258, *269*
Vogel, G. W., 115, *129*
Vogt, R. A., 246, 260, *264, 268*
Volavka, J., 63, *80*
Vollrath, M., 112, 118, *129*
Volpicella, J. R., 217, 224, *236, 237*
Von Korff, M., 111, *129,* 139, *159*
Vranizan, K. M., *269*

Wachtel, H., 133, *159*
Wadden, T. A., 239, 245, 246, 252, 253, 260, *261, 262, 263, 264, 267, 268*
Wadland, W. C., *211*
Wadworth, A. N., 116, *129*
Wager, S. G., *157*
Wagner, E. F., 138, *154*
Wald, E. R., *80*

Subject Index

About the Editors

Morgan T. Sammons, PhD, received his undergraduate degree from Georgetown University and his doctoral degree in counseling psychology from Arizona State University. He is a graduate of the first cohort of the Department of Defense Psychopharmacology Demonstration Project and has been a prescribing psychologist since 1994. Currently he is a Commander on active duty in the U.S. Navy. Dr. Sammons lectures extensively and is the author of numerous papers and book chapters on prescriptive authority for psychologists. He is a Fellow of the American Psychological Association, a member of the Board of Directors of the National Register of Health Service Providers in Psychology, and has been elected president of the Maryland Psychological Association.

Norman B. Schmidt, PhD, is an associate professor of psychology and director of the Anxiety and Stress Disorders Clinic at The Ohio State University. Dr. Schmidt has published over 60 articles and book chapters. Most of these articles focus on the nature, causes, and treatment of anxiety problems as well as the medical or health consequences of pathological anxiety. He currently serves on the editorial boards of the *Journal of Abnormal Psychology* and *Behavior Therapy*. He has received a number of honors and was recently awarded the American Psychological Association's Distinguished Scientific Award for Early Career Contributions to Psychology in the area of applied research.